Marketing Management Technology as a Social Process

EDITED BY
GEORGE FISK

PRAEGER

New York
Westport, Connecticut
London

Library of Congress Cataloging-in-Publication Data

Marketing management technology as a social process.

   "Significant issues . . . analyzed by purpose of
publications of Reavis Cox compared to papers in this
book" — P.
   Includes bibliographies and index.
   1. Marketing — Management.   2. Marketing — Social
aspects. 3. Cox, Reavis, 1900–.   I. Fisk, George,
1922– .
HF5415.13.M356   1986   658.8   86-8202
ISBN 0-275-92177-8 (alk. paper)

Library of Congress Catalog Card Number: 86-8202
ISBN: 0-275-92177-8

First published in 1986

Praeger Publishers, 521 Fifth Avenue, New York, NY 10175
A division of Greenwood Press, Inc.

Printed in the United States of America

The paper used in this book complies with the Permanent
Paper Standard issued by the National Information Standards
Organization (Z39.48-1984).

10 9 8 7 6 5 4 3 2 1

Preface

"Spillover" consequences or "marketing externalities" have been the subject of debate since Aristotle declared that "trade is barren." In contemporary society the impacts of marketing have produced "spillover" consequences prompting reactions by consumerists, environmentalists and trade protectionists among others. These responses to the technologies of marketing render the study of marketing management increasingly dependent on advances in knowledge about marketing as a social process. More importantly, perhaps, the publics impacted by marketing externalities need to understand the social benefits as well as the social costs they experience as a result of marketing activity. Thus, the need to identify and evaluate "spillover" effects of marketing on the members of society offers a compelling reason for collecting a set of essays exploring the relationships between marketing management technologies and their social consequences.

The desire to provide a clear focus on these issues for new generations of marketing investigators is a second reason motivating this collection of essays. Despite the advantages of understanding marketing as a social process, research on this topic has languished in recent decades. Instead, greater interest in improving management applications of marketing technology has claimed attention by a majority of marketing investigators. Yet, the interdependent nature of complex societies cannot be understood without identifying the interactions between marketing managers and the social groups who respond to the effects of marketing activities on their lives. These "publics" of marketing affect the opportunities and constraints available to marketing decision makers. Hence the influence of these marketing publics on marketing opportunities and constraints requires continuous study.

Finally, it is the desire of the authors of these essays to recognize a major contributor to the ideas around which this book is organized. Reavis Cox, Professor Emeritus at the Wharton School of the University of Pennsylvania, his colleagues and students posed questions beginning in the year 1948 that continue to engage the efforts of a number of present day investigators. In that year Wroe Alderson and Reavis Cox published "Toward a Theory in Marketing" (*Journal of Marketing*, 13, Oct, 137 - 152.) Cox's identification and exploration of these questions relating marketing management technology to social processes continued to occupy his research and teaching efforts until publication of *Distribution in a High Level Economy* in 1965 (Cox, Reavis in association with Charles S. Goodman and Thomas Fichandler, Englewood Cliffs, N.J. Prentice-Hall, 1965.) Cox's contributions to marketing theory and to the understanding of marketing as a social process merit recognition by students and practitioners of marketing alike.

In seeking to acknowledge these contributions it has been necessary to ask a number of busy people to do something for nothing. The generous responses of the contributors to this book deserve appreciation by all members of the marketing profession. No only have our authors paid tribute to Cox's contributions to the marketing discipline, but they have demonstrated the enduring viability of the social systems paradigm of marketing behavior. At a time when prevailing fashions focus attention on more limited managerial perspectives in marketing, this collection of essays may prove to be of more value in orienting new generations of marketing students than rival paradigms now claiming the loyalties of many marketing management technologists.

Contents

PART III
CHANNEL NETWORK BEHAVIOR

PART IV
METHODS FOR ADVANCING MARKETING KNOWLEDGE

Overview: Challenging Managerial Perspectives on Marketing

GEORGE FISK

Most marketing literature maintains that marketing is a social process (Hunt 1976), but it commonly treats marketing as a management technology. Problems of marketing operations managers dominate the journals devoted to marketing practice, policy, and science. Hence, the adjustment of the economic infrastructure of trade and service industry to market demands receives scant attention. As a widely quoted business journal article describes current U.S. practice, we are "Managing Our Way to Decline" (Hayes and Abernathy 1980).

Global trade now depends more on national policies and marketing strategies than in the heyday of the American Challenge by U.S. multinational corporations in the 1960s. As the emergence of Japan, Inc., and its rivals in developing nations engenders protectionist responses from the U.S. and European governments, the lack of knowledge about the problems faced by firms in the domestic markets of these economies is rendering industries as well as firms incapable of dealing with their declining markets. If protectionist measures are enacted to shelter domestic industries, the secondary impacts of globally interdependent markets are unforeseeable but predictably serious.

CHALLENGE TO MANAGERIAL PERSPECTIVES

In a world largely ignorant of the complex processes by which standards of living are delivered by marketing organizations, the assumption that applying the knowledge of marketing professionals will advance the well-being of society is true only if it includes the marketing infrastructure as well as the marketing tactics of individual firms. The marketing system of interest is not only that of the ad, sales, or product manager but that of the economy. Adjusting the network of all firms to meet aggregate demand entails more than the study of cooperative synergies in a marketing department. It requires examination of the interacting processes by means of which marketing serves final and intermediate demands of a society. The focus on marketing management in professional literature creates the illusion that marketing achievements result solely from applying technical skills to the marketing problems of firms.

Knowledge about the macrosystem is a prerequisite to understanding how to achieve optimal performance of the national, international, and global organization of the marketing function in society. As the chronic existence of famine and glut illustrates, there is much improvement needed in world organization of the marketing task. Marketing must be practiced as a cooperative social process in order to grapple with issues of economic system effectiveness and efficiency. Thus, analysis of intersystem competition must embrace more than the marketing strategy or price policy of a firm. The time period for analysis has to extend far beyond the life cycle of an industry or product. By embracing stages of economic development and including questions of interregional and even global optimization, the analysis of marketing systems may yield insights into the institutional performance of marketing as a provisioning technology.

The study of society by political scientists, economists, and sociologists has rarely addressed issues of marketing organization. Hence, the study of the relationship between marketing and other social processes is an appropriate domain for marketing investigation. To understand institutional phenomena, the questions marketing scholars need to answer about marketing as a social process are at a higher level of aggregation than those addressed by the marketing manager. Hence, to define significant issues and to indicate methods for their investigation, the present volume focuses on marketing behavior in aggregate or macromarketing systems. These pertain to cooperation and competition as social processes and to the "spillover" social benefits and costs of marketing activity. The questions to be considered include the following:

1. What ends should marketing services serve compared with the ends they do serve?
2. How well do domestic marketing systems provide levels of living under prevailing political and economic system organizations?
3. How should marketing networks be organized for optimal service delivery compared with how they are currently organized?
4. By what methods of learning more about marketing as a social process (metamarketing) can reliable knowledge be accumulated?

The fastest avenue of entry for examining these significant but neglected questions is to identify the work of scholars who have explored them previously. Among strategies appropriate to answer these questions, the role model approach offers a rapid and effective means to enhanced understanding because great scholars often specialize in an area whose blind alleys they describe for future generations.

Few marketing thinkers have explored marketing as a social process in recent years. Among the last of these is Reavis Cox, Sebastian S. Kresge Professor of Marketing, Emeritus, of the University of Pennsylvania. Marketing problems he viewed as significant continue to challenge the interests of his former colleagues and students, more than 20 years after his last major work appeared in 1965. As Cox himself observed: "A scholar is remembered, if at all, for a few of his major ideas that other people find interesting."

Among the contributions of Reavis Cox to the organization of this volume are conceptualization of marketing as a social process and as a field for theory building. Cox's analyses of the conduct of transactions, marketing activity flows, and comparative studies were his method for developing a body of testable hypotheses about marketing. First among his contributions Cox recognized the technology-specific activities in the equation of exchange as early as 1952 (Vaile, Grether, and Cox 1952). Without naming exchange as the essence of marketing behavior as it was subsequently identified by Kotler (1972) and Bagozzi (1975), Cox expanded his analyses to measure dollar day transaction flow costs for specific commodities (Cox and Goodman 1954, 1956). Cox's contributions to the marketing flow concept are noted in Part II of this book by his coauthor, Ewald T. Grether.

Third, although Cox did not publish comparative studies, his suggestion that such studies be initiated (1965) has been one of the most widely cited statements in the comparative studies area. It motivates several essays in this collection. Few suggestions in the international studies area have drawn such a tenacious following, an almost certain sign of a powerful paradigm.

Fourth, the methods Cox proposed for comparative studies were in keeping with his earlier call to the development of marketing theory, an area that has enjoyed continuous support from marketing scholars since it was first enunciated in 1948 (Alderson and Cox 1948). Few ideas in the history of marketing thought have engaged the interest of so diverse a group as the development of marketing theory. By 1950 Cox and Alderson coedited a volume on *Theory in Marketing*, and with their student Stanley J. Shapiro they coedited a second series in 1964. Cox's own research culminated in the publication of *Distribution in a High-Level Economy* (1965), a study of the costs, social effectiveness, and productivity of the marketing institution. This study along with other studies of the productivity and efficiency of wholesaling, retailing, and transportation industries provides baseline data as well as methodological insights for answering such momentous questions as, How should marketing networks be organized for optimal efficiency compared with how they are presently organized? The following table outlines the relationship between ideas investigated by Reavis Cox and their extension by the present contributors.

Significant Issues Concerning Marketing Management Technology as a Social Process Analyzed by Purpose of Publications of Reavis Cox Compared with Essays in this Book

Title and Purpose of Publications by Reavis Cox

Title and Purpose of Papers in this Book

1. MARKETING: MANAGEMENT TECHNOLOGY AS SOCIAL PROCESS

Cox, Reavis, with Charles S. Goodman and Thomas C. Fichandler, *Distribution in a High-Level Economy* (1965) Englewood Cliffs, N.J. Prentice-Hall. Cox and his associates examine the part distribution plays in performing functions allotted to it in the highly developed U.S. economy.

"The Marketing Concept: A Déjà Vu"

Stanley C. Hollander examines common errors in interpreting relationships between characterizations of marketing and economic development during production, sales, and marketing stages of the U.S. economy.

Part III. *How Good a Job Does Distribution Do?* in same reference as above. Cox explores critical issues in the Evaluation of Distribution with respect to efficiency fairness, and social abusiveness.

"Marketing: Management Technology or Social Process at the Twenty-First Century?"

Robert Bartels speculates about the consequences of preoccupation with marketing as a management technology to supply consumption demands without consideration of the range of social expectations. Contributions of marketing based on the definition of man as a market for consumables could yield to conceptions that provide opportunities for broader commitments to social needs.

"The Search for Universals in Comparative Studies of Domestic Marketing Systems" (1965) in Peter Bennett (ed.), *Marketing and Economic Development, Proceedings of the 1965 Fall Conference,* Chicago, American Marketing Assn, 143–162. Cox sought a reconceptualization of marketing behavior that could be identified in disparate cultures across time and amenable to cross culture comparisons under different forms of economic organizations to answser the question "What is marketing?"

"What Is Marketing? The Search for Universals"

Jean J. Boddewyn compares Cox's economic and social perspectives on market exchange with the views of behavioral scientists.

2. COMPARATIVE STUDIES OF MARKETING OUTPUTS

See "The Search for Universals in Comparative Studies of Domestic Marketing Systems" (1965) Same reference as above.

"Marketing as a Provisioning Technology: Fueling World Development from Finite Resource Base," Nikhilesh and Ruby Roy Dholakia pose the issue of rising expectations. Given the appetite for rising levels of living, what is the appropriate role for marketing under circumstances of rising populations, decreasing natural resources, and rising environmental hazard?

Ch. 15 "Marketing in a Trillion-dollar Economy" in ——, Charles S. Goodman and Thomas C. Fichandler (1965). Same references as above. Examines assumption that the discrepancy between the level of aspiration and level of achievement of higher levels of consumption will continue in light of social pressures for public sector "expenditures on highways, health education, defense and perhaps even war."

"Consumption Expenditures and Economic Development," Edward W. Cundiff tests the hypothesis that marketing increases consumption thereby leading to further increases in levels of economic development using national income statistics from developing nations.

"The Search for Universals in Comparative Studies of Domestic Marketing Systems" (1965) in Peter D. Bennett (ed.), Chicago, *American Marketing and Economic Development: Proceedings of the 1965 Fall Conference*, Chicago, American Marketing Association, 143–162.
Cox underscores the importance of comparative research in identifying universals of marketing which apply...not only in macrostudies of marketing systems, but also in relation to microstudies of areas such as consumer behavior.

"Contributions of Comparative Research to the Study of Consumer Behavior," Susan P. Douglas and C. Samuel Craig set rules for comparing concepts and constructs used in consumer research, their methods and limitations of measurement together with ideas for the improvement of such measures, in studies of domestic marketing systems.

3. CHANNEL NETWORK BEHAVIOR

Cox viewed channel systems as relational networks in several publications. For example: "Looked at from the point of view of the consumer, the channel of

"Flow Analysis in Marketing," Ewald T. Grether gives an historical account of Reavis Cox's work in developing flow analysis concepts.

distribution is...(a) complicated set of relationships among agencies of marketing," (1965, p. 72) same reference as above. See also R.S. Vaile, E.T. Grether, and —— (1952), *Marketing in the American Economy*, N.Y. Ronald Press.

Cox diagrams and flow charts the direction of interorganizational network interactions in various marketing flows based on theories developed by Ralph F. Breyer.

——, with Charles S. Goodman and Thomas C. Fichandler (1965), same reference as above. Cox and his associates sought global estimates of aggregate marketing contributions to the national economy including wholesale and retail trade based on the assumptions that marketing begins with heterogeneous conglomerations found in nature and transforms them into assortments fitted for consumption by the efforts of marketing intermediaries.

—— (1948), "The Meaning and Measurement of Productivity in Distribution," *Journal of Marketing*, 12 (April), 433–441.

——, with Charles S. Goodman, *Channels and Flows in Marketing Housebuilding Materials* (1954), Washington, Producers Council, Three Volumes and —— and Charles S. Goodman, "Marketing of Housebuilding Materials," *Journal of Marketing* (1956), 21, July, 36–51. Identifies dollar-day costs of performing marketing services required to construct a single house on a single site. See also ——, Charles S. Goodman and Thomas C. Fichandler (1965) same reference as above.

"Consumer Convenience and the Retail Structure of Cities" (1959), *Journal of Marketing*, 23, April, 355–362.
Retail structure is defined by Cox as the

"Shared Symbols, Meanings, and Ways of Life in Interorganizational Networks, Johan Arndt augments the interaction episodes in exchanges within relational network structures with three conceptions drawn from organization theory: shared values, beliefs, and ways of life comprising the organization culture.

"Distribution in a High-Level Economy: Twenty Years After," Charles S. Goodman assesses viability of assumptions and accuracy of estimates which he and Cox developed in this base line study of marketing performance, and relate their effort to issues addressed in this collection of papers.

"Trade Flows in a Developing Region," Roger A. Layton uses a linear equation set to transform an input/output table into a trade flow table based on a sector structure similar to that used in *Distribution in a High-Level Economy*.

"Determining the Distribution of Retail Store Types Within a Metropolitan Area: Macroretail Structure," Charles A. Ingene examines the interaction between distribution and clustering of individual stores into planned and unplanned shopping districts within metropolitan areas. Cox traces the influence of retail structure on the convenience with which consumers purchase goods and services, but demonstrates that socioeconomic characteristics of consumers affects the long term structure of retailing.

"The Dark Continents of Marketing" (1960) in Richard M. Hill (ed.) *Marketing Concepts in Changing Times*, Chicago, American Marketing Association, 239. Cox suggests that cities emerge to foster trade.

the nature of retail distributive space and the socioeconomic forces responsible for existing distributive patterns.

"Cities as Agencies of Distribution: The Vital Role of Exports"

Richard F. Wendel reviews three millenia of historical data to test the hypothesis that the pace and timing of city development are determined by city forming export marketing.

4. METHODS FOR ADVANCING MARKETING KNOWLEDGE

——, and Wroe Alderson (1950), *Theory in Marketing*, Chicago, R.D. Irwin.
——, Wroe Alderson and Stanley J. Shapiro (1964), *Theory in Marketing, Second Series*, Homewood, IL, R.D. Irwin for American Marketing Association. Editors collected papers reflecting scope, method and content of marketing theory at two points in time.

Wroe Alderson and —— (1948), "Towards a Theory of Marketing," *Journal of Marketing*, 13, Oct, 137–152.
The authors explain the need for development of marketing theory and suggest sources for and directions which such theoretical studies might take.

"Time, Space, and Competition: Formulations for the Development of Marketing Strategy"

Ronald Savitt grapples with analyses of spatial and temporal aspects of competitive behavior analysis based on Cox's contributions from 1952 to 1965 to spatial and longitudinal analysis.

"Parameter Theory and Science in Marketing"

Stig Ingebrigtsen and Michael Pettersson examine the Alderson and Cox paper in comparison with Danish parameter theory involving optional combinations of major marketing variables. Their purpose is to question the marketers' image of man, the methods by which marketing behavior is studied and to develop a more fluid language than that of mathematics for the study of marketing behavior.

———, with Charles S. Goodman and Thomas C. Fichandler, *Distribution in a High-Level Economy* (1965), Englewood Cliffs, N.J. Prentice-Hall. Cox and his associates consider effectiveness, social benefits and social costs in attaining social objectives

"Externality Focus of Macromarketing Theory"

Robert W. Nason applies the idea of decision choice to marketing externalities based on strategies for their remediation.

REFERENCES

Alderson, Wroe, and Reavis Cox. 1948. "Toward a Theory of Marketing." *Journal of Marketing* 13 (October):137–52.

Bagozzi, Richard. 1975. "Marketing as Exchange." *Journal of Marketing* 39 (October):32–39.

Cox, Reavis. 1965. "The Search for Universals in Comparative Studies of Domestic Marketing System." In *Marketing and Economic Development: Proceedings of the 1965 Fall Conference*, edited by P. D. Bennett, pp. 143–62. Chicago: American Marketing Association.

Cox, Reavis, and Wroe Alderson, eds. 1950. *Theory in Marketing*. Chicago: Richard D. Irwin.

Cox, Reavis, Wroe Alderson, and Stanley Shapiro, eds. 1964. *Theory in Marketing*, 2nd series. Homewood, IL: Richard D. Irwin.

Cox, Reavis, and C. S. Goodman. 1956. "Marketing of Housebuilding Materials." *Journal of Marketing* 21 (July):36–61.

———. 1954. *Channels and Flows in the Marketing of House Building Materials*, 3 vols. Mimeo., Philadelphia.

Cox, Reavis, C. S. Goodman, and T. C. Fichandler. 1965. *Distribution in a High-Level Economy*. Englewood Cliffs, NJ: Prentice-Hall.

Hayes, Robert H., and William J. Abernathy. 1980. "Managing Our Way to Economic Decline." *Harvard Business Review* 58 (July–August):67–77.

Hunt, Shelby. 1976. "The Nature and Scope of Marketing." *Journal of Marketing* 40 (July):17–28.

Kotler, Philip. 1972. "A Generic Concept of Marketing." *Journal of Marketing* 36 (April):46–54.

Vaile, Roland S., Ewald T. Grether, and Reavis Cox. 1952. *Marketing in the American Economy*. New York: Ronald Press.

PART I

Marketing Management Technology as Social Process

CHAPTER 1

The Marketing Concept: A Déjà Vu

STANLEY C. HOLLANDER

THE RECEIVED DOCTRINE

Most current teachers and practitioners of marketing seem to believe that something called "the marketing concept" emerged in the 1950s (or later). Moreover, and more importantly, they believe that it marked a radical transformation of U.S. business rather than simply being a new label for long-established practices. This viewpoint is expressed in almost all introductory texts that serve as primary sources of knowledge and attitudes for marketing students. We are concerned here with whether business has indeed gone through the "production," "sales," and "marketing concept" steps as conventionally described. Table 1.1 reflects perspectives found in a convenience sample of 25 general marketing and marketing management textbooks with copyright dates from 1980 through 1984. The sample includes many widely known as well as some less popular works. The summary in Table 1.1 is, of course, rough and it does ignore citations of exception and reservations, but it provides a generally fair sense of the prevailing textual account of how U.S. marketing has changed over time.

Those textbook histories, as shown in the table, differ somewhat in details, dating and terminology. Yet with few exceptions [for example, Kotler (1984) and to some degree Boone and Kurtz (1983)] they depict a drastic change in marketing after about 1950. Most adhere to what may be considered the standard chronology:

1. Up until about 1930 (or in a few citations up to 1920), business focused upon production to satisfy shortages and an intense hunger for goods. In a variant approach, industry is seen through the nineteenth and probably into the early

TABLE 1.1 Changes in Business Orientation as Presented in Marketing Textbooks, 1980–84

Year	1	2	3	4	5	6	7	8	9	10	11	12
1910	Production	*Production	Production	Production	Production	Production	Production	Production	Production	Sales	... undated Sales	Distribution
*1915	Mktg Concept											
1920				Sales			Sales	Sales	Sales		Production undated	Production
1925		Mktg Concept	Sales		Sales							
1930												Sales
1935						Sales			Sales	Sales Modified by War and Depression	Mktg <Mktg^a Concept^e	
1940			Mktg PCD	Mktg Concept	Mktg Concept	World War II	World War II	Mixed	World War II		World War II	
1945												
1950			Mktg Control /Mktg Co.		Mktg Concept	Mktg Concept	Mktg Concept	Mktg Concept (except Korean War)	Mktg Concept	Mktg Concept	Mktg Concept	Managerial Mktg Consumer Orientation
1955												
1960												
1965												

McDaniel (1982) pp.9-11	Markin (1982) pp.24ff	Stanton (1981) p.11E	Berman and Evans (1982)	Pride and Ferrell (1980) pp.14-16	Rachman and Romano (1980) pp.13-15	Nickels (1984) pp.54-62	Hartley (1984) pp.17-18	Russ and Kirkpatrick (1982) pp.9-10	Cunningham and Cunningham (1981) pp. 14-17	Boone and Kurtz (1980) pp.13-15	Lazer and Culley (1983) p.23
		Zikmund and D'Amico (1984) p.19	Diamond and Pintel (1980) pp.11-14						Gaedke and Tootelian (1982)		
		Kinnear and Bernhardt (1983) pp.13-16	Enis (1980) pp.44-51						Schewe and Smith (1983) pp.13-14		
		McCarthy and Perrault (1984) pp.35-36							Schoell and Ivy (1982) pp.15-17		

TABLE 1.1 (continued)

Notes: Some of the above authors cite some exceptions and approximations. Much of the dating is approximate. Authors in many instances say, "The marketing concept [emerged] [was adopted] [spread] [etc.] in the 1950s." Most authors also discuss subsequent modification of the marketing concept or state that a [social] [broadened] marketing concept [emerged] [prevailed] in the [1960s] [1970s]. PCD, planning/concept/department.

[a]Boone and Kurtz (1980) recognize considerable marketing in the years 1932–42 but regard it as an extension of a sales orientation. They see it as subordinate to and subsequent to production in the firm, and substantially different from the marketing concept.

Texts Without Chronologies
Cundiff, Still, and Giovanni (1980, ch. 1, "The Emergence of Marketing") note that recent environmental, competitive, and technological changes have made movement toward the marketing concept increasingly relevant.
Dalrymple and Parson (1980, p. 7). "One of the most amazing things about the marketing concept is that it has been an effective management tool for almost 30 years" that is, since around 1950).
Neidell (1983): "Over the past three decades since General Electric became the first company to widely publicize the marketing concept. . . ."
Runyon (1982, p. 205): "This growth [in marketing research following World War II] was stimulated by the emergence of the marketing concept as a fundamental philosophy of product competition."

But Somewhat at Variance
Kotler (1984, p. 20): "Although the marketing concept has a long history, its central tenets did not fully crystalize until the mid-1950s."

twentieth century as trying to move a low-level economy with little discretionary purchasing power away from concentration upon basic food, clothing, and shelter (Kinnear and Bernhard 1983; also seé Tosdal 1933).

2. The collapse of consumer demand during the Great Depression of the 1930s forced a shift from a "production era" to a "sales era." During the latter period, industry did not consider consumer desires but used hard, aggressive, high-pressure sales methods to move its output.

3a. After 1950 industry embraced the "marketing concept." That is a vague term but it implies close attention to consumer or user desires, integration or coordination of all of the firm's marketing-related activities with appropriate planning, and a focus upon profit rather than sales volume. The literature has gone on to credit marketing executives with numerous other attributes that distinguish them from sales executives (Kotler 1977; Vizza, Chambers, and Cook 1967). The marketer regards credit, transportation, and packaging as customer services and sales opportunities rather than as simply product requisites or necessary evils, and is interested in segmenting the market. The marketer's advertising stresses customer benefits, not product features or the seller's ego. Marketing involves emphasis on analysis and planning.

3b. Authors who rely upon the experience of the Pillsbury Company as detailed in a frequently quoted article (Keith 1960) distinguish between the 1950s and the 1960s. The 1950s are considered "the marketing department era," when companies invested substantially in marketing activities and converted sales, advertising, and related departments into marketing departments. But the 1960s are seen by this group as the period when a marketing philosophy permeated corporate management and decision making.

3c. Some texts depict a shift in corporate attitudes during the last decade to take into account broader social responsibilities. The 1980s are sometimes described as the era of "social marketing."

As the page citations in Table 1.1 indicate, most of these chronologies are presented as introductory material. Textbook presentation can easily be both oversimplified and platitudinous. By definition, platitudes are generally accepted beliefs. If the statement that corporate orientation changed from a production to a sales focus in the 1930s and to a marketing focus in the 1950s or 1960s is a cliché, it represents what people think did happen.

Belief in the two historical transformations has also received acceptance in more advanced academic circles. Bartels's *History of Marketing Thought* (1976) refers to the "marketing concept" as a contribution of the 1950s (pp. 177, 228). Blackwell and Talarzyk (1983, p. 8) speak of "the marketing concept which emerged in the 1960s marketing literature." The belief in the 1950 shift is also voiced in Myers, Massy, and Greyser's American Marketing Association-sponsored assessment of the sources of marketing thought and science (1980, pp. 13, 24).

Consequently, we are justified in accepting the "standard versions" referred to earlier as a falsifiable hypothesis about the process of change in business management philosophy and in searching for contradictory evidence. The now-standard chronology deals with large-scale trends in U.S. business, and thus cannot be either proven or disproven by citing one or a few exceptions. Instead, we must turn to what limited macroscopic evidence is available and to the accumulation of numerous more or less "representative" cases to judge how well the chronology fits.

This approach warrants a caveat. The evidence cited on some macromarketing topics, such as the general nature of the economy from 1850 to 1890 to 1940, is not selective. But part of the discussion of some of the other topics is. I deliberately sought out reports and citations of companies that were using market research or that had developed effective means for coordinating marketing functions. Moreover, the literature from which these examples are drawn was itself selective. Authors and publishers were (and are) naturally more interested in the new and successful than in the stale and declining business methods. Yet, I think the names of the companies that were using market-oriented approaches before 1940 add up to what would have been most of the consumer goods sector (and some of the industrial goods sector) or a prewar *Fortune 500* list. In all of the reading that I did, only a fraction of which is cited in References,[1] I came across only two cases of conscious attempts by past businesspeople to alienate customers or to ignore their desires. With regard to one incident, Reavis Cox often remarked that Commodore Vanderbilt's statement, "The public be damned," was a response to a reporter's importunate inquiry during the small hours of the morning. The other, Henry Ford's decision to offer only black cars, was both idiosyncratic and enormously helpful to his competition, General Motors.

SOME PROBLEMS OF FIT

A historical review indicates several points of divergence between the hypothesized standard and the actual business scene.

The Economic Climate

The first half of the century included two war periods, when demand far outran supply, and the Great Depression, during which demand shriveled. But most of it seems to have been a time of frantic buying.

Personal saving, putting aside the contrasting war and crash years, remained remarkably constant at about 10 to 10.5 percent of personal income (Goldsmith 1955, pp. 73–88, 155–57). The figure contrasts with post-World War II rates of about 6.5 to 9.5 percent (U.S. Bureau of the Census 1982, p. 428). This suggests that marketing required more effort than now, a view that is substantiated further by evidence of price trends from 1890 on (U.S. Bureau of the Census 1975).

In spite of the lower propensity to consume, people purchased far more than minimal food, clothing, and shelter. Cox (1949) concludes that from 1860 on, U.S. consumers generally enjoyed a growing discretionary margin above basic food, clothing, and shelter costs.

Marketing Education and Professionalization

Marketing courses appeared in U.S. colleges and universities in the early years of the century, and they flourished after 1920 (Bartels 1976; Beckman, Maynard, and Davidson 1957, p. 12). They were preceded or accompanied by growing marketing employment and publication and by the formation of professional associations in marketing.

The proliferation of marketing-related organizations is indicated in Table 1.2, which shows the dates cited by some current associations for either their own establishment or the birth of the societies from which they have evolved. Undoubtedly, many of these had quite limited memberships in the early years. However, in judging the significance of these fledgling groups, allowance must be made for the smaller absolute size of the economy, the greater role of small business, and the concomitant relatively smaller number of staff specialists. The Associated Advertising Clubs of America, founded in 1905, had more than 15,000 members by 1916 (Schudson 1984).

There were other marketing-interested organizations as well. By 1931 the Society of Industrial Engineers included a Distribution Research Committee and a Sales Managers Group ("Summary of the 18th National Convention" 1931). A number of salesmen's organizations were formed in the late nineteenth century and apparently attracted substantial membership (Hollander 1964).

The volume of marketing-related books and monographs during the early years of the century was substantial, as shown by Table 1.3. The rows should

TABLE 1.2 Founding Dates of Some Currently Existing Marketing-Related Associations or Their Antecedents

Outdoor Advertising Association	1891
Advertising Club of New York	1906
Association of National Advertisers	1910
Promotion Marketing Association of America	1911
Newspaper Advertising Association	1913
American Marketing Association	1915
Bank Marketing Association	1915
American Association of Advertising Agencies	1917
Direct Marketing Association	1917
Sales and Marketing Executives International	1936
Advertising Research Foundation	1936

Source: *Encyclopedia of Associations 1985* (Detroit: Gale Research, 1984).

not be added horizontally to derive totals for the entire period because of the slight possibility of some duplication of listings and because the criteria for listing changed with the 1928–32 volume.

The sheer number and magnitude of marketing activities and institutions, even before 1950, suggest that there must have been many people in contact with, and sensitive to, consumer markets.

Market Orientation

Within the context of a dynamic, even though at times troubled, economy, the years prior to 1950 (or really those prior to 1940 and World War II) saw acceptance and adoption of many aspects of the marketing concept—interest in and interaction with consumers; product planning to meet customer pereferences; integration of promotional, customer service, and merchandising functions; and (probably to a lesser degree) employment of a profit rather than a volume criterion.

As early as the second half of the nineteenth century, large manufacturing firms had developed continuous process methods of production or that were handling perishables integrated forward to get closer to the market. They developed extensive branch house systems to service clearly defined compact territories. Branch house personnel were responsible for local sales. They also telegraphed headquarters information about competition, demand, sales, and inventory for use in coordinating production and distribution with market opportunities. The list includes such firms as American Tobacco, Diamond Match, Quaker Oats, Washburn–Crosby (General Mills), Borden, Proctor & Gamble, and Swift and Armour (Chandler 1977, pp. 287–314).

This forward integration suggests strong efforts in coordinating marketing and nonmarketing functions. Moreover, there were exceptions to the use of jobbers. Many manufacturers sold directly to the blossoming mass retailers, such as the mail order houses and department stores, and Eastman Kodak ultimately established its own chain of retail stores. It seems unlikely, whether they worked through jobbers or not, that successful, intelligent businesspeople could have remained oblivious to market desires. Product and other management decisions must have rested, Tosdal's words (1950), "on intelligent guesses, based on experience, as to what the public really desired." Perhaps sometimes the executive guess was wrong, but the aim was commendable.

Manufacturers of more complex, technologically advanced products such as sewing machines, automated business machines, and the like moved even closer to the market and sold directly to users. In at least some companies, such as John Deere and General Electric, feedback information from the branch houses strongly influenced product design (Broehl 1984, pp. 174–92; Chandler 1977, pp. 287–314, 424–31).

Market orientations also appeared in other, less "basic" industries. For example, a careful student of the silverware trade has written of the early years

TABLE 1.3 Number of Book and Pamphlet Titles Listed Under Selected
Marketing-Related Subject Headings in Selected Volumes of the *United States Catalog*

	1912	1912–17	1918–21	1921–24	1924–25	1925–26	1927	1928–32	1933–37	1938–42
Advertising	71	125	73	72	21	70	36	175	157	150
Marketing	3	13	7	15	4	19	22	53	43	52
Marketing Research	—	—	—	—	—	—	—	2	9	3
Marketing Surveys	—	—	—	—	—	—	—	3	9	11
Marketing, Cooperative	—	—	7	8	9	8	2	12	5	6
Salesmanship	48	108	60	62	28	50	23	101	96	116
Merchandising	—	3	2	2	1	2	2	9	5	5
Retailing/Retail Trade	4	37	26	41	16	23	11	94	74	85
Wholesale	4	1	3	3	1	1	—	—	8	4

Source: United States Catalog: Books in Print. 4th ed. (New York: H. W. Wilson, 1928). 3d ed. (Minneapolis: H. W. Wilson, 1912); 2d ed. (Minneapolis, 1912); 1st ed. (Minneapolis:1899). Supplements to the United States Catalog, *Cumulative Book Index,* annual 1924–1927; cumulative: 1928–1932, 1921–1924, 1918–1921, 1912–17; cummulative: 1906–1910; cummulative: 1902–1905. After 1933, issued as: *Cummulative Book Index: A List of Books in the English Language.* (New York: H. W. Wilson, 1933—).

11

of this century: "The art of merchandising was being born and sales campaigns were launched with verve and imagination, and keen insight into the whims of consumer demand. The industry explored with enthusiasm the meaning of the new phrases, 'market appeal', 'buying motives', 'brand policy'" (Gibbs 1943).

The United States was tardy, say, in comparison with Great Britain, in developing a system of traveling salesmanship. After 1850, however, following improvements in passenger transportation, manufacturers of apparel, hardware, and other consumer goods began sending salesmen out to call on the trade. One estimate is that 100,000 salesmen were on the road by 1882–85 and 300,000 in 1903. These figures probably were exaggerations, but the Census enumerations of 59,000 in 1890 and 93,000 in 1900 may well have been undercounts (Hollander 1964; also see Atherton 1947; Marburg 1948). Selling and salesmanship, of course, are not tantamount to marketing, but the growth of sales forces, even before 1900, does indicate the way in which firms reached out to their customers and competed for business.

The accolade for an early market orientation, however, might well go to a heterogeneous group of industries and firms that did not try merely to sense their markets, but rather literally created them. Some members of this group, such as the railroads, are not usually praised for market acumen. Yet the early transcontinental railroads actively sponsored western settlement in order to obtain agricultural production and, to a lesser extent, consumer demands for goods that would result in significant freight volume (Hazard 1977). Local streetcar companies built amusement parks, usually on the outskirts of cities, to obtain additional off-peak ridership as well as to profit from the revenues the parks themselves generated. Manufacturers of domestic, commercial, and agricultural machinery and other products conducted classes to develop users and customers.

To create customers, General Electric financed local power companies, and then in the 1920s and 1930s, many utilities sold electrical appliances to consumers at reduced prices to increase the demand for power. Curtis Publishing Company was not only a pioneer in using market research. Its editors and some of the competitors changed U.S. magazines from elitist publications that relied on voluntary submissions to manuscripts, gentlemanly editorial taste, and small readership to carefully packaged collections of commissioned and in-house-crafted articles and stories that would attract the large audiences their potential advertisers desired (Wilson 1983).

Marketing Research

The increasing professionalization of marketing and the growth of advertising agencies were associated with substantial developments in marketing research and analysis. C. C. Parlin began his market research work for Curtis Publishing Company in about 1911 (Bartels 1976, pp. 124–25, 38). By 1931, the

University of Illinois Bureau of Business Research was able to publish a 75-page annotated market research bibliography that listed probably 1,000 to 1,500 items.

It must be admitted that, by contemporary standards, much of the marketing research of the 1920s and 1930s seems cold and impersonal. The sources in the Illinois bibliography, for example, seem mainly repositories for facts and figures about markets and about the distribution of goods. Aside from an occasional study of, for instance, the returned goods problem, the annotations hardly even hint at such topics as motives and attitudes.

However, even prior to the 1930s, many large companies were doing consumer surveys and were obtaining consumer reactions to their current and potential offerings.

Starch (1923) also felt that much marketing research was too mechanistic and statistical, rather than psychological and attitudinal, but he published examples of consumer questionnaires on raisins, dentifrices, paints, fountain pens, and retail services. These questionnaires asked for product attribute evaluations and saliency ratings. Blanchard (1921), a practitioner, likened market research to medical diagnosis, a prerequisite to prescribing treatment. He said it was customary for an advertising agency that handled a large account to send skilled interviewers to obtain opinions from jobbers, retailers, and consumers before preparing the campaign. This provided a good basis for selecting copy appeals, as well as serving other marketing policy purposes, according to Converse (1927, p. 400).

The 1922 Montgomery Ward catalog said: "Our buyers have been spending part of their time visiting many of our customers in their homes. Our representatives are constantly calling upon many of you, getting your ideas, your criticisms, your suggestions." The statement at the very least showed recognition of the yet-unformulated marketing concept. Similarly, in 1917 R. H. Macy and Company engaged a full-time interviewer to question customers as to what they liked and disliked about the store (Hower 1943, p. 373). Carman and Uhl (1973), who differ from most general textbook writers, cite the early "purchasing agent of the public" philosophy of wholesalers and retailers as one indication of "pre-war marketing orientation." Bartels (1976, p. 228) and Blackwell and Talarzk (1983) also find marketing concept counterparts among retailers in, respectively, "the customer is king" philosophy of the 1920s and the close customer contact enjoyed by nineteenth-century small merchants.

Turning to manufacturers, Frey (1940, pp. 368–76) cites consumer surveys and panel projects conducted in the 1930s for General Motors, Proctor & Gamble, General Electric, Kendall Mills, Bendix, International Silver, Dennison, Westinghouse, American Safety Razor, Life Savers, General Foods, Swift, and Beechnut Packing Company. In the 1920s, Corning Glass interviewed 3,448 housewives to find out what Pyrexware items they used most and why; Gorton Pew Fisheries Ltd. asked 10,000 women what they would think of canned codfish cakes and then ran a product test in 2,000 homes; while the United Hotel Corporation used surveys of businesspeople to find good communities for hotel building (Converse 1927). The advertising manager of the Kellogg Company spearheaded a cooperative magazine readership study in 1911 (Lockley 1950). Over the years, advertising agencies, both anxious to absorb a greater marketing role and pressured by their clients to do so in return for their commissions, sponsored much proprietary marketing research. N. W. Ayer's collection of market statistics for its client Nichols–Shepard in 1879 was a pioneering bit of market research.

The agency-sponsored studies ultimately included much psychologically oriented work. Hurwitz (1984, pp. 3-4) describes the alliance between advertising agencies and marketing researchers. The agencies funneled much of the research findings back to their clients and their campaigns. Pollay's careful content analysis of consumer ads appearing in large circulation magazines from the 1900s through the 1970s (1983) shows that the focus upon user benefits and other hallmarks of a "marketing concept" orientation peaked in the 1930s and have since declined markedly.

Internal Coordination

The indications are the advertising, sales, promotion, and merchandising people in industry worked together more closely than is commonly thought.[2]

The Taylor Society (now the Society for the Advancement of Management) studied a selective and possibly unrepresentative sample of about 100 companies in 1920 and 1921. It found that almost all coordinated the various marketing functions through committees, through making the other functions subordinate to, and a part of, the sales department, or by having all report to the same senior executive. A small number had specialized sales engineering units responsible for much marketing planning and budgeting (Taylor Society 1920, 1921). Among 62 corporate respondents to a 1922 study, 18 had "commercial research" departments. Half of those departments reported to the firm's sales manager, the other half to a higher executive (Weld 1922).

While the Taylor Society and Weld surveys did not identify individual respondents, coordination arrangements have been reported for some companies. Both the outbound freight and the advertising manager reported to the sales manager at U.S. Rubber Company as early as 1902. At about the same time, DuPont's sales department included both the advertising and information (that is, market intelligence) bureaus. Even earlier, about 1895, product managers at General Electric branch houses reported to higher-level product managers at headquarters. Those national managers in turn served on a sales committee along with the director of foreign sales and the director of advertising. That committee was chaired by the company vice-president (a very senior title in the days before the proliferation of vice-presidential hierarchies) who today would be called "VP-Marketing." This committee considered "pricing, competitors' activities, market conditions, customers' needs and concerns, and the processing of major orders" (Chandler 1977, pp. 424–31).

During the 1920s, many industrial equipment companies were reported to have responded to intensified competition by, among other things, combining their selling and merchandising (that is, product planning) staffs. Apparently this did not always work out well because merchandising often became very subordinate to sales and overly devoted to short-run activities connected with prospective individual orders. Consequently, a number of companies established or reestablished merchandising as a separate function (Moore 1937). Probably such a separation was instituted at the Dennison Manufacturing Company (paper products) (Keir and Dennison 1929b).

Businessmen who made a deliberate decision to separate the two functions, whether well advised or not, were clearly far more sensitive to the nature of the total marketing task than the the the decision-by-default-and-ignorance stereotypes depicted by the modern view of the revolutionary nature of the marketing concept.

Moreover, even though many of the general marketing books then did not discuss the coordination of marketing activities, the subject was by no means absent from the literature. The lack of consistent definitions and distinctions between such terms as "distribution," "marketing," "sales," and "merchandising" in those days (see Reilly 1929) caused some of the discussion of managerial coordination to appear in more specialized books on sales, such as Hayward (1926; also see LaLonde and Morrison 1967), and merchandising, such as Frey (1940). To some extent, coordination was also seen as a general management obligation, particularly at a time of much personal ownership–management, and was discussed in general business administration books such as Marshall (1921).

Diversification and Simplification

The simplification movements of World War I and of the 1920s provide inverse evidence of the product diversification and segmentation inherent in the conventional marketing concept. To historians, laws and corrective movements often demonstrate the existence of whatever those laws or movements were designed to correct. That is the case with the national simplification program.

Rather than seeking only maximum physical output prior to 1930, U.S. industry often produced an enormous *variety* of objects. Herbert Hoover, upon becoming secretary of commerce in 1921, launched a campaign for industrial efficiency that embraced the ideas of voluntary, industry-wide standardization and simplification. This crusade continued until the end of the decade. Then the main thrusts of public and industry attention turned to other things and the appropriation for the national Bureau of Standards was severely curtailed. Moreover, the voluntary programs fell apart as individual firms increasingly sought competitive advantage through product diversification (U.S. Library of Congress 1974, pp. 10–15).

The simplification movement produced numerous temporary and some permanent successes (Hudson 1928). Some individual consumer goods companies carried out their own internal simplification programs. For example, Cherington and Roddick (1940) cite the case of a candy bar manufacturer who eliminated many slow-selling varieties, discouraged the sale of mediocre ones, and vigorously promoted the best portion of his product portfolio with very beneficial effects on sales and profits.

But most writers (for example, Soule 1934) noted, or complained, that the simplification programs had little effect on final consumer goods. Cracker and biscuit bakeries were, for instance, reported to be producing between 150 and 350 varieties in 1925, and it is not at all clear whether those figures include all different packing case sizes and whether they include sweet goods such as cookies and cakes (Stevens 1927). The tendency toward diversification has been ascribed to many motives, including an overeagerness to satisfy consumer whims (Hudson 1928; McCullough 1928). But basically the issue centers around the recurring tension between trying to satisfy market demands with a low-priced standardized product and trying to approach the market with the advantages of a full and differentiated line.

The tendency of U.S. industry to proliferate product variations to match customer desires (and to obtain competitive differentiation) during the 1930s is demonstrated by simplification efforts that the government again mounted during the 1940 war years. As a minor functionary in the Office of Price Administration, the author participated peripherally in an arduous but more or less successful effort to induce the cotton work glove industry, which had customized its offerings to meet climatic variations and the preferences of every craft from corn-huskers to oyster-shuckers, to concentrate on about 80 to 125 styles instead of the pre-War 500 or 600.

Credit, Packaging, and Transportation

The marketing concept has been credited with changing the pre-1950 view that credit, transportation, and packaging were necessary evils into a post-1950 appreciation of their use as selling tools (see Vizza, Chambers, and Cook 1967). With regard to credit, it should be sufficient to quote Cox on installment buying. After pointing out (1949, pp. 5–18) that the formal installment buying arrangement appeared in the United States during the early nineteenth century, and that its growth paralleled the rise in purchases of mass-produced consumer durables, Cox says somewhat retrospectively (p. 394):

> And many producers and distributors do use it [installment credit] as a form of sales promotion. This is why some of the largest producers have gone to great pains to set up financing agencies to serve their distributors. It is probably the

principal reason why many retailers are determined to keep installment financing in their own hands rather than let it be taken over by banks, finance companies and other cash lenders.[3]

The pre-World War II attitude toward packaging is summarized by Frey (1940, p. 256):

> Just as increased attention in recent years has been devoted to the manufacture of products suited to the market, so too has stress been laid upon the development of appropriate packaging. Recognition of the importance of the package as a sales and profit factor has led to an increase in the number and variety of products offered for sale in packages as well as improvement in existing packages.

As early as 1886, Quaker Oats placed sales messages and recipes on its packages (Schudson 1984, p. 166). Kiernan (1985, p. 261) believes competitive, promotional packaging first emerged in the 1800s among toilet paper manufacturers.

Attitudes toward transportation are demonstrated by the numerous ingenious pricing schemes designed to widen market outreach, described by Nelson and Keim (1941). Clearly, executives were not treating remote customers on a purely "Here it is—if you want it, pay to haul it" basis. Many companies included the traffic or outbound freight manager as part of the sales executive's staff, and numerous branch house systems were established to bring inventory close to the customers.

Profit Orientation

Recent presentations of the marketing concept often stress its emphasis on a *profit*, rather than a *volume*, orientation. The late nineteenth-century antitrust fervor reflected a popular belief that at least some corporations restricted output to enhance profits. Similarly, the businesspeople of the 1930s would be very much surprised to learn that they are now being castigated for a supposedly reckless pursuit of volume. Then they were often excoriated fairly or unfairly for restricting output ("plowing under little 'pig irons'") to maintain prices and unit profits. "A great deal of criticism was directed at the imperfections of markets organized around administered prices" (McKittrick 1957, p. 71). This contrasted with an agricultural situation where pure competition forced each farmer to maximize output and thus depress agricultural prices. The claimed resultant disparity between the prices farmers paid and the prices farmers received was advanced as an argument for government crop control and price support programs (Gee 1930, pp. 50–53, 156–58).

In fact, McKittrick, whose 1957 American Marketing Association (AMA) conference paper is often cited in discussions of the marketing concept, but who seems to have been often misread or not read, faulted the owner–managers of pre-1940 corporations for over- (not under-) concentration on profits. This, he felt, contrasted with the more statesman-like role of the contemporary hired corporate manager who acted as mediator between various stakeholders, such as stockowners, workers, customers, the government, the environments, and the public. The main weakness of the older companies was, in his view, insufficient attention to long-term strategic planning.

Considerable ground exists for believing that many pre-World War II businesspeople were able to distinguish between profitable and unprofitable activities, and pursued the former. Accounting historians agree that fairly sophisticated cost-accounting tools were available and were used before 1940 (Chatfield 1977, p. 172; Jackson 1952, p. 228). Sales analysis was also widely utilized before 1940. Consequently, it is difficult to believe that business executives did not make cost and revenue comparisons. The Federal Trade Commission did find that many manufacturers were ignorant of the costs of serving particular customer classifications, specific territories, and/or product markets (Edwards 1940, p.108). But Palamountain (1955, p. 64, n. 26) believed that the 1936 Robinson–Patman Act had the paradoxical effect of causing many suppliers to engage in more careful cost accounting, which showed that their small customers were being charged less than justified by costs of serving such accounts. Aside from this development, there was considerable evidence (Palamountain 1955, pp. 62–73 and sources cited therein) that many producers had some reasonable appreciation of the cost and revenue relationships attached to various-sized accounts.

Cowan (1940, p. 77), perhaps talking about the blue ribbon companies, said, "Classifications are made to show volume, expenses, gross profits and net results by products, periods, regions and persons." (If he had substituted "places" for regions, he would have invented his own 4 P's.) The author of this chapter has heard Cowan lecture on how he introduced selective concentration on the more profitable accounts at Swift & Company in the early years of the Great Depression. The "DuPont Model," a well-known set of equations for estimating and explaining return on investment, still taught today, was instituted at DuPont before World War I (Chandler 1977, p. 446). It must have also been available to General Motors through Donaldson Brown, a senior DuPont financial executive who subsequently transferred to the automaker.

The 1920 movement for standardization and simplification, discussed elsewhere in this chapter, involved for many companies, even much smaller enterprises, the elimination of unprofitable lines. A producer of men's felt hats went from 1,684 styles and color permutations to the 70 on which it did 90 percent of its business, and a shoe firm reduced its offerings from approximately 2,500 styles in three grades to 100 in one. Both increased their profits (Frey 1940, pp. 180, 186).

Many reasons may induce business firms to concentrate, reluctantly or eagerly, on volume objectives, which in the long run may turn out to be profit objectives. This leads to the final point, expressed by Filene (1927, pp. 80–82). He held that while it was common practice to measure costs and add them up to determine a (profitable) price, it was much better practice to set a price that would increase volume and then use it as both a means and a goal to cost reduction. Filene's approach seems closer to a true market orientation than any mandate for profit seeking.

A Note on "High-Pressure" Selling

The standard chronology describes the 1930s as a period of "high-pressure" selling. This characteristic is seen primarily as a response to the Great Depression and the presumed shift from a seller's market to one in which the buyers assumed power. "High pressure" is not always well defined, but it is represented by stereotypes such as the "Music Man," the sly Yankee trader, and P. T. Barnum; in other words, in personal salesmanship fast-talking insistence upon immediate purchase, in advertising constant boastful repetition, and in both little regard for full and candid disclosure.

One may well raise some questions about the validity of the stereotypes. Many pre-1950 salesmen had long continuing relationships with their customers. Wholesalers dominated much of nineteenth-century consumer goods business (Porter and Livesay 1971). The growth in the 1930s of voluntary chains that united large numbers of small retailers under wholesaler leadership is evidence of the continuation of at least some of that influence. Although wholesalers sometimes acted in a cavalier fashion toward dealers, those relationships and semi-integrated arrangements could not have continued as long or as successfully as they did if they had not been based upon mutual trust and cooperation. High-pressure tactics would have been self-defeating in the long run. "Diamond Jim" Brady, the apparent extreme exemplar of another "high-pressure" type, the ostentatious, vulgar, free-spending "good-time Charlie," best known for his liaison with the actress Lillian Russell, was actually a skilled salesman of railroad equipment. His ornate dress, hail-fellow-well-met manner, opulent parties, and lavish gifts were elements of a sales approach that was based upon an encyclopedic knowledge of the railroads. Through personal inspection and through acquaintanceships down to the section gang level, Brady became familiar with the roads' trackage, rolling stock, motive power, personnel, and operating problems and needs (Burke 1972, pp. 67–69).

This is not to deny the use, probably the widespread use, of high-pressure tactics before 1940. The critical question for this chapter, however, is not whether high pressure was existent or nonexistent prior to 1940, but rather whether the pre-1940 condition was radically different from that of modern time. The nature of many television commercials and recent controversies over so-called "junk mail" and over children's television advertising illuminate the fact that high-pressure selling did not permanently disappear in 1940. Nor, to cite one more example, did it permanently leave the used car lot (Browne 1973). So, in practice it becomes hard to distinguish the 1930s from the 1970s or the 1980s as representative of the ''hard'' and ''soft'' sell. As Reavis Cox might remark, we cannot seek a vigorously competitive society, in the business rather than the economic sense of competition, in which people compete only softly.[4]

Social Marketing

As noted earlier, the term ''social marketing'' has come into vogue as an extension and improvement on the marketing concept. It has at least two quite different meanings. One is a desire for normative judgments, a concern for the societal impact of marketing actions and systems. But that is certainly not new to the literature. Lack of a holistic view can hardly be charged against the early writers who are constantly accused of being insufficiently managerial. It also cannot be levied against a pre-World War II literature that produced such volumes as Stewart and Dewhurst's *Does Distribution Cost Too Much?* (1939) and Borden's *Economic Effects of Advertising* (1942). The question of whether managerial attitudes have changed is beyond the limits of this essay.

The other meaning of social marketing is the application of marketing techniques to nonprofit organizations and to social and political causes. Again, this is hardly new. An advertising textbook published in 1917 (Martin) contains a chapter on ''Public Sentiment Campaigns.'' It includes sections on political advertising; advertising a city, a state, and a nation; advertising to win strikes; and general goodwill advertising. One has only to read even such self-serving reports as George Creel's *How We Advertised America* (1920) to sense the planning, organization, and analysis behind the government effort to mold public opinion during World War I. Social marketing was, and still to a large extent is, done by people who called themselves fundraisers, publicists, propagandists, and public relations counsel. A supposed distinction is that the social marketer works with more knowledge of the potential audience(s), draws more careful plans, and is more likely than the other specialists to shape the offering as well as its description. These, however, are more matters of individual stature and competence than of specialization. Lasswell, an authoritative observer, said (1935, p. 190): ''Business and nonprofit groups may handle propaganda through the law department, the marketing division or the office of the chief executive and the official title of the propagandist may be descriptive or deceptive.'' Similarly, Edward Bernays, a well-known public relations counsel, wrote (1928) that he used the same techniques of managing events to further the interests of the government of Lithuania that he used to create new markets for silk textiles.

In Retrospect

Recapitulating the evidence presented thus far may be helpful. Macrostatistics show that, war and depression notwithstanding, the U.S. public absorbed a substantial and increasing volume of discretionary products over the years between

1900 and 1941. Many new products such as radios, oilburners, air conditioning, electric refrigerators, new packaged foods, and passenger air transport were introduced or popularized, and many product modifications took place.

This chapter has not explored the difficulties of fashioning markets for those innovations, and in retrospect they may seem so convenient and necessary that consumer resistance would appear to have been impossible—but that is historical error. The consumer who never knew an electric refrigerator had to be convinced that it would work, that it would not explode, that it would not harm the food, and that it was worth both the monetary cost and the effort of change. All of this discretionary spending and new product adoption took place in a setting in which personal savings remained high. Yet price behavior, which involved only a fairly moderate upward trend from 1890 to about 1915 and a generally declining one from 1920 to 1940, indicates that the high savings rate did not result from a shortage of consumer goods on which to spend the money. (The 1915–20 inflation was an exception to this observation.) Clearly customers had to be obtained and business did not enjoy a runaway sellers' market.

Marketing professionalization grew during the period. This becomes especially apparent if one recognizes that many people who performed marketing management or marketing staff functions bore such titles as sales manager, merchandising manager, or sales engineer. Professional societies developed, although their memberships were much smaller than their modern counterparts'. Business school marketing courses grew, and advertising agencies became marketing agencies.

With their marketing orientation, major companies offered very extensive choices to cater to intersegment variations in product demands. They used a variety of mechanisms to coordinate advertising, selling, sales promotion, product design, and production. They used market analysis, test marketing, and survey research. They lacked some of the current market researchers' psychological tools and many of their statistical ones, but those are matters of technique, not orientation. They understood the use of credit and transport as marketing tools, and insofar as practicable (then as well as now) sought profit rather than sheer volume. Even social marketing can easily be traced to the early years of the century. As an aspect of a world marked by great political, religious, and moral movements, its history stretches into the very distant past.

Some perceptive writers now say that only a few or some companies adopted the marketing concept after World War II and reconversion. Even more perceptive writers say that the concept adopted was flawed and limited, at least in what came to be its simplistic interpretation. Similarly, the pre-World War II business press contains many generalized, unsubstantiated statements about business marketing inadequacies. But that is normal. Accountants, controllers, personnel managers, traffic managers, product designers, and all other types of specialists as well as marketers usually devote their nontechnical speeches to the subject of how unappreciated they are. The record suggests that the differences between marketing before and after World War II are matters of degree rather than of kind, and that many of those boil down to differences in technology and terminology, not in basic philosophy. The standard chronology does not fit.

EXPLANATION

How can one explain the prevalence and popularity of the standard chronologies in the face of so many contrary facts?

The idea of the marketing concept has been popularized within the academic community through introductory textbooks and within the business community through trade press articles and after-dinner speeches. Many publishers, authors, and speakers believe that these media call for easily remembered, absolutist presentations, with little subtlety or reservation. One modern view of good historical pedagogy calls for very distinctive labeling of discrete time periods organized around easily remembered dates, such as the decennial years. This does produce the best results on machine-graded examinations.

In fairness, it should be noted that many of the texts cited in Table 1.1 contain statements about exceptions to the chronologies. A few journal articles cast doubt on either the novelty or the pervasiveness of the marketing concept (LaLonde and Morrison 1967; Bell and Emory 1971). Professor Ronald Fullerton (1985) prepared a paper (which I have by agreement not seen as I write this essay) that will agree with what has been said here. The point is that I cannot claim to be a lone voice crying in the wilderness.

The idea of moving from a production to a sales to a marketing orientation is the marketer's version of the belief in *progress* that characterizes Western, and particularly U.S. culture. The so-called "marketing concept era" came immediately after the 1940s' war and reconversion decade—the most pronounced "production era" of the century. The war years may have obscured marketers' impressions of earlier times.

Marketing is particularly ahistorical or even antihistorical. Marketing scholars typically quote only very recent sources in their journal articles (Goldman 1979). There are two journals in the history of accounting; *The Academy of Management* has a strong historical section. Although some small signs of change have appeared, marketing lags far behind the other business disciplines in historical research. A large proportion of what has been made available on the history of marketing thought [for example, Bartels (1976) and a now out-of-print and mostly unknown or forgotten series of reprints offered by Arno Press] is based upon college textbooks. These are very useful and informative sources, but they constitute only a part of the story. We need a much more extensive literature that explores the marketing academics' more scholarly output and the thoughts and actions of marketing practitioners, critics, and regulators.

The standard chronology has probably hindered research into marketing history by more or less denying that there is any. It has been enormously self-satisfying, however. It tells marketing students, and academics, and practitioners that they are the first people in history to fully understand marketing.

IMPLICATIONS

The historical record, in addition to its intrinsic value, has important implications for current research, teaching, and practice.

Whether one agrees with the thesis of this chapter or not, any reader must find in any detailed historical account evidence of the richness, diversity, and complexity of marketing in an industrialized world. The standard chronologies are, I submit, gross oversimplifications. That still leaves open the question of what the harm of oversimplification is in this connection.

First, it provides an entirely false sense of progress. The euphoria over the supposed emergence of the marketing concept out of the primeval muck of production and sales orientations may have had some positive benefits. It may have temporarily stimulated morale, encouraged enrollment in marketing courses, and enhanced the status and budgets of some corporate marketing divisions. To the extent that that enthusiasm rested upon an erroneous base, it held out a false promise. It clouded the profession's eyes to how little basic progress had been made in solving fundamental micro and macro problems.

Drucker's familiar remark (1969) that consumerism was the shame, the failure of the marketing concept, is more than a catch-phrase. It indicates the gap between what marketers thought they were providing in the way of new and increased consumer satisfactions and what substantial segments of the market felt had really been accomplished. It also suggests that the gap will not be permanently closed by bandying about other slogans, such as "social marketing." Perhaps that gap can never be eliminated in a society that must accept some of the costs and frictions as well as the benefits of competition and that encourages constantly rising expectations. Any serious attempt to understand or deal with it must pass from sloganeering to detailed consideration of a topic familiar to all of Reavis Cox's students: detemining the cost and value of marketing.

Second, the dominance of the marketing concept, as a prime paradigm for marketing academics, tended to divert scholarly attention away from some of the social and macroscopic implications of marketing activity.[5] Marketing teaching and research will probably always remain primarily managerial. There have been both many exceptions to an exclusively managerial orientation in the past and signs of growing current interest in macromarketing and social issues. Nevertheless, the enthusiasm for the marketing concept is likely to have been the cause of some imbalance in academic interest.

Third, the belief in the emergence of the marketing concept as a new and efficacious solution to marketing managerial problems may well have reduced marketing managers' attention to many aspects of their craft. It certainly overshadowed academic attention to such matters as marketing strategy (Day and Wenseley 1983) and negotiation (Mitchell and Dickinson 1985). Some writers believe that it led to oversegmentation, the creation of overly extensive product lines, and the loss of important economies of scale (Levitt 1983; Resnick, Turney, and Mason 1979a,b). Both marketing management and, to an even greater degree, business management are complex operations. Stressing one or two or three aspects of either process to the neglect of the rest of the task inevitably becomes dysfunctional. One wonders if all of the proclaimed emphasis on marketing has not led to the slighting of other manufacturing considerations besides the oversegmentations discussed above.

Caution should temper enthusiasm for any one swift panacea that is supposed to resolve marketing problems. The marketing concept, simplification, diversification, centralization, decentralization. portfolio theory, emphasis on volume, market share or profit, and absorption of Japanese marketing techniques all seem to have their uses and limitations. But none are "cure-alls" and most are less novel than they first seem. History may help us determine what works when and under what conditions.

Acknowledgment. I am not entirely certain that Reavis Cox will agree with all of the points made in this chapter, but he always encouraged considerable diversity of opinion among his students. Once, after I gave a paper at an AMA session in which he presided, someone approached him and in an attempt at academic one-upmanship said, "Your own student disagrees with you." I was prepared to defend my paper as purely Coxian, but Reavis ended the matter by saying, "That is the point of education." Moreover, Reavis always encouraged my interest in a historical approach. I do wish to acknowledge the assistance of Mr. Jeffrey Thompson and Mrs. Kathy Rassuli in connection with the tables and of Mrs. Jan Thelen in preparing the manuscript. The essay has been edited by incorporating suggestions made by Prof. Ronald A. Fullerton.

NOTES

1. The documentation has been curtailed by remembrance of Reavis Cox's literary admonition that a desire to incorporate every 5 by 8-inch bibliography card in the manuscript is the Achilles' heel of graduate student writing.

2. At the same time I have been drafting this essay, Prof. Ronald I. Greenwood and Charles D. Wrege prepared a paper, "Introducing Marketing to Scientific Management 1921–1927," for presentation at the Second Workshop on Historical Research in Marketing, East Lansing, Michigan, April 18–30, 1985, which appeared in the workshop proceedings.

3. Cox goes on to predict that when installment selling becomes so widespread as to offer no differential advantage, many retailers will be quite willing to let third parties handle their credit ar-

rangements. That is exactly what has happened today; so in some ways it is the modern, not the pre-1950, merchant who regards consumer credit as a necessary evil.

4. This is a paraphrase of a remark in class or conversation that I am now unable to quote verbatim.

5. Both Prof. Roger Dickinson of the University of Texas at Arlington and Prof. Fisk have suggested this in personal correspondence.

REFERENCES

Atherton, Lewis E. 1947. "Predecessors of the Commercial Drummer in the Old South." *Bulletin of the Business Historical Society* 21 (February):17ff.

Bartels, Robert. 1976. *The History of Marketing Thought,* 2nd ed. Columbus, OH: Grid.

Beckman, Theodore, Harold H. Maynard, and William R. Davison. 1957. *Principles of Marketing,* 6th ed. New York: Ronald Press.

Bell, Martin, and C. William Emory. 1971. "The Faltering Marketing Concept." *Journal of Marketing* 35 (October): 37–42.

Berman, Barry, and Joel Evans. 1982. *Marketing.* New York: Macmillan.

Bernays, Edward J. 1928. "Manipulating Public Opinion." *American Journal of Sociology* 33 (May): 958–71.

Blackwell, Roger D., and W. Wayne Talarzyk. 1983. "Life-Style Retailing: Competitive Strategies for the 1980s." *Journal of Retailing* 59 (Winter):7ff.

Blanchard, Frank L. 1921. *The Essentials of Advertising.* New York: McGraw-Hill.

Boone, Louis E., and David L. Kurtz. 1980. *Contemporary Marketing,* 3rd ed. Hinsdale, IL: Dryden.

Borden, Neil H. 1942. *The Economic Effect of Advertising.* Chicago: Richard D. Irwin.

Broehl, Wayne G., Jr. 1984. *John Deere's Company.* Garden City, NY: Doubleday.

Browne, Joy. 1973. *The Used Car Game.* Lexington, MA: Lexington Books.

Burke, John. 1972. *Duet in Diamonds.* New York: Putnam.

Carman, James M., and Kenneth P. Uhl. 1973. *Phillips and Duncan's Marketing Principles and Practices.* Homewood, IL: Richard D. Irwin.

Chandler, Alfred. 1977. *The Visible Hand.* Cambridge, MA: Belknap/Harvard University Press.

Chatfield, Michael. 1977. *A History of Accounting Thought,* rev. ed. Huntington, NY: Krieger.

Cherington, Paul T., and Harrison A. Roddick. 1940. "Strategies and Policies in Marketing." *Annals of the American Academy of Political and Social Sciences* 209 (May): 79–83.

Converse, Paul D. 1927. *Selling Policies.* New York: Prentice-Hall.

Cowan, Donald R. G. 1940. "The Function of Management in Marketing." *Annals of the American Academy of Political and Social Science* 209 (May):71–78.

Cox, Reavis. 1949. *The Economics of Installment Buying.* New York: Ronald Press.

Creel, George. 1920. *How We Advertised America.* New York: Harper (reprinted, New York: Arno Press, 1972).

Cundiff, Edward W., Richard R. Still, and Norman A. Giovanni. 1980. *Fundamentals of Marketing,* 2nd ed. Englewood Cliffs, NJ: Prentice-Hall.

Cunningham, William, and Isabela Cunningham. 1981. *Marketing*. Cincinnati: South-Western.

Dalrymple, Douglas J., and Edward J. Parsons. 1980. *Marketing Management: Text and Cases*. New York: John Wiley & Sons.

Day, George S., and Robin Wensley. 1983. "Marketing Theory with a Strategic Orientation." *Journal of Marketing* 47 (Fall): 79–89.

Diamond, Jay, and Gerald Pintel. 1980. *Principles of Marketing,* 2nd ed. Englewood Cliffs, NJ: Prentice-Hall.

Drucker, Peter. 1969. "The Shame of Marketing." *Marketing Communications* (August):60–64.

Edwards, Corwin D. 1940. "Pricing Processes and Policies," in Howard T. Houde, ed, *Marketing in our American Economy: The Annals of the American Academy of Political and Social Science* 209 (May): 108–21.

Enis, Ben. 1980. *Marketing Principles*, 3rd ed. Santa Monica, CA: Goodyear.

Filene, Edward A. 1927. *The Way Out*. Garden City, NY: Doubleday/Gage.

Frey, Albert W. 1940. *Manufacturer's Product, Package and Price Policies*. New York: Ronald Press.

Fullerton, Ronald A. 1985. "Was There a 'Production Era' in Marketing History? A Multinational Approach." In *Marketing in the Long Run*, edited by S. C. Hollander and T. R. Nevett, pp. 388–400. East Lansing: Department of Marketing and Transportation, Michigan State University.

Gaedke, Ralph M., and Dennis H. Tootelian. 1982. *Marketing: Principles and Applications*. St. Paul: West.

Gee, Wilson. 1930. *The Place of Agriculture in American Life*. New York: Macmillan.

Gibbs, George S. 1943. *The Whitesmiths of Taunton*. Cambridge, MA: Harvard University Press.

Goldman, Arieh. 1979. "Publishing Activity in Marketing as an Indicator of Its Structure and Interdisciplinary Boundaries." *Journal of Marketing Research* 16:485–94.

Goldsmith, Raymond W. 1955. *A Study of Savings in the United States*, Vol. 1. Princeton, NJ: Princeton University Press.

Gray, James. 1954. *Business Without Boundaries*. Minneapolis: University of Minnesota Press.

Hartley, Robert E. 1984. *Marketing Fundamentals*. New York: Harper & Row.

Hayward, Walter S. 1926. *Sales Administration*. New York: Harper.

Hazard, John L. 1977. *Transportation: Management, Economics Policy*. New York: Cornell Marine Press.

Hollander, Stanley C. 1964. "Nineteenth Century Anti-Drummer Legislation in the United States." *Business History Review* 38 (Winter):479–500.

Holleran, O. C. 1935. *Checksheet: Introduction of New Consumer Products,* U.S. Department of Commerce, Market Research Series No. 7. Washington, D.C.: U.S. Government Printing Office.

Hower, Ralph M. 1943. *History of Macy's of New York*. Cambridge, MA: Harvard University Press.

Hudson, Ray M. 1928. "Organized Effort in Simplification." *Annals of the American Academy of Political and Social Science* 137 (May):1–8.

Hurwitz, Donald. 1984. "U.S. Market Research and the Study of Radio in the 1930s." Paper presented at the International Association for Mass Communications Research Congress, Prague, August.

Jackson, G. Hugh. 1952. "A Half Century of Cost Accounting Progress." *National Association of Cost Accounting Bulletin* 34 (September):3–17 (Reprinted in Michael Chatfield, ed. *Contemporary Studies in the Evolution of Accounting Thought.* Belmont, CA: Dickinson).

Keir, John A., and Henry S. Dennison. 1929a. "Merchandising Standards." In *Scientific Management in America,* edited by H.S. Person, pp. 163–74. New York: Harper.

——. 1929b. "Control of Sales Operations." In *Scientific Management in America,* edited by H.S. Person, pp. 291–307. New York: Harper.

Keith, Robert J. 1960. "The Marketing Revolution." *Journal of Marketing* 24 (January):35–38.

Kiernan, Thomas. 1985. *The Road to Colossus.* New York: Morrow.

Kinnear, Thomas C., and Kenneth L. Bernhardt. 1983. *Principles of Marketing.* Glenview, IL: Scott, Foresman.

Kotler, Philip. 1984. *Marketing Management: Analysis Planning and Control,* 5th ed. Englewood Cliffs, NJ: Prentice-Hall.

——. 1977. "From Sales Obsession to Marketing Effectiveness." *Harvard Business Review* 55 (November–December):68–69.

Kurtz, David L., and Louis E. Boone. 1984. *Marketing,* 2nd ed. New York: Dryden.

LaLonde, Bernard J., and Edward J. Morrison. 1967. "Marketing Management Concepts Yesterday and Today." *Journal of Marketing* 31 (January):9–13.

Lasswell, Harold D. 1935. "The Person, Subject and Object of Propaganda." *Annals of the American Academy of Political and Social Science* 179 (May):187–93.

Lazer, William, and James Culley. 1983. *Marketing Management: Foundations and Practices.* Boston: Houghton Mifflin.

Lazerfield, Paul F. 1934. "The Psychological Aspect of Market Research." *Harvard Business Review* 13 (October): 54–71.

Levitt, Theodore. 1983. "The Globalization of Markets." *Harvard Business Review* 61 (May–June):92–102.

Lewis, E. St. Elmo. 1931. "Let the Customer Plan Your Product." *Society of Industrial Engineers Bulletin* 13 (May): 17.

Lockley, Lawrence C. 1950. "Notes on the History of Marketing Research." *Journal of Marketing* 14 (April):733–35.

Lyons, Leverett S. 1926. *Salesmen in Marketing Strategy.* New York: Macmillan.

Marburg, Theodore F. 1948. "Manufacturer's Drummer 1852." *Bulletin of the Business Historical Society* 22 (April):52ff.

Markin, Rom. 1982. *Marketing Strategy and Management,* 2nd ed. New York: John Wiley & Sons.

Marshall, Leon C. 1921. *Business Administration.* Chicago: University of Chicago.

Martin, Mac. 1917. *Advertising Campaigns.* New York: Alexander Hamilton Institute.

McCarthy, E. Jerome, and William O. Perrault, Jr. 1984. *Basic Marketing,* 8th ed. Homewood, IL: Richard D. Irwin.

——. 1981. *Basic Marketing,* 6th ed. Homewood, IL: Richard D. Irwin.

McCullough, E. W. 1928. "The Relations of the Chamber of Commerce of the United States to Simplification Programs in American Industry." *Annals of the American Academy of Political and Social Science* 137 (May):9–12.

McDaniel, Carl, Jr. 1982. *Marketing,* 2nd ed. New York: Harper & Row.

McKittrick, J. B. 1957. "What Is the Marketing Management Concept?" In *The Frontiers of Marketing Thought and Science,* edited by Frank M. Bass, pp. 71–81.

Mitchell, Ted J., and Roger Dickinson. 1985. "Introducing Negotiation to the Basic Marketing Course." Paper presented at the 1985 Western Marketing Educators Association Conference.

Moore, C. W. 1937. "The Integration of Merchandising and Selling in Marketing Industrial Equipment." *Harvard Business Review* 15 (Summer):497ff.

Myers, John G., William F. Massy, and Stephen A. Greyser. 1980. *Marketing Research and Knowledge Development.* Englewood Cliffs, NJ: Prentice-Hall.

Neidell, Leonard A. 1983. *Strategic Marketing Management.* Tulsa: Pennwell.

Nelson, Saul, and Walter F. Keim. 1941. *Price Behavior and Business Policy,* Temporary National Economic Committee Monograph No. 1. Washington, D.C.: U.S. Government Printing Office.

Nickels, William G. 1984. *Marketing Principles,* 2nd ed. Englewood Cliffs, NJ: Prentice-Hall.

Palamountain, Joseph C. 1955. *The Politics of Distribution.* Cambridge, MA: Harvard University Press.

Pollay, Richard W. 1983. "The Subsiding Sizzle." In *Proceedings of the First Workshop in Historical Research in Marketing,* edited by Stanley C. Hollander and Ronald Savitt, East Lansing: Department of Marketing and Transportation Administration, Michigan State University.

Porter, Glenn, and Howard C. Livesay. 1971. *Merchants and Manufacturers.* Baltimore: Johns Hopkins University Press.

Pride, William L., and O. C. Ferrell. 1980. *Marketing,* 2nd ed. Boston: Houghton Mifflin.

Pyle, John F. 1936. *Marketing Principles.* New York: McGraw-Hill.

Rachman, David J., and Elaine K. Romano. 1980. *Modern Marketing.* Hinsdale, IL: Dryden.

Reilly, William J. 1929. *Marketing Investigations.* New York: Ronald Press.

Resnick, Alan J., Peter B. Turney, and J. Barry Mason. 1979a. "Marketers Turn to Countersegmentation." *Harvard Business Review* 57 (September–October):100–6.

———. 1979b. "Reconciling Marketing and Production Factors: A Neglected Area of Segmentation Theory." In *Theoretical Developments in Marketing,* edited by O. C. Ferrell, S. W. Brown, and C. W. Lamb, pp. 346–57. Chicago: American Marketing Association.

Runyon, Kenneth E. 1982. *The Practice of Marketing.* Columbus, OH: Merrill.

Russ, Frederick A. and Charles A. Kirkpatrick. 1982. *Marketing.* Boston: Little, Brown.

Schewe, Charles D., and Reuben N. Smith. 1983. *Marketing,* 2nd ed. New York: McGraw-Hill.

Schoell, William F., and Thomas T. Ivy. 1982. *Marketing.* Boston: Allyn and Bacon.

Schudson, Michael. 1984. *Advertising: The Uneasy Persuasion.* New York: Basic Books.

Soule, George. 1934. "Standardization." In *Encyclopedia of the Social Sciences, vol. 14,* pp.319–22. New York: Macmillan.

Stanton, William J. 1981. *Fundamentals of Marketing,* 6th ed. New York: McGraw-Hill.

Starch, Daniel. 1923. *Principles of Advertising.* Chicago: A. W. Shaw.

Stevens, W. H. S. 1927. "Marketing Biscuits and Crackers." *Harvard Business Review* 6 (October):20–31.

Stewart, Paul W., and J. Frederick Dewhurst. 1939. *Does Distribution Cost Too Much?* New York: Twentieth Century Fund.

"Summary of the 18th National Convention." 1931. *Society of Industrial Engineers Bulletin* 13 (October):4.

The Taylor Society. 1921. "Abstract of a Preliminary Report of a Committee on the Organization and Function of the Sales Operating Department." *Bulletin* (October).

——. 1920. *Bulletin* (December).

Tosdal, Harry. 1950. *Introduction to Sales Management*, 3rd ed. New York: McGraw-Hill.

——. 1933. "Some Recent Changes in the Marketing of Consumer Goods." *Harvard Business Review* 11 (January):156–64.

University of Illinois, Bureau of Business Research. 1931. *A Marketing Research Bibliography*, Bulletin No. 38. Urbana: The Bureau of Business Research.

——. 1975. *Historical Statistics of the United States: Colonial Times to 1970*, bicentennial edition. Washington, D.C.: U.S. Government Printing Office.

U.S. Bureau of the Census. 1982. *Statistical Abstract of the United States (1982–1983)*. Washington, D.C.: U.S. Government Printing Office.

U.S. Library of Congress Legislative Reference Service. 1974. "Voluntary Industrial Standardization in the United States," Report to Committee on Science and Astronautics, U.S. House of Representatives, 93rd Cong., 2d Sess. Washington, D.C.: U.S. Government Printing Office.

Vaile, Roland S., E. T. Grether, and Reavis Cox. 1952, *Marketing in the American Economy*. New York: Ronald Press.

Vizza, Robert F., Thomas E. Chambers, and Edward J. Cook. 1967. *Adoption of the Marketing Concept: Fact or Fiction?* New York: Sales Executive Club of New York.

Walker, Amasa. 1913. "Scientific Management Applied to Commercial Enterprises." *Journal of Political Economy* 21 (May):388–99.

Weld, L. D. H. 1922. "The Progress of Commercial Research." *Harvard Business Review* 1 (January): 175–86.

White, Percival. 1927. *Scientific Marketing: Its Principles and Methods*. New York: Macmillan.

Wilson, Christopher P. 1983. "The Rhetoric of Consumption: Mass Market Magazines and the Demise of the Gentle Reader." *The Culture of Consumption: Critical Essays in American History 1880–1980*, edited by Richard Wightman Fox and T. J. Jackson Lears. pp. 39–64. New York: Pantheon.

Zikmund, William, and Michael D'Amico. 1984. *Marketing*. New York: John Wiley & Sons.

CHAPTER 2

Marketing: Management Technology or Social Process at the Twenty-First Century?

ROBERT BARTELS

Throughout this century, appreciation has been expressed for men who have developed the marketing discipline and advanced what may be known as the "century of marketing." They have been praised for insight and foresight that turned daily events of the marketplace into structures of thought for business-persons and citizens. Human thought has been enriched, business improved, and consumers better served by their efforts. The subject of marketing has been introduced into the curricula of universities and schools of business, and systems of distribution have been created where none existed before.

Tribute to individuals is always due, but it is timely at the century's end to assess the role of marketing itself. The place it now occupies was not foreseen at the outset, for there was no pattern or precedent for such an activity in human society. Like other developments, marketing was shaped not only by circumstances, but by old conventions, new ideas, personal interests, and the sanction of society in general. It is a conception born of the nineteenth century and given form and expression in the twentieth. As we now witness its fruition, we can consider what role it may play in the next century.

A focal question is whether marketing has become what society may have expected of it. A society's needs are met by its patterns of behavior known as social institutions—the economic institution, to meet consumption needs. Institutional needs, on the other hand, are met by relevant technologies. Marketing emerged, at a particular time and place, as part of the economic institution, to meet the need for *consumption*; it has evolved more as a technical means of meeting the economic business need for *distribution*. Whether the two are congruent, that it may be said that marketing is meeting the social as well as the institu-

30

tional need, is an issue debated and of concern. As social objectives are broader than technical objectives, the expectation of ethical and spiritual, as well as material, satisfactions in consumption exceeds the mere providing of goods and services. The contribution of marketing in this respect has varied, coinciding with prevailing concepts of marketing—of what is and of what is expected of it. When narrowly conceived, marketing has served business interests more than social expectations; when broadly conceived, it has approximated the service expected of the social institution itself. How it is viewed will determine the role of marketing in the century ahead.

SOCIAL INSTITUTION VERSUS TECHNOLOGY

Whether marketing is an institution or a technology is sought in the history of human consumption. Until the Industrial Revolution of the eighteenth century, the meeting of consumption needs was not formally instituted. Trade was deemed exploitive, deceptive, and profiteering; society expected little more of it. The economy functioned with minimal consideration, for preference was given to religious, military, and political institutions. The economy evolved slowly.

In ancient times, the supplying of consumables was simply an activity, not a business, and much less a technology. The extended family provided for its own needs, and what it did not self-supply it obtained by formal and informal exchanges. In communal societies, the collected common products were redistributed. Market distribution began in barter and local market trade, but purchase for resale was frowned upon, and market intermediaries were held low in esteem and in social class. Skill in distributive activity was self-learned, unconceptualized, and guarded as "secrets of the trade."As production and consumption became further separated, and distribution more complex, apprenticeship was sponsored by merchant guilds. During the nineteenth century, means of supply became more organized, but there was still little technical intelligence and no technology. Not until the end of the nineteenth century did market economy outgrow traditional economic theory and require reformulation of how consumption was being and should be supplied. But with the increase of supplies was also a rising expectation of social acceptability of distribution, and not merely the providing of material goods. In these circumstances, the discipline and practice of marketing were conceived.

The new expectations and the emergence of marketing, however, were not merely the outgrowth of nineteenth-century economic conditions and thought. They stemmed from an intellectual and spiritual renaissance occurring throughout society and throughout the century, which gave people vision of a better society and hope of achieving it. Liberty, freedom, and human rights, which had motivated the American Revolution, characterized the mental atmosphere and inspired a new intellectualism. This flowered in confidence that the scientific method was a means of solving all problems. Marketing was such an intellectual approach to problems of supply and distribution. Industry flourished with new technologies, aggressive entrepreneurship, and new markets. At the same time, new religious convictions raised standards of morality and ethics that decried the tyrannies of trade. In these and other respects, the beginning of the twentieth century was a turning point in economic history, a point at which the distribution of consumption products was expected to conform to higher spiritual values, while at the same time catering to the satisfaction of material needs.

The rising voice of society on behalf of its role as consumer became institutionalized as a philosophy of "consumerism," which asserted that "the consumer is king." No society had gone so far before to express the primacy of demand over supply interests, although economists had long professed that "consumption is the end and object of production." Trade restriction began, albeit on behalf of competitors rather than consumers, with enactment of the Sherman Act in 1890. By the 1920s, abuses of consumers' expectations—for reliability of products, honesty in advertising, and truthfulness in labeling—gave rise to a consumer protest movement. Throughout the 1930s, corrective and protective marketing legislation was passed, but even throughout the 1940s consumer protests continued. The fact that essentially the same protections were asked for, although under different immediate circumstances, was evidence that the market mechanism, although supplying goods and services, was not complying with the spiritual consumption expectations of society. The subordination of economic to social interests, which anthropologist Karl Polanyi saw as the century-end "great transformation" of our society, was not achieved by the middle of this century.

The implications of the transformation in progress seem not to have been recognized by early marketing scholars, whose interests were less with society's spiritual and material expectations and more with the specific and respective interests of producers and consumers. For some years the dichotomy was not apparent, for benefits to consumers were tantamount to benefits to society, so urgent was the need for better product distribution. For it to become apparent required a much later critical judgment of marketing, a new scholarly discipline, a new body of thought. It began as the age-old process of people finding supplies, and of producers finding customers, and became the object of study, conceptualization, theorization, and application. Inductive studies were conducted of activities of producers, consumers, and the increasingly prevalent middleman, both of their individual actions and of their broad market patterns. However, unlike the past when consumers' search efforts to find scarce supplies dominated distribution, the new increase of supplies made producers' disposal problems the focus of marketing interest. Evidently, in the eyes of early researchers, the ultimate interests of producers and consumers were the same.

Until midcentury, marketing academics generally accepted the coincidence of social and economic, consumer and producer, interests. After 1950, however, management behavior became the primary object of marketing interest, and consumers were studied more to understand their market behavior than their market need. Concern for the latter, especially for the spiritual expectations of consumers, shifted to federal and state legislators, voluntary consumer protest groups, administrative agencies, consumer educators, and consumer research organizations. Thus became more evident the discrepancy between the capability of an institutional technology and the satisfaction of social need. It is on the point of this division that marketing stands at the threshold of the twenty first-century.

BASIC CONTRIBUTIONS OF MARKETING

Although marketing may not have fulfilled all of society's or consumers' expectations, its potential for the twenty-first century cannot be judged without understanding what its contribution to this century has been. The principal contributions of marketing as a technology lie in four areas of understanding: consumer behavior, market characteristics, management techniques, and the mathematics of marketing. These must be judged in terms of four criteria:

1. The importance of the subject
2. The evolution of concepts in the environment of market change
3. The universality of the technology developed
4. The adequacy of the technology for fulfilling future demands

Consumer Behavior

Throughout this century, much attention has been given to understanding consumers' motivation and behavior. This was requisite for disposing of the increasing industrial production, especially inasmuch as economists' and psychologists' concepts of consumers seemed inadequate statements of market behavior. Moreover, consumers' behavior changed as they became more adept in the marketplace, and as they became better-educated citizens. Researchers, at the same time, became more analytical, as new concepts of human nature gave fresh interpretation to behavior. The following are some of the concepts that were formed:

1. Role self-interest. A premise of economic theory was that consumers are hedonistic, seeking to maximize satisfaction in a conflict relationship in which haggling and bargaining are inherent. It was also presumed that consumers have knowledge of what is available in the market, and, knowing what is best for themselves, they arrive rationally at a purchase decision. This has remained a basic concept of consumer behavior.

2. Rational–emotional. As the complexity of markets increased, the assumption that consumers knew the market became less valid, especially their knowledge of product quality. Moreover, not all market behavior evidenced rational-

ity. Often decisions were made not by weighing costs against satisfactions, but in consideration of satisfactions alone. This was deemed emotional behavior.

3. Market interaction. With the introduction of sociological, rather than only economic or psychological, concepts in buying, consumer behavior was interpreted as interaction rather than just as action. Thus, initiative and response, negotiation and compromise, became aspects of role behavior, rather than the unconceptualized process of haggling.

4. Mutuality of interests. As marketing became routinized and transactions were more impersonal, consumers gained appreciation of sellers' positions and practices, and confrontation in the buyer–seller relationship diminished. Mutuality of interests was realized. This became an essential element of fixed pricing and mass marketing.

5. Multiple influences. Socialization of behavior gave recognition also to multiple external influences upon purchasing decisions. Consumers' referents included others in the family unit, friends, peers, image groups, and trend setters. This perception increased the field for research of consumer motivation.

6. Postsale evaluation. Market behavior was seen also as not terminating with the consummation of a sale but as extending to some time thereafter, during which the decision might be reconsidered or a subsequent decision influenced. The tentativeness of sales resulting from payment with credit and from liberal return policies and product warranties increased the importance of postsale behavior.

Many models of consumer decision making have been drawn, evidencing the subjectivity of theorization as well as reliance upon different interdisciplinary interpretations of the market mentality. Moreover, they reflect the consumer in different environments of economics and social change, providing comparative rather than absolute interpretations of behavior. In this fact lies the continuing validity of this technology for enhancing consumer satisfaction. In it lies also the applicability of the research methodology to consumer behavior in other cultures.

Segmentation of Markets

Another contribution of marketing has been the infusion of economic theory with classification of markets. The classes resemble somewhat the types of buyer motivation, but they have been used more for market planning than for buyer influencing. The following are principal types of markets identified:

1. Markets and absolute scarcity. In economies of scarcity, all persons have more or less a common motivation: survival. The problem of society is to achieve through its marketing system some feasible distribution of products. Systems of allocation, barter, or queuing have determined the distribution of scarce products, with control resting in the hands of suppliers. To rise out of this condition is still the goal of many nations, and even of groups of individuals within more affluent nations.

2. Economic stratification. As national affluence increased, markets became classified on the basis of personal income as low, middle, and high-income markets. The availability of discretionary income and spending made possible the offering of different, and of differentiated, products and services, through new patterns and plans of distribution.

3. Social stratification. Toward midcentury, markets were conceived and differentiated by social, rather than only economic, factors. Heritage, affiliations, peer group, social class, acquired standard of living, and the like were recognized as determinants of market differences.

4. Service markets. Further segmentation was made as markets for service, with or apart from physical products, became evident. In economically less-developed areas, or where convention militates against the purchase of intangibles, services are rarely deemed worth payment. The rise of desire and demand for convenience, image, ambiance, credit, and delivery evidenced the mental character of consumption in the more affluent, educated, and sensitive markets.

5. Self-fulfillment. Markets characterized by self-interest are today supplemented by markets motivated by desire for self-fulfillment through altruism, charity, benevolence, humanitarianism, gift giving, and the like. These are non-consumption markets, so far as the buyer is concerned. Their appearance coincides with economic sufficiency, satiety with material consumables, and expression of life in its more generous dimensions.

Although markets are socially economic phenomena, they are scientifically conceptual creations. Their classifications represent markets perceived in the process of change and from a variety of scholastic viewpoints. In the hands of marketing practitioners, these concepts are technical tools. They have become a standard framework in which our economy is seen.

The Management Process

Throughout this century, the concept of management in marketing also has evolved. Its initial conception was derived from theories of management in industrial concerns, but the distinct character of marketing functions and systems led to more relevant concepts of management. The following are some of the stages through which the management technology has come:

1. Function management. In both wholesaling and retailing, management originally consisted more or less of doing "intelligently" what had to be done. Performance of management and performance of a function were not at first differentiated, but as this distinction was made, theories of management began to appear. Although broader concepts have appeared, management of function performance, which consists of planning, organizing, supervising, and evaluating, remains basic.

2. Coordinative management. During the second decade of the century, marketing management was further seen as not simply the supervision of function

performance, particularly selling, but as the coordination of all activities essential to the presentation of products to the market. Although this was an abstraction at first incomprehensible to many managers, this concept has been classic in marketing and marketing theory.

Coordination, which was limited at first to the internal marketing functions, became extended to include those external as well: relations with suppliers, customer, competitors, resources, government, and technically unrelated organizations in the community.

3. Integrative management. At another stage, marketing management was integrated with management of other functions with a business. It imputed to marketing managers responsibility for cooperation with production, finance, research, and personnel departments for the origination and creation of marketable products, as well as for the marketing of them. This, too, was a concept accepted slowly by managers who thought of production as *preceding* marketing, rather than as being coexistent and coordinate with it.

4. Societal marketing. Still further broadened, the concept of marketing management included coordination of marketing processes of the firm with the public environment in which it operates. This implied acknowledgment of responsibility to society in its various institutions and roles, such as governmental, educational, religious, recreational, artistic, civic, and international. Many of those institutions have in turn sought closer relations with business, not only for financial support but for the management expertise that business can share. In this dimension of management, the marketing manager approaches more nearly the responsibility of person to person—rather than of marketer to consumer—of which the material consumption satisfactions are but part.

The process of marketing management today represents a more encompassing intelligence than it did earlier in this century, broadening with the scale and complexity of the task, and with acquiescence to society's larger consumption demands. Ability to fulfill these demands, however, derives not only from the progressive conceptual stages of management, but also from development in the state of the arts for information intelligence. Coordination of both internal and external factors has improved with technical development of office systems, communication, transportation, and data retrieval. On the threshold of innovative electronics, management will experience new measures of interaction with customer, suppliers, and the public at large through computer linkages, electronic records, interbusiness financial and inventory systems, and videotex. These fast tracks for management afford new opportunities for management expertise.

Mathematics of Marketing

A significant talent of marketing managers is the ability to evaluate past performance from evidence of operating data and to foresee the possible operational efffects of contemplated plans and policies. These evidences appear in financial, sales, and other statistical data of a company. The conception of the statistical anatomy of marketing activity in terms of measurable components so that performance could be evaluated in quantitative relationships gave unprecedented objectivity to management. The following are some of the mathematical concepts devised for this purpose:

1. Components of profit. At the turn of the century, management, especially in wholesaling and retailing establishments, was guided by the meager records of conventional bookkeeping. In the 1920s and 1930s, literature on many phases of retailing emanating from New York University placed operations on a more informative quantitative basis. It dealt with the collection and use of such data as cost of goods sold, markups and markdowns, maintained margins, operating costs, inventory composition and turnover, gross and net profits, and sales per square feet of floor space. Similar information for wholesalers and manufacturers' sales branches was published by Harvard University. In due course, studies of physical distribution provided comparable bases for evaluating storage and transportation activities. This created vocabulary for a language in marketing management.

2. Function allocation. While such data made possible judgment of past activities, they served also for basing future plans, especially the determination of what activities should be performed and what could be shifted to others. As operating data for all types of middlemen became available from the Census of Distribution, the composite costs of selectively composed channels could be determined. Function allocation and institutional specialization introduced a plasticity into marketing management. Performance of the entire marketing task could then be thought of in terms of alternative channels. Services of wholesaling and retailing could be judged in different categories, as could the separate functions of selling, financing, advertising, risk bearing, and the like. The availability of such data gave structure to the marketing system, rather than merely to the marketing establishment.

3. Unit integration. Internal and external operating data led also to decisions, not to specialize by function allocation, but to assume more of the marketing task through integration of operating units, horizontally and vertically. This gave rise to chain organizations and to multilevel combinations of distributive units.

4. Discretionary profit cycles. Simplistically stated, mathematical guidelines facilitate managers' efforts to realize profit by combinations and recombinations of—by adding or by subtracting—variables determining profit: products, services, functions, units, volume, markets, etc. In a competitive market system, entrepreneurs find a market niche by differentiating their offerings through such selections. Opposite courses may be taken simultaneously by operators, each thinking that the mathematics of their offering is best for them at a given time. With the change of circumstances, opposite decisions may be made. Whatever the case, the entire marketing system has been translated into a mathematical construction. As both an evidence of policy applied and a guide to policy contemplated, the mathematical concept has been an important contribution to marketing.

Reduction of marketing to its technology and of the technology to these few critical topics is an oversimplification. It has been done for a twofold purpose: first, to show more clearly the difference between technology and concern for social values; second, to facilitate evaluation of the technology in terms of its universality and adequacy.

CONTINUITY AND UNIVERSALITY OF MARKETING TECHNOLOGY

The merit of marketing cannot be judged only from its contribution in the United States during the twentieth century. That it has not found ready acceptance and equally constructive utilization elsewhere has resulted not from the limitations of marketing, but from its rejection elsewhere and from our own reticence to advocate it properly abroad.

It has been rejected, and often where constructive marketing technology is most needed, for several reasons. Foremost is ignorance. The uneducated, unscientific mentality of more primitive people does not think in terms of technology, but rather of patterns and routines of action. Individual initiative is limited by lack of objectivity, resources, or incentive. Thus, for example, where in some Africans countries traditional and educational attitudes eschew tradesmanship, foreign expatriates more of a mind to trade assumed the marketing and merchandising functions. Central-planning economic developers there also have not seen the ways in which marketing may contribute to, rather than passively follow, economic development.

In the People's Republic of China, where communalism and control have dominated, the awakening to enterprise has aroused search for techniques of free marketing applicable to their industrialization goals. In the Soviet Union on the other hand, Western marketing technology has been disdained as capitalistic, and rejection of the most rudimentary principles has, by policy, deprived consumers of needed products, promoted unsalable goods, severed vital distribution channels, and implemented adverse production and pricing policies. By further contrast, in countries such as Brazil, Japan, Singapore, and Hong Kong, modern marketing has been a concomitant to industrialization and social urbanity.

Unfamiliarity with marketing throughout the world, however, is not due solely to rejection. It has resulted also from our own lack of interest in making it properly known. This, too, is an indictment for not meeting more widely the world's consumption needs as well as our own. Most marketing academics are, because of institutional and peer constraints, not prepared to teach or research marketing apart from their ethnic environment. Their marketing "principles" are principles only within a limited sphere. Our unilinguisticality and our satisfaction with being "the most advanced" have dulled our broader vision. And marketing practitioners also have too often seen foreign markets as extensions of domestic ones, misapplying principles that really do have universal applicability.

The presumption of universality—of useful relevance at different times and places—is based upon the fact that in our own milieu marketing has developed through a span of time and in a diversity of circumstances that are currently found throughout the world. The technology evolved here was a function of prevailing circumstances. Progressive refinement supplemented but did not supplant earlier, less advanced techniques, and the applicability of inherent principles is proportionate to the stage of circumstances existing anywhere. However, because technology is related more to economic than to social management, culture factors must be considered in order to provide more than a technical satisfaction of any society's consumption needs. This does not invalidate the universality of the marketing technology or principles.

THE ADEQUACY OF MARKETING

Notwithstanding the universality of marketing technology, the adequacy of marketing to fulfill society's expectations should also be considered. The discipline emerged as a scholastic response to problems of both supply and demand, to problems of both business and society. To meet society's consumption needs was the principal objective of marketing, and earliest writings expressed this. This dual interest continued until the middle of the century.

Progressively, however, concentration on the marketing of manufactured goods narrowed the field of interest and study. Programs for marketing agricultural products were assumed by colleges of agriculture, where their interest, too, was specialized. This reduced the competence of marketing theorists later to assist the development of marketing in industrializing agricultural countries. Reduction of interest in physical distribution per se turned this area to specialists skilled in operations research techniques. And although consumer and market studies facilitated management, they contributed little to the actual satisfying of consumers.

After 1950 other developments that could have spurred marketing to broader competence passed with little effect. As government "management" of marketing increased through legislative, administrative, and judicial action, marketing concerned itself mainly with management in the private sector. As marketing activities raised questions of ethical and social responsibility, marketing dealt mainly with technical aspects of distribution. As the world market became global, marketing concerned itself with marketing at home. As international trade expanded, marketing limited its interest to domestic distribution. As developing nations needed new systems of production and distribution, marketing offered them what was relevant and applicable in the United States. As national systems evolved under different ideologies, marketing remained a capitalist, market-oriented system of thought. As consumer rejection of products and marketing practices increased, marketing allowed public and semipublic agencies to put it in a defensive position.

By narrowing its field of interest and not pursuing new opportunities, marketing has avoided responsibility that earlier in the century it might have been expected to assume, namely, for improving both the quality and the quantity of consumption at home and for extending its technology abroad wherever it might apply. This has resulted from a viewpoint that was narrow, technical, and provincial, rather than broad, philosophic, and global. The marketing process has been seen as *business* meeting society's needs rather than as *society* meeting its needs through the institution of business. Marketers have held themselves to be dominant and independent of what did not concern them directly, and profitably. During the nineteenth century, the narrower viewpoint prevailed. That has broadened, but had it done so to a larger extent, greater concern might have been shown in the twentieth century for opportunities that have been neglected.

If such has been the twentieth-century response of marketing to society's expectation of ethical and spiritual standards in the supplying of goods and services, what are the prospects for the century ahead? Two trends are in progress that may be expected to increase: first, a growing demand for respect of social and spiritual values in supplying consumption needs; second, an increasing conviction of the coincidence of global consumption needs and our own.

The domestic expectation continues to be met with some indifference by marketing. The continued marketing of inferior and harmful products remains an unsolved problem. Some regard this as a problem of production quality control, but inasmuch as such products may be distributed without warranty or subject to recall, it becomes a marketing problem. Products publicly deemed detrimental to human well-being, such as alcohol, tobacco, and drugs, are among the most prominently marketed and advertised. Degrading appeals of chauvinism and sexism, as well as the questionable influencing of children, also continue. Against such practices, the expectations of society today are higher than they were a century ago.

The role that marketing may play abroad lies more in the realm of opportunity than of demand at this time. New demographics indicate that in the next century population masses will shift, power blocs be altered, and resource utilization more controlled than at present. The demand for products will increase in a multiple of population growth, for social and economic expectations are rising everywhere. International trade will expand, for the world community cannot exist without interdependence. Living standards and market patterns will become more similar, but cultural differences will still have to be considered by marketers. Less-developed countries will improve their domestic marketing by application of universal marketing techniques. As marketing has responded more to economic than social expectations, willingness to meet demands elsewhere that it has not met here cannot be confidently predicted.

THE ULTIMATE CHALLENGE

The issue is whether marketing is an economic technology responsible to markets for distribution of goods and services, or an institution responsible to society for meeting those consumption needs in the context of society's ethical and spiritual expectations. At the beginning of this century, there was no such question, for the demand for both appeared simultaneously, and marketing scholars seemed aware of this. It has become a consideration because marketing has pursued the lesser of the two obligations. And one wonders whether in years ahead marketing will assume the larger responsibility.

That marketing should have adopted the narrower view arises not from fault but from accepting the business definition of *human* as a *market*, characterizing humans economically, physically, psychologically, and socially. Creationists' and evolutionists' concurrence that the human is material has been basic to the practice of marketing. But those beliefs that the human is *divinely* created material, or *materially* created material, are both challenged by the more inspired conviction that humans are divinely created *spiritual*, and not material. This concept gained credence and expression in the nineteenth-century renaissance of religious thought. Directly and indirectly, it has inspired the expectation that humans should be viewed holistically, and their consumption needs supplied with respect to their spiritual nature and their endowed rights. Without integrity in the market, honesty in representation, and fairness in market dealings—as well as in all walks of life—it is the spiritual and not just the psychological nature of humans that is violated.

The implications of perceiving human spiritual nature are far reaching for marketing. They require acknowledgment that the morals of marketing must be equal to the expectations of society. They portend full meeting of consumption needs. And they further suggest the ultimate supplying of human provisions solely by prayerful spiritual recognition of humans, as exhibited by ancient seers and prophets who prolonged supplies and fed multitudes with provisions not produced or distributed by usual economic means. Human destiny must tend in that direction, to a stage in which neither production nor distribution may exist as it does now, although humans' material needs will be met so long as they have those needs.

Progress toward the ultimate is slow, but society's present expectations of marketing suggest that in the twenty-first century they will continue and increase. The role that marketing will play in this fulfillment remains to be seen, but it is already evident that marketing will have to constitute more than a technology to contribute what it is capable. As society conceives the consumer as a whole person whose spiritual as well as physical needs must be fed, so it conceives the marketer as a whole person, whose consideration of the consumer must correlate with the view of society in general. To the extent that this unity is achieved, marketing may meet the full consumption expectations of society. To the extent, on the other hand, that marketing continues as a technical aid to distribution rather than as an institutional aid to consumption, society will invoke other institutional means of satisfying its demands for safety of products, preservation of ethnic values, and maintenance of integrity, honesty, fairness, and human dignity in market relationships. The government, the school, the family, and the church are institutions that have asked of marketing more than "bread alone." Moreover, extension of the hand of marketing to the underprivileged and underdeveloped of the world will come from either the U.S. marketing community or from others, at home or abroad, who see the global consumption need as the marketing opportunity of the next century.

Whether marketing academics, practitioners, and social administrators will guide marketing into the broader commitment remains to be seen. If the inevitable changes do not occur under the aegis of marketing, they will occur under some other one or several headings. The challenge is great, but the satisfaction of using the technology of marketing for broader service to humanity is greater.

REFERENCES

Boulding, Kenneth E. 1964. *The Meaning of the Twentieth Century.* New York, Harper & Row.

Cavanagh, Gerald F. 1976. *American Business Values in Transition.* Englewood Cliffs, NJ: Prentice-Hall.

Clark, Lincoln H. 1958. *Consumer Behavior.* New York: Harper & Bros. (Reprinted, New York: Arno Press, 1978).

Converse, Paul D. *The Beginnings of Marketing Thought in the United States.* Austin: University of Texas Press (Reprinted, New York: Arno Press, 1978).

Coolsen, Frank G. 1960. *Marketing Thought in the United States in the Late Nineteenth Century.* Lubbock: Texas Tech Press.

English, Wilke. 1984. "Why Are Marketing Academicians So Cowardly?" *Journal of Marketing Education* 6 (Summer):2.

Hurst, James W. 1982. *A Politics of Markets and a Market of Politics.* Madison: University of Wisconsin Press.

McNair, Malcolm P. 1958. "Significant Trends and Developments in Postwar Retailing." *Sales Management* (November 21, 1958).

Novak, Michael. 1982. *The Spirit of Democratic Capitalism.* New York: American Enterprise Institute/Simon & Schuster.

Polanyi, Karl. 1957. *The Great Transformation. The Political and Economic Origins of Our Time.* Boston: Beacon Press.

Ross, Christopher A., and Ronald McTavish. 1984. "The Marketing Education Task in Third World Countries." *Journal of Marketing Education* 6 (Spring 1984):20–27.

Terry, Samuel H. 1869. *The Retailer's Manual.* Newark, NJ: Jennings Brothers (Reprinted, New York: Arno Press, 1978).

CHAPTER 3

What Is Marketing?
Reavis Cox's Search
for Universals

JEAN J. BODDEWYN

Reavis Cox's venture into the field of "comparative marketing" provides a useful springboard for examining the economic and social dimensions of marketing.[1] Cox may not have invented the distinction between (1) "universals" found everywhere, (2) "limited generalizations" valid only for some countries, and (3) "specific differences" proper to a single nation, but he was the first one to apply it to marketing.[2] He wrote:

> I hope to demonstrate that the greatest weakness in our attempts to make effective comparisons of domestic marketing systems lies in the shortcomings of the concepts with which we are trying to work. (p. 144)
>
> Paradoxical though it may seem, what we stand to gain most from comparative studies of domestic marketing systems is not what they tell us about others but what they force us to learn about ourselves in order to understand what we see abroad. (p. 162)

COX'S CENTRAL QUESTION: WHAT IS MARKETING?

Cox had trouble answering the question, What is marketing? In his 1965 paper he correctly acknowledged that U.S.-type "marketing" could be only a subset of some more encompassing concept or institution, but he could not find an overarching term for it:

> If we like, we can say that the Western world uses a system of marketing; but we then need to invent phrases to denominate each of the other possible alter-

native systems and a general term to denominate all of the systems collectively. At one time I thought we could say that all the countries in question have systems of distribution (the universal); that in our country, and perhaps in other Western countries, the specific form taken by distribution is marketing; and that in still other countries such as Russia, distribution takes further forms for which we have not yet selected names. (p. 153)

For many years, I have felt that the term Cox was looking for was *exchange*, but he does not use it once in his paper. This is puzzling since the term had long been used in economics, anthropology, and sociology; it was discussed in the *Encyclopedia of the Social Sciences*, which he quoted; and by 1965, the seminal work of Karl Polanyi (1944) and other students of exchange systems was readily available (for example, Smelser 1959).[3] What is known about the economic and social dimensions of "exchange"?

Exchange is a "universal" because division of labor (specialization) itself is a universal practice—whether based on sex, age, skill, or any other criterion—required by the universal scarcity condition and other factors. In turn, specialization everywhere generates separations that have to be bridged by exchange, so that the latter is the "general term to denominate all of the systems collectively," for which Cox was groping. It is necessary for purposes of comparative analysis of different kinds of exchange to distinguish between economic and social exchanges.

The Social View

Cox's search for "phrases to denominate each of the . . . possible alternative systems" could have been satisfied by the typologies of economic exchange systems developed by anthropologists, economic geographers (Wagner 1960), and sociologists (Polanyi, Smelser, etc.). They identify three major principles ruling all economic activities, including exchange: *tradition* (based on the community), *command* (the state), and *bargaining* (the market). What is to be produced, who is going to get it, how exchange will be conducted, and how consumption will take place are all ruled by these alternative but actually complementary bases of the "social order."

In this light, Western-style "marketing" is that form of economic exchange based on "self-regulating" bargaining (Adam Smith's "invisible hand") that takes place in the "market" rather than under the rules of tradition or command. *Marketing* is thus an appropriate label for one of the "limited generalizations" for which Cox was searching, together with *reciprocative exchange* (based on traditional community values and relationships) and *redistributive and mobilizative exchange* (based on state commands)—to use Smelser's terminology.

Economic exchange has always existed among humans, but it has been significantly of the "marketing" type for only a relatively short period of time (since the mid-1800s). Economic exchange does not predominate in the world: Wagner (1960, p. 132) estimated around 1960 that "perhaps only 10 percent of the world's population lives in fully *commercial* countries [although] the influence of commercial market relations is very much wider."[4]

At other times and places, economic exchange has been overwhelmingly ruled by reciprocity (as among the members of a family or clan, or with gifts among friends) and/or by mobilization–redistribution (as when the state owns the factors of production, allocates the resulting goods among people, and controls their exchange and consumption). Modern Western economies exhibit a mixture of these types, of course (Pandya 1984).

But why do some countries (or sectors) rely more on the market than others? There is no simple answer to that question, which brings us to Cox's search for explanations of "specific differences." Anthropologists and historians (Polanyi was both) typically analyze a set of environmental factors—natural resources, value system, social and political structure, etc.—to explicate each situation. For example, marketing is linked with "associational" (*Gesellschaft*) societies where inter- and intraagency bonds are voluntary and typically based on contracts (Nicosia 1962, p. 411).

"Marketing" as a "social institution" exists to the extent that it is valued, promoted, tolerated, prohibited, and controlled in a particular country on account of its interfaces with other societal institutions. As Polanyi pointed out in *The Great Transformation*, capitalism was accepted reluctantly and has enjoyed a relatively short unadulterated life (circa 1850–1914) in a few Western countries because it has threatened traditional social relations by stressing competition more than cooperation and cohesion. By divorcing economic activities ("disembedding" them, in economic–anthropological terminology) from the community and the polity (Dixon 1984; Fullerton 1984; Hirschman 1982),[5] market exchange contended with the earlier socially reciprocative, redistributive, and mobilizative (state-directed) exchanges. Nowadays, most countries exhibit various mixes of market, reciprocal, and redistributive exchanges.

The Economic View

Economics is built around four issues: (1) production (What is to be produced?, based on the allocation of the scarce factors of production); (2) distribution (Who gets the goods produced?);[6] (3) exchange (How do people get what they really want or need in exchange for what they already have?); and (4) consumption (How are goods used up?).

When can an exchange or transaction be called "economic" or "commercial"? Economic acts of exchange are of the marketing type only if they are related to "price-making markets."[7] Every society studied by anthropologists and historians has an "economy" of some sort because personal and community life requires the structured provision of material goods and services. As Polanyi put it:

> [The] empirical economy...can be briefly (if not engagingly) defined as an instituted process of interaction between man and his environment, which results in a continuous supply of want-satisfying material means. Want-satisfaction is "material" if it involves the use of material means to satisfy ends; in the case of a definite type of physiological wants, such as food and shelter, this includes the use of so-called services only. (Dalton 1968, p. 145)[8]

COX AND THE TRANSFER OF OWNERSHIP

Cox raised an important question in his 1965 paper. Referring to a Soviet-type of exchange where the state owns or uses all the factors of production from manufacturing to retailing, and where it dictates all of most product, price, promotion, and place decisions, Cox observed that "if there is no transfer of ownership [among the various levels], then marketing...can be said to disappear from the system altogether" (p. 152).

Cox was right. As argued above, such an exchange system is not of the "self-regulating" type based on bargaining in the market. It is of the "command" variety. However, commanded exchanges are not unique to centrally planned economies but can also be found in Western economies—and not just in the case of Western state enterprises either.

What Cox was referring to can be subsumed under the concepts and phenomena of "markets vs. hierarchies" and "internalization."[9] In other words, firms—in the East or in the West—do not always use "external" markets to source their inputs or to dispose of their outputs, but they also rely on "internal" markets to "transfer" goods and services through vertical integration and other devices—with imposed "transfer prices" being used in lieu of freely bargained "market prices" among the organization's units. Polanyi also referred to "external vs. internal organization" to differentiate between "transactions" and "appropriations" (Dalton 1968, p. 146). In the Soviet Union, the organization is as large as the economy and thus represents a limit case, although even there one finds free markets tolerated for the exchange of certain goods (for example, fresh food).

Market-driven economies are "mixed" *economies* where different types of exchange coexist, but these various types can also be found within the same firm when it engages not only in true external "marketing" but also in internal "commanded exchanges."[10] In this context, "private ownership" and the concomitant freedom of entering into "private contracts" must be closely and even exclusively related to market exchanges. In the Soviet and internal market cases, "user" rather than "ownership" rights pass through the various layers of the system until the goods reach the ultimate buyer and consumer.

The debate about the nature of marketing was revived after 1965, but Cox's comparative paper was hardly referred to thereafter. As a way of touching base with recent theoretical issues and developments related to Cox's query about the nature of marketing, the rest of this chapter focuses on (1) the recent discussion of "exchange and marketing" and (2) the "micro–macro" split in marketing.

The "Marketing and Exchange" Controversy

Cox had ignored "exchange" in 1965, but it came to the fore on account of Kotler and Bagozzi in the early 1970s.[11] The terms of reference are throwing the "What is marketing?" question into even more confusion because substituting concepts such as "exchange" and "transactions" for "marketing" does not resolve anything if they are not well understood and differentiated.

For example, observing that "give-and-take behavior" or "human-exchange relationships" are found everywhere (for example, "Vote for me and I'll take care of your interests") does not justify the conclusion that "all exchange can be marketing." People "trade" words, blows, and calling cards, but none of these exchanges is of the marketing type. Similarly, all sorts of "transactions" ("the exchange of values between two independent parties") take place among people and organizations, but not all of them are of the "marketing" type even though the same separations of time, space, perception, etc., do exist outside of marketing and need to be bridged.

Behind acknowledging the valid argument that marketing techniques (locating potential "trading partners," making contact, evoking interest, etc.) can be used outside of marketing proper lies a very important assumption or definition. That is, the concepts of exchange and transaction can be applied only to consummated or completed ones. We do not call "production" what could have been produced but only what was actually produced. Similarly, "exchange" can refer only to what was finally exchanged—not to what people would have liked to get or give, were tempted to do, or tried to achieve. This requirement applies even to true but unsuccessful marketers: Like the little piggies in the nursery rhyme, they "went to market," but in failing to exchange their goods or services, they did not ultimately engage in "economic exchange."

To understand the rationale for a typical marketing exchange, think of all the times someone goes into a store, talks to a salesclerk, feels inclined to buy the product—but does not buy. Can we call these activities "exchange" or "transacting'? In a loose sense, yes; but the gross sales line on the store's income statement and the value-added statistics of the gross national product (GNP) certainly do not count them. The criticism that GNP statistics do not include all "economic" transactions is well known, but would anyone argue that they should cover "unterminated" exchanges and transactions (since marketing also includes the "terminating" function)?[12]

In "social exchange," by contrast, "each participant obtains something of value from the other" (Storer 1980, p. 235) by many forms of interaction. It is appropriate to differentiate them, to label some forms of them as "economic exchanges," and, within that category, to isolate those of the "marketing" type—as was attempted above.

Thus, there is a difference between joining (1) a trade association or a business club and paying dues in return for immediate "commercial" information, exposure, and personal contacts and (2) a church where the quid pro quo (salvation, happiness, etc.) is indefinite and where a tithe or even regular assessments remain legally unenforceable.

The same applies to joining a consumerist or environmentalist association. The rules and tests applied by the U.S. Internal Revenue Service provide a good yardstick for differentiating between the "economic" and the "noneconomic." The distinction depends on the relevant motivation: For example, firms join consumer associations in order to obtain public affairs information and access, and they consequently deduct membership fees as a business expense; while a non-businessperson may not do so, but is allowed to deduct them as a donation.

Underground Markets

Continuing with the definition of economic exchange, one can observe that societies have always forbidden or restricted the "marketing" of certain goods and services. As Polanyi and other economic historians and anthropologists have pointed out, the "market system" has been opposed because it implies that everything can be exchanged through bargaining—compared with other systems that dictate that certain goods or services cannot be exchanged at all, or only at rates of exchange set by tradition and/or command. The notion that brides, heirlooms, affection, respect, votes, loyalty, affiliation, etc., can be freely bought and sold through an immediately enforceable contract spelling out the quid pro quos has offended all religious and moral systems for ignoring, threatening, and jeopardizing the social relations based on "community" as well as the power relations monopolized by the "state." In other words, "economic" exchanges are not "socially" acceptable for certain transactions, which therefore cannot be labeled as being of the "economic" and "marketing" types.

Hence, the boundaries of what can enter the "marketplace" and be freely bargained and terminated within it will always be elastic. Yes, there are politicians who exact explicit and immediate bribes for their services; yes, people buy marijuana—and they are truly economic transactions that should be recorded in

GNP statistics. However, the important thing to observe is that community values usually stress that such "commercial" exchanges are wrong; and laws proscribe or severely restrict many of them[13] even though these bounds evolve: Prostitution and marijuana may be legalized while the list of drugs that can be freely sold keeps shrinking in the United States and elsewhere. In other words, at any particular point in time, society sanctions certain transactions and determines what constitutes "economic" exchange so that no universal or permanent definition of the latter can be developed.

The Micro–Macro Distinction in Marketing

Cox examined marketing at the *macro* level. Just to limit ourselves to his 1965 paper, he reiterated there his faith in flow analysis—an application of the functional approach (pp. 156–59). His appeal went largely unheeded (but see Jaffe 1969), although his concrete suggestions for research using this kind of analysis remain very appealing and deserving of renewed attention for the macro study of comparative marketing and other forms of economic exchange because it is central to conceptualizing them in their entirety. In particular, it helps us visualize and even measure how each exchange transaction creates particular utilities that aggregate into the total structured "flows" that constitute an exchange system—a macro view par excellence.

Going beyond this Coxian insight, it is appropriate to conclude by addressing a few other "universals" related to the endless quest about the content of marketing.

Macromarketing has attempted to distance itself from an exclusive concern with the "firm" and its immediate "task environment" to examine marketing (and other forms of economic exchange) as a societal institution—that is, as both a creation of society and a participant–contributor to societal processes, structures, and performances (Fisk 1982).

Implicit in the macromarketing endeavor is the much-needed recognition of various levels of marketing (and other types of economic exchange) analysis that are not otherwise sufficiently distinguished. While individual buyers and sellers bring to their transacting all sorts of "demographics" and "sociographics" that reflect their broader societal environment, these environmental data do not make the analysis "macro." It is still "micromarketing" at the level of the "firm" (the buyer is also a "firm" in economic theory—as is particularly obvious when the buyer is another organization). Therefore, true macromarketing analysis rises above the "firm" to look at "aggregates" such as all firms in a particular economy or even industry, although the term "mesomarketing" may be more appropriate for the latter.[14]

Macromarketing cannot be overconcerned with consumption as if it were the only touchstone of marketing–exchange, but must relate consumption to all economic functions (production, distribution, and exchange)[15] as well as to other societal goods—power, solidarity, respect, justice, etc.—besides wealth (Parsons and Smelser 1956).

CONCLUSION

Cox contributed to the "What is marketing?" debate by raising extremely valid questions, thereby helping us to evaluate newer views. Although he failed to provide answers to some of his own questions, the quest for marketing theory must continue to mine his multiple contributions—as is done here in the context of his 1965 search for universals.

Acknowledgement. The assistance of the following scholars is gratefully acknowledged: Johan Arndt (Norwegian School of Economics and Business Administration, Bergen), J. M. Carman (Berkeley), Nikhilesh Dholakia (Rhode Island), O. C. Ferrell (Texas A & M), George Fisk (Emory), Stanley C. Hollander (Michigan State), Shelby D. Hunt (Texas Tech), D. J. Luck (Delaware), F. M. Nicosia (Berkeley), Anil Pandya (Northeastern), N. G. Papadopoulos (Carleton), Norman W. Storer (Baruch), and Gloria Thomas (Baruch).

NOTES

1. This chapter is a shortened version of "What Is Marketing: In the Footsteps of Cox's Search for Universals" (New York: Baruch College, May 1985). Unless otherwise indicated, all references to Cox will be to his 1965 paper.

2. I suspect that this distinction can be traced back to personality psychology: "In some ways, I am like everybody else; in other ways, I am like some other people; in still other ways, I am like nobody else." One year before Cox, Clark Kerr et al. had used similar concepts ("the universal, the related and the unique") to compare industrial relations systems in their book *Industrialism and Industrial Man* (p.10).

3. Karl Polanyi's major relevant work is *The Great Transformation* (1944), but see also George Dalton's collected essays of Karl Polanyi (1968).

4. "Long-distance" trade has a much longer history, but this chapter is about "local" or "domestic" exchange. For a history of early marketing, see Mund (1948).

5. For a fuller treatment of the concepts of economy, polity, community, and other bases of "society," see Parsons and Smelser (1956) and Levy (1952). Franco Nicosia has pointed out, however, that cooperation and cohesion are not totally foreign to economy theory—including game theory (private communication). It remains that capitalism, as an economic institution, has often been perceived and criticized as socially disruptive.

6. The economist's concept of "distribution" (of the fruits of production among the factors of production that generated it—land, labor, capital, entrepreneurship, technology, etc.) is obviously different from that of the Western marketing scholar, for whom it means either the totality of marketing or some physical aspect of it, such as transportation.

7. "Only in the presence of a system of price-making markets will exchange acts of individuals result in fluctuating prices that integrate the economy" (Polanyi in Dalton 1968, p. 151).

8. The resemblance to Wroe Alderson's definition of marketing as being "directly concerned with the material culture embodied in exchangeable products" is obvious (1965, p. 303). The reference to services in the quotation reveals that exchange also encompasses such transactions as consultants selling their advice to a firm [see Dalton (1968, pp. 23, 27, 93, 137) for further discussions of "services"].

9. This topic is, of course, associated with Williamson (1975), but see also the "internalization" literature developed in the context of foreign direct investment and the multinational enterprise (for example, Rugman 1981).

10. I am not arguing here that state enterprises—in the East as well as in the West—cannot or do not engage in true marketing or use marketing techniques. On the other hand, I cannot recognize much "marketing" going on in the Soviet Union when the state dictates who will distribute what to whom, at what time, place, price, etc.

11. I am relying here on recent review and discussion papers that refer extensively to the relevant literature: Papadopoulos (1984), Farrell and Shaikh (1984), and Foxall (1984).

12. What about expenses incurred in contemplation of an economic transaction? Incorporation and other expenses connected with the launching of a business are normally tax deductible because a real economic exchange did take place for these expenditures. The situation gets trickier when a would-be "commercial" painter deducts the money spent on canvas, oils, and other supplies on the ground that the resulting paintings will ultimately be sold on the market. The U.S. Internal Revenue Service accepts such a deduction if there is "a reasonable expectation of profit," but is likely to reject it if no sale (that is, a commercial transaction or exchange) materializes within some reasonable period of time.

13. The Sherman Act stated that "labor is not a commodity" clearly to exempt trade unions from antitrust laws but also as a reaction against considering human beings as transactionable objects, as was also true in the cases of slavery and indentured labor.

14. The literature on "corporatism" (see "association" as "private interest government") as an intermediate institution and level of analysis between the firm (or individual) and society (as represented by the community and the state) is very relevant here. See Streeck and Schmitter (1985).

15. An essential part of the self-regulating type of exchange is that it "organizes" production, which in turn affects distribution and ultimately exchange and consumption in an interactive manner.

REFERENCES

Alderson, Wroe. 1965. *Dynamic Marketing Behavior*. Homewood, IL: Richard D. Irwin.

Boddewyn, J. J. 1981. "Comparative Marketing: The First Twenty-Five Years." *Journal of International Business Studies* 12 (Spring–Summer):61–79.

Cox, Reavis. 1965. "The Search for Universals in Comparative Studies of Domestic Marketing Systems." In *Marketing and Economic Development, Proceedings of the 1965 Fall Conference,* edited by P. D. Bennett, pp.143–62. Chicago: American Marketing Association (Reprinted in J. J. Boddewyn, ed. 1969. *Comparative Management and Marketing,* pp. 142–60. Glenview, IL: Scott, Foresman).

Dalton, George, ed. 1968. *Primitive, Archaic and Modern Economics; Essays of Karl Polanyi.* Garden City, NY: Anchor Books.

Dixon, D. F. 1984. "Macromarketing: A Social Systems Perspective." *Journal of Macromarketing* 4 (Fall): 4–17.

Farrell, O. C., and Karim Shaikh. 1984. "Exchange as a Framework for Understanding Marketing: New Directions." In *1984 AMA Educators' Conference Proceedings,* edited by R. W. Belk and R. Peterson, pp. 341–45. Chicago: American Marketing Association.

Fisk, George. 1982. "Editor's Working Definition of Macromarketing." *Journal of Macromarketing* 2 (Spring):3–4.

Foxall, Gordon. 1984. "Marketing's Domain." *European Journal of Marketing* 18:25–40.

Fullerton, R. A. 1984. "Capitalism and the Shaping of Marketing." Mimeograph, Rhode Island College, Providence.

Hirschman, A. O. 1982. "Rival Interpretations of Market Society: Civilizing, Destructive or Feeble?" *Journal of Economic Literature* 20 (December):1463–84.

Hunt, S. D., and J. J. Burnett. 1982. "The Macromarketing/Micromarketing Dichotomy: A Taxonomical Model." *Journal of Marketing* 46 (Summer):11–26.

Jaffe, E. D. 1969. "A Flow Approach to the Comparative Study of Marketing Systems." In *Comparative Management and Marketing,* edited by J. J. Boddewyn, pp.160–70. Glenview, IL: Scott, Foresman.

Kerr, Clark. 1964. *Industrialism and Industrial Man.* New York: Oxford University Press.

Levy, M. J., Jr. 1952. *The Structure of Society.* Princeton, NJ: Princeton University Press.

McInnes, W. C. 1964. "A Conceptual Approach to Marketing." In *Theory in Marketing: Second Series,* edited by Reavis Cox, Wroe Alderson and Stanley J. Shapiro, pp.51–67. Homewood, IL: Richard D. Irwin.

Mund, V. A. 1948. *Open Markets.* New York: Harper.

Nicosia, F. M. 1962. "Marketing and Alderson's Functionalism." *Journal of Business [Chicago]* 35 (October):403–13.

Nicosia, F. M., and R. N. Mayer. 1976. "Toward a Sociology of Consumption." *Journal of Consumer Research* 3 (September):65–75.

Pandya, Anil. 1984. "The Relationships Between Forms of Distribution: Exchange and Reciprocity." Mimeograph, Northeastern University, Boston.

Papadopoulos, N. G. 1984. "Exchange and the Marketing Concept: Conflicts and Promises." In *Proceedings of the XIIIth Annual Conference of the European Marketing Academy.* pp.132–50. Breukelen: Netherlands School of Business.

Parsons, Talcott, and N. J. Smelser. 1956. *Economy and Society.* New York: Free Press.

Piatier, André. 1970. "Préface." in Reader's Digest, *Radioscopie de l'Europe,* pp.i–xviii. Paris.

Polanyi, Karl. 1944. *The Great Transformation.* New York: Rinehart.

Rugman, A. M. 1981. *Inside the Multinationals: The Economics of Internal Markets.* New York: Columbia University Press.

Smelser, N. J. 1959. "A Comparative View of Exchange Systems." *Economic Development and Cultural Change* 7 (January):173–83.

Storer, N. W. 1980. *Focus on Society: An Introduction to Sociology.* Reading, MA: Addison-Wesley.

Streeck, Wolfgang, and P. D. Schmitter. 1985. "Community, Market, State—and Associations?" In *Private Interest Government and Public Policy,* edited by Wolfgang Streeck and Ph.D. Schmitter (in press). London: Sage.

Wagner, Ph.L. 1960. "On Classifying Economies." In *Essays on Geography and Economic Development,* Research Paper No. 62, edited by Norton Ginsburg, pp.49–62. Chicago: Department of Geography, University of Chicago (Reprinted in J. J. Boddewyn, ed. 1969, *Comparative Management and Marketing,* pp.122–35. Glenview, IL: Scott, Foresman).

Williamson, O. E. 1975. *Markets and Hierarchies.* New York: Free Press.

PART II

Comparative Studies of
Marketing Outputs

CHAPTER 4

Marketing as a Provisioning Technology: Fueling World Development from a Finite Resource Base

NIKHILESH DHOLAKIA
RUBY ROY DHOLAKIA

INTRODUCTION

Consider the following two news items about the global petroleum situation, one circa the early 1970s and the other circa the mid-1980s:

> In virtually every company in the country this week, top management was trying to measure how the continued shutoff of Arab oil might affect business next year.... If the shutoff continues for several months, economists are predicting a cut in output ranging from 10% to 15%. Labor is fearful of widespread layoffs.... As the oil and gas shortage bites deeper, a host of products will disappear from the market.... They could include such products as plastic drinking straws, plastic pens, fertilizer, aluminum windows, water purifying chemicals, buttons, plastic milk cartons, and firewood. (*Business Week* 1973, pp. 56, 58, 59)

> As the [OPEC] ministers gathered, worries over sliding North Sea oil prices sent the British pound and stock market reeling.... In the U.S., March crude-oil futures contracts on the New York Mercantile Exchange hit a record-low $24.66 per bbl. before bouncing back. Some analysts wondered anew if a break to $20 might be in the offing.... At the market's peak in 1981, the average OPEC crude sold for nearly $35. (Taggiasco and Glasgall 1985, p. 29)

The nature of the global "oil crisis" has changed dramatically in less than 15 years. The greatest economic and resource crisis of the industrial world since the Second World War has "ended" in a whimper rather than in a bang. Of course, the petroleum crisis has abated rather than "ended." But the turnaround is quite spectacular and yields some important marketing insights for a resource-constrained world:

1. Demand and supply are highly flexible notions, even for a nonrenewable fossil resource like petroleum. For instance, technological innovations and greater geologic knowledge have led to increased estimates of crude oil and the status of deposits has been revised from "hypothetical" to "conditional" to "reserves." The classification of estimated supplies is both a function of knowledge of deposits as well as a function of prices at which they can be recovered (Leonardo Scholars 1975). Similarly, demand estimates for electricity have varied depending on assumptions regarding prices, population growth, etc. (Chapman, Tyrell, and Mount 1972).
2. Changes in consumer behavior on a macro scale, though difficult, are possible. For example, the average annual rate of growth in energy consumption fell dramatically after 1974. In Japan, it fell from 11.3 percent between 1960 and 1974 to 1.5 percent between 1974 and 1981. Similar declines have been observed in the Netherlands (from 9.8 to 0.1 percent) and the United States (from 4 to 0.7 percent).
3. Market opportunities for substitute resources can substantially improve under the combined influence of rising demand and increasing investment incentives.
4. Conservation-oriented marketing practices proliferate in periods of shortages, although their effectiveness as yet is considerably less than of stimulational marketing practices.

A schematic view of the unfolding of the petroleum crisis is presented in Figure 4.1. The various actions listed under the heading "Responses" in the figure illustrate the marketing effects of the resource crisis.

The Problematique

The petroleum crisis is a special case of the general problematique this chapter addresses: the relationships among resources, consumption, marketing, and development. In general, marketing activities as well as the process of economic development stimulate consumption levels in a society (see Figure 4.2). As consumption levels increase, resources are depleted. When resources are abundant, renewable, and evenly distributed, this process continues without serious disruptions. But when resources are scarce, nonrenewable, and unevenly distributed, disruptions may arise. A resource crunch may create "feedbacks" (see dashed lines, Figure 4.2), which could alter the role of marketing from one of stimulation to one of conservation. There could even be pressure to alter or reverse the development process.

We take up the four variables of Figure 4.2—resources, consumption, development, and marketing—as our major discussion categories in this chapter. Although the substantive discussion on "marketing" is reserved to last, we highlight the role of marketing practices and institutions throughout the essay.

FIGURE 4.1 The Petroleum Crisis and Responses to It

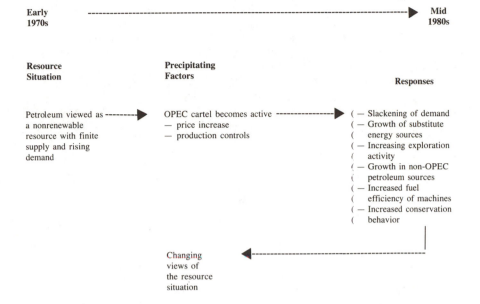

RESOURCE BASES

Resources are finite. This is what constrains resource-depleting activities like consumption and development. The quantity of resources, however, is not always determinate. Petroleum is a case in point. The acute shortage of the 1970s has given way to the comfortable "glut" of the 1980s. The amount of petroleum under the earth's crust has not changed. But the proven reserves and the extraction efforts have. To explain this "indeterminacy" of the quantity of resources, let us examine the notion of a "resource frontier."

The Resource Frontier

The resource frontier represents the boundary to which it is economically feasible to extract resources. For instance, estimates of recoverable copper in the United States range from 81 million tons at a price of $0.50 per pound to 198 million tons at $1.50 per pound (House Committee Hearings 1970). The ocean bed, the Amazon rain forest, a five-mile-deep mine shaft, the moon, etc., can all become resource frontiers under appropriate economic conditions.

The resource frontier is an economic and not an ecological concept. Technology, access to markets, and intensity of resource use affect the boundaries of the resource frontier. What is a resource frontier for one entity may not be

FIGURE 4.2. **Relationships Among Marketing, Consumption, Development, and Resources**

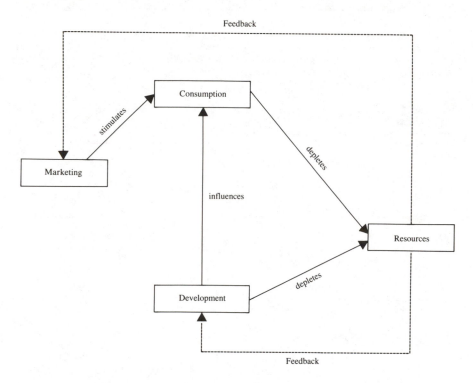

so for another. The ocean bed may be a resource frontier for firm X, which possesses deep-sea exploration technology, but not for firm Y, which is land bound. The outer space may be a frontier for a country that has the technological and military capability to build and defend space systems, but not for a country that has no space technology.

Like technology, access to markets also shapes the perception of an economic frontier. What is just another stretch of farmland to a cocoa farmer in Africa may represent the source of important raw material for $25-a-pound confections to Godiva Chocolatier. What is just sand on the beach in Mauritius may be the appropriate high-grade silicon source for an electronics firm in Santa Clara. What is waste fish for a fishing village in India may be just the right stuff to make "Surimi" fish paste for a Japanese food conglomerate (King and Durkin 1985).

Intensity of resource use also affects the resource frontier. When countries like the United States consume a disproportionate share of the world's resources (for example, 63 percent of combined natural gas, 30 percent of metal, 33 percent of petroleum) (see Meadows et al. 1974), then the pressures are greater to expand the resource frontiers. In the case of petroleum, depletion of land sources of U.S. oil has led to costlier exploitation of off-shore oil.

As the resource frontier is extended, it leads to accelerated depletion of the world's resources and greater degradation of the environment (DuBoff 1974). With increased international movement of oil, spillage has become a worldwide problem threatening aquatic life (Ketchum 1971; Longgood 1972). It is also achieved at increasingly higher costs and resource use. A ton of copper, for instance, can be produced with 15,193 kilowatt-hours from 1.0 percent ore; however, energy requirements almost double (29,766 kilowatt-hours) as the quality of ore declines to 0.3 percent (Leonardo Scholars 1975). A gloriously expanding resource frontier can therefore represent an ecological disaster in the making. This is precisely what is happening in the case of tropical rain forests (McNeil 1972; Young 1972). There are limits to which the resource frontier can be extended, and it becomes a macro challenge to achieve consumption and development goals without reaching those limits. The political–social–economic organization of a society will determine the ways in which these limits are approached and managed (Matthews 1976; Schnaiberg 1980).

The Question of Access

The question of access to resources, so vital to both developed and developing countries, is really a question of an integrated access to resources, technology, and markets. The Japanese have very limited resources on their soil. But they do have good technology and access to a vast market, domestic and international. Because of this, Japanese investments in resource-producing sectors have been strategically directed at resource-abundant regions like Africa, Australia, Alaska, Brazil, Canada, and the Middle East (Kojima 1978). The fact that this resource-poor country has emerged as a premier value-adding society of the industrial world calls into question the conventional notions about resources and development. While resources and development do go hand in hand, the Japanese experience shows that "resource access" can be managed if technology and marketing are mastered first (Kotler, Fahey, and Jatusripitak 1985). An important aspect of resource management, of course, is the pattern of resource use.

Resource Use and Quality of Life

From the vast gap in incomes and resource use between First and Third Worlds, it would appear that there is a direct link between economic development and resource use (Mazur and Rosa 1974). The relationship is not as straightforward as it appears, particularly within high-income countries (Mazur and Rosa

1974). Table 4.1 shows the per capita income, per capita energy consumption, and the physical quality-of-life index (PQLI) developed by Morris (1979) for the 15 richest industrialized countries. Per capita income and per capita energy consumption are poorly correlated ($r=0.25$). The "outliers" in energy consumption—Norway, the United States, and Canada—are in fact energy-rich countries. It should be noted that per capita income and PQLI are less poorly correlated ($r=0.42$), and PQLI and energy consumption are negatively correlated ($r=-0.11$).

Generalizing from energy to all resources, it appears that quality of life depends on how wisely resources are used rather than on how intensely they are used. Since relative late developers like France and Japan are also frugal energy users, it can be surmised moreover that there is some social "learning" regarding resource use. Clearly, in "learning societies" resource use patterns are likely to be quite different from the patterns found in societies that are slow to learn (Fisk 1978). The challenge for marketing is to facilitate and accelerate forms of social learning that foster development without jeopardizing the world's resources and environment.

TABLE 4.1. Relationships Between Income, Energy Consumption and Physical Quality-of-Life Index (PQLI) in High-Income Countries

Country	Per Capita GNP[a] (1982 in U.S dollars)	Per Capita Energy Consumption[a] (1,000 kg oil equivalent)	PQLI[b]
Switzerland	17,010	3,755	96
Norway	14,280	8,305	97
Sweden	14,040	6,138	98
U.S.A.	13,160	7,540	95
Denmark	12,470	3,616	97
W. Germany	12,460	4,342	94
France	11,680	3,619	96
Canada	11,320	9,208	95
Australia	11,140	4,908	95
Netherlands	10,930	4,908	97
Finland	10,780	5,793	95
Belgium	10,760	4,636	94
Japan	10,080	3,087	97
Austria	9,880	3,398	94
U.K.	9,660	3,541	94

[a]*Source:* World Bank, *World Development Report 1984* (New York: Oxford University Press, 1984).

[b]*Source:* From John W. Sewell, *The United States and World Development: Agenda 1980* (New York: Praeger, 1980). Table A-4.

CONSUMPTION CHANGES

Every act of consumption depletes resources. Not only are resources directly used up in the process of consumption (for example, cooking, driving), but vast amounts of resources are required to make available products for consumption and to support the socioeconomic infrastructure of an industrial society. There is a quantum jump in resource requirement as a country progresses from an industrially underdeveloped to an industrially developed state. Consider energy consumption once again. In terms of thousands of kilograms of oil equivalent consumed per capita, low-income countries consumed 253 units, middle-income countries consumed 721 units, and advanced industrial economies consumed 4,985 units in 1981. The differences are quite dramatic.

The consumption of resources has grown most rapidly in the last 50 years with withdrawals and use of resources accelerated by the developments in the high-income economies. Because of these factors, today's low-income countries may never progress from the current 250 units of energy consumption to the nearly 5,000-unit level of the advanced industrial countries. Nonetheless, a substantial increase can be expected as today's low-income countries industrialize. The world's resources will be severely strained by the future consumption changes of the low-income countries, compounding the resource pressures created by the currently resource-intense life-styles of the affluent countries. These strains can be minimized only if consumption patterns and aspirations are modified to reflect the realities of resource constraints.

Consumption Patterns

We have argued that high-resource use intensity is not neccessarily associated with high quality of life. Yet there are built-in pressures in advanced industrial societies to adopt consumption patterns that are resource intensive and even wasteful (Uusitalo 1982). According to Wilensky (1964), to be socially integrated in the United States is to accept advertising and speedy obsolescence in consumption. The dominant consumption pattern in advanced industrial societies is individual (rather than collective), based on private (rather than public) goods, and slanted toward passive (rather than active) forms of consumption (Firat and Dholakia 1977, 1982). This is exemplified by the organization of life around the single-family detached home, located at considerable distances from the workplace, and supported by individualized transport systems and private ownership of major household durables.

It so happens that this dominant pattern is among the most energy- and resource-intensive patterns possible. It is estimated that in 1972 it took 42,500 pounds of materials (organic, metals, mineral fuel, and nonmetallic), exclusive of food, to support one U.S. citizen (Leonardo Scholars 1975). The consumer "discretion" in deviating from the dominant consumption pattern is very limited:

Once the commitment has been made to a suburban residence, in reality there is very little choice in matters like owning two automobiles, washer–dryers, etc. (Schnaiberg 1980). The individual costs of deviating from this pattern are also high (Dholakia and Dholakia 1985, and Firat and Dholakia 1982). Rather than pay these high economic, social, and psychological costs, people in advanced industrial countries—quite naturally—prefer to "fit in" with the dominant consumption pattern.

Consumption Aspirations

Trends worldwide indicate shifts in consumption patterns toward the individual–private–passive direction. Preferences for the single-family detached home continue to persist in the advanced economies (Dillman, Tremblay, and Dillman 1979) along with two cars and other amenities (Dholakia and Levy 1984; *Marketing News* 1980; Perry 1976). Even the socially and ecologically concerned consumers who are likely to be younger, liberal, economically upscale (Belch 1979) appear to be moving away from their past choices of multifamily dwellings (*Providence Evening Bulletin* 1984). Similarly, greater consumer expenditures for services have not resulted in less resource-intense life-styles. Instead, goods-intensive services such as recreation and fast food have developed fastest with large utilization of capital, energy, and resources promoting a private individual mode of consumption (Landsberg 1976; Schnaiberg 1980). Such consumer aspirations in the affluent economies continue to strain the world's critical resources.

Add to these the rising consumption aspirations of the populous Third World. Consider China. A country with nearly a quarter of the world's population, China maintained an austere economic style for three decades. Now the floodgates are being thrown open to new products, ideas, and technologies (Butterfield 1978; Jones et al. 1985; Kraar 1985). The prospect of a television set, a washer, or a refrigerator in every Chinese household is absolutely staggering. It is no wonder that multinational companies are lining up to tap the Chinese market, despite the presently high cost of doing business with China (Kraar 1985). But what brings a gleam to the eye of the General Electric executive looking at China also very likely strikes terror in the heart of the environmentalist. The resource impact of rising consumption levels in China, and the Third World in general, will be phenomenal.

But the tide of rising consumption aspirations in the Third World is not one that can be rolled back. The world has become a global village linked by electronic communications. What is in vogue in New York today will surely reach Nairobi in just a few weeks. Moreover, people and governments of the Third World resent the sermons for simplicity from the high-living First World, even while recognizing the virtues of ecologically adapted indigenous economic styles

(Schumacher 1973). Most importantly, however, many corporations in the First World realize that their market frontier lies in the Third World. Their corporate strategies rest on the premise of rapidly expanding consumption in the Third World (Matthews 1972). Given these pro-consumption forces, it is unlikely that consumption aspirations in the Third World will abate. These aspirations, however, can be creatively channeled in ecologically sounder avenues—a point we return to later in the chapter.

Simplicity in consumption, of course, is also very germane to the First World. The energy intensity of alternative modes of transport can be seen in Table 4.2. When both energy intensity and load factors are considered, there is considerable scope for improving resource utilization and efficiency by shifting to more efficient modes of transport as well as increasing the load factors of each mode (Hannon 1975; Leonardo Scholars 1975). There is limited evidence that consumers in the First World have "ecologized" their life-styles to some extent and have often resorted to voluntary simplicity (Elgin and Mitchell 1977; Mitchell 1980). More importantly, as Ferguson (1980) argues, a "new mind" with humanistic–ecological values has quietly replaced the older Western mentality of acquisition and exploitation. Counterbalancing these trends are the self-indulgence of the "me generation" and the vigorous pursuit of la dolce vita by the young urban affluents (Alder 1984; Gelman 1984). It is difficult to say which way the scale will tip in the high-level economies, but marketing will have a role in determining the resource-intensity of future consumption patterns.

TABLE 4.2. Energy Consumption and Savings in U.S. Transportation

Transportation Mode	Energy Consumption (BTU/passenger mile)		Energy Savings (%)	
	Actual Load Factor	100% Load Factor	Within Mode[a]	Between Modes[b]
Urban Auto	8,100	2,300	252	
Urban Mass Transit	3,800	760	400	113
Intercity Auto	3,400	1,600	112	
Intercity Bus	1,600	740	116	112
Airplane	8,400	4,100	164	
Rail	2,900	1,100	105	189

Source: The Leonardo Scholars (1975, p. 94, Table 7.3), reproduced with permission.

[a]If changes made from actual to 100% load factor.

[b]If changes made from urban auto to urban mass transit; from intercity auto to intercity bus; from airplane to rail.

Influencing Consumption

Marketing is the primary instrument for influencing consumption in modern societies. Studies in both Asia and Latin America indicate aspiration for modern goods such as air conditioners and television sets to be most influenced by mass media and exposure to foreign tourists (Freedman 1972; Lauterbach 1972). Although theoretically it is possible to use marketing techniques for reducing or simplifying consumption (Kotler 1973; Kotler and Levy 1971), practically this is a much more difficult task than stimulational marketing.

From an ecological perspective, marketing—the provisioning technology of the modern era—has its challenges cut out. In the Third World, the challenge is to canalize rising consumption aspirations into ecologically sane avenues. In the First World, the challenge is to make people aware of the ecological insanity of their consumption patterns. The challenge for "responsible marketing" (Fisk 1973) is much greater, in our view, in the First World than in the Third World. It is much more difficult to resurrect Calvin than to escape the possible shadow of Malthus.

But the reigning perspective in the contemporary world is economic, not ecological. There are few conditions supporting the emergence of "responsible marketing." The imperatives of development favor the conventional forms of marketing. Such "marketing" is concerned primarily with demand stimulation, at the micro level, and socializing consumers into the dominant consumption patterns, at the macro level. To learn new forms of marketing, contemporary societies must first adopt new perspectives on development.

PERSPECTIVES ON DEVELOPMENT

Development is a state as well as a process. The state of development refers to the socioeconomic conditions prevailing in contemporary advanced industrial countries. These countries have "achieved" development and are often labeled "developed" countries. Others are struggling to achieve it and are generally called "developing" countries.

The notion of development as a state is useful for describing desirable levels of living. But it says little about how these levels of living are achieved. For this, we need the notion of development as a *process*. Of course, the "developed" countries are not static and "development-as-a-state" is a moving target. The process of development is of as much interest to "developed" countries as it is to "developing" countries. There has been, in fact, a resurgence of development agencies and projects in the industrially advanced nations (Beaudoin et al. 1984). We will deal with development primarily in the process sense, and only secondarily in the state sense. To avoid the labeling problems, we continue to refer to First and Third Worlds as denoting the two polar states of development.

View of Development in Marketing

In the marketing literature, a widely held but rather lopsided view of development prevails. As a state, development is defined and measured by per capita income. As a process, development occurs when per capita incomes rise; that is, *economic growth* is the process of development (Drucker 1958; Layton 1982).

Contemporary theory and practice of development have moved considerably beyond the "growth" view of economic development, a fact that has received scant recognition in marketing literature (Dholakia and Dholakia 1984). From a contemporary perspective, there are four views of development, each having a different implication for marketing (Dholakia and Dholakia 1984):

1. The growth view
2. The growth-with-diversification view, which emphasizes economic diversification in addition to growth
3. The growth-with-equity view, which emphasizes the redistribution of the benefits of growth
4. The quality-of-life view, which focuses on the consequences of the development process

All these views are valid and important for development planners. From a marketing and resource perspective, the quality-of-life view is especially important. This view personalizes the notion of development. By interpreting development in terms of personal quality-of-life factors, we convert development from an abstract notion to a high-involvement issue. This quality-of-life perspective appeals not only to people in the First World but also to those in the Third World, who are increasingly interpreting development in the so-called "basic needs" framework (Burki and Haq 1981; Singh 1979).

Development and Resources

The process of development demands and depletes resources. This is an inescapable ecological fact. But some forms of development deplete fewer resources—they are less wasteful. For example, a cluster of multifamily dwellings and services ("the dense city") is much less resource intensive than the suburban, single-family, detached dwelling pattern. Furthermore, some forms of development generate resources. Activities like afforestation, wind mills, solar plants, etc., harness and husband resources that are otherwise unavailable for human use. In a broader sense, many development activities upgrade human resources, a phenomenon—which if appropriately managed—can have favorable multiplier effects for the economy and the ecology.

The marketing challenge is to foster forms of development that are resource conserving and resource generating. Sachs (1976) calls these *ecodevelopment* strategies, which look at long-term as well as immediate needs and use cultural as well as ecological data to develop self-reliant, adaptive, and specific solutions to problems of each ecoregion. This is difficult. Just as marketing is easily geared to resource-intensive consumption, it is also easily put in the service of resource-intensive development. Once again "responsible" forms of marketing are easy to articulate but difficult to operationalize. To this issue, we turn next.

MARKETING

A dominant metaphor in marketing is that of promotion. Marketing techniques have been successfully used for promoting or furthering a variety of products, places, persons, ideas, and causes (Kotler 1971; Levy and Kotler 1970). It is in this "promoting" sense that marketing relates to consumption and development. Figure 4.3 enlarges our basic model of Figure 4.2 by incorporating the links between marketing and development. Marketing is widely used for promotion consumption. Cox (1965) sees marketing's task to be one of increasing consumption aspirations in order to create demand for various goods. Marketing has been strongly recommended, but not widely used, for promoting development (Etemad 1984).

The basic logic of Figure 4.3 is difficult to alter. It is unrealistic to put drastic brakes on either consumption or development. It is much less realistic to expect marketing to provide these brakes. But marketing can help in promoting forms of consumption and development that are less resource destructive or are even resource generative.

FIGURE 4.3   An Enlarged View of the Role of Marketing

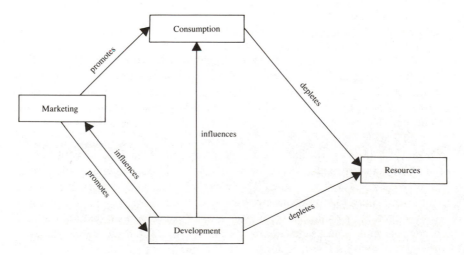

Forms of Consumption

In addition to increasing the level of production and consumption, marketing has succeeded in reducing diversity in production and consumption forms. This drive towards *homogenization* has created resource-depleting and environment-degrading economic activities that need to be altered. For instance, the "green revolution" with its reliance on chemical fertilizers, pesticides, and mechanization has created global dependence on single-crop farming with serious social and biological consequences in various parts of the world (Farvar 1976; Sachs 1976). This emphasis on monoculture has resulted in the world's dependence on a mere 15 kinds of food plants (Stockholm Conference 1972) and increased vulnerability to pests and other diseases. Similar trends are visible in food animals.

Reduction in diversity of manufactured goods is frequently masked by the increase in brand choice (Dholakia and Dholakia 1985) and "unimportant" product attributes (Dickson 1975). The resource intensities of the dominant consumption form are further exacerbated by the "upgrading" of products through features such as increased power, speed, weight, convenience in cars, refrigerators, air conditioners, etc. (Hirst 1972; Newman and Day 1975). This search for ever-increasing levels of speed, power, convenience, and novelty has meant greater intensities of energy and resource use. This is evident, for example, in the trend toward disposable, all-aluminum beverage cans, which are the most energy intensive of all beverage container choices (Hannon 1973), and continual introduction of new and "improved" models of automobiles and other durables (Scitovsky 1976).

Promoting diversity has become an important ecodevelopment strategy, and marketing has to play an important role. Alternative energy sources need to be supported, such as proposals for "soft" energy paths (Schumacher 1973) and production systems based on labor intensity and decentralization (Hannon 1975; Schnaiberg 1980). Varied consumption patterns need to be promoted, for example, different ways of organizing working and living arrangements such that travel is reduced or achieved through low-energy systems (Firat and Dholakia 1982). Alternatives to individual ownership through community ownership and leasing need to be fostered to reduce levels of resource intensities (Fisk 1974).

The Agency Dilemma

Marketing techniques work well when put in the hands of well-identified agencies with well-defined goals. Nonprofit organizations have been quite successful, for example, in promoting environmental and resource conservation causes (Lovelock and Weinberg 1977, pp. 7–17, 183–96). But the success of a Sierra Club or an Earthwatch is not enough to guarantee that responsible development and responsible resource use will occur on a global scale. Fundamentally, the problem is that there is no identifiable agency to champion the causes of eco-logically sound resource use and development patterns. The likely "agencies" for these causes—the future generations, the society, Nature, etc.—are too re-mote or too nebulous to be effective. These "agencies" cannot act as purposive organizations with driving entrepreneurial energy, which seems essential for mar-keting strategies to work. While the contributions of individual ecology-oriented interest groups are often of societal value, the macro-level issue of selecting and promoting responsible resource use and development strategies is difficult to resolve.

A Strategic Approach

For fueling global development from a limited resource base, a strategic ap-proach to responsible marketing is needed. Marketing strategies have to be designed in which the eco-logic reinforces economic and political logic. In the final section, we briefly discuss such strategies.

STRATEGIC AND RESPONSIBLE MARKETING

From the earlier discussion, it can be surmised that marketing techniques aid in the promotion of ecologically sound development patterns when the fol-lowing occur:

1. An identifiable agency exists.
2. Ecological objectives make economic and political sense.
3. Entrepreneurial opportunities for ecologically sound strategies exist or can be created.

The strategies discussed below strive to create conditions for successful forms of responsible marketing. Each category listed can be the subject of consider-able research and action; hence, only brief and illustrative discussion is provided here.

Macro-Level Marketing Programs

Campaigns for fire prevention (Smokey the Bear), crime prevention (McGruff the Hound), etc., in the First World and family planning, nutritional education, etc., in the Third World are examples of macro-level marketing pro-grams designed to create major, long-term behavior changes in the society. Ex-perience has shown that such programs are successful if they are based on valid assessment of consumer needs and are well administered and funded (Bloom and Novelli 1981). Typically, such programs are administered by a government agency or other macroentity.

Similar programs can be created for promoting ecologically sound patterns of development and resource use. Where such programs are already in place, greater marketing expertise can be injected to improve program effectiveness. A danger in such strategies is trying to "sell" ecological behavior patterns when no economic or social rationale for adopting such behavior exists. Careful need assessment must precede the design of such programs.

Licensing Eco-entrepreneurs

A strategy of licensing capitalist entrepreneurs for ecological purposes may be useful in some cases. Licensing has become a tremendous growth industry in industrially advanced countries. As an example, consider the appearance of Halley's comet in 1986—an astronomic event that happens once every 76 years. An entrepreneur has created a licensable property with a sales potential based on Halley's comet (Dunkel 1985). On one plane, this represents a crass commercial exploitation of a natural phenomenon. On another plane, this shows how entrepreneurship may be harnessed to any cause—ecological ones included. Forward-thinking governments and environmental organizations can create such licensing opportunities, with appropriate safeguards to ensure that a reasonable share of profits is ploughed back for ecological development.

Marketing a Consumption or Development Ethic

The inspiration for Schumacher's *Small Is Beautiful* (1973) was Mahatma Gandhi's campaign of decentralized rural development undertaken in preindependence India. Gandhi was not "marketing" his ideas of decentralized development by appealing to the long-term self-interest of the people or advancing complex arguments about intergenerational equity. He was simply promoting an ecological consumption and production style with a strong moral appeal.

In today's world, the marketing of such consumption and developmental "ethics" has been largely appropriated by religious sects and groups. This greatly limits the appeal of such "ethics." Secular organizations with ecological objectives, including governments, can greatly expand the "market" for ecologically sound consumption and development "ethics." The great advantage in marketing such "ethics" is that if the moral appeal strikes a resonant chord in the society, the appeal regenerates and propagates by its own momentum.

Riding Megatrends

Naisbitt's labeling of major social trends as "megatrends" (1982) has been quite influential, at least in a semantic sense (Sheth 1984). Such trends can be interpreted in terms of emerging business opportunities. Environmental groups can make it their business to identify "ecotrends"—trends toward responsible consumption and resource use patterns—and interpret these as business opportunities. In this way, incipient pro-ecology trends can be accelerated by chan-neling business interest and investment in their direction.

Creating Ecological Interdependence

The First and the Third Worlds have become heavily interdependent in an economic sense. Similar interdependences can be created on an ecological plane. For example, a substantial portion of the so-called "waste" of the First World can be recycled as raw material or intermediate goods for the Third World. Remanufacturing and refurbishing of discarded First World machines and other goods for Third World use can become viable business propositions (Walle 1984). There are clear marketing opportunities for creating and managing such recycling channels.

Promoting Industrial Adjustment

The transition to a postindustrial era is already quite pronounced in the First World (Bell 1973). Such industrial restructuring is painful but inevitable. In terms of resources, the postindustrial era relies increasingly on the intangible and self-regenerating resource called "information." To the extent that the transition to the information age can be made smoother, the impact on tangible resources (fos-sil fuels, metals, etc.) will be favorable. In fact, the countries of the Third World are entering a resource-intensive phase just as the countries of the First World are becoming information intensive. To the extent that the transfer of conven-tional manufacturing activities to the Third World can be smoothly accomplished, the resources freed from an information-seeking First World can be made avail-able to a resource-seeking Third World. At present, such transitions occur through a wrenching process of social and economic dislocations. The political rhetoric of "export of jobs" masks the fundamental technological shift under-way. Many First World countries, the United States especially, do not have co-herent policies to deal with such transitions. Marketing techniques can be use-ful in smoothing such transitions, both in terms of analyzing shifting global market opportunities and in terms of "social marketing" to bring about neces-sary social changes within the First World.

Concluding Note

Marketing concepts and techniques can be adapted to the needs of global de-velopment in a resource-constrained world. But it is not easy to usher in such "responsible" forms of marketing. This type of marketing cannot be legislated into existence or normatively prescribed. A strategic and entrepreneurial approach is needed. The strategies suggested above are illustrative. Singly, such strate-gies will have only limited impact, but collectively, they can create a form of ecological marketing that goes beyond rhetoric.

REFERENCES

Alder, Jerry. 1984. "The Year of the Yuppies." *Newsweek,* December 31, pp.14–24.
"American 'Trading Off' to Combat Inflation, Tight Credit, High Gas Costs." *Marketing News* (November 14 1980):1.
"Baby-Boom Adults Buy Older Homes." *Providence Evening Bulletin* April 11, 1984, p. C-6.
Beaudoin, D. B., N. Dholakia, D. W. McLeavey, and R. W. Nason. 1984. "Regional Redevelopment: A Macromarketing Perspective." Presented at the Ninth Annual Macromarketing Seminar, Vancouver, August.
Belch, Michael A. 1979. "Identifying the Socially and Ecologically Concerned Segment Through Lifestyle Research: Initial Findings." In *The Conserver Society,* proceedings series, edited by Karl E. Henion II and Thomas C. Kinnear, pp. 69–81. Chicago: American Marketing Association.
Bell, Daniel. 1973. *The Coming of Post-Industrial Society: A Venture in Social Forecasting.* New York: Basic Books.
Bloom, Paul N., and William D. Novelli. 1981. "Problems and Challenges in Social Marketing." *Journal of Marketing* 45 (Spring):79–88.
Burki, Javed, and Mahbub ul Haq. 1981. "Meeting Basic Needs: An Overview." *World Development* 9 (February):167–82.
Butterfield, Fox. 1978. "Peking's Postwar Warriors Are Not Just Paper Tigers." *New York Times,* November 26, p.E-3.
Chapman, L. P., T. J. Tyrell, and T. D. Mount. 1972. "Electricity Demand Growth and the Energy Crisis." *Science* 178 (November):703–8.
Cox, Reavis. 1965. *Distribution in a High-Level Economy.* Englewood Cliffs, NJ: Prentice-Hall.
Dholakia, Nikhilesh, and Ruby R. Dholakia. 1985. "Choice and Choicelessness in the Paradigm of Marketing." In *Changing the Course of Marketing: Alternative Paradigms for Widening Marketing Theory,* edited by N. Dholakia and J. Arndt. Greenwich, CT: JAI Press.
———. 1984. "Missing Links: Marketing and the Newer Theories of Development." In *Marketing in Developing Countries,* edited by G. S. Kindra, pp. 57–75. London: Croom Helm.
Dholakia, Ruby R., and Sidney J. Levy. 1984. "The Changing Economic Environment and Consumption Values in the U.S.: An Exploratory Analysis." Presented at the Ninth Annual Macromarketing Conference, Vancouver, B.C., August.
Dickson, David. 1975. *The Politics of Alernative Technology.* New York: Universe Books.
Dillman, Don A., K. R. Tremblay, Jr., and J. J. Dillman. 1979. "Influence of Housing Norms and Personal Characteristics on Stated Housing Preferences." *Housing and Society* 6:2–19.
Drucker, Peter F. 1958. "Marketing and Economic Development." *Journal of Marketing* 22 (January):252–59.
DuBoff, Richard B. 1974. "Economic Ideology and the Environment." In *Man and Environment Ltd.,* edited by Hans G. T. van Raaj and Ariel E. Lugo, pp.203–20. The Hague: Rotterdam University Press.
Dunkel, Tom. 1985. "Pennies from Heaven." *Northwest Orient* 16 (March):13–16.

Elgin, Duane, and Arnold Mitchell. 1977. "Voluntary Simplicity." *Co-Evolution Quarterly* 14 (Summer):4–18.

Etemad, Hamid. 1984. "Is Marketing the Catalyst in the Economic Development Process?" In *Marketing in Developing Countries,* edited by G. S. Kindra, pp. 29–56. London: Croom Helm.

Farvar, M. Taghi. 1976. "The Interaction of Ecological and Social Systems." In *Outer Limits and Human Needs,* edited by William H. Matthews, pp. 67–81. Uppsala: Dag Hammarskjold Foundation.

Ferguson, Marilyn. 1980. *The Aquarian Conspiracy.* Los Angeles: J. P. Tarcher.

Firat, A. Fuat, and Nikhilesh Dholakia. 1982. "Consumption Choices at the Macro Level." *Journal of Macromarketing* 2 (Fall):6–15.

——. 1977. "Consumption Patterns and Macromarketing: A Radical Perspective." *European Journal of Marketing* 11:291–98.

Fisk, George. 1978. "Marketing in Learning Societies." In *Future Directions for Marketing*, Report No. 78–104, edited by G. Fisk, J. Arndt, and K. Grønhaug, pp.78–104, 52–73. Cambridge, MA: Marketing Science Institute.

——. 1974. *Marketing and the Ecological Crisis.* New York: Harper & Row.

——. 1973. "Criteria for a Theory of Responsible Consumption." *Journal of Marketing* 37 (April):24–31.

Freedman, Deborah S. 1972. "Consumption Aspiration as Economic Incentives in a Developing Country—Taiwan." In *Human Behavior in Economic Affairs,* edited by B. Strumpel, J. N. Morgan, and E. Zahn, pp.229–59. San Francisco: Jossey-Bass.

Gelman, Eric. 1984. "They Live to Buy." *Newsweek* December 31, pp. 28–29.

Hannon, Bruce. 1975. "Energy Conservation and the Consumer." *Science* 189 (July 11):95–102.

——. 1973. *System Energy and Recycling: A Study of the Beverage Industry,* Center for Advanced Computation, Doc. No. 23. Champaign–Urbana: University of Illinois.

Hearings Before House Committee on Interstate and Foreign Commerce. 1970. "Copper Pricing Practices," Document Y4.IN 8/4: 91–97; HR.17657, 149–57.

Hirst, Eric. 1972. *Energy Consumption for Transportation in the U.S.,* Report NSF-EP-15. Oak Ridge, TN: Oak Ridge National Laboratory.

"How the Energy Crisis Will Hit Industry." *Business Week* No. 2304 (November 24, 1973):56–60.

Jones, Dorothy E., and others. 1985. "Capitalism in China." *Business Week* No. 2876 (January 14):52–59.

Ketchum, Bostwick H. 1970. "Biological Implications of Global Marine Pollution." In *Global Effects on Environment Pollution,* edited by S. Fred Singer. New York: Springer-Verlag.

King, Resa W., and Amy Durking. 1985. "Surimi Could Become 'The Hot Dog of the Fish Business'." *Business Week* No. 2882 (February 25): 106.

Kojima, Kiyoshi. 1978. *Japanese Direct Foreign Investment.* Tokyo: Charles E. Tuttle Co.

Kotler, Philip. 1973. "The Major Tasks of Marketing Management." *Journal of Marketing* 37 (October):42–49.

——. 1971. "Metamarketing: The Furthering of Organizations, Persons, Places and Causes." *Marketing Forum* (July–August):13–23.

Kotler, Philip, Liam Fahey, and S. Jatusripitak. 1985. *The New Competition.* Englewood Cliffs, NJ: Prentice-Hall.

Kotler, Philip, and Sidney J. Levy. 1971. "Demarketing, Yes, Demarketing." *Harvard Business Review* 49 (November–December):74–80.

Kraar, Louis. 1985. "China After Marx: Open for Business?" *Fortune* 3 (February 18):28–33.

Landsberg, Hans H. 1976. "Materials: Some Recent Trends and Issues." *Science* 191 (February 20):637–41.

Lauterbach, Albert. 1972. "The Social Setting of Consumer Behavior in Latin America." In *Human Behavior in Economic Affairs,* edited by B. Strumpel, J. N. Morgan, and E. Zahn, pp. 261–88. San Francisco: Jossey-Bass.

Layton, Roger A. 1982. "A Theory of the Role of Marketing Systems in Economic Growth." Presented at the American Marketing Association Annual Educators' Conference, Chicago.

The Leonardo Scholars. 1975. *Resources and Decisions.* N. Scituate, MA: Duxbury Press.

Levy, Sidney J., and Philip Kotler. 1969. "Beyond Marketing: The Furthering Concept." *California Management Review* 12 (Winter):67–73.

Longgood, William. 1972. *The Darkening Land.* New York: Simon and Schuster.

Lovelock, Christopher H., and Charles B. Weinberg. 1977. *Cases in Public and Nonprofit Marketing.* Palo Alto: Scientific Press.

Matthews, Roy A. 1972. "The Multinational Firm and the World of Tomorrow." In *The Multinational Firm and the Nation State,* edited by G. Paquet, Ontario: Collier-Macmillan.

Matthews, William H. 1976. "The Concept of Outer Limits." In *Outer Limits and Human Needs,* edited by W. H. Matthews, pp. 15–37. Uppsala: Sweden: Dag Hammarskjold Foundation.

Mazur, Allan, and Eugene Rosa. 1974. "Energy and Lifestyle." *Science* 183 (November 15):607–10.

McNeil, Mary. 1972. "Lateristic Soils in Distinct Tropical Environments: Southern Sudan and Brazil." In *The Careless Technology-Ecology and International Development,* edited by M. T. Farvar and J. P. Milton, New York: National History Press.

Meadows, D. H., D. L. Meadows, J. Randers, and W. W. Behrens III. 1974. *The Limits to Growth,* 2nd ed. New York: Universe Books.

Mitchell, Arnold. 1980. *Changing Values and Lifestyles.* Menlo Park, CA: SRI International.

Morris, Morris D. 1979. *Measuring the Condition of the World's Poor.* New York: Pergamon Press.

Naisbitt, John. 1982. *Megatrends: Ten New Directions Transforming Our Lives.* New York: Warner Books.

Newman, D. K., and D. Day. 1975. *The American Energy Consumer.* Cambridge, MA: Ballinger.

Perry, Donald L. 1976. *Social Marketing Strategies.* Pacific Palisades, CA: Goodyear Publishing.

Sachs, Ignacy. 1976. "Environment and Styles of Development." In *Outer Limits and Human Needs,* edited by William H. Matthews, pp. 41–65. Uppsala: Dag Hammarskjold Foundation.

Schnaiberg, Allan. 1980. *The Environment: From Surplus to Scarcity.* New York: Oxford University Press.

Schumacher, E. F. 1973. *Small Is Beautiful: Economics as if People Mattered.* New York:

Harper & Row.

Scitovsky, Tibor. 1976. *The Joyless Economy: An Inquiry into Human Satifaction and Consumer Dissatisfaction*. New York: Oxford University Press.

Sewell, John W. 1980. *The United States and World Development: Agenda 1980*. New York: Praeger.

Sheth, Jagdish N. 1984. "Marketing Megatrends." *Journal of Consumer Marketing* 1:1.

Singh, Ajit. 1979. "The Basic Needs Approach to Development vs. the New International Economical Order: The Significance of Third World Industrialization." *World Development* 7 (June):585–606.

The Stockholm Conference. 1972. *Only One Earth*. London: Friends of the Earth.

Taggiasco, Ronald, and William Glasgall. 1985. "OPEC Still Hasn't Faced up to Reality." *Business Week* No. 2880 (February 11):29.

Uusitalo, Liisa. 1982. "Environmental Impact of Changes in Consumption Styles." *Journal of Macromarketing* 2 (Fall):16–30.

Walle, A. H. 1984. "Remanufacturing in Less Developed Regions: A Challenge to Macro Marketers." Presented at the Ninth Annual Macromarketing Seminar, Vancouver, B.C.

Wilensky, Harold L. 1964. "Mass Society and Mass Culture: Interdependence or Independence?" *American Sociological Review* 29 (April):173–97.

The World Bank. 1984. *World Development Report 1984*. New York: Oxford University Press.

Young, Allen. 1972. "Ecology and Development in Brazil." *Win Magazine* 8 (August).

CHAPTER 5

Consumption Expenditures and Economic Development

EDWARD W. CUNDIFF

Since the publication of Drucker's article on ''Marketing and Economic Development'' in 1958, marketers have explored various ways in which particular aspects of marketing have affected the levels of economic development in different economies. Over 120 articles have been published describing how marketing and economic development are interrelated and how each affects the other. The premise underlying much of this research is that marketing creates or increases consumption, and consumption in turn increases the level of economic development. It is the intent of this chapter to explore the relationship between consumption and economic development in nations at various levels of development. Are such relationships coincidental or interrelated? If interrelated, what effect does one have on the other?

MEASURING ECONOMIC DEVELOPMENT

Economic development is a complex concept involving many possible dimensions. Sethi (1970) measured levels of development in 91 countries, using 29 different variables to classify them, and Mentzer and Samli (1981) described a more limited list of 14 variables. Accurate and comparable statistical data on most such variables are simply not available for the majority of nations in the world. As a consequence, Mentzer and Samli found it necessary to recommend that a separate panel of experts familiar with each country be formed to evaluate the level of economic development of the countries of the world. This lack of comparable data is particularly true of the less-developed nations. Yet, any attempt to compare rates of development between nations must include as large a sample as possible of all nations. In addition, many of the variables used to define level of development among nations are not really economic factors. Instead, they may measure social or cultural differences.

One economic measure that is available through U.N. sources for most nations in the world is gross domestic product (GDP). This statistic, which includes government and private consumption, capital formation, and imports and exports, is gathered in fairly standardized (and hence comparable) form for nearly all member nations of the United Nations. Thus, it provides a useful basis for comparing the relative economic wealth of each, particularly during the decades of the 1960s and 1970s, an important period of widespread economic development.

TRENDS IN ECONOMIC DEVELOPMENT
IN OPEN MARKET ECONOMIES

During the 1960s, there was a clear pattern of differential development between rich and poor nations. Nations with per capita GDP of $1,000 (U.S.) or more (as of 1970) showed increases in GDP of 100 percent during that decade. Countries with per capita GDP of $500 to $999 showed increases of only 60 percent, and countries with GDP less than $500 per capita showed 45 percent or less growth (see Table 5.1). These data supported the hypothesis that the rich get richer, and although the poor may not all get poorer in an absolute sense, they do in a relative sense.

The decade of the 1970s showed a much more balanced growth between the richer and poorer nations. With the exception of the most underdeveloped coun-

TABLE 5.1. Changes in Gross Domestic Product (GDP) During the 1960s and 1970s

GDP Per Capita as of 1970	Increase in GDP (%)	
	1960–70	*1970–80*
Under $200 (U.S.) per capita	42.6	295.6
$200 to $499 (U.S.) per capita[a]	45.3	390.6
$500 to $999 (U.S.) per capita[b]	61.7	417.2
$1,000 to 1,999 (U.S.) per capita	114.0	406.5
$2,000 (U.S.) and above per capita	103.7	405.1

[a,b]Omitting Oman and Saudi Arabia respectively, because each experienced growth in excess of 1,500 percent during the 1970s because of OPEC earnings.

Source: Computed by author from tables in U.N. *Yearbook of National Account Statistics* vol.1, part 2. (United Nations, 1971, 1981).

tries (those with less than $200 GDP per capita), which showed less than 300 percent growth during the decade, all nations showed a growth of approximately 400 percent per capita. Actually the "take-off" nations in the $500 to $999 per capita category showed a slightly faster rate of growth. However, these data are expressed in relative terms, and in actual or dollar terms the rich were still getting richer than the poor.

THE ROLE OF CONSUMPTION IN DEVELOPMENT

Marketing theoreticians have claimed that economic development theoreticians have largely ignored or underplayed the role of marketing in development. The major focus of development experts has been on production as a contributor to development. As more products are produced, more products are consumed, and the general wealth of the nation is raised accordingly. Thus, factors that will increase the production capacity of a nation will have the effect of increasing economic development. Marketers have criticized this production emphasis for two reasons. First is the assumption that if goods are produced, they will be consumed. Marketers know that only goods for which there is a felt need or demand will be consumed, and then only if the product is available where the consumer can buy it at acceptable prices and the consumer is aware of this. Only if these marketing inputs are in place will production drive consumption. The second assumption of the production-oriented development economists is that consumption is a result rather than a cause of production. Yet, it can be argued just as logically that increases in consumption in a developing country may channel the flow of capital into new productive capacity to serve the market demand. It is the purpose of this chapter to more closely examine this relationship between consumption and economic development.

THE DEVELOPMENT OF HYPOTHESES

The assumption that consumption is a major factor contributing to economic development requires the development and testing of a number of hypotheses about this relationship. They are as follow:

1. *Personal consumption comprises a greater share of GDP in less-developed than in developed open market economies.* The assumption here is that a larger proportion of population in a less-developed nation is living at subsistence level, and therefore a larger share of GDP is devoted to such subsistence-level consumption.

2. *The share of GDP spent on private consumption is growing in all nations, but the rate of growth is faster in the highly developed economies.* This hypothesis is based on the fact that improvements in transportation and communications in

all societies, even the least developed, improve consumer access to goods and hence their ability to consume. Differential pressures for saving and investment would account for differences in the rate of growth in consumption depending on the current levels of development.

3. *Personal consumption has a smaller share of GDP in planned economies than in open market economies.* The underlying assumption of this hypothesis is that the planners in planned economies place a high priority on government expenditures and investment in capital goods, so they allocate a small share of the GDP to personal consumption than would result from the interaction of natural forces in an open market economy.

4. *The rate of growth in personal consumption is slower in planned economies than in open market economies.* This would also result from the lower priorities placed on personal consumption by planners.

5. *A higher proportion of personal consumption expenditures for services reduces the rate of economic development. The rate of growth in expenditures for services will be higher in more developed economies.* This is based on the assumption that the production of goods requires a higher investment in production facilities and hence greater accumulation of wealth than the production of services.

6. *A lead or lag relationship between government consumption, personal consumption, and gross capital formation might help to explain the impact of each factor on economic development.* If changes in one or more of these factors lead to changes in the other(s) on a regular basis, it could be argued that there may be at least a partial cause-and-effect relationship.

7. *Per capita personal consumption increases at a faster rate relative to total consumption in the more highly developed nations.* Since the less-developed nations generally experience higher rates of population growth, their per capita growth in consumption could be expected to be less than that of highly developed nations.

It has also been argued that higher per capita consumption expenditures for public goods leads to a higher quality of life. It would have been interesting to test such a hypothesis, but since no objective measures of quality of life in a larger number of nations were available for this study, it was not attempted.

TESTING OF HYPOTHESES

It is possible to test the above hypotheses for most of the nations of the world with objective and highly comparable data, because most nations are members of the United Nations and as such are expected to report annually on a number of economic variables. Data submitted by the more highly developed nations are detailed and are probably prepared with considerable care and accuracy. In general, the less economically developed a nation is, the less complete (and probably the less accurate) are its reports to the United Nations. Data from a number of the least-developed nations are too incomplete to be of use in testing the above hypotheses. In general, the less-developed nations submitting adequate data to the United Nations are those that inherited efficient civil services from former colonial governments. Thus, the hypotheses have been tested on what amounts to an almost complete census of the developed nations and a sample of the less-developed nations.

The first step in testing the hypotheses was to develop a system for ranking the nations of the world with respect to their stages of economic development. The statistic used to differentiate the nations was GDP per capita. Thus, even though segments of a society may enjoy an economic life-style considerably above or below the majority, the nation was ranked with other nations according to the average. Perhaps the most dramatic example of such dichotomous life-styles is South Africa, where 15 percent of the population have a per capita GDP that ranks with the most highly developed nations; and the economic infrastructure and life-style for that portion of the population are clearly like those of the highly developed nations. Nevertheless, since the remaining 85 percent of the population has a very low per capita GDP, the average GDP for the nation places it among the less-developed nations.

In order to trace changes in levels of economic development, it is necessary to have access to comparative data over a period of years. Since 1960 a large number of nations have reported fairly detailed economic data to the United Nations. Prior to that date, the number of reporting nations was much smaller, and the extent and comparability of the data were limited. So, most of the comparisons cover a 20-year period from 1960 to 1980. In 1960, 107 nations were making economic reports in sufficient detail to be included in this study. These were ranked into groups of nations with GDP per capita of less than $500 (U.S.), $500 to $999 (U.S.), $1,000 to $1,999 (U.S.), and over $2,000 (U.S.). Later it was decided to further differentiate the lowest and highest levels of development, so the nations were ranked into the following categories:

Under $200 (U.S.) per capita—13 nations
$200 to $499 (U.S.) per capita—32 nations
$500 to $1,000 (U.S.) per capita—22 nations
$1,000 to $1,999 (U.S.) per capita—7 nations
$2,000 to $2,999 (U.S.) per capita—12 nations
$3,000 (U.S.) and above per capita—7 nations

All of the above nations can be classified at least to some extent as open market economies. In addition, U.N. data were available on seven planned economies (Communist nations). General statistical data on these countries are presented in Table 5.2.

TABLE 5.2. Gross Domestic Product (GDP) and Its Distribution Among Reporting U.N. Member Nations in 1970

Nations by Amount of GDP Per Capita	Population (Millions)	GDP Millions of $ 100%	Government Consumption Total	Percentage	Personal Consumption Total	Percentage	Gross Formation Total	Percentage
Under $200								
Burma	27,748	10,260						
Haiti	4,235	1,656						
India	543,132	402.63	31.71	7.9	298.03	70.0	71.77	17.8
Indonesia	119,467	3,238.0						
Kenya	11,247	572.66	93.10	16.3			38,905	15.6
Madagascar	6,932	249,761						
Malawi	4,360	267,072						
Mauritania	1,162	11,330.0						
Pakistan	60,449	50,487	5,270	10.4				
Philippines	37,604	42,448			29,552	69.6	8,992	21.1
Sierra Leone	2,644	348.6	54.26	15.6	267.7	76.8	53.3	15.3
Sri Lanka	12,514	14,161.1	1,679.7	11.9	10,165.3	71.8	2,746.1	19.4
Thailand	35,745	136,060	15,620	11.5	92,429	79.3	35,606	26.2
$200 to $499								
Algeria	14,330	24,073					8,752	36.4
Bolivia	4,780	12,370	1,324	10.7			2,111	17.1
Columbia	22,075	130,361					28,660	21.9
Dom. Rep.	4,343	1,485.5					284.3	19.1
Ecuador	6,031	35,019					6,371	18.2
Egypt	33,329	3,145.5					437.0	13.9

Country								
El Salvador	3,516	2,571			1,935	75.3	341	13.3
Fiji	520	192	28	14.6	125	65.1	43	22.4
Guatemala	5,298	1,904.0					244.2	18.8
Guyana	709	535,550					121,863	22.8
Honduras	2,553	1,446	166	11.5	1,061	73.4	312	21.6
Iran	28,349	841.5						22.0
Ivory Coast	4,310	414,862					91,311	12.7
Jordan	2,280	174.4	58.7	33.7	152.8	87.6	22.1	26.9
Korea, Rep.	31,365	2,672.1	165.9	6.2	1,939.1	72.6	719.1	19.0
Liberia	1,523	407.8	220.7		395.5		246.3	18.5
Malaysia	10,466	10,588	1,742	16.5	6,349	60.0	2,016	
Morocco	15,126	20.02					3.70	
Oman		106.8						
Papua N.G.	2,413	621.7	183.1	29.5	387.1	62.3	91.6	14.7
Paraguay	2,301	74,921					11,034	14.7
Senegal	3,925	240.1						
Solomon Is.		28.6						
Sri Lanka	12,514	14,161.1	1,679.7	11.9	10,165.3	71.8	2,746.1	19.4
Swaziland	409	76.8	10.9	14.2			18.5	24.1
Syria	6,247	6,848						
Thailand	35,745	136,060	15,620	11.5	92,429	67.9	35,606	26.2
Turkey		144,634	18,719	12.9			28,825	19.9
Upper Volta	5,384	98,749	6,835	6.9			9,750	9.9
Yemen		1,527					215.0	14.1
Zambia	4,295	1,278.0	205.5	16.1	489.7	38.3	367.6	28.8
Zimbabwe		1,080.0	106.1	9.8	715.5	66.3	222.0	20.6
$500 to $999								
Argentina	23,748	88						
Brazil	95,204	210,118					47,694	22.7

TABLE 5.2. *(continued)*

Nations by Amount of GDP Per Capita	Population (Millions)	GDP Millions of $ 100%	Government Consumption Total	Percentage	Personal Consumption Total	Percentage	Gross Formation Total	Percentage
Chile	9,369	97					15.1	15.6
Costa Rica	1,737	6,524.5					1,339.9	20.5
Cyprus	633	226.6	21.6	9.5	171.5	75.7	55.2	24.4
Gabon	500	93,100						
Guadeloupe	328	1,330.0					244.2	18.4
Hong Kong	3,942	19,214			13,462	70.0	369.7	31.6
Jamaica	1,882	1,171.1						
Lebanon	2,469	4,866						
Malta	326	94,821	18,350	19.4	73,855	77.9	31,034	32.7
Martinique	338	1,600.5					366.5	22.9
Mexico	50,313	444,271			319,522	71.9	100,956	22.7
Panama	1,458	1,045.8	149.8	14.3	654.7	62.6	275.9	26.4
Peru	13,248	267,121	30,372	11.4			35,411	13.3
Portugal	8,628	177,338	25,245	14.2	122,370	69.0	41,806	23.6
Reunion	447	2,013.4					539.4	26.8
Saudia Arab.	7,740	22,921						
Singapore	2,075	5,804.9						
S. Africa	21,500	12,908			7,760	60.1	3,684	28.3
Trinidad & Tobago	955	1,734						
Uruguay	2,955	601					69	11.5
$1,000 to 1,999								
Austria	7,447	375.88	55.22	14.7	205.29	54.6	111.69	29.7
Greece	8,793	298,917	37,742	12.6	205,888	68.9	84,009	28.1

Ireland	2,954	1,620.2			1,116.0	68.9	396.5	24.5
Israel	2,958	1,961	714.8	36.5	1,133.9	57.8	537.3	27.4
Italy	53,565	62,883	8,664	13.8	39,371	62.6	14,511	23.1
Spain	33,779	2,576.2	219.2	8.5	1,751.9	68.0	629.0	24.4
Venezuela	10,559	52,309	6,889	13.2	27,548	52.7	15,456	29.5
$2,000 to $2,999								
Australia	12,552	33,737	4,198	12.4	20,404	60.5	9,221	27.3
Belgium	9,638	1,280,924	175,300	13.7	769,013	60.0	307,511	26.3
Denmark	4,929	118,627	23,137		68,078		30,431	
Finland	4,606	44,858			25,859		13,220	
France	50,670	782,560			469,338		204,098	
Iceland	204	43,663			28,183		10,118	
Japan	104,331	73,285	5,647		38,272		28,617	
Kuwait	760	1,026	139				124	
Netherlands	13,032	114,573	18,706		65,589		32,363	
New Zealand	2,820	5,609	794				1,521	
Norway	3,877	79,876	13,533		43,046		24,325	
Puerto Rico	2,743	5,678.5			4,295.3		1,707.5	
U.K.	55,480	50,930	8,972		31,507		9,891	
$3,000 and Over								
Canada	21,406	86,454			49,753		18,120	
Denmark	4,929	118,627	23,137		68,078		30,431	
Germany	60,700	678,750	108,110		367,550		189,090	
Luxembourg	339	54,043			27,717		13,877	
Sweden	8,043	170,836	36,844		91,270		43,685	
Switzerland	6,267	90,665			53,455		29,245	
U.S.	204,879	988,704	189,506		621,612		175,524	

Hypothesis 1: Personal Consumption Comprises a Greater Share of GDP in Less-Developed than in Developed Open Market Economies

This hypothesis is supported by the material presented in Table 5.3. It shows that the lower the level of economic development, as measured by GDP per capita, the higher is the share of GDP going into personal consumption. Although the difference between the most highly developed and the least-developed nations is not a dramatic one, it is consistent with respect to stage of development. In 1980 the nations with under $200 (U.S.) GDP per capita allocated an average of 63.8 percent of GDP to personal domestic consumption: whereas the nations with $3,000 (U.S.) or more GDP per capita spent only 57.3 percent of GDP on personal domestic consumption. The difference between the highest and lowest figures was only 11.3 percent, but the direction of change was consistent; that is, each higher stage of economic development spent a smaller share of GDP on personal consumption than the preceding stage.

Hypothesis 2: The Share of GDP Spent on Private Consumption Is Growing in All Nations, but the Rate of Growth Is Faster in the Highly-Developed Economies

The data presented in Table 5.4 provide complete support for the first half of Hypothesis 2. During both the decade of the 1960s and the decade of the 1970s, per capita personal consumption (in constant values) showed average increases at every level of economic development. The second part of the hypothesis, that the rate of growth is faster in the highly developed economies, seems to hold true for all but the least-developed countries—those with less than $200 GDP per capita. These countries showed abnormally high growth in per capita personal consumption in comparison with the next level of GDP. During the 1960s, the variation was just between the two lowest levels of development, and the hypothesis that the rate of growth in personal consumption is higher in the

TABLE 5.3. Share of Gross Domestic Product (GDP) Spent on Personal Consumption in 1980

Countries by Stage of Development— Amount of GDP	Percentage of GDP Spent on Personal Consumption
Under $500 (U.S.) per capita	63.8
$500 to $999 (U.S.) per capita	62.7
$1,000 to $1,999 (U.S.) per capita	61.2
$2,000 to $2,999 (U.S.) per capita	60.9
$3,000 and over per capita	57.3

Source: Yearbook of National Account Statistics (United Nations, 1981).

developed economies is supported. Again, in the 1970s, the hypothesis is supported at all levels except under $200 GDP per capita, but at that level the increase in consumption is at more than twice the rate of nations at other levels. This 94.1 percent growth figure was inflated by the extraordinarily high increases in consumption in four nations: Kenya (201.5 percent), Indonesia (110.4 percent), Madagascar (117.9 percent), and Pakistan (139.3 percent). All four of these countries experienced growth in GDP well above the average in the 1970s, which, for societies near subsistence level, provided incentive and opportunity for increased consumption at levels higher than what might otherwise have been expected.

Hypothesis 3: Personal Consumption Has a Smaller Share of GDP in Planned Economies than in Open Market Economies

The Communist bloc Eastern European countries do not use the term "gross domestic product" in the statistics they submit to the United Nations; instead they use the term "net material product." However, the two terms seem to be essentially synonymous. Net material product is the summation of personal consumption, government expenditures, capital investment, and exports and imports. Since these are exactly the same elements that make up GDP, it seems reasonable to use the terms interchangeably in comparing Communist and open market economies.

Table 5.5 shows personal consumption expenditures as a percentage of net material product in six Communist nations of Eastern Europe. Comparable data

TABLE 5.4. Changes in Per Capita Personal Consumption by Stage of Development Between 1960 and 1980

Countries Classified by Amount of GDP Per Capita	Increase in Personal Consumption Per Capita (%)	
	1960–70	*1970–80*
Under $200 (U.S.)	35	94.1
$200 to $499 (U.S.)	8.2	17.6
$500 to $999 (U.S.)	52.7	32.9
$1,000 to $1,999 (U.S.)	53.9	39.1
$2,000 to $2,999 (U.S.)	65.7	38.9
$3,000 (U.S.) and above	45.5	40.7

Note: GDP, gross domestic product.

aMexico was not included in this average because its abnormally large rate of growth (566.5 percent distorted the figure to 72.2 percent.

Source: Yearbook of National Account Statistics (United Nations, 1971, 1981).

are not available for other planned economies, that is, China, Cuba, and North Korea. These data do not support Hypothesis 3. In fact, every country except Yugoslavia spends a higher percentage of national product on personal consumption than any of the categories of open market economies shown in Table 5.3. The average personal consumption share in the open market economies is 62.4 percent, whereas in the planned economies it is 67.3 percent. Personal consumption is apparently a more important influence on planned than open market economies, because it consumes a slightly greater share of national product.

Hypothesis 4: The Rate of Growth in Personal Consumption Is Slower in Planned Economies than in Open Market Economies

U.N. data do not seem to support Hypothesis 4. During the decade of the 1960s, personal consumption per capita increased by 49.6 percent in the Eastern European Communist bloc nations, only slightly less than the 50.7 percent increase in the countries of Western Europe and more than in the less-developed open market economies. During the 1970s, the growth in personal expenditures in Eastern Europe was clearly greater than in Western Europe, 56.7 percent as compared with 39.0 percent. This 56.7 percent rate of growth was higher in the 1970s than in all but the nations with under $200 GNP (see Table 5.4).

Hypothesis 5: A Higher Proportion of Personal Consumption Expenditures for Services Reduces the Rate of Economic Development. The Rate of Growth in Expenditures for Services Will Be Higher in More-Developed Economies

Data for testing this hypothesis were available for only 33 nations, and for most of these nations only for the decade from 1970 to 1980. There seems to

TABLE 5.5 Share of Net Material Product (NMP) Spent on Personal Consumption in 1980

Planned Economies	Personal Consumption Expenditures as a Percentage of NMP
Bulgaria	67.6
Czechoslovakia	65.3
Hungary	69.1
Poland	72.5
Soviet Union	74.9
Yugoslavia	54.2
Average	67.3

Source: Yearbook of National Account Statistics (United Nations, 1981).

be some positive support for the hypothesis, but the numbers are too small to be able to place reliance on the results. If we compare the five years 1970–75 with the five years 1976–80, only five nations experienced an increase in the proportion of personal consumption expenditures allocated to services. Of these, three experienced sizable decreases in GDP, one remained about the same (4.7 percent increase), and one experienced a 54 percent increase. Thus, three times as many nations experienced a reduction in rate of economic development (as measured by GDP) as experienced an increase when consumption of services increased.[1]

Negative support for the hypothesis is much more reliable, because the numbers involved are much greater. Twenty-eight nations experienced reductions in the proportion of personal consumption expenditures allocated to services. Of these, 15 showed increases in GDP and 6 more showed very small reductions of less than 5 percent. Only six nations showed large decreases in GDP: France, 56.7 percent; Korea, 10.9 percent; Malta, 38.7 percent; Norway, 9.7 percent; Singapore, 13.6 percent; and Zimbabwe, 17.0 percent. Thus, well over twice as many nations experienced decreases in GDP when consumption of services increased and increases in GDP when consumption of services decreased, as hypothesized.

The second part of Hypothesis 5, that the rate of growth in expenditures for services will be higher in more-developed countries, was not supported. In fact, the data supported a reverse relationship: The rate of growth in expenditures for services was higher in the less-developed countries, and it increased fairly consistently with decreases in level of development. These data are presented in Table 5.6.

Hypothesis 6: A Lead or Lag Relationship Between Government Consumption, Personal Consumption and Gross Capital Formation Might Help to Explain the Impact of Each Factor on Economic Development

The data seem to indicate that instead of a lead–lag relationship between total consumption (government and private) and gross capital formation, there is a current or simultaneous relationship. Table 5.7 shows that in all stages of economic development a preponderance of changes in consumption are accompanied by changes in the same direction in gross capital formation. For example, in the least-developed countries (those with less than $200 GDP per capita), year-to-year comparisons of percentage changes in consumption and investment were made for the 1970s in 13 countries. Of the 87-year intervals on which data were available, 50, or 69 percent, showed consistent movement between consumption and capital formation; that is, when total consumption increased, gross capital formation increased, and when total consumption decreased, gross capital formation decreased. This higher-than-chance relationship was true at fairly consistent amounts across all levels of development.

**TABLE 5.6 Average Rate of Growth in
Consumption by Level of Economic Development**

GDP Per Capita	Number of Nations	Average Rate of Growth in Consumption of Services (%)
$3,000 and above	7	3.8
$2,000 to $2,999	9	4.2
$1,000 to $1,999	5	3.1
$500 to $999	6	7.9
Under $200	6	21.2

Note: GDP, gross domestic product.
Source: Yearbook of National Account Statistics, vol. 1. part 2. (United Nations, 1981).

It was hypothesized that the effect of increases in consumption on capital formation might not be an immediate one, that is, that it might not occur for a few months. For this reason, changes in consumption were compared not only with the current years, but with two subsequent years. However, the only consistent relationship between the factors was a current one. There was no pattern of relationship between changes in consumption in one year and changes in capital formation in either of two succeeding years.

Hypothesis 7: Per Capita Personal Consumption Increases at a Faster Rate Relative to Total Consumption in the More Highly Developed Nations

The hypothesis that per capita personal consumption increases at a faster rate relative to total consumption in more highly developed economies is supported

**TABLE 5.7 Relationship Between Changes in Total
Consumption and Changes in Gross Capital Formation**

GDP Per Capita	Number of Nations	Number of Comparisons	Number of Matched Changes	Percentage of Matches
Under $200	13	87	50	69.0
$200 to $499	28	229	130	56.8
$500 to $999	14	72	45	62.5
1,000 to $1,999	6	52	39	75.0
$2,000 and above	17	148	96	64.9

Note: GDP, gross domestic product.
Source: Compiled from data in Yearbook of National Account Statistics (United Nations, 1981).

by the U.N. statistical data, as presented in Table 5.8 for the decade of the 1970s. During this decade, although every country listed in the table showed a growth in both total consumption and per capita consumption, the rate of growth of the latter was less than that of the former in every country.

In countries with under $500 GDP per capita, the growth in per capita consumption was only 50 percent of the growth in total consumption (45 percent if we do not average in Korea with its take-off stage of development), and it was even lower in countries with GDP per capita of $500 to $999. Yet, in the wealthier nations, increases in per capita consumption were much nearer to increases in total consumption: 83.3 percent for the $1,000 to $1,999 GDP level, 74.9 percent for $2,000 to $2,999, and 74.1 percent for $3,000 and over. These differences between richer and poorer nations are accounted for by differential rates of population growth. The higher rates of population growth in the less-developed countries diluted much of the effect of growth in total consumption.

TABLE 5.8 Comparison of Growth in Total Consumption with Consumption Per Capita in 36 Nations

Nations by GDP Per Capita	A Changes in Total Consumption in 1970–80 (%)	B Changes in Per Capita Consumption in 1970–80 (%)	B as a Percentage of A
Under $200			
Honduras	+51.3	+26.8	32.3
India	+31.0	+6.0	19.4
Korea	+99.5	+84.7	85.1
Paraguay	+111.5	+59.3	28.0
Philippines	+59.8	+20.5	34.3
Sri Lanka	+78.3	+51.7	66.0
Thailand	+89.5	+43.8	48.9
Zimbabwe	+69.9	+44.9	64.2
			49.8
$500 to $999			
Hong Kong	+162.6	+127.1	43.3
Malta	+147.0	+55.2	37.6
Mexico	+79.8	+22.7	28.4
Panama	+43.3	+9.8	22.6
Singapore	+107.2	+79.8	74.4
South Africa	+45.4	+ 0.2	0
			34.4

TABLE 5.8 (*continued*)

Nations by GDP Per Capita	A Changes in Total Consumption in 1970–80 (%)	B Changes in Per Capita Consumption in 1970–80 (%)	B as a Percentage of A
$1,000 to $1,999			
Austria	+45.4	+45.6	100.0
Ireland	+35.3	+26.4	74.8
Israel	62.8	+45.4	72.3
Italy	+35.0	+27.0	77.1
Greece	+53.8	+45.8	85.1
Spain	+46.2	+32.1	98.4
			83.3
$2,000 to $2,999			
Australia	+38.2	+30.2	79.6
Belgium	+44.9	+36.0	80.2
Finland	+36.0	+33.3	92.5
France	+52.8	+44.4	84.1
Japan	+58.0	+38.9	67.1
Netherlands	+68.6	+55.2	80.5
Norway	+112.3	+99.6	88.7
Puerto Rico	+36.7	+1.9	5.2
United Kingdom	+23.3	+22.5	96.6
			74.9
+4,000 and above			
Canada	+59.3	+42.4	71.5
Denmark	+16.9	+15.7	92.9
Germany	+36.2	+45.5	125.7
Luxembourg	+44.4	+41.1	92.6
Sweden	+19.7	+15.9	80.7
Switzerland	+21.1	+23.7	91.9
United States	+37.5	+23.7	63.2
			88.4

Note: GDP, gross domestic product.
Source: Compiled from data in *Yearbook of National Account Statistics* (United Nations, 1981).

CONCLUSIONS

U.N. statistical data provide considerable evidence to support a long-standing claim of marketers that both personal and government consumption are closely related to economic development, often in a causal relationship. Marketing theorists have taken issue with the strong production orientation of economic theorists, but the evidence to support their view is often more conjectural than real. It is hoped that these data will provide objective support for the role of consumption in economic development.

The data provide support for the old axiom that the rich get richer and the poor get poorer. GDP increased, on the average, at all levels of development, but in the decades of both the 1960s and the 1970s the GDP in constant dollars increased more rapidly in the richer nations than in the poorer nations. Less-developed nations find it necessary to spend a larger proportion of GDP on personal consumption. Although the difference between the highest- and lowest-GDP nations was not great, the relationship of GDP to consumption was consistent—the lower the level of economic development, the higher the percentage spent on personal consumption. Yet, personal consumption per capita is growing more rapidly in the more highly developed nations because of their generally lower rates of growth in population. Even though total personal consumption is growing rapidly in the poorer nations, each individual may be consuming less. It is also interesting to note that the planned economies (the Eastern European Communist nations) spent, on the average, more than even the lowest-GDP level open market economies in all parts of the world. During these two decades, there was a worldwide increase in economic wealth, as evidenced by increases in GDP at all levels of economic development. However, in general, the less-developed nations showed a slower increase in consumption, perhaps because there was more need for capital investment and public works than for discretionary spending. The one exception was in the least-developed nations, those with per capita GDP of less than $200. Much of the population in these nations is living at or below subsistence levels, and the dramatic increases in GDP during the 1970s was necessarily spent on personal consumption.

Development theoreticians disagree about the relative impact of consumption of products and consumption of services. Services are perceived by some as making less of a contribution to the growth of an economy. Those data provide some support for a negative relationship between consumption of services and economic development; countries increasing their consumption of services are more likely to experience decreases in GDP, and countries decreasing their consumption of services are more likely to experience increases in GDP. These less-developed nations that could benefit the most from increased levels of economic growth are experiencing the most rapid increases in the consumption of services, a factor that may be retarding that economic growth.

A basic point of disagreement among development theorists is whether personal consumption reduces the amount of capital available for investment in capital goods and hence slows the rate of development, or whether it generates more capital and hence accelerates development. The study provides support for the latter view. Year-to-year changes in consumption were in the majority of cases accompanied by like changes in gross capital formation. At the very least, increases in consumption seemed to have no negative effect on capital formation.

There seems to be little doubt from the evidence of U.N. statistical data that personal consumption and economic development are interrelated. It also seems clear that this effect is sometimes a positive one and sometimes a negative one. It was not possible in this analysis to evaluate the relative impact of consumption and other economic factors on development, but merely to demonstrate that consumption is one of the influencing factors. Since the actions of marketers impact heavily on levels of personal consumption, the impact of marketing should be recognized as a major input to economic development planning.

NOTE

1. These nations, classified by level of GDP per capita, were as follow: $3,000 and above—Canada, Denmark, Germany (Federal Republic), Luxembourg, Sweden, Switzerland, and the United States; $2,000 to $2,999—Australia, Belgium, Finland, France, Japan, the Netherlands, Norway, Puerto Rico, and the United Kingdom; $1,000 to $1,999—Austria, Israel, Italy, Greece, and Spain; $500 to $999—Malta, Mexico, Panama, Singapore, South Africa, and Hong Kong; under $500—Honduras, India, Korea, Sri Lanka, Thailand, and Zimbabwe.

REFERENCES

Bartels, R. 1976. "Marketing and Economic Development." In *Macromarketing: Distribution Processes from a Societal Perspective,* edited by C. Slater, pp. 211–17. Boulder: University of Colorado Press.

Cundiff, E. 1982. "A Macromarketing Approach to Economic Development. *Journal of Macromarketing* 2 (Spring):14–19.

Dixon, D. F. 1981. "Role of Marketing in Early Theories of Economic Development." *Journal of Macromarketing* 1 (Fall):19–27.

Drucker, Peter. 1958. "Marketing and Economic Development." *Journal of Marketing* 22 (January):251–59.

Hilger, M. 1977. "Theories of the Relationship Between Marketing and Economic Development: Public Policy Implications." In *Macromarketing: Distributive Processes from a Societal Perspective, an Elaboration of Issues,* edited by Philip D. White and Charles C. Slater, pp.333–50. Boulder: University of Colorado Press.

Hirsch, L. V. 1961. "The Contribution of Marketing to Economic Development—A Generally Neglected Area." In *The Social Responsibility of Marketing,* edited by W. D. Stevens, pp.413–18. Chicago: American Marketing Association.

Mentzer, J. T., and A. C. Samli. 1981. "A Model for Marketing in Economic Development." *Columbia Journal of World Business* 16 (Fall):91–101.

Moyer, R. 1965. *Marketing in Economic Development: International Occasional Paper No. 1.* East Lansing: Bureau of Business and Economic Research, Michigan State University.

Nielsen, Richard P. 1974. "Marketing and Development in LCD's." *Columbia Journal of World Business* 9 (Winter):46–49.

Sethi, S. Prakash. 1970. "Comparative Cluster Analysis for World Markets." *Journal of Marketing Research* (August):348–54.

CHAPTER 6

Contributions of Comparative Research to the Study of Consumer Behavior

SUSAN P. DOUGLAS
C. SAMUEL CRAIG

INTRODUCTION

Twenty years ago, in a seminal article, Cox (1965) pointed out the potential contribution of comparative studies of marketing systems. He noted their role not only in broadening understanding of marketing systems, through the investigation of their form and functioning in different societies, but also in refining concepts used in the study of domestic marketing systems. In particular, he underscored the importance of comparative research in identifying "the universals" of marketing, which apply in all societies throughout the world. This applies not only in relation to macro studies of marketing systems, but also in relation to micro studies of areas such as consumer and organizational behavior. Here, the importance of environmental or societal variables in influencing behavior suggests that comparative research can have a major contribution in improving understanding of such concepts. This chapter focuses on examining the nature of this potential specifically in relation to consumer behavior.

Comparative research is widely recognized as playing an important role in many of the social sciences, from which consumer behavior concepts are derived, including sociology (Bendix 1963; Elder 1976; Marsh 1967), psychology (Brislin, Lonner, and Thorndike 1973; Triandis, Malpass, and Davidson 1973; Brislin 1983), and cognitive anthropology (Ember 1977). In all these areas, cross-cultural or comparative studies are acknowledged to be central to theory development. They are, for example, viewed as a means of examining the universality of theories or concepts developed in one sociocultural setting to another; of examining how these vary or are expressed in different societal contexts or conditions; and ultimately, therefore, of identifying the impact of societal factors on individual or group behavior.

In the case of consumer behavior, comparative research can help in examining whether specific concepts and constructs used in consumer research, typically derived from research conducted in the United States, are also applicable in other countries and contexts. Insights can also be gained into the way in which constructs may best be measured and the limitations associated with different measurement procedures. Further, ideas for improved research design and methodology may be generated, and in some cases more refined concepts and measurement procedures developed.

Yet, despite their rich potential, relatively few comparative studies of consumer behavior have been conducted. In the 12 years since the *Journal of Consumer Research* was established, only five comparative studies have been published (Anderson and Engledow 1977, Jolibert and Baumgartner 1982; Douglas 1976; Clarke and Soutar 1982; Green et al. 1983). In these the primary emphasis has essentially been descriptive, focusing on comparing differences and similarities in consumer segments and behavior patterns in various countries and thus their universality or generality.

The relatively limited number of comparative studies appears to stem in large measure from the inherent difficulties in conducting such research. In particular, difficulties arise owing to the need to establish the equivalence or comparability of the research in the different countries studied, first in terms of the concepts, constructs, or theories examined and second, in terms of measurement procedures. As Church (1952) has pointed out, in making a comparison, objects, systems, and other units can be compared only with respect to properties that are common to both. An orange and a lemon can be compared as fruit with respect to sweetness, juiciness, shape, and size, but not with respect to the degree of orangeness. This implies that an important first step in conducting comparative consumer research is the commonality or concept equivalence of the dimensions of behavior in all the countries or contexts studied, as well as the equivalence of the measurement instrument(s) used.

Since each country has certain idiosyncratic features and is characterized by a unique pattern of sociocultural behavior patterns and values, attitudinal and behavioral phenomena may be expressed in unique ways. Consequently, some constructs may be unique to a given country. On the other hand, insofar as there is commonality between countries, comparable constructs and concepts can be identified. Similarly, in some cases equivalent and standardized measures of concepts may be developed, but in other cases idiosyncratic or country-specific measures may be required.

This suggests the need for research methodologies that not only examine or test the universality and equivalence of a concept and its measurement in different countries and contexts, but also allow for the identification of concepts and measurement procedures specific or unique to a given country and context. In the past, research methodologies have tended to focus predominantly on the first concern, namely, testing the applicability of concepts and measures developed in one country in other contexts. Often the reliability and validity of a measure, as for example, its internal consistency, scalar equivalence, or external validity, are examined in each context. This procedure does not, however, take into consideration that certain concepts may be "culture specific," or manifested in different ways in different contexts, and equally that the effectiveness of a given measurement procedure may vary from one context to another.

The purpose of the present chapter is thus to suggest a hybrid methodological approach to the conduct of comparative consumer research that aims as far as possible to develop "universal" concepts and measures, but at the same time allows for the possibility of culture-specific concepts and measurement procedures. This, it is hoped, will provide improved guidelines for the conduct of such research and facilitate realization of its full potential in refining existing consumer concepts and measures. Some areas of consumer behavior where the conduct of comparative research appears likely to be the most fruitful are identified and how such studies may advance the current state of consumer research is illustrated.

The chapter is divided into three major sections. First, key issues relating to the establishment of construct and measure equivalence in comparative consumer research are discussed. The proposed methodological approach for dealing with these issues is then outlined. Finally, the potential contributions of comparative studies to further understanding of consumer behavior are identified and areas or topics where application of this approach seems most promising highlighted.

ISSUES IN COMPARATIVE CONSUMER RESEARCH

The central importance of establishing equivalence in comparative studies is widely recognized throughout the social sciences (Anderson 1967; Berrien 1967; Manaster and Havighurst 1972; Preworski and Teune 1970; Sears 1961). Various types of equivalence have been identified. Berry and Dasen (1974), for example, identify three types of equivalence: functional, conceptual, and metric. Functional equivalence implies that a behavior, system, or concept has the same role or function in all contexts studied. Conceptual equivalence (Sears 1961), on the other hand, is concerned with the meaning of stimuli, concepts, and behavior in different contexts. This has been considered to include aspects such as linguistic or translation equivalence (Berry 1980; Brislin 1970, 1983) and category equivalence (Price-Williams 1974). Metric equivalence requires that the psychometric properties of data from two societies exhibit the same underlying structure (Poortinga 1975). In addition, Straus (1969) has pointed out that the establishment of conceptual equivalence also requires determining not only whether concepts and research materials are equivalent, but also whether their actual measurement, that is, codes, scores, norms, or scoring procedures, are identical.

In the present context, for the purpose of simplification, two major categories of equivalence are identified: construct equivalence and measure equivalence. In the case of construct equivalence, three types of equivalence are considered: (1) *functional* equivalence, that is, whether a given concept or behavior has the same role or function in society from one country to another; (2) *conceptual* equivalence, that is, whether the interpretation and meaning attached to different objects or behavior are the same; and (3) *category* equivalence, that is, whether categories, such as product classes or occupations, are the same from one country to another. In the case of the measurement instrument, three types of equivalence may be identified: (1) *calibration* equivalence, that is, whether the measurement units, such as points on a scale, use of metric versus other measuring systems, etc., are comparable; (2) the equivalence of the *translation* and translation procedures used; and (3) the metric or *scalar* equivalence of the response scores. Equivalence of procedures used in the administration of the instrument should also be considered, as, for example, sampling, data collection, the timing of research, and the context in which it is conducted. These are covered in detail elsewhere (Douglas and Craig 1983) and hence are not examined here.

Construct Equivalence

The establishment of construct equivalence is a first consideration in the design of comparative research. In essence, this amounts to assessing whether the market structure and relevant parameters, including, for example, objects, use of objects, habit patterns, attitudes, and value standards, are the same or equivalent from one country to another, as well as factors that condition these, such as, for example, the distribution structure, the degree of competition, etc. The various aspects of this, namely, functional, conceptual, and category equivalence, are next considered in more detail.

Functional Equivalence

First, it is important to remember that the concepts, objects, or behaviors studied may not necessarily be functionally equivalent, that is, have the same role or function in all countries studied (Berry 1969). Thus, for example, while bicycles and motorcycles are predominantly used for recreation in the United States, in many Far Eastern countries, such as Taiwan and Thailand, they are a basic mode of transportion. This implies that the relevant competing product set must be defined differently. In the United States, it will include other recreational products, while in the Far East, alternative modes of transportation may need to be considered.

Apparently similar activities may also have different functions. In some countries such as the United States, for example, adult education courses may be regarded primarily as a leisure activity designed to provide broader cultural awareness. In other countries, such as Japan, adult education is geared primarily to improving work performance. Similarly, while for many U.S. families grocery shopping is a chore and a work activity to be accomplished as efficiently and conveniently as possible, in other countries it plays an important social function. Interaction with local shopkeepers and vendors and with other neighbors and acquaintances in stores or in the marketplace is thus an integral part of day-to-day living.

Conceptual Equivalence

While functional equivalence is concerned with the role of objects and behavior in society at a macrocultural level, conceptual equivalence is concerned with the interpretation that individuals place on objects, stimuli, or behavior and whether these exist or are expressed in similar ways in different countries and cultures. Thus, while the same object or behavior may occur in two different countries, it may not have the same interpretation or significance in different countries or cultures, or may be manifested in different types of behavior. Similarly, an attitude, behavior, or object may be unique to a specific country or occur in some countries but not in others.

Personality traits such as aggressiveness, authoritarianism, alienation, and affiliation needs may not be relevant in all countries and cultures, or may be expressed in different types of behavior, hence requiring different measures. Some attitudes or behavior may be unique to a specific country. The concept of *philotimo*, or behaving in the way members of one's in group expect, for example, is unique to the Greek culture (Adamopoulos 1977; Triandis and Vassilou 1972). This includes meeting obligations and sacrificing self to help in-group members, which include family, friends, or guests.

Even where the same concept or construct is identified, it may be expressed by different types of behavior in different culture settings. For example, a physical male-oriented life-style may be defined in the United States in terms of attitudes such as wanting to be a professional football player and liking war stories and behavior such as reading the sports page in the daily paper or *Playboy* (Plummer 1977). In Canada, it is defined not only in terms of liking war stories but also in liking hunting and fishing, while in Mexico, it is expressed in terms of wanting to be a soccer star, liking sports events, liking to go to bullfights and fiestas, and admitting to being a girl watcher.

Category Equivalence

A third type of construct equivalence relates to the category in which objects or other stimuli are placed. This depends to a large extent on the level at which categorization is compared across countries and cultures. Rosch (1978) has, for example, identified three major levels of categorization: (1) a *superor-dinate* level of the most general or abstract concepts (for example, furniture); (2) a *basic* level of more concrete–specific concepts (such as chair); and (3) a *subordinate* level of most concrete–specific concepts (such as dining room chair). This hierarchy has been found to exist in a variety of cultures (Szala and Deese 1978).

Researchers of consumer behavior are, however, typically more concerned with making comparisons about the specific content of these categories, rather than examining the existence of such hierarchies. For example, they may be concerned with comparing behavior relative to specific product classes, as, for example, soft drinks or detergents, or the behavior of specific consumer segments. Consequently, the primary focus is on the establishment of equivalence or comparability relative to the *content* of a category rather than its position in the hierarchical structure.

In establishing category content equivalence, a number of problems may arise. Relevant product class definitions may, for example, differ from one country to another. In the soft drink and alcoholic beverage market, for example, forms of soft drinks such as carbonated sodas, fruit juices, and powdered and liquid concentrates vary significantly from one culture to another, and hence how these are defined and delineated differs. In Mediterranean cultures, for example, beer is considered to be a soft drink (Berent 1975). Similarly, in the dessert market, items that are included will vary substantially, ranging from apple pie, jellies, and ice cream to baklava, rice pudding, and zabaglione. In some societies, cakes or cookies are included as desserts, while in China sweet items do not form part of the meal. This implies that what is included in the relevant competing product set will vary. Careful attention to such factors is thus an important consideration when developing product-related measures. In addition, the characteristics or attributes perceived by consumers as relevant in evaluating a product class may differ from one country to another. In France, for example, the hot–cold continuum is a key attribute characterizing consumers' perceptions of fragrances. In the United States and the United Kingdom, however, this is not an attribute that is perceived as relevant by consumers.

Differences in background or sociodemographic characteristics have also to be considered. In the case of marital status, for example, in various African countries it is not uncommon for a man to have several wives, and in some cases women may have several husbands. Occupational categories also do not always have strict equivalence in all countries. The counterpart of the U.S. lawyer, the English barrister, or the Japanese subway packer may be difficult to find. Occupations may also differ in status from one country or society to another. Being a priest, religious minister, or teacher is, for example, often more prestigious in less-developed than in the more-literate industrialized nations. Similarly, the social prestige attached to government administrative positions or to being a lawyer varies from society to society.

Measurement Equivalence

In addition to establishing the equivalence of the constructs to be examined, the equivalence of the measurement instrument has also to be determined (Straus 1969). Measurement and construct equivalence are highly interrelated insofar as the measure operationalizes the conceptual definition of the construct. It is nonetheless useful to separate the conceptual definition from actual measurement insofar as the conceptual definition indicates what the researcher aims to measure, while the measure is the instrument used to tap that construct. Here, equivalence with regard to three aspects has to be considered: (1) the calibration system used in measurement; (2) the translation of the research instrument; and (3) the metric or scalar equivalence of the instrument.

Calibration Equivalence

In developing a research instrument, equivalence has to be established with regard to the calibration system used in measurement. This includes not only equivalence with regard to monetary units and measures of weight, distance, and volume, but also other perceptual cues, such as color, shape, or form, which are used to interpret visual stimuli.

The need to establish equivalence with regard to monetary and physical measurement units is clearly apparent. Standard procedures or tables for conversion are readily available. Comparability with regard to measurement standards and procedures needs also to be considered, however, as these may vary from one context to another. For example, comparability with regard to standards such as product grading or product quality and safety regulations should be investigated, since these are not uniform from one country to another.

More subtle differences in instrument calibration, which are particularly relevant in the case of nonverbal instruments, relate to perceptual cues such as color, form, and shape. Studies in cognitive and cross-cultural psychology suggest that a substantial degree of commonality exists with regard to the manifestations of these in different countries and cultures (Derogowski 1980; Pick 1980). However, ability to differentiate and to develop gradations in these schema appears to differ.

Studies of color have shown the existence of an identical color spectrum throughout different cultures (Berlin and Kay 1969), but the ability of cultures to differentiate between different points on the color spectrum varies. Berlin and Kay claim that there are never more than 11 basic color classes but there may be less. Western subjects, for example, typically have more color classes than African subjects, and some primitive people have only a two-term color language (Heider 1971, 1972). The Bantu of South Africa, for example, do not distinguish between blue and green. Consequently, they do not discriminate between objects or symbols in these colors. Awareness of such nuances is thus an important consideration in instrument design and development, especially in relation to visual stimuli.

Translation Equivalence

A second aspect of measure equivalence concerns translation of the instrument so that it is understood by respondents in different countries and has equivalent meaning in each research context. The need for translation of questionnaires and other verbal stimuli where research is conducted in countries with different languages is readily apparent. The need to translate nonverbal stimuli to ensure that they evoke the desired image and to avoid problems of miscommunication is less widely recognized.

Translation equivalence is a central issue in the establishment of construct validity in survey research, since this is the stage in the research design at which the construct is defined in operational terms (Brislin 1970, 1983). The translation procedure thus frequently helps to pinpoint problems with regard to whether a concept can be measured by using the same or similar questions in each cultural context, and whether a question has the same meaning in different research contexts. If different questions are used, then issues arise with regard to the minimal level of equivalence necessary for two questions to be considered the same and the criteria for equivalence that can be established.

Translation of nonverbal stimuli requires attention to how perceptual cues are interpreted in each research context. Misunderstanding may arise because the respondent is not familiar with a product or other stimuli, for example, an electrical appliance, or the way in which it is depicted. Alternatively, respondents may misinterpret stimuli because the associations evoked by the stimuli, such as, for example, those associated with color or shape, differ from one country or culture to another.

Interpretation of meaning attached to colors may vary from one culture or cultural context to another. White, for example, is a color of mourning in Japan. In Chinese culture, red is a symbol of happiness and plays a focal role in weddings, from invitations being printed in red, monetary gifts given in red envelopes, to the red dresses worn by the bride. Green, in Malaysia, symbolizes the jungle and hence has connotations of danger. Translation of verbal and nonverbal stimuli thus plays a key role in the establishment of equivalence. Often it proves a focal point both for uncovering and for making pragmatic decisions as to how to resolve construct equivalence issues.

Metric Equivalence

A final concern is metric equivalence. This is the scoring or scalar equivalence of the measure used (Poortinga 1975). Two aspects have to be considered in determining metric equivalence. The first concerns the specific scale or scoring procedure used to establish the measure and whether relationships among these are patterned similarly in different contexts, the second the equivalence of responses to a given measure in different countries. The greater the emphasis placed on quantitative measurement and data interpretation, the more important the establishment of metric equivalence becomes. It is thus an integral part of decisions relating to data analysis, especially where attitudinal scaling or multivariate procedures are entailed.

Metric equivalence in scales and scoring procedures is of particular relevance insofar as the most effective graduation of scales or scoring procedures may vary from one country or culture to another. This depends essentially on the type of scales and scaling procedures most commonly used in a country or culture. While in the United States, use of a five- or seven-point scale is common, in other countries, 20- or 10-point scales may be more typical. Use of nonverbal response techniques such as latency measures, that is, speed of response, also requires consideration of their applicability in each country or cultural context.

Considerable attention has also been drawn to the need to establish similarity in the patterning of relationships among independent variables, particularly where multiple items are used to measure a given construct. Following the Campbell–Fiske logic (1959), establishment of convergent and discriminant validity may influence confidence in conceptual or construct equivalence.

A second aspect of metric equivalence concerns the response to a score obtained on a measure. Here, the question arises as to whether a score obtained in one research context has the same meaning and interpretation in another. Response set biases or differences in social acquiescence or sensitivity to various topics may result in the use of different parts of a scale from one country to another. Consequently, a position on a Likert scale may not have the same meaning in all cultures.

The existence of such conceptual and measurement issues in conducting comparative consumer research suggests the importance of considering their implications in terms of the specific topic to be studied prior to the establishment of a research design. Such considerations should guide the extent to which methodological procedures examine and test theories, concepts, measures, and scales developed in one country as opposed to developing concepts, measures, and scales specific to a particular country. A methodological approach encompassing both facets of comparative research design is next discussed in more detail.

A METHODOLOGY FOR COMPARATIVE CONSUMER RESEARCH

Given the conceptual and measurement issues raised in the preceding section, the proposed guidelines for developing a comparative research design allow for the existence of both universal concepts, measures, and measurement procedures as well as culture-specific concepts and measures. As far as possible, the focus is on developing "pan-cultural" or "universal" concepts or measures in order to facilitate comparison, but the possibility of "culture-specific" concepts is not ignored. This implies an iterative procedure comprising a number of steps.

First, relevant concepts and hypothesized linkages to be examined—or, in other words, the underlying conceptual framework—must be identified. In some cases, this may include concepts thought to be specific to a given country or cultural context, as well as those that are hypothesized to be universal. Next, operational definitions of these concepts for each country are developed and multiple measures for each concept designed. These might include both country-specific and universal measures. These measures are then administered and tested for validity, reliability, and equivalence in the various countries and contexts studied. Based on this analysis, appropriate multiple measures of the concepts to be studied are selected. As far as possible, these should be pan-cultural, though some country-specific measures may also be required. These measures are then applied to examine the comparability of the behavior or attitudes studied, in terms of the relationship between attitudes and behavior both within countries and across or between countries. A flow chart of this procedure is shown in Figure 6.1.

Identifying Relevant Constructs and Concepts in Each Country or Culture

The first step in the proposed approach is to establish the conceptual framework for the study and to determine relevant components of this or constructs to be examined in each country or culture. Operational definitions of these concepts have then to be developed, and alternative measures of these designed. These may include country-specific measures and pan-cultural or universal measures adapted to a specific country, as well as measures hypothesized to be pan-cultural, or universal measures adapted to a specific country, as well as measures hypothesized to be pan-cultural.

For example, in order to compare behavior or characteristics of innovators in the United States with those of innovators in other countries, the concept of innovation and of an innovator has first to be defined. If this is defined as a person who is the first to buy or adopt a new product innovation in a country, a list of new products or innovations has to be established. What is perceived as an innovation may, however, not be the same in different countries. In a study comparing characteristics of innovators in France and the United States, for example, 15 grocery products and 8 retail services were identified as innovations in both countries (Green and Langeard 1975). However, only one of the grocery products (freeze-dried coffee) and three of the retail services (a delicatessen section in supermarkets, self-service gasoline stations, and self-service dry-cleaning establishments) were the same in both.

An alternative definition might be based on the perceived innovativeness of an individual based on self-perceptions or those of others. Self-reported innova-

FIGURE 6.1   Steps in Establishing Comparability in Comparative Consumer Research

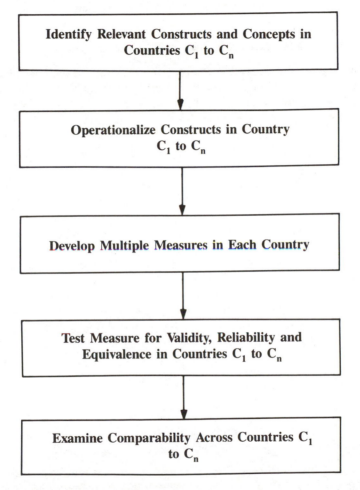

tiveness could thus be assessed based on attitudinal measures such as whether they perceived themselves as likely to be among the first or last among their friends to purchase a new product or service or their degree of interest in new products and services. Use of reports of others might, on the other hand, require the application of sociometric techniques.

Similarly, procedures for identifying new concepts and alternative definitions of a concept need to be developed. For example, in developing definitions of life-style, use of focus groups as well as examination of the appropriate sociological literature might suggest the existence of dimensions specific to a particular country. Studies of life-style in other countries have, for example, identified aspects such as antimaterialism and environmental concern in the United Kingdom and reaction to manipulation and social constraints in France—aspects that have not been identified as key trends in the United States.

Developing Measures in Each Country or Context

The next step is to develop operational measures and measurement procedures for each concept in each country or research context. Here, following the spirit of the Campbell–Fiske multitrait, multimeasure approach (1959), it is desirable to develop multiple measures of each concept in each country. This enables not only comparison of the reliability and validity of different measures in a given country, but also examination of the equivalence and reliability of measures across a range of measurement contexts.

Use of a multiple-measure approach is particularly desirable in comparative research insofar as a given measure may be subject to different types of measures in different countries and cultural contexts. Verbal rating scales such as Likert scales may be subject to more pronounced response set bias (that is, checking of extreme points) or yea-saying, nay-saying bias in some countries than others. Similarly, use of self-report measures may be subject to social desirability response-style bias or topic sensitivity, which again may vary from country to country.

Thus, in examining innovativeness in different countries, a number of different measures might be used. These might include the type of behavioral measures discussed previously, based on purchase or use of products and services perceived as innovations. Self-report attitudinal measures might also be developed as well as sociometric or other observational measures.

Testing Measures for Reliability, Validity, and Equivalence Across Countries

Once multiple measures of relevant concepts have been developed, the next step is to examine their reliability and validity in each country and also to compare their equivalence across countries.

In examining reliability, various tests can be used. These include external measures such as test–retest reliability where repeated measures are available or interjudge reliability where multiple judges have been used. Alternatively, where multiple-item measures are used, internal measures such as split-half reliability or measures such as Cronbach's alpha can be compared. In both cases, levels of reliability can be compared across countries to assess equivalence of measures in each context. Where multiple measures are used, convergent validity can also be examined in each country and then compared across countries. Both types of tests can aid in assessing the degree of bias associated with use of a specific type of measure in various countries.

In addition, where multiple-item measures are used, their scalar equivalence in different countries may be examined. This focuses on the extent to which the patterning of responses to a given measure is the same in all contexts. This can be examined using confirmatory factor analysis or more simply patterns of intercorrelation among variables.

If, as the result of this analysis, the same measure appears to be effective in measuring a given construct in all countries considered, then a pan-cultural concept might be identified and used in subsequent stages of research. If, on the other hand, different measures appear to be most effective in tapping a given construct in various countries, then use of the most reliable or effective measure in each country may be desirable. If feasible, it may, however, also be desirable to retain equivalent measures across all countries studied in order to be able to compare bias due to a specific type of measure more systematically.

Examining Comparability with and across Countries

Once the relevant conceptual framework has been determined, including appropriate concepts and hypothesized relationships among these, and alternative measures of these identified, the final step is to apply these to examine the relevant behavioral phenomena.

If, for example, attention were centered on comparing information-seeking behavior of innovators in various countries, appropriate conceptual definitions and measures of innovative behavior would first need to be developed and examined in each country. Appropriate sources of information, such as personal influence and mass media, would also need to be identified in each country or culture. For example, in closed societies, relevant sources of personal influence might include merely the immediate family and close friends. In Chinese societies, the family network might be considerably more influential and extensive. In child-oriented societies, the family might also include children. In mobile or open societies, personal sources might also include neighbors and a broader circle of acquaintances. Similarly, in the case of mass media, relevant media would need to be identified. In some societies with high levels of television ownership, this might include television, while in societies where television ownership is low, it might focus on radio and print media.

Application of this approach can thus aid in planning comparative consumer research and particularly in improving its methodological underpinnings in terms of the measures and measurement instruments used. Thus, such research may help not only in identifying the universality of different consumer concepts and behavior, but also in developing improved conceptual definitions and measures of these concepts. These potential contributions are next examined in more detail.

CONTRIBUTIONS OF COMPARATIVE STUDIES TO CONSUMER BEHAVIOR

Comparative studies can thus make an important contribution to research in consumer behavior. In the first place, they may provide a vehicle for testing the universality and generality of theories and concepts relating to consumer behavior in a wide range of different countries and sociocultural contexts. In addition, where rigorous methodological procedures are applied, they may also stimulate development of improved conceptual definitions and better calibrated measures of these concepts. Areas where such contributions may prove fruitful are highlighted below.

Testing the Universality and Generality of Theories and Concepts of Consumer Behavior

Examination of the applicability of a theory or concept of consumer behavior developed in one country or culture in other countries or cultures can shed light on the validity and universality of this theory or concept. Much of the research relating to consumer behavior (as in other social sciences) has been conducted in the United States. The relevance of this research and the resultant theories and concepts of consumer behavior in other countries and cultural contexts is thus open to question. For example, the two-step flow of influence model, which hypothesized that the impact of mass media was filtered by "opinion leaders" who influence opinions of others, was developed initially by Katz and Lazarsfeld (1955) based on research conducted in the United States. In testing this theory in Sweden, Cerha (1974) found the flow of information tended to be horizontal, that is, across similar interest groups, rather than vertical as in the United States. This link in the model has subsequently been included in research on personal influence in the United States.

Similarly, "innovators" in a given product class in the United States have been found to have a higher rate of exposure to information related to the product class and to be more likely to be "active" communicators, that is, initiate product-related conversations, than noninnovators and provide information to friends and neighbors about new products and brands. In other countries where innovation is less highly valued, there is less tendency to converse about new products. A comparison of U.S. and French homemakers (Green and Langeard 1975), for example, found that the French rarely discussed new product purchases with others. This was attributed to a tendency to adhere to traditional food habits in France.

Stimulating More Rigorous Conceptual Definitions

The importance of establishing the equivalence of concepts and their definitions in different countries or sociocultural contexts may also help to inject greater rigor at this stage of the research process. Establishment of conceptual equivalence requires careful reflection to determine a clear-cut definition that can be operationalized in a variety of different contexts. Furthermore, independent conceptualization or operationalization of relevant aspects of consumer behavior to be examined in each country or culture may help in broadening perspectives with regard to the nature of a given concept and how it may be related to consumer behavior.

A comparison of trends in value orientations or life-style patterns in different countries may, for example, result in the identification of values and aspects of life-style that might not emerge from a single-country study. For example, studies of value trends in France resulted in the identification of trends toward acceptance of self-directivity and openness to others and in the United Kingdom of skepticism of consumers, and environmental concerns and opposition to social discrimination, trends that do not appear to characterize persons in the United States (Douglas and Macquin 1977).

Similarly, in examining life-style patterns of women in the United States, the United Kingdom, and France, factors characterizing perceptions and attitudes toward a woman's role have been found to be somewhat different in the first two as compared with the last (Douglas and Urban 1977). While in the United States and the United Kingdom, attitudes toward a woman's role were characterized predominantly by interest and orientation toward the home, in France another aspect was involvement in household tasks and food perparation. This suggests that attitudes toward a woman's role are multifaceted and characterized not only by general perceptions or a woman's role in society but also attitudes toward the performance of household tasks.

Developing Improved and Better-Calibrated Research Instruments

Similarly, insofar as the equivalence as well as the reliability of research instruments in different countries and cultural settings need to be examined, this may lead to improvement and finer tuning of measures. Where measures of a concept are developed independently in each country or context, ideas for new and different ways of measuring specific concepts may be generated. Development and testing of multiple measures may help in pinpointing more effective and reliable measurement instruments.

For example, studies of life-style trends in France have made use of projective techniques as opposed to a battery of attitudinal statements, the approach most commonly used in the United States. Pictures of prototypical life-style patterns are developed. These are shown to respondents, who are then requested to indicate which appears to correspond most closely to their own or an "ideal" life-style. This approach is said to be particularly effective in indicating future trends in life-style patterns.

Comparative studies of life-styles in the United States and Europe have also used time allocation measures on the grounds that these provide a more objective measure of life-style and are more appropriate in comparative studies than attitudinal statements. It is argued that the latter are likely to be susceptible to subjective bias as well as different types of respondent or response bias in various countries, which may make them less suitable for comparative studies.

Comparative research is thus a methodology that offers considerable potential in studying consumer behavior. It can aid not only by examining consumer behavior and decision making in a broader sociocultural context, but also by stimulating greater thought with regard to the research methodology used to study these phenomena.

CONCLUSION

The contribution of comparative studies appears likely to be most significant in understanding the impact of the sociocultural influences and patterns of interaction on behavior of consumers. In this context, comparative studies may aid in understanding the role of sociocultural value orientations in influencing consumer behavior, as well as how the consumption of products and services is used to express or enhance life-style patterns. Similarly, they may shed light on the extent to which the dominance of certain personality types in various countries or cultures results in certain patterns of interpersonal influence. Understanding of the nature of communication processes in different societal contexts may also be improved, as well as of the impact of the marketing infrastructure on the formation or evolution of consumer behavior patterns. Some illustrations of potential contributions in each of these areas are next highlighted.

Comparative studies can aid in identifying different dimensions of *value orientations* and in broadening understanding of their impact on consumer behavior. In some cases, identification of an emergent trend in one country and its impact on consumer behavior may provide pointers as to future trends in another country. Examination of whether the emergence of similar value orientations such as concern with health and fitness appears to be associated with similar consumption trends in other countries, such as, interest in health foods, vitamins, jogging, etc., might, for example, shed light on the link between sociocultural value orientations and behavior as consumers.

Comparison of the behavior patterns of *life-style segments* or *demographic groupings*, such as upscale consumers, teenagers, or working versus nonworking wives, may also provide insights into the attitudes and behavior of these segments. One might, for example, expect similar demographic groups such as teenagers (or working wives), faced with similar problems and with similar motivations, to demonstrate similar behavior irrespective of their national origin. Existing studies suggest, however, that this is not always the case. Behavior is likely to be conditioned by position relative to existing sociocultural norms. For example, in countries characterized by traditional sex role norms, only working wives with liberated sex role attitudes feel free to make use of convenience products and services (symbols of a "poor" housewife) (Douglas 1976). Working wives with traditional views feel guilty about the limited time available for household duties and overcompensate by spending time in food preparation and performance of household tasks.

The dominant *personality types* characterizing a society, such as inner-directed or other-directed personalities or externally versus internally controlled types, may also affect behavior in consumer roles. For example, sociable and outer-directed personalities may be expected to be more susceptible to personal and other marketer-controlled influences and more likely to indulge in symbolic production consumption than other personality types, though this may be conditioned by the role of the media and the nature of social interaction as well as the rigidity of the social hierarchy.

Examination of *communication processes* and information-seeking behavior relating to purchase decisions in different societal contexts may also shed further light on the nature of these processes. Reliance on, and hence effective, visual versus verbal versus written communication may, for example, vary from one country to another as also the effectiveness of emotional versus informational appeals. The nature and extent of information-seeking behavior may also be influenced by factors such as purchasing power, consumer mobility, time availability, and levels of literacy, and also the degree of product or brand differentiation and the homogeneity of prices within a country.

Finally, the impact of the *marketing infrastructure*, such as, for example, the retail environment and the physical and media infrastructure, on consumer decision-making and purchase behavior can be investigated under a wider range of alternative scenarios than would be feasible in a single country. This may therefore aid in understanding to what extent the marketing environment conditions behavior. The degree of self-service or nonstore retailing may, for example, be anticipated to affect the role of salespersons in purchase decisions, as also the importance of point-of-purchase stimuli such as displays or promotions in consumer purchase decisions. Similarly, the integration and coverage of the media network as well as the degree of exposure to external influences may influence interest in innovation and rate of adoption of new products and services.

Comparative studies offer a wealth of new insights into understanding consumer behavior patterns and the way in which the societal setting and patterns of social interaction condition this behavior. They enable examination of these phenomena in a much wider range of societal contexts and conditions, and as such enable examination of a wider degree of variation in relevant variables than would be feasible in a single-country or -culture study. This perspective can aid not only in assessing the extent to which findings in one country, often the United States, can be generalized to other countries and contexts, but also in stimulating ideas with regard to new concepts and measures and ways of studying consumer behavior.

REFERENCES

Adamopoulos, John. 1977. "The Dimensions of the Greek Concept of Philotimo." *Journal of Social Psychology*. 10:313–14.

Anderson, R. 1967. "On the Comparability of Meaningful Stimuli in Cross-Cultural Research." *Sociometry* 30:124–36.

Anderson, Ronald, and Jack Engledow. 1977. "A Factor Analytic Comparison of U.S. and German Information Seekers." *Journal of Consumer Research* 3 (March): 185–96.

Bendix, Reinhard. 1963. "Concepts and Generalizations in Comparative Sociological Studies." *American Sociological Review* 28.

Berent, Paul-Howard. 1975. "International Research Is Different." In *Marketing in Turbulent Times and Marketing: The Challenges and the Opportunities—Combined Proceedings*, edited by Edward M. Mazze, pp. 293–97. Chicago: American Marketing Association.

Berlin, B., and P. Kay. 1969. *Basic Color Terms: Their Universality and Evolution*. Berkeley: University of California Press.

Berrien, F. Kenneth. 1967. "Methodological and Related Problems in Cross-Cultural Research." *International Journal of Psychology* 2:33–43.

Berry, John W. 1980. "Introduction to Methodology." In *Handbook of Cross-Cultural Psychology, Vol. 2*, edited by Harry C. Triandis and John W. Berry, pp. 1–28. Boston: Allyn and Bacon.

———. 1969. "On Cross-Cultural Comparability." *International Journal of Psychology* 4:119–28.

Berry, J. W., and Pierre Dasen. 1974. *Culture and Cognition*. London: Methuen.

Brislin, Richard. 1983. "Cross-Cultural Research in Psychology." *Annual Review of Psychology* 34:363–400.

———. 1970. "Back-Translation for Cross-Cultural Research." *Journal of Cross-Cultural Psychology* 1 (September): 185–216

Brislin, Richard, Walter J. Lonner, and Robert M. Thorndike. 1973. *Cross-Cultural Research Methods*. New York: John Wiley & Sons.

Campbell, Donald T., and Donald W. Fiske. 1959. "Convergent and Discriminant Validation by the Multi-Trait Multi-Method Matrix." *Psychological Bulletin* 26 (March):81–105.

Cathelat, Bernard. 1977. *Les Styles de Vie des Francais*. Paris: Stanke.

Cerha, Jarko. 1974. "The Limits of Influence." *European Research* 2 (July):141–51.

Church, R. 1952. *An Analysis of Resemblance*. London: George Allen & Unwin.

Clarke, Yvonne, and Geoffrey N. Soutar. 1982. "Consumer Acquisition Patterns for Durable Goods: Australian Evidence." *Journal of Consumer Research* 8 (March):456–60.

Cox, Reavis. 1965. "The Search for Universals in Comparative Studies of Domestic Marketing Systems." In *Marketing and Economic Development: Proceedings of the 1965 Fall Conference*, edited by P. D. Bennett, pp. 143–162. Chicago: American Marketing Association.

Derogowski, Jan B. 1980. "Perception." In *A Handbook of Cross-Cultural Psychology,*

Vol. 3: Basic Processes, edited by Harry C. Triandis and Walter Lonner, pp. 21–117. Boston: Allyn and Bacon.

Douglas, Susan P. 1976. "Cross-National Comparisons and Consumer Stereotypes: A Case Study of Working and Non-Working Wives in the U.S. and France." *Journal of Consumer Research* 3 (June):12–20.

Douglas, Susan P., and C. Samuel Craig. 1983. *International Marketing Research*. Englewood Cliffs, NJ: Prentice-Hall.

Douglas, Susan P., and Anne Macquin. 1977. "L'Utilísation du Style de Vie dans le Media-Planning." The Jours de France Gold Medal for Advertising Research. Paris: Jours de France.

Douglas, Susan P., and Christine Urban. 1977. "Life-Style Analysis to Profile Women in International Markets." *Journal of Marketing* 41 (July):46–54.

Elder, Joseph W. 1976. "Comparative Cross-National Methodology." *Annual Review in Sociology*.

Ember, Carol R. 1977. "Cross-Cultural Cognitive Studies." *Annual Review of Anthropology* 6:33–56.

Green, Robert T. et al. 1983. "Societal Development and Family Purchasing Roles: A Cross-National Study." *Journal of Consumer Research* 9 (March):436–42.

Green, Robert T., and Eric Langeard. 1975. "A Cross-National Comparison of Consumer Habits and Innovator Characteristics." *Journal of Marketing* 49 (July):34–41.

Green, Robert T., and Phillip D. White. 1976. "Methodological Considerations in Cross-National Consumer Research." *Journal of International Business Studies* 7 (Fall, Winter): 81–87.

Heider, E. R. 1972. "Universal in Naming and Memory." *Journal of Experimental Psychology* 93:10–20.

———. 1971. "Focal Color Areas and the Development of Color Names." *Developmental Psychology* 4:447–55.

Jolibert, Alain J., and Gary Baumgartner. 1981. "Toward a Definition of the Consumerist Segment in France." *Journal of Consumer Research* 8 (June):114–17.

Katz, Elihu, and Paul F. Lazarsfeld. 1955. *Personal Influence*. New York: Free Press.

Manaster, Guy J., and Robert J. Havighurst. 1972. *Cross-National Research: Social-Psychological Methods and Problems*. Boston: Houghton Mifflin.

Marsh, R. M. 1967. *Comparative Sociology: A Modification of Cross-Societal Analysis*. New York: Harcourt, Brace & World.

Pick, Anne D. 1980. "Cognition: Psychological Perspectives." In *A Handbook of Cross-Cultural Psychology, Vol. 3: Basic Processes*, edited by Harry C. Triandis and Walter Lonner, pp. 117–54. Boston: Allyn and Bacon.

Plummer, Joseph. 1977. "Consumer Focus in Cross-National Research." *Jouranl of Advertising* 6 (Spring):5–15.

Poortinga, Ype H. 1975. "Limitations on Intercultural Comparison of Psychological Data." *Nederlands Tijdschrift van de Psychologie* 30:23–39.

Preworski, A., and M. Teune. 1970. *The Logic of Comparative Social Inquiry*. New York: Wiley-Interscience.

Price-Williams, D. 1974. "Psychological Experiment and Anthropology: The Problem of Categories." *Ethos* 2:95–114.

Rosch, Eleanor. 1978. "Principles of Human Categorization." In *Cognition and Categori-*

zation, edited by E. Rosch and B. Lloyd, pp. 28–48. Hillsdale, NJ: Lawrence Erlbaum.

Sears, Robert R. 1961. "Transcultural Variables and Conceptual Equivalence." In *Studying Personality Cross-Culturally*, edited by Bert Kaplan, pp. 445–55. Evanston, IL: Row, Peterson.

Straus, Murray A. 1969. "Phenomenal Identity and Conceptual Equivalence of Measurement in Cross-National Comparative Research." *Journal of Marriage and the Family* 31 (May):233–39.

Szalai, Lorand P., and James P. Deese. 1978. *Subjective Meaning and Culture*. Hillsdale, NJ: Lawrence Earlbaum.

Triandis, Harry. 1972. *The Analysis of Subjective Culture*. New York: John Wiley & Sons.

Triandis, Harry C., Roy S. Malpass, and Andrew R. Davidson. 1973. "Psychology and Culture." *Annual Review of Psychology* 23:355–78.

Triandis, Harry, and V. Vassilou. 1972. "A Comparative Analysis of Subjective Culture." In *The Analysis of Subjective Culture*, edited by Harry C. Triandis. New York: John Wiley & Sons.

Van Raaij, W. Fred. 1978. "Cross-Cultural Research Methodology as a Case of Construct Validity." In *Advances in Consumer Research, Vol. 5*, edited by H. Keith Hunt, pp. 693–701. Ann Arbor: Association for Consumer Research.

Wind, Yoram, and Susan P. Douglas. 1982. "Comparative Consumer Research: The Next Frontier." *Management Decision* 2:24–35.

PART III

Channel Network Behavior

CHAPTER 7

Flow Analysis in Marketing

EWALD T. GRETHER

Over the years, I have been fortunate to have been associated with Reavis Cox in a number of major and minor ways. First was an appointment as Visiting Professor in Marketing at Wharton in 1938–39 when he was the Chairperson of the Marketing Department. Second was an association as editors of the *Journal of Marketing*. Roland S. Vaile had been managing editor in 1937–38 and editor-in-chief in 1939–40. I succeeded Vaile as managing editor in 1939–40 and editor-in-chief in 1941–43. Cox became managing editor in 1941–42 and editor-in-chief in 1943–44. This trilogy in the editorship of the *Journal of Marketing* became the basis for our most important association as joint authors of Vaile, Grether, and Cox, *Marketing in the American Economy*, published in 1952. In this association, Vaile and I remarked frequently that "Reavis has a very sharp pencil"—fortunately for his coauthors.

Cox had been marketing editor of the New York *Journal of Commerce*, 1927–31, an experience that no doubt helped both to sharpen his pencil and arouse his interest in the field of marketing, and to establish his writing interests. Over the years he has been a prolific writer.

It is important to note a few important aspects of his career and associations by way of background. Cox was not interested in conventional economic theory, as had been true of numerous other scholars in the field of marketing. The assumptions of the formal models and approaches of current economic analysis in his view dpearted from the world of marketing he had come to know as marketing editor of the *Journal of Commerce* and in general. His own bent was toward a more realistic approach not only in general terms but especially in the analysis of pricing. Chapter 19 in Vaile, Grether, and Cox (1952) on "The

Mechanics and Procedures of Pricing" is an excellent example of how he related pricing to the actual procedures and setting of transactions in contrast with the formal models of economic analysis. Of equal importance was his empirical field work stress in all his studies. He was anything but a closet philosopher barricaded behind his books manipulating formal models.

Very important in interpreting Cox and his writings was his association with a Wharton and Philadelphia colleague, Wroe Alderson. In the October 1948 issue of the *Journal of Marketing*, Alderson and Cox collaborated on a paper, "Towards a Theory of Marketing," which may well be one of the most important papers published in that journal. The authors discussed the "lively interest in marketing theory" and interpreted its nature and possible content. Seven categories of opportunity and need were enunciated, including (1) "Problems of Price Discrimination," (2) "Spatial Aspects of Marketing," and (3) Temporal Aspects of Marketing." Among the possible approaches to an "integrated theory of marketing," group behaviorism was highly recommended. And, important for this discussion, an exploratory survey of the productivity of marketing in Philadelphia just begun was mentioned. Even more important, it was stated: "In order to measure some aspects of effort expended and work done, reliance can best be put upon concepts of movement or flow through some one or more varieties of space and time" (p. 150).

This 1948 article, among other things, provided the background for the two influential volumes edited by Cox and Alderson on *Theory in Marketing*, published in 1950 and 1964. But from the standpoints of this particular essay, it also clearly enunciated Cox's interest and plans for his researches in flow analysis.

By way of background for this chapter, it is important to note that Reavis Cox, although a colleague and associate of Wroe Alderson, was not "Aldersonian." This is not the place to appraise the work of Wroe Alderson, who was also one of my friends and associates at the Marketing Science Institute and in other enterprises (see Grether 1967). The point that must be made is that Cox developed his own approach, which was neither Aldersonian nor conventional. Insofar as any direct influences are concerned, it would appear that there may have been two such sources. First was A. W. Shaw in his *Approach to Business Problems*, published in 1916, and his paper, "Some Problems in Market Distribution," published in 1912. Shaw had stressed the "application of motion to materials." Second, and much more important, most likely, was Cox's association with Ralph E. Breyer on the Wharton faculty. Breyer in his *Marketing Institution* (1934) had enunciated a flow concept based on the simile of electric circuitry with both space and time elements. Regardless of possible sources of inspiration, the fact is that flow analysis became most important in Cox's own approach to the analysis of marketing. We turn therefore to brief expositions of the applications and nature of this analysis.

Flow analysis was used very helpfully in the discussion of channels of distribution in Vaile, Grether, and Cox, *Marketing in the American Economy* (1952).

The flows through the channels of distribution were developed in terms of forward, background, and two-way flows. The analysis was bolstered by statistical tables and flow charts. Looking backward now with the hindsight of 33 years, it is evident that this part of our analysis has been well received by students and instructors. It is clear, too, that, looking at the volume as a whole, we did not ourselves as coauthors relate to it as we should have in the six parts of the volume.

In the meantime, Cox and Goodman were at work on their major study, *Channels and Flows in the Marketing of House-Building Materials*, which appeared in three volumes, mimeographed in 1954. The mammoth study was reported in the *Journal of Marketing* in July 1956. In his *Commissioned Commemorative Paper* prepared at the request of the American Marketing Association (AMA) for its Fiftieth Anniversary International Symposium (1965), Cox gave a clear-cut, helpful statement of flow analysis. His final observation is well worth quoting: "I shall not here evaluate flow analysis in detail. It has strengths; it has weaknesses; it has limitations. . . . If we are going to make effective international comparisons of domestic marketing systems we are going to have to throw off the shackles of conventional ways of thinking about marketing and experiment with new approaches such as the one I have described briefly" (p. 162).

DISTRIBUTION IN A HIGH-LEVEL ECONOMY

Probably Cox's most important publication, which appeared in 1965, was, *Distribution in a High-Level Economy* (Cox, Goodman and Fichandler 1965) the volume supported by the Twentieth Century Fund as a followup of the well-known 1939 book by P. W. Stewart, J. F. Dewhurst, with the assistance of L. Field, *Does Distribution Cost Too Much?* The Cox book also was an overall view and appraisal of marketing or "distribution." For the purposes of this essay, it is important to note that Chapter 3, "The Flow of Goods and Services Through the American Economy," was a very basic aspect of the approach. Here, as elsewhere, the flows or movements through geographic space and time were stressed together with the so-called intangible flows. In the front inside cover of the volume, there is a beautiful color chart depicting "The Flow of Ownership in the United States Economy." Chapter 1 is intended to (1) portray the complicated network of interconnections among the major buying and selling groups and (2) measure the relative size of the different flows of goods and services. It is noted in Appendix A that "the distribution system is infinitely more complex than the chart implies" (p. 165).

In succeeding chapters the analysis is focused upon the marketing agencies that distribute the goods and services and their organization into channels and cities as agencies of distribution. It is most interesting that Cox came to consider markets also as agencies of distribution. In other words, markets were not merely passive intermediaries as depicted in much of economic analysis but positive forces. This had come to be the view also of Edwin G. Nourse, first chairperson of the Council of Economic Advisers. Space will not be taken here to discuss the applications of the basic analysis to the overall appraisal of distribution and the look into the future. It is in this part of the volume that important comparisons are made with the earlier 1939 study, *Does Distribution Cost Too Much?*

For the purposes of this chapter, the important consideration is the relative feasibility of the flow approach especially in applications, say, to the entire economy or major sectors. Not only are there important problems of data availability but also of aggregation in the broader applications. Cox and his associates, of course, were thoroughly aware of the problems and difficulties. Cox, for example, indicated that the application to relatively clear-cut transvection analysis of a single product as shoes, although complex, was usually feasible (1978). For broader applications he expressed confidence ultimately in computerization, especially of point-of-sale computers (1981). As of now there are sharp differences of opinion as to whether Cox's hopes in terms of computerization are well supported. There should be a much better basis for judgment within a few years. Fortunately, an application in Australia suggests that Cox's approach could be generalized as the basis for making international comparisons, as he suggested in his AMA-commissioned commemorative paper in 1965. In this paper, Cox stated, "Comparative marketing seems to me to be one of the great frontiers of marketing today" (p. 162). He made some cautious comparisons between the United States and Europe. But as things have turned out, the most significant comparisons have been made between the Australian economy and that of the United States. Roger A. Layton, Professor of Marketing at the University of New South Wales, in three important papers dealing with "Trade Flows in Macromarketing Systems" (1981, 1981, 1984), made specific comparisons between the Australian economy in 1968–69 and 1974–75 and the Cox, Goodman, and Fichandler estimates for 1947 for the United States in *Distribution in a High-Level Economy* (1965).

Layton's studies and publications tend to support Cox's hopes for systematic international comparisons. On the whole, the Layton studies expressed a more optimistic view about such studies than did Cox himself. The structural contrasts between the United States and Australia clearly demonstrated the value of such international comparisons, even though at different time periods, 1947 in the United States and 1968–69 and 1974–75 in Australia. The most significant observation was "the evident structural similarity between the two systems, separated as they are in both space and time" based upon the 1947 and 1968–69 data.

FINAL OBSERVATIONS

The flow concept, of course, is not new, and it was not invented by Reavis Cox and his associates. Thus, for example, Alfred Marshall in his *Principles of*

Economics (1927) stated in the preface, "The element of time which is the centre of the chief difficulties of almost every economic problem is itself continuous" (p.vii). Marshallians will recall that this was a very important aspect of Marshall's economic analysis.

The original Twentieth Century Fund study, *Does Distribution Cost Too Much?* (Stewart, Dewhurst, and Field 1933), had a brief chapter on "The Flow of Goods Through Distribution Channels." This 1939 study also enclosed a very elaborate chart based on 1929 data on "The Flow of Goods in the United States," not unlike the chart in *Distribution in a High-Level Economy*. The Cox chart, however, was limited to the flow of ownership. The 1939 chart displayed only the flow of movable tangible commodities from the point of origin to the point of final sale as commodities—not the total volume of trade. The crucial difference between Cox and the many others who have recognized the flow concept is that he and his associates put it to work in their house-building materials study. And, of course, scholars in many fields continue to grapple with continuities of time, space, etc., in their studies. Ronald Savitt, in his chapter in this volume reports upon the work of the Swedish School at Lund.

In the Fall 1983 *Journal of Marketing*, I reported upon developments in regional–spatial analysis and noted especially the systematic interdisciplinary relationships that "bode well for the future of scholarship." The works and writings of Reavis Cox have had and will continue to have an influence in these interdisciplinary developments.

REFERENCES

Alderson, Wroe, and Reavis Cox. 1948. "Towards a Theory of Marketing." *Journal of Marketing* 13 (October):137–52.

Balderston, F. E., J. Carman, and F. M. Nicosia. 1981. *Regulation of Marketing and the Public Interest.* New York: Pergamon Press.

Breyer, Ralph F. 1934. *The Marketing Institution.* New York: McGraw-Hill.

Cox, Reavis. 1965. "The Search for Universals in Comparative Studies of Domestic Marketing Systems." In *Marketing and Economic Development: Proceedings of the 1965 Fall Conference*, edited by P. D. Bennett, pp. 158–62. Chicago: American Marketing Association.

Cox, Reavis, and Wroe Alderson, eds. 1950. *Theory in Marketing.* Chicago: Richard D. Irwin.

Cox, Reavis, Wroe Alderson, and S. J. Shapiro, eds. 1964. *Theory in Marketing.* Homewood, IL: Richard D. Irwin.

Cox, Reavis, and C. S. Goodman. 1956. "Marketing of Housebuilding Markets." *Journal of Marketing* 21 (July):36–61.

———. 1954. *Channels and Flows in the Marketing of House Building Materials*, 3 vols. Mimeo., Philadelphia.

Cox, Reavis, C. S. Goodman, and T. C. Fichandler. 1965. *Distribution in a High-Level Economy.* Englewood Cliffs, NJ: Prentice-Hall.

Grether, E. T. 1983. "Regional-Spatial Analysis in Marketing." *Journal of Marketing* 47 (Fall):36–43.

——. 1967. "Chamberlin's Theory of Monopolistic Competition and the Literature of Marketing." In *Monopolistic Competition Theory: Studies in Impact*, edited by R. E. Kuenne, pp. 307–28. New York: John Wiley & Sons.

Grether, E. T., Reavis Cox, and W. T. Tucker. 1978. "Perspectives of Marketing: Past Present and Future," Working Paper 78-46. University of Texas at Austin, Graduate School of Business, May.

Layton, Roger A. "Trade Flows in Macromarketing System." *Journal of Macromarketing* "Part I, A Macromodel of Trade Flows" 1 (Spring 1981):35–48; "Part II, Transforming Input, Output Tables into Trade Flow Tables." 1 (Fall 1981):48–55; "Part III, Trade Flows in Australia, 1974–75, An Assessment of Structural Change" 4 (Spring 1984):62–73.

Marshall, A. 1927. *Principles of Economics*. 1st ed. London: Macmillan.

Shaw, A. W. 1916. *An Approach to Business Problems*. Cambridge, MA: Harvard University Press.

Shaw, A. W. 1912. "Some Problems in Market Distribution." Reprinted in *Changing Perspectives in Marketing*, edited by Hugh G. Wales, pp. 32–54. Urbana, Illinois: University of Illinois Press.

Stewart, P. W., J. T. Dewhurst, and L. Field. 1939. *Does Distribution Cost Too Much?* New York: Twentieth Century Fund.

Vaile, R. W., E. T. Grether, and Reavis Cox. 1952. *Marketing in the American Economy*. New York: Ronald Press.

CHAPTER 8

Shared Symbols, Meanings, and Ways of Life in Interorganizational Networks

JOHAN ARNDT

INTRODUCTION

Conceptualizations in marketing tend to develop from simple imperatives to more complex, ambiguous, and sometimes contradictory formulations. The purpose of this chapter is to contribute to such a development by merging two important traditions of thought, the traditions of marketing networks and organizational culture. This theme is much inspired by Reavis Cox, who throughout his career worked diligently to develop new conceptualizations of marketing networks.

At first, such a conceptual merger may appear strange. However, a new stream in culture research addresses the rituals and shared understandings, norms and values of modern organizations and other forms of "civilized tribes" (Levy 1978). This tradition throws new light at organizational phenomena by introducing concepts and metaphors such as symbols, language, and social drama, emphasizing interactive, ongoing recreative aspects of organizational life (Jelinek, Smircich, and Hirsch 1983, p. 331). This essay first examines the evolution of the marketing network. The second section addresses the field of organizational cultures. The sections that follow deal with managerial implications and the research imperatives of the conceptual framework developed here.

THE EVOLUTION OF MARKETING THOUGHT

The truncated review below covers only the time after World War II. More complete reviews can be found in Bartels (1970), Hunt (1976), and Arndt (1978).

Here, the recent developments in marketing thought are classified into three main periods: The marketing concept, the broadened marketing concept, and the new institutional concept periods. As will be shown, the trend has been in the direction of expanding both the scope and the applications of marketing, hence responding to the call to arms for better theory by Alderson and Cox (1948).

The Marketing Concept Period

The traditional selling concept in marketing took the product (and often the customers as well) as given and emphasized promotional activities such as advertising and personal selling. This paradigm, however, was found inadequate when conditions changed from a seller's to a buyer's market in postwar North America. With increasingly fiercer competition, the emerging new paradigm, the so-called marketing concept, advocated focus on customers and customer needs and argued for integrated analysis, planning, and control of all elements of the marketing mix. This concept was popularized as the 4 P's (Product, Price, Promotion, and Place) by McCarthy (1960). Hence, the main avenue to profits went through developing, producing, and distributing products satisfying customer wants (McKitterick 1957; Kotler 1967).

The Broadened Marketing Concept

In a pioneering article in the late 1960s, Northwestern University professors Kotler and Levy (1969) noted perceptively that marketing behavior was manifest in a wide range of situations beyond the regular economic exchanges in the marketplace. Consequently, marketing techniques were used and should be used by all organizations needing favorable responses from external interest groups. Kotler and Levy asserted that marketing was relevant for churches, schools, police departments, labor unions, and political campaigns. Not surprisingly, such a codification of marketing's expansion into the area of nonprofit organization is already well covered in managerially oriented textbooks (Kotler 1981).

This development is less a change than may be apparent at the first look. As pointed out by Stidsen (1979), this broadening is mostly a widening of application rather than theory, transplanting existing theory (mainly relating to promotional activities) into new settings. Another limitation is that the broadened marketing concept, like its predecessors, is mainly a stimulus–response formulation using what Johnston and Bonoma (1977) term the "unit paradigm," focusing on the individual social unit, the firm or the consumer.

New Institutionalism

As seen in the recent literature review by Carman (1980), a common feature of the main traditions in the emerging new institutionalism in marketing is the strong emphasis on the patterns of interactions between two or more parties and the structural mechanisms established for facilitating and implementing such interactions. Perhaps the most important streams of thought are the marketing-as-exchange notion, the transaction cost formulation, and the political economy approach. As will be shown, all these streams of thought contribute to the emerging network paradigm.

Marketing as Exchange

The chief architect of the exchange notion in marketing is Bagozzi (1975), who creatively extended thoughts earlier developed by Alderson (1957). In Bagozzi's view, the two main questions facing marketing theory are (1) Why do people and organizations engage in exchange relationships? and (2) How are exchanges created, resolved, or avoided? Building on work in anthropology, Bagozzi identified three types of exchange: restricted, generalized, and complex. Later, the notion developed in a more normative direction, building on microeconomic reasoning (Bagozzi 1978) at the same time as Bagozzi became more oriented toward causal modeling (Bagozzi 1980). The theoretical development of the exchange tradition seems to occur mainly in the applications area. For instance, Swedish researchers at the Stockholm School of Economics and the Universities of Linkoping and Uppsala have over time developed an interaction model for industrial and international marketing (for example, Hakansson 1982; Mattsson 1984). This approach, partly the result of and partly the guide for many empirical studies, isolates four basic elements of marketing and purchasing processes: (1) the interaction process, (2) the participants in the interaction process, (3) the environment within which interaction takes place, and (4) the atmosphere affecting and affected by the interaction.

Transaction Cost Economics

One of the most provocative and widely discussed theories in the organizational field is the transaction cost economics approach formulated by Williamson (1975), integrating parts of microeconomics, contract law, and organization theory. According to this view, transaction costs may become particularly high in markets characterized by a small number of buyers and sellers, opportunism, uncertainty, and bounded rationality. When such conditions prevail, the market fails. It is then more cost-efficient to handle transactions through administrative procedures in integrated networks. Though allowing for imperfections in the market, this notion is a rational and economic approach, which does not capture power and conflict processes well. It should also be underscored that Williamson has the *transaction* rather than *relationship* as his unit of analysis.

This conceptualization of marketing relationships is shown in Figure 8.1. It underscores the mutual dependence of episodes and structure that follows from institutionalized and routinized episodes. The boundary is not absolute but will depend on the rigor of criteria for network membership.

FIGURE 8.1 Chief Components of Marketing Network

NETWORK BOUNDARY

INTERACTION EPISODES

PROPERTIES OF TRANSACTION	TRANSACTIONAL CONTENT			
	Product or Services	Affect	Information	Financial Resources
Direction				
Scope				
Complexity				
Intensity				
Variability				
Reciprocity				

NETWORK STRUCTURE

CONTENT OF THE TIES	STRUCTURE FOR GOVERNANCE OF TIES		
	Causality	Formalization	Differentiation
Technical			
Information			
Affect			
Economic			
Legal			

124

The Political Economy Approach

The political economy approach centers on the interplay of power, the goals of the power wielders, and the productive exchange systems (Buchanan 1964; Zald 1970; Wamsley and Zald 1976). The following three dimensions are particularly often used in the analyses of organizations: polity (power and control phenomena) versus economy (implementation of productive and distributive functions); external (to the organization) versus internal; and substructure (pattern of ownership and dominance) versus superstructure (behaviors and sentiments). It has become customary to develop typologies for political economy components on the basis of the first two dimensions. Hence, the resulting framework distinguishes between political environment, economic environment, internal polity, and internal economy (Stern and Reve 1980; Arndt 1983). A limitation so far is that researchers in the political economy tradition (Reve 1980; Achrol, Reve, and Stern 1983) have been interested mainly in *dyads* rather than in *networks*.

Marketing Systems as Relational Networks

The concept of interorganizational networks has become increasingly important in organization theory (Pfeffer 1982, pp. 371–1277; Reve 1980, pp. 12–21). Most transactions are effected not through ad hoc market encounters but in the context of stable relationships within networks. In such networks, each transaction may be termed an *episode*, as proposed by Hakansson (1982). These transactions are embedded in long-lasting relationships among all parties involved. Moreover, viewed differently, the exchanges as they occur over time form recurring patterns of transactions. These patterns then result in ties of dependency, hence forming the *structure* of the network (Mattsson 1984).

There are two different dimensions of interaction episodes: transactional *content* and *properties* of the transaction. Regarding content, Figure 8.1 distinguishes between four main flows: (1) goods and services, (2) affect, (3) information, and (4) financial resources. Similar listings have been proposed by Tichy, Tushman, and Fombrun (1979) and Hakansson (1982, pp. 16–17). Process properties include direction, scope, complexity, intensity, variability, and reciprocity (Reve 1980, pp. 31–33).

Similarly, the framework features two structural dimensions. The first dimension, *governance*, includes the properties of centrality, formalization, and differentiation. Centrality is the degree to which decision making is concentrated in one part of the network. Formalization is the degree to which decision making is governed by explicit rules and fixed policies. Differentiation is the degree to which there are differences in decision-making patterns across the network. The second dimension of network structure includes the *content* of the structural ties. These structural ties include five kinds of mutual dependencies: dependence on other members of the network for production and exchange processes; information and ideas; cognitive; affect and liking; economic resource ties such as credit, risk absorption, etc. These ties may also be formalized through legal contracts.

The notion of marketing networks has also a normative–managerial dimension. Hence, the corresponding concept of network management ("the management of management") refers to the analysis, planning, implementation, and maintenance of viable networks satisfying the needs and wants of internal and external interest groups (Arndt 1979; Stern and El-Ansary 1982).

In marketing as well as in the other behavioral sciences, the metaphors used reflect dominating assumptions and perspectives brought to the study of the discipline. As in organization theory, instrumental, managerial views show up in the metaphor of the "machine" consisting of multiple parts as can be found in the marketing concept, the broadened concept, and transaction cost views. Similarly, the metaphor "organism" is important in ecological formulations such as that of Alderson (1957), bringing in concepts such as "niche," "resources," etc. The network tradition also uses metaphors from economics or the physical world, such as tasks, efficiency, ties, harmony, control, and output. Physical and biological metaphors focus on certain properties but neglect others. While not inappropriate, metaphors are partial truths. Such is the case for organizational cultures and their research traditions, to be discussed next. The concept of network culture incorporates elements that add a metaphorical dimension alluded to but not employed in traditional marketing analysis of network interaction patterns. Hence, organizational culture can be conceptually incorporated into traditional network analysis without discarding the existing "network paradigm."

THE RESEARCH TRADITION OF ORGANIZATIONAL CULTURES

The budding tradition of organizational cultures adds new conceptual tools to the area of marketing as well as organization theory. The metaphor of culture focuses on organizational behavior as a social process. This means using dynamic and interactive models of *organizing* viewed as a process conditioned by the nature of the human mind that seeks to interpret or make sense of a stream of events (Jelinek, Smircich, and Hirsch 1983, p. 338). In accounting for the cultural approach to organization behavior, this section starts by commenting on the use of anthropology in marketing. The role of culture in contemporary organization theory is then discussed before different approaches to organizational cultures are outlined.

The Organizational Cultures Research Tradition

As vividly demonstrated by Levy (1978), a variety of conceptions of culture exist within the discipline of anthropology. For instance, the followers of White (1959) emphasize cultural evolution expressed in technological terms. An almost opposite tradition exemplified by Geertz (1973) stresses the role of culture as a system of symbols and argues for the study of people's conscious and unconscious ideas.

The concept of culture has been increasingly linked with the study of contemporary organizations. The recognition of the symbolic aspects in human interaction led to a call for a cultural perspective or organization (Smircich 1983). This may imply treating management as symbolic activity (Peters 1978) or a language game (Pondy 1978) and calling attention to organizational legends, myths, and ceremonies (Trice and Beyer 1983). In a way, this development has much in common with the celebrated "rediscovery of people" in the mass communications area several decades earlier (Katz and Lazarsfeld 1955). Again, prevailing paradigms and approaches are being challenged.

This challenge was recognized by *Business Week*, which in its October 1980 issue featured a cover article on corporate cultures. The authoritative scholarly journal *Administrative Science Quarterly* devoted its entire September 1983 issue to the organizational cultures area. The resurging interest in the subject matter is more than an academic phenonemon. The best-seller status of recent popular books such as *Theory Z* (Ouchi 1981), *The Art of Japanese Management* (Pascale and Athos 1981), and *In Search of Excellence* (Peters and Waterman 1982) confirms the widespread recognition of the importance of corporate cultures.

While the literature reveals little agreement on how organizational cultures should be defined, the following definition proposed by Uttal (1983, p. 66) summarizes important common elements of the many conceptions. According to this definition, a corporate culture is (1) a system of shared values (what is important) and (2) beliefs (how things work) that interact with (3) a company's people, organizational structures, and control systems to produce (4) behavioral norms (the way we do things around here). In other words, the "antecedent conditions" are the shared values and beliefs and the final "consequent variable" is the resulting behavioral norms influencing and controlling behavior and ways of life in organizations and networks of organizations.

The different concepts and perspectives of culture from anthropology can be linked to organizational research orientations as shown in Figure 8.2, which to some extent builds on Smircich (1983). In turn, these research orientations have parallels in the interorganizational network area.

As suggested by Figure 8.2, conventional studies in the economics traditions on channels of distribution are instrumentally oriented and focus on task accomplishment (Stern and Reve 1980, p. 53). In essence, culture is viewed as a *set of environmental factors* acting as independent variables, imported to the network through organizational or individual members. The research agenda inspired by this view is to chart the differences among cultures and to relate the structure, process, and functions of the network to these differences (Boddewyn 1966).

The next category views corporate culture as an *internal variable*. The interorganizational marketing systems are seen as social and societal instruments

FIGURE 8.2 Intersections of Culture Theory, Themes in Organization and Management Research, and Concepts of "Interorganizational Networks"

CONCEPTS OF "CULTURE" FROM ANTHROPOLOGY	CONTENT AREA IN ORGANIZATION AND MANAGEMENT RESEARCH	CONCEPT OF "INTER-ORGANIZATIONAL NETWORKS"
Culture as an instrument serving human biological and psychological needs. Example: Malinowski's functionalism	Cross-cultural or comparative management	Organized networks as instruments for the efficient distribution of products and services; e.g., traditional view of channels of distribution
Culture as an adaptive–regulatory mechanism uniting individuals into social structures. Example: Radcliffe–Brown's structural functionalism	Corporate culture	Interorganizational networks as adaptive organisms existing by processes of exchange with the environment; e.g., contingency theory of channel management
Culture as a system of shared cognitions and meanings. Examples: Goodenough's ethnoscience and Geertz's symbolic anthropology	Organizational cognition and symbolism	Networks as systems of knowledge and patterns of symbolic discourse; e.g., management of meaning within interorganizational networks

Source: Adapted from Smircich (1983, p. 342).

128

to produce satisfaction and value through exchanges. At the same time, as a by-product they produce distinctive cultural entities such as myths, legends, and sagas. Though the networks are recognized as being embedded in wider cultural contexts, the emphasis of researchers is on the development of sociocultural qualities within networks (Smircich 1983, p. 344). Researchers in this tradition try to discover patterns of contingent relationships among the variables describing the different "spheres" or dimensions of networks or organizations such as goals, technology, and structure.

The third more complex concept leaves the physical images of the first two conceptions. Instead, it starts with the assumption that culture is something a network is rather than something it has (Smircich 1983, p. 347). As a *root metaphor*, culture accounts for networks as expressive or symbolic forms and manifestations of human consciousness, emphasizing the subjective aspects of marketing networks.

There are two main streams of thought in the third construct.[1] The first one emphasizes the role of interorganizational networks as systems of shared cognitions and beliefs, as underscored in Uttal's definition (1983) quoted earlier. In other words, network culture is seen as a unique system for perceiving and organizing material phenomena, things, events, behaviors, and emotions (Smircich 1983, p. 348). The other stream of thought conceptualizes networks as shared symbols and meanings. The application of the symbolic perspective to marketing networks leads to a need for "interpreting," "reading," or "deciphering" the symbolism relating to a given network. Hence, interorganizational governance may be viewed as the management of meaning and the sharing of interpretations (Peters 1978).

A COMPREHENSIVE VIEW OF MARKETING NETWORKS

Figure 8.3 shows the expanded notion of interorganizational network, which is a result of merging the network conceptualization in Figure 8.1 with the idea of network cultures. The "net value" of the cultural network notion is the underscoring of the importance of shared goals and values, cognitions, and meanings.

The core of the definition of interorganizational cultures developed here is the homogeneity of the elements or members of the culture. This leads to the issues of manifest as well as latent, unintended functions of network cultures. There are three main functions of culture: demarcation, identification, and control.

An important theme in anthropology is the role of the common features within the culture of giving the boundary of the network dichotomizing members and nonmembers who belong to the environment, including consumers,

FIGURE 8.3 A Composite View of Marketing Networks

NETWORK BOUNDARY

NETWORK STRUCTURE

CONTENT OF THE TIES	Causality	Formalization	Differentiation
Technical			
Information			
Affect			
Economic			
Legal			

STRUCTURE FOR GOVERNANCE OF TIES

INTERACTION EPISODES

TRANSACTIONAL CONTENT

PROPERTIES OF TRANSACTION	Product or Services	Affect	Information	Financial Resources
Direction				
Scope				
Complexity				
Intensity				
Variability				
Reciprocity				

NETWORK CULTURE

Shared goals and values
Shared cognitions
Shared earnings

competitors, regulators, etc. What distinguishes a network from a random collectivity of organizations is the fact that the superorganization of the network retains its identity when individual member organizations interact with one another and with "outsiders." This view parallels important anthropological views of the role of boundaries of ethnic groups (Barth 1969).

The second function follows from the first one. By defining network boundaries, the culture also constitutes the glue creating intranetwork cohesion and shared understandings of the network as a social reality. These shared understandings and meanings reduce uncertainty and enable network members to cope with turbulent environments.

Third, the network culture canalizes behavior of system members by providing norms and guidelines complementing and in some cases neutralizing formal controls such as contracts, job descriptions, budgets and sales quotas, etc. In this capacity, the culture often works through the mechanism of internalization.

The final task of this chapter is to discuss the implications of the network culture conceptualization. Some managerial implications will be outlined before implications for research are spelled out.

MANAGERIAL IMPLICATIONS

Conceptual and empirical research on corporate cultures suggests that such cultures are often firmly entrenched and not easily manipulated by management. While much of the research is flawed by simplifications and resort to anecdotal evidence, it nevertheless establishes that a progressive organizational culture is associated with success (Peters and Waterman 1982; Deal and Kennedy 1982). In this case, as always, correlation should not be mistaken for causation. It is just as plausible that the management styles and value configurations are results of corporate successes as it is that they are the cause. Unfortunately, available studies do not reveal the direction of the causal flow.

Direct Manipulation of Network Cultures

Although culture serves as a sense-making device that can guide and shape behavior (Pfeffer 1981), there is little evidence that culture can be easily changed by managerial manipulation. For example, it has not been established that the road to success for organizational and interorganizational management is to cast managers in the role of "cheerleader, facilitator, and keeper of the bureaucratic mickey-mouse off the productive peoples' backs," as put provocatively, but overoptimistically, by Peters (1984, p. 33).

Network culture is a phenomenon having its own existence in the subjective, shared experiences of members of the organizations and the network, and not as the result of molding efforts from top management. When top management has been shown to rejuvenate values, this has more often than not occurred in the context of top management changes, as in the case of Lee Iacocca at Chrysler and Jan Carlzon at Scandinavian Airlines System. Furthermore, most organizations do not have one dominating culture. Instead, they have multiple cultures and even countercultures, all competing for the power to define reality (Smircich 1983, p. 346; Gregory 1983). While the direct use of culture as a managerial tool may prove infeasible, culture may prove managerially meaningful in at least two ways: as a conceptual facilitator in adaption and as the underpinnings of strategic management.

The Culture Notion as an Adaptive Device

There are several theories of life cycles of organizations and marketing networks. For instance, Greiner (1972) hypothesizes that companies as they grow go through a fixed sequence of problems needing different solutions in terms of corporate organization and controls. It is likely that such transitions and passages must also involve cultural changes to create "cultural fit" (Wilkins and Ouchi 1983). For instance, the culture "should" be different when the problems are in the area of efficient production as contrasted with the case of problems in establishing a functioning white-collar bureaucracy (Jones 1983).

Another adaptive function is the activities of interpreters placed strategically at the boundary between the network and its environment. The role of such interpreters, usually played by boundary persons (Adams 1976) such as agents in international business, is to bridge two or more cultures. Because of their sheer size, comprehensive marketing networks often have more profound impacts on external interest groups than do individual members of traditional channels. The network culture concept facilitates the bridging of management technologies with goals and social processes in the environment. The idea of organization development (French and Bell 1978) may be extended to network development, referring to the use of various intervention techniques by the channel captain to bring values and shared meanings in different parts of the networks in line with demands of the environment.

Culture as Strategic Underpinnings

The network culture notion may also be used as a framework for strategic management of interorganizational systems.

One implication, following the conclusion of Peters (1978) and Pfeffer (1981), is to view management as the task of creating, recreating, and changing meanings. This can be done through the systematic use of symbols. The idea of corporate identity can well be applied to interorganizational settings as "network identity.'' Such identity can then be achieved by the coordinated use of visual or oral symbols used in advertising and point-of-purchase communications, as exemplified by the network constituted by the McDonald and 7–11 franchise systems. Internally, identification with the network can be developed by using the special language of common promotion, budget, and control systems and in the unusual application of certain words and phrases. Another solution is ''visible leadership,'' implying that leaders should be seen and heard by as many employees as possible. One variant of this principle is management-by-walking-around. Mass communications channels may also be used, as dramatically demonstrated by Chrysler's Iacocca.

In synchronizing network strategy and network culture, it is not the relationship between strategy and structure that determines success, but the interactive nature of network strategy and network culture. Bourgeois and Jemison (1983) have proposed a multistep procedure for analyzing corporate culture in a strategic context. Though the authors have individual organizations in mind, their procedure seems also applicable in the area of interorganizational management. Applied in a workshop format for the top management of an unidentified Indonesian company, it started with a forecast of environmental trends and an analysis of industry and competition. The next step consisted of analyzing past and current strategies with a view to corporate strengths and weaknesses. In the third step, existing corporate cultures were identified by having participants develop lists of adjectives describing the perceived culture before the evidence or clues bearing on each cultural factor were marshalled. A fourth step called for developing strategic alternative courses of action. In this way, it was possible to locate mismatches between environmental trends and culture and between strategies and culture. The final result was a comprehensive plan for changes in culture, systems, and structure to facilitate strategy implementations.

If the notion of network cultures is to become a useful managerial tool, the problems relating to measuring and diagnosing such cultures need to be solved. This leads to the area of research on organizational cultures.

RESEARCH IMPLICATIONS

The metaphors emanating from the corporate culture tradition, such as ''myths,'' ''symbols,'' ''shared understandings,'' and ''ways of life,'' lead to necessary changes in research design. These involve alterations in the concepts researched, the time perspective of the study, and the degree of researcher involvement with the respondents.

The emphasis on subjective worlds and shared interpretations directs the attention to interpretive approaches to extract meaning from symbols or systems of signs employed. Barley (1983) has demonstrated the power of the area of semiotics (the study of signs or systems of signs) to understand the processes and impacts of events, behaviors, and objects in the context of funeral work. It is tempting to adapt this methodology to the study of communication and shared codes in interorganizational networks, such as channels of distribution.

The metaphors derived from the corporate culture tradition suggest research strategies different from the currently popular single-shot, cross-sectional surveys of network members. To examine the dynamics of processes, it is clear that longitudinal designs need more emphasis. Such analyses may make it easier to examine how network systems are developing and changing and to isolate the role of the various influential forces. An example is Pettigrew's longitudinal analysis of the social dramas associated with the leadership succession in a British school (1979).

To come closer to anthropological ways of data collection through participant observation, it is not only necessary for students of marketing networks to examine processes over time. It is also necessary that they become so much involved with the objects (persons or organizations studied) that they are able to describe in fairly accurate terms personal interpretations, values, meanings, and understandings in a phenomenological way. In the words of Malinowski (1922, p. 25), the role of the researcher is "to grasp the native's point of view, his relation to life, to realize his vision of his world." This, of course, would force the researcher to leave the convenient distance to the respondents and become a part of the process. Such involvement creates problems of objectivity and nonreproducible results. In some cases, unobtrusive methods such as documentary sources may be used (Pettigrew 1975, 1979).

CONCLUDING COMMENTS

This chapter has attempted to widen perspectives on marketing channels and other networks by merging two important research traditions: institutionalism in marketing and the developing corporate cultures tradition. Such a widening creates opportunities for incorporating new metaphors such as sagas, myths, rituals, and shared meanings as complements or challenges to existing formulations of the network flow paradigm in marketing. Network culture is envisioned as both product and process, a shaper as well as an outcome of human interaction within organizations and interorganizational systems. The notion of culture may be even more applicable for the analysis of interorganizational relations than the problems of behavior within individual organizations.

In several ways, networks may have properties similar to those of tribes and ethnic groups. For instance, in both a crucial function is boundary maintenance. Moreover, the boundary between the network and its environment canalizes behavior and social life. More often than not, the boundary is a subjective phenomenon defined by shared understandings, rather than being a legal matter. Inside marketing networks as well as ethnic groups, there may be considerable diversity and differentiation. The surface similarities may well attract researchers from social anthropology to the study of marketing phenomena. These similarities also challenge marketing academics to use anthropological approaches such as longitudinal case studies, participant observation, and semiotic analyses.

NOTE

1. Smircich (1983) furthermore defines a third stream of thought viewing culture as a projection of the mind's universal unconscious infrastructure, building on Levi–Straussian structuralism.

REFERENCES

Achrol, Ravi Singh, Torger Reve, and Louis W. Stern. 1983. "The Environment of Marketing Channel Dyads: A Framework for Comparative Analysis." *Journal of Marketing* 47 (Fall):55–67.

Adams, J. Stacy. 1976. "The Structure and Dynamics of Behavior in Organizational Boundary Roles." In *Handbook of Industrial and Organizational Psychology*, edited by Marvin D. Dunnette, pp. 1175–99. Chicago: Rand McNally.

Alderson, Wroe. 1957. *Marketing Behavior and Executive Action*. Homewood, IL: Richard D. Irwin.

Alderson, Wroe, and Reavis Cox. 1948. "Toward a Theory of Marketing." *Journal of Marketing* 13 (October):137–51.

Arndt, Johan. 1983. "The Political Economy Paradigm: Foundation for Theory Building in Marketing." *Journal of Marketing* 47 (Fall):44–54.

———. 1979. "Toward a Concept of Domesticated Markets." *Journal of Marketing* 43 (Fall):69–75.

———. 1978. "The Marketing Thinking of Tomorrow." In *Future Directions for Marketing* edited by George Fisk, Johan Arndt, and Kjell Gronhaug, pp. 4–27.

Bagozzi, Richard P. 1980. *Causal Models in Marketing*. New York: John Wiley & Sons.

———. 1978. "Marketing as Exchange: A Theory of Transactions in the Marketplace." *American Benavioral Scientist* 21 (March–April):535–56.

Barley, Stephen R. 1983. "Semiotics and the Study of Occupational and Organizational Cultures." *Administrative Science Quarterly* 28 (September):393–413.

Bartels, Robert. 1970. *Marketing Theory and Metatheory*. Homewood, IL: Richard D. Irwin.

Barth, Fredrik. 1969. "Introduction." In *Ethnic Groups and Boundaries*, edited by Fredrik Barth. Oslo: Universitetsforlaget.

Boddewyn, Jean J. 1981. "Comparative Marketing: The First Twenty-Five Years." *Journal of International Business Studies* 12 (Spring–Summer):61–79.

——. 1966. "A Construct for Comparative Marketing. *Journal of Marketing Research* 3 (May):49–53.

Bourgois, L. J., and David B. Jemison. 1982. "Analyzing Corporate Culture in Its Strategic Context." *Exchange: The Organizational Behavior and Teaching Journal* 7:37–41.

Buchanan, James A. 1964. "What Should Economists Do?" *Southern Economic Journal* 30:213–22.

Carman, James M. 1980. "Paradigms for Marketing Theory." In *Research in Marketing, Vol. 3*, edited by Jagdish N. Sheth, pp. 1–36. Greenwich, CT: JAI Press.

Deal, Terrence E., and Allan A. Kennedy. 1982. *Corporate Cultures: The Rites and Rituals of Corporate Life*. Reading, MA: Addison-Wesley.

Engel, James F., and Roger D. Blackwell. 1982. *Consumer Behavior*, 4th ed. New York: Dryden Press.

French, W. L., and C. H. Bell. 1978. *Organization Development*, 2nd ed. Englewood Cliffs, NJ: Prentice-Hall.

Geertz, Clifford. 1973. *The Interpretation of Cultures*. New York: Basic Books.

Gregory, Kathleen. 1983. "Native View Paradigms: Multiple Cultures and Culture Conflicts in Organizations." *Administrative Science Quarterly* 28 (September):359–76.

Greiner, Larry E. 1972. "Evolution and Revolution as Organizations Grow." *Harvard Business Review* 50 (July–August):37–46.

Hunt, Shelby D. 1976. "The Nature and Scope of Marketing." *Journal of Marketing* 40 (July):17–28.

Hakansson, Hakon, ed. 1982. *International Marketing and Purchasing of Industrial Goods*. Chichester: John Wiley & Sons.

Jelinek, Mariann, Linda Smircich, and Paul Hirsch. 1983. "Introduction: A Code of Many Colors." *Administrative Science Quarterly* 28 (September):331–38.

Johnston, Wesley J., and Thomas V. Bonama. 1977. "Reconceptualizing Industrial Buying Behavior." In *Contemporary Marketing Thought*, edited by Barnett A. Greenberg and Danny N. Bellenger, pp. 247–51. Chicago: American Marketing Association.

Jones, Gareth R. 1983. "Transaction Costs, Property Rights, and Organizational Culture: An Exchange Perspective." *Administrative Science Quarterly* 28 (September):454–67.

Katz, Elihu, and Paul F. Lazarsfeld. 1955. *Personal Influence*. New York: Free Press.

Keegan, Warren J. 1980. *Multinational Marketing Management*. Englewood Cliffs, NJ: Prentice-Hall.

Kotler, Philip. 1981. *Marketing for Nonprofit Organizations*, 2nd ed. Englewood Cliffs, NJ: Prentice-Hall.

——. 1967. *Marketing Management*. Englewood Cliffs, NJ: Prentice-Hall.

Kotler, Philip, and Sidney J. Levy. 1969. "Broadening the Concept of Marketing." *Journal of Marketing* 33 (January):10–15.

Levy, Sidney J. 1978. "Hunger and Work in a Civilized Tribe." *American Behavioral Scientist* 21 (March–April):557–70.

Malinowski, Bronislav. 1922. *Argonauts of the Western Pacific*. New York: Dutton.

Mattsson, Lars-Gunnar. 1985. "An Application of a Network Approach to Marketing—Defending and Changing Market Position." In *Changing the Course of Marketing*, edited by Nikhilesh Dholakia and Johan Arndt. Greenwich, CT: JAI Press.

McCarthy, E. Jerome. 1960. *Basic Marketing*. Homewood, IL: Richard D. Irwin.

McKitterick, J. B. 1957. "What Is the Marketing Concept?" In *The Frontiers of Marketing Thought and Science*, edited by Frank M. Bass, pp. 71–81. Chicago: American Marketing Association.

Ouchi, William G. 1981. *Theory Z*. Reading, MA: Addison-Wesley.

Pascale, Richard T., and Anthony G. Athos. 1981. *The Art of Japanese Management*. New York: Warner.

Peters, Thomas J. 1984. "Interview." *Harvard Business School Bulletin* April, 33.

———. 1978. "Symbols, Patterns and Settings: An Optimistic Case for Getting Things Done." *Organizational Dynamics* 7:3–23.

Peters, Thomas J., and Robert H. Waterman, Jr. 1982. *In Search of Excellence*. New York: Harper & Row.

Pettigrew, Andrew. 1979. "On Studying Organizational Cultures." *Administrative Science Quarterly* 24 (December):570–81.

———. 1975. "The Industrial Purchasing Decision as a Political Process." *European Journal of Marketing* 9 (March):4–19.

Pfeffer, Jeffrey. 1982. *Organizations and Organizations Theory*. Boston: Pittman.

———. 1981. "Management as Symbolic Action: The Creation and Maintenance of Organizational Paradigms." In *Research in Organizational Behavior, Vol. 3*, edited by Larry L. Cunnings and Barry M. Staw, pp. 1–52. Greenwich, CT: JAI Press.

Pondy, Louis R. 1978. "Leadership Is a Language Game." In *Leadership: Where Else Can We Go?* edited by Morgan W. McCall, Jr., and Michael M. Lombardo, pp. 87–99. Durham, NC: Duke University Press.

Reve, Torger. 1980. "Interorganizational Relations in Distribution Channels: An Empirical Study of Norwegian Distribution Channel Dyads," Unpublished Doctoral Dissertation. Evanston, IL: Northwestern University.

Stern, Louis W., and Adel I. El-Ansary. 1982. *Marketing Channels*, 2nd ed. Englewood Cliffs, NJ: Prentice-Hall.

Stern, Louis, W., and Torger Reve. 1980. "Distribution Channels as Political Economies: A Framework for Comparative Analysis." *Journal of Marketing* 44 (Summer):52–64.

Smircich, Linda. 1983. "Concepts of Culture and Organizational Analysis." *Administrative Science Quarterly* 28 (September):339–58.

Stidsen, Bent. 1979. "Directions in the Study of Marketing." In *Conceptual and Theoretical Developments and Marketing*, edited by O. C. Ferrell, Stephen W. Brown, and Charles W. Lamb, Jr., pp. 383–98. Chicago: American Marketing Association.

Tichy, Noel M., Michael L. Tushman, and Charles Fombrun. 1979. "Social Network Analysis for Organizations." *Academy of Management Review* 4:507–19.

Trice, Harrison M., and Janice Beyer. 1983. "The Ceremonial Effect: Manifest Function and Latent Dysfunction in Dynamic Organization." Paper presented at the Conference of Myths, Symbols, and Folklore: Expanding the Analysis of Organizations, University of Claifornia, Los Angeles.

Uttal, Bro. 1983. "The Corporate Culture Vultures." *Fortune* 110 (October 17):66–72.

Wamsley, Gary L., and Mayer N. Zald. 1976. *The Political Economy of Public Organi-*

zations. Bloomington, Indiana University Press.

White, I.A. 1959. *The Science of Culture*. New York: Farrar, Strauss & Giroux.

Wilkins, Alan L., and William G. Ouchi. 1983. "Efficient Cultures: Exploring the Relationship Between Culture and Organizational Performance." *Administrative Science Quarterly* 28 (September):468–81.

Williamson, Oliver E. 1975. *Markets and Hierarchies: Analysis and Antitrust Implications*. New York: Free Press.

Winick, Charles. 1961. "Anthropology's Contribution to Marketing." *Journal of Marketing* 25 (July):53–60.

Zald, Mayer N. 1970. "Political Economy: A Framework for Comparative Analysis." In *Power in Organizations*, edited by Mayer N. Zald, pp. 221–61. Nashville, TN: Vanderbilt University Press.

CHAPTER 9

Distribution in a High-Level Economy: Twenty Years After

CHARLES S. GOODMAN

When it appeared in 1965, *Distribution in a High-Level Economy*, on which Tom Fichandler and I assisted Professor Cox, the more significant reviews were clearly mixed. While Charles Collazzo (*Journal of Marketing*, October 1965) was highly favorable and Harold Barger (*Journal of Marketing Research*, May 1966) favorable but with a few reservations, David Revzan (*Journal of Business*, 1966, pp. 413–17) was highly critical on a number of counts.

Absent a more recent comprehensive attempt to measure the nature, aggregate contribution, and cost of distribution in the United States, it seems appropriate now to look back to see what we and our critics did not foresee. With the benefit of hindsight, how well–poorly did we do? Where should macromarketers go in advancing understanding and measurement of the total system?

The reader should be forewarned that in attempting to review–assess our work of two decades ago, the present author is not an unbiased observer and the positions and observations herein might well be viewed as self-serving.

Any contribution that *Distribution in a High-Level Economy* may have made to the marketing literature of the 1960s would seem to lie in three areas:

1. Measurement of the role of and costs imposed–value added by the distribution system and its components
2. Concept building: adding to the understanding of marketing phenomena and relationships, including explanation of trends or suggesting ways of perceiving of or thinking about marketing phenomena (for example, suggesting relationships from which others might construct more formal theories—this was not intended to be a theory book)
3. Appraisal of the social performance of marketing

MEASUREMENT OF THE ROLE AND COSTS IMPOSED-VALUE ADDED BY THE DISTRIBUTION SYSTEM AND ITS COMPONENTS

Our measurement of the contribution of the distribution industries (Chapter 8) and of distribution activities (Chapters 9 and 10) and the construction of the flow charts were developed largely from the Bureau of Labor Statistics (BLS) interindustry relations (input–output) study using 1947 data. Distribution industries were defined broadly to encompass the support industries such as transportation and storage in addition to retail and wholesale trade. This provided an aggregative approach not available to the authors of the earlier 1939 study (Stewart and Dewhurst, with the assistance of Field, *Does Distribution Cost Too Much?*), who had to rely on piecing together data from the 1929 census and numerous other sources to make aggregate estimates for that year. When in Chapter 9 we extended our study from the measurement of distribution industries to embrace also the distribution activities of other industries such as farmers and manufacturers, we, too, had to rely on diverse ratio-type measures.

Professor Revzan was unhappy that we failed to attribute differences between our results using 1947 data and the earlier study to trends rather than methodology and that we failed to use later data. Although it would have been nice to use later data, unfortunately the 1947 input–output data were the most recent available at the time the study was undertaken. To this writer's knowledge, no one has made similar estimates for the United States for any more recent year based on input–output data. Our study did, however, become the basis for the work by Layton (1980, 1981a, 1984) in developing trade flow tables for Australia and his continuing efforts to develop both longitudinal data for Australia and cross-country comparisons. The time may well be ripe for a new attempt to measure the global role of distribution, especially with so much current attention to the service sector, and for substantial attempts to make comparisons across economies despite the enormous problems arising from data inadequacies.

Other Attempts to Measure Distribution Costs

Some scholars have attempted to measure the total costs of distribution activities, while still others have been concerned with the margins of the distribution industries alone, commonly just retailing and wholesaling.

MEASUREMENT OF DISTRIBUTION ACTIVITIES

Paul Converse, drawing on data from the 1929 Censuses of Manufactures and Distribution and a myriad of other sources, estimated that production created 47.8 percent of total value produced by the economy in that year while marketing created 52.2 percent. Converse developed his estimate by first determining the value of products of various sectors and then using available data to estimate the proportions of such product value that represented "production" and "distribution" costs. Thus, he estimated that marketing costs represented 10 percent of the value of product for coal and other mineral products in 1929 (Converse and Huegy 1940, p. 817; 1946, p. 693). Converse made a similar estimate of 15 percent for manufacturers for 1929 (1940, p. 818), but he subsequently reduced this to 10 percent based on a variety of studies of costs for advertising and other selling expenses and allocating an estimated portion of general and administrative costs (Converse and Huegy 1946, p. 694). Similar estimates were made for the marketing content of farming, fishing, and the other "production" sectors.

For 1939, Converse's corresponding figures were 49.5 percent and 50.5 percent and for 1948 51.9 percent and 48.1 percent. Converse warns the reader, however, that these differences are more likely the result of improved estimating procedures than reflective of real changes. Indeed, in the 1952 edition (Converse, Huegy, and Mitchell), he revises his 1929 estimate for distribution's share downward from 52.2 to 49.2 percent.

Perhaps the most widely cited early study of distribution costs was that by Stewart Dewhurst, with the assistance of Field, *Does Distribution Cost Too Much?* (1939), which, like Converse's study, drew heavily on 1929 data. Stewart, and Dewhurst, and Field used national aggregates of gross sales by industry and census data on distribution of manufacturers' sales as starting points but, lacking the kind of interindustry analysis that was not available until the 1950s, had to rely very heavily on ratios of one sort or another to determine the distribution content embodied in various dollar transaction aggregates.

As part of an attempt to measure productivity in marketing and productivity changes over time, Bucklin (1975) used value added to determine the proportions that each of the six sectors that perform most of the marketing work contribute to total value added by marketing. The study was confined to commodities, exclusive of construction materials. He concluded that the two trade sectors contributed 72 percent of the total value added in 1967, up from 67 percent in 1948, as shown in Table 9.1. The most noteworthy changes over this period are the growing role of wholesaling as a proportion both of the trade sector and of the total and the declining relative role of transportation.

MEASUREMENT OF THE DISTRIBUTION INDUSTRIES

The costs incurred or value added by the distribution industries narrowly defined to encompass only wholesaling and retailing presents fewer problems. Thus, by limiting his study to consumers' goods and defining distribution as consisting solely of retailers and those wholesalers who sold to retailers, Barger (1955) was able to make reasonable estimates of the role of distribution in the economy over the period 1869–1948.

More recently, Bucklin (1970) used national accounts data to derive a dis-

TABLE 9.1 Value Added in Marketing of Commodities Exclusive of Construction Materials by Major Contributing Industries, in 1948 and 1967

Industry	Percentage of Value Added by Marketing	
	1948	1967
Retailing	45.1	46.0
Wholesaling	22.1	26.3
Transportation	19.7	14.1
Manufacturing	11.8	12.3
Minerals	0.5	0.3
Advertising	0.7	1.0
	100.0%	100.0%

Source: Louis P. Bucklin, "A Synthetic Index of Marketing Productivity," *Proceedings of the 58th International Conference of the American Marketing Association,* April 1975, pp. 556–60.

tributive trade cost ratio, which relates value added (at factor costs) by wholesalers and retailers to total value added in the economy, exclusive of the finance, services, and government sectors and adjusted for exports. If his results (pp. 17–18) are adjusted to remove the effects of the war years, distributive trade costs do appear, as Barger indicated earlier, to be remarkably stable over long periods of time. Bucklin's data also confirm our observation in Chapter 4 of the growing role of wholesalers, a phenomenon that has been continuing at least since 1929, Wholesale trade, measured in terms of national income originated, represented only 35 percent of the total wholesale and retail trade contribution in 1954. This had grown to 38 percent by 1967 and represented more than 42 percent in 1982 (Figure 9.1).

Problems with Ratio Analyses

Ratio analysis is relatively straightforward in dealing with distribution institutions such as retailers and wholesalers where gross margins can either be used as a measure of distribution cost or be adjusted by deducting costs of purchased supplies, fuels, etc., to create a value-added figure similar to that used in calculating value added in manufacturing. There are, unfortunately, a number of problems associated with the use of ratios to determine changes in aggregate marketing costs–value added over time or between economies.

One set of problems concerns the availability of relevant and consistent data. Such general sources of data on income and expenses as Internal Revenue Service *Statistics of Income,* the Censuses of Manufactures, Mining, and Business, the consolidated income statement reports available from organizations such as

FIGURE 9.1   National Income Originated by Wholesale Trade

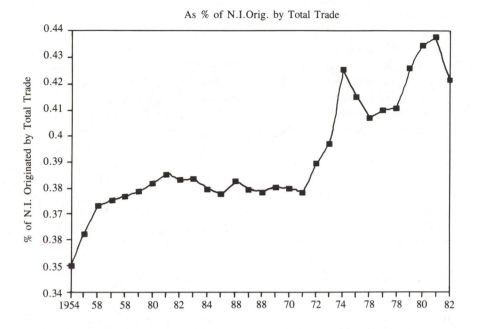

As % of N.I.Orig. by Total Trade

Robert Morris Associates, the various income statement statistics collected by trade groups, and the annual statements of corporations do not provide data in a form that identifies distribution costs as such. We can frequently obtain data for some categories such as advertising or bad debts, but rarely for the full range of costs. Thus, we are forced to assemble data piecemeal. Studies sometimes provide data for one function for one or more industries at one point of time. Rarely, if ever, are they available over a broad set of industries or over time. To fill the needed gaps, we fall back on often crude estimates or heroic assumptions that a relationship observed at some time in the past still holds. For example, even if one identifies vegetable farmers' marketing costs (for example, transporting goods in their own trucks) from a particular study, one can make only (often crude) judgments as to the extent that the numbers will apply to other types of farms or to the same type at a later date.

Over the years, the data available for ratio estimates have improved as more studies and statistical sources have become available. But these improvements themselves create problems of comparability over time. In Chapters 9 and 10 of *Distribution in a High-Level Economy*, we sought to go beyond measuring value added by the distribution *industries* to the broader and socially more relevant issue of value added by distribution *activities*, by whomever performed. Like our predecessors, we were forced to rely on ratio-type analyses for many of our inputs. We developed our estimates for 1954 to obtain maximum comparability, given the data problems, with Converse's most recent figure of 48.1 percent for 1948. We calculated that marketing accounted for 45.3 percent of the cost of producing and distributing goods in 1954. Using the best available data, we calculated marketing's share as 46.3 percent for 1958, the next census year. We found, however, that newer data, additional adjustments, and refined concepts and data collection methods *used by the underlying sources* made accurate comparisons over time risky.In fact, a revision of 1958 data estimates to 1954 concepts would have increased the 1958 value added by marketing by roughly two percentage points. An effort to develop a recent measure based on an updating of 1958 data revealed that some of the data are no longer available and that others would require significant adjustment even to approach comparability.

In sum, and especially because the distribution share seems itself so stable, the estimating errors in studies heavily dependent on ratio analysis make it difficult if not impossible to isolate real changes in aggregate value added by distribution. Analysis derived primarily from input–output data as used to measure the role of distribution industries in *Distribution in a High-Level Economy* and in Layton's work would appear to be a more fruitful direction. Ratios will probably still be needed to estimate the internal distribution activities of other firms.

Other Problems Involved in Evaluating Changes in the Role and Performance of Distribution

In addition to the problems of measuring the role of distribution or the performance of institutions across time periods (or countries), there are a number of problems in interpreting any results. These arise because of possible changes in (1) the product mix within individual institutions (for example, stores), (2) the mix of stores in the economy, and (3) changes in the real output of distribution institutions and the distribution system.

1. Innovative forms of retailing may start as short-line operations concentrating on volume. As competition squeezes profits and/or as opportunities appear, items carrying higher margins are added. These are likely to entail higher operating costs. The higher gross margin does not mean that distribution costs for particular products or services have increased, but merely that the product mix has changed in the particular store. An undetermined portion of the increase in gross margins and operating expense of supermarkets in recent years is believed to be the result of adding more higher-margin, slower-turn items.
2. Even if all stores maintain their gross margins and operating ratios, the aggregates for the economy will change as the mix of stores changes, reflected in the mix of goods bought by consumers. Thus, if average operating expenses of wholesale merchants increase (Bucklin 1970, p. 19), this might signify lower productivity. But alternatively it may simply reflect the fact that an increasing share of wholesale trade is in support of industrial and institutional customers, segments

that require relatively high levels of services, rather than in support of retailers, which tends to be a more routinized, lower-cost operation.

3. The difficulty of measuring *the real output* of distribution poses an even more difficult problem. It is not unusual for studies of distribution costs to note the fact that consumers may perform such duties as selecting merchandise from shelves, carrying it home, etc. Some have noted that a portion of the decline in margins in food retailing, for example, may be attributed to the consumer foregoing credit, delivery, or clerk service. But we have yet to measure the *real service output* of a store, much less the system. Suppose, for example, that a retailing store or entire sector (a) installs self-service, (b) triples assortments offered consumers, and (c) changes operating hours to those that customers find more suitable. At least the last two changes, and quite possibly the first as well, represent clear increases in the service output of the system, but unless margins are increased it will not be reflected in our measure of value added. We may, in fact, have a Marshallian consumer surplus, which we conveniently ignore. If the entire industry in a market adapts, consumers may in fact receive more service, but our measures will not detect it. Or, take the converse: A category of stores maintains its margin but reduces the *value of service* provided customers by providing only indifferent clerks, and inconvenient locations and hours. Again, we have no measure, although one would expect that, given time and absent governmental protections of established firms, consumers would shift patronage and thus eliminate such institutions. Rather, we assume that market-determined value added is the appropriate proxy. This is not a trivial problem. One may regard retailing as primarily a service business in which the merchandise itself is no more than an ingredient waiting to be converted to a total product that embraces the total of the retailer's offering. This is obvious in eating places in which ambience is an ingredient often more potent than the physical ingredients on the customer's plate. A valid measure of output must recognize the total of what the consumer receives. Is the concept any less relevant for other retailers?

Lacking measures of the real output of institutions and of the system, we have, of course, no benchmark from which to measure changes.

CONCEPT BUILDING

Regarding concept building, I believe we have a fundamental difference of viewpoint with Professor Revzan and possibly more generally with those who seek to view marketing phenomena as applied economics, frequently in the context of received, often neoclassical, economic doctrine. In his review, Professor Revzan refers to our failure to use available theoretical materials. Although he does not cite examples of material he had in mind, his references to "the vast theoretical and location-applied locational studies" and to studies of price determination and price-making efficiency, his concern with our failure to distinguish organized from nonorganized wholesale markets, and his thrust to treat market contacts largely in terms of price determination and price-making efficiency suggest that he is tied to that neoclassical thought that views products as desirably homogeneous and physical presence as the important element in price-making efficiency, thus confining the risk of insufficient information to price elements alone.

Our view, in contrast, was, and remains, that marketing theory is best advanced in the A–B–C (Alderson–Breyer–Cox) basically inductive tradition of attempting to infer relationships from observation in the marketplace and in the behavior of marketing and other social systems and of the individuals and organisms composing them.

Most of the concepts relevant to modern marketing theory come not from neoclassical economics but initially from Breyer and extensions by Alderson. In *The Marketing Institution* (1934), Breyer defined a market as "such potentialities as compose an opportunity for the purchase or sale of goods" (p. 54). He recognized the heterogeneity of both buyers and sellers, noting that each producer is somewhat different even from others producing the same product (p. 57), although it remained for Alderson more than two decades later to introduce the concept of niche.

Breyer seems also to have adopted an Austrian, as opposed to neoclassical, view of competition: "Each [producer] desires to outstrip their associates by producing such products as will gain them *maximum* returns. At the same time (buyers) desire to get the *maximum* from their purchases. So there follows constant competition to *discern, create, and realize upon* the best opportunities to buy and sell" (p. 65, emphasis added). Although Schumpeter had pointed out many years earlier that the competition that really matters to society is innovative competition that threatens or destroys the old, it is unlikely that Breyer was familiar with his work, which was little read in the United States until later and considered outside the mainstream by U.S. economists who then, as today, fall largely within the neoclassical tradition of viewing competition in terms of an ideally static, perfectly homogeneous world.

It remained for Alderson, raised in the institutionalist rather than the neoclassical tradition, to recognize differential advantage as a market phenomenon and thus provide an explanation of market behavior. In the Aldersonian tradition, differential advantage arises from superior perception of opportunities in discrepant markets. This contrasts with the neoclassical view that conceives of differential advantage in terms of production costs or in terms of Chamberlin's "selling costs."

In seeking to develop marketing theory inductively, Breyer was also well ahead of his colleagues in observing the role of the marketing function in determining product strategy and developing new products: "The marketing institution is charged with initiating the development of better products" (p. 75).

Developments since 1965 increasingly support our view. The Aldersonian view "that the market process can only be understood in terms of choice and perception of opportunity" (Reekie and Savitt 1982) has been increasingly recognized. Marketing has drawn increasingly on the behavioral disciplines. We study, rather than make deductive assumptions about, not only consumer behavior but the behavior of channels and channel members and industrial and other organizations and their components. Research has moved increasingly to the formulation and testing of models that are basically inductive, rather than deductive. We have been freed, at long last, from the chains by which many of us were bound by our early training as economists examining "applied economics."

Distribution in a High-Level Economy was more closely related to such basically Aldersonian concepts as the role of organized behavior systems, the heterogeneity of wants and resources, and the central role of sorting functions in the marketplace. We did not, however, anticipate Alderson's notion of discrepant markets cleared by innovation.

Nothing that has developed in the last two decades has changed this writer's view that Aldersonian concepts provide a more valid basis for constructing theory than neoclassical economic doctrine with its perspective of a static world of (ideally) homogeneous wants, universally free information, and rigid behaviors.[1] Modern economists, such as Liebstein, Baumol, Williamson, von Mises, and the other Austrians, have moved away from these restrictions in the direction of a broader view. They have modified their concepts to reflect work in the behavioral and organizational sciences and the greater role now possible for statistical inference and hypothesis testing. Many economics texts, however, continue to ignore the roles of information and innovation rather than price as the central clearing mechanism, ignore or downplay the role of value to the user in determining price and ultimately costs, and regard consumption and supply uniformity (the so-called "ideal" of perfect competition) rather than user benefit in appraising social performance.

The idea of buyers as active rather than passive participants in searching both for information and for solutions was well understood by marketing theorists prior to 1965 (Breyer 1934; Alderson 1957; Bauer 1960). We attempted to add to this flow of thought through the examination of the role of cities as aids to collection of a standard of living. This view contrasted with the more traditional locational studies of that time, which tended to be tied either to neoclassical locational economists such as Alfred Weber or to location-of-industry concepts that recognized a balancing of supply and market considerations in industrial location. Except for the work by Mitchell and Rapkin (1954), these studies tended to take the market as given and did not see it primarily from the buyer's perspective. Even the work of city planners up to that period tended to downplay the value to consumers of such amenities as a wide selection of goods and resources. Public housing and other publicly planned housing developments provided overly restrictive commercial choices in such communities. Even Dewhurst (Stewart and Dewhurst, with the assistance of Field 1939) complained that consumers had too much choice. Professor Cox's notion of efficient congestion, though introduced earlier (1959), was extended in *Distribution in a High-Level Economy*. In retrospect, we might well have carried the notion further and indicated its ramifications for marketing structure and urban planning.

In any event, this is a different direction from that suggested by the reviewer who had hoped for a more traditional approach. The increasing customer orientation of retail developments and the difficulties of many well-intentioned planners who substituted supply-dominated criteria in projects in recent years would seem to support our view that meaningful understanding of urban development must devote considerably more emphasis to the cities' role as source of supply of goods and services and rather less on their more narrowly defined production functions.

That the role of searching and sorting is critical is surely demonstrated by structural developments in the last 20 years. One notes, for example, the growing role of trade shows and the continuing growth of wholesale firms and establishments as buyers find these increasingly more effective as supply sources in a world of growing information needs. The latter in turn has been brought about by the greater variety of products available from a world economy and rapid rates of change in what is, or could be made, available. This is especially true in the industrial sectors, so that the growing role of intermediaries in serving these markets is not surprising.

Professor Revzan was unhappy that we focused on final demand and did not devote separate treatment to industrial marketing. But a macro study must concern itself with the support of final, not intermediate, demand. We reported market value added by various industry segments to both household purchases and total final demand. In view of the increased interest in industrial marketing, it might be useful in future studies to also calculate value added by various industry segments to private nonhousehold capital formation.

APPRAISAL OF SOCIAL PERFORMANCE

We proposed that appropriate tests of social performance were efficiency, fairness, and consumers' orientation. Our treatment of the efficiency problem attempted to use an engineering-like output–input notion of efficiency. It focused on the difficulties of measuring output when the real output of distribution systems consists of services rather than the goods being distributed. This makes it difficult to determine whether a system with fewer stores, for example, would be more efficient. We know it would use fewer resource inputs; we do not know how the service outputs (consumer benefits) would be altered.

A similar type of problem is involved in determining socially desirable levels of consumer choice. Among Dewhurst's recommendations (Stewart and Dewhurst, with the assistance of Field 1939) was the reduction in the number of brands on the market, a position taken by those who advocate restrictions on supermarket size in inner cities on the grounds that inner city consumers ("they") do not need so many brands and varieties from which to choose. The underlying premise behind these positions seems to rest on neoclassical econonics assumptions that product homogeneity as postulated in the purely competitive model, rather than product diversity, is a desirable economic–social goal. Rarely, if ever, do such advocates attempt to determine if consumers, the supposed beneficiaries, would prefer such limitations. Concerns related by inner city consumers about inadequate choice in local stores would suggest quite the contrary. In the light of increased emphasis today on "quality-of-life" factors and on individual preferences and prerogatives, the notion that social ends are best achieved by moving away from market-determined assortment breadths to administratively imposed ones seems even more dubious now than in 1965.

We also noted the difficult conceptual problems involved in trying to improve the buying efficiency of consumers without introducing compulsions that adversely affect those to be helped. We noted that regulatory attempts to provide an "efficient" system with the "right" numbers of supply sources selling at the "correct" prices tend to result in a system that reduces both efficiency and consumer welfare, citing the highly regulated milk industry as an example. We observed that the few studies of efficiency from a social perspective to that time had seriously flawed output and, macroeconomic concepts (Galbraith and Halton 1955) or were limited to productivity studies of retailers and wholesalers. Barger's study of the latter (1955) indicated rising productivity in distribution over time but at a rate slower than that in manufacturing and agriculture. Thus, sound judgments about either the level of efficiency in distribution or changes over time could be partial at best.

Revzan was disappointed that we did not compare efficiencies of alternative channels and did not deal with price-making efficiency (neoclassical microeconomics again!), although he makes no mention of what now appears a more significant shortcoming, our failure to give greater attention to information provision efficiency. As marketing is essentially an *information-sorting* as well as a *goods-sorting* process, this would have been a more cogent critique.

Barger (1966, p. 202) was concerned that, with respect to advertising as a tool of interbrand competition, "Madison Avenue brain power...often just has no social product at all." Unless we are able to separate that portion of the advertising effect that is useful for the buyer in making judgments, not only about the relative worth of various brands but also about the worth of various aspects of his or her life-style, from those portions that contain no meaningful content for the viewer, it is difficult to evaluate this statement. Suffice it to say that advances in consumer behavior and advertising research suggest that the problem is much more difficult than the critics have suggested.

Revzan's point that we should not have confined our treatment of "unfairness" to the complaints of farmers may be well taken. In today's social milieu, we should probably want to consider whether the system is unfair to ghetto residents, various minorities, women, or some special interest group. The conceptual and basically ethical problem of determining what is "unfair" as well as the very substantial problems of measurement remain. Is it unfair to charge airport users more for coin box phone calls than inner city residents?

On one issue both the critics and ourselves made a common error: We failed to fully grasp the great difficulties of using government to deal effectively with the problems of improving social performance. Many of the interventions designed to improve social performance and eliminate abuses over the last two decades have been disappointing and in some cases counterproductive. Only in part does this represent the old problem of the regulators being influenced by the regulated. We understand now that regulators have a life and goals of their own, quite apart from the nominal beneficiaries of regulation. As the goal of the businessperson is maximum profits while, it is hoped, providing society with useful goods and services, so the agencies of the state seek to maximize their power while, it is hoped, providing constructive regulation. Like our contemporaries interested in improving the social performance of marketing, we tended to think that the regulatory process suffered from insufficient scope, power, and funding. Although one of our reviewers thought we should have made recommendations in this area, we did not do so because of the difficulties of specifying unambiguous regulatory goals and effective regulatory means. With the greater understanding of the regulatory process and the development of theories of regulation in recent years, perhaps we underestimated these difficulties.

In addition to the costs of regulation and restrictions on consumer freedom of choice, Venkatesh and Burger (1984) note that regulators have their own interests, which may conflict with consumers' interests. Mitchell (1977) is even more pessimistic. He classifies theories of regulation into three categories:

(1) Public interest theories, which assert that industries are regulated to compensate for the shortcomings of non-competitive markets; (2) producer-protection theories, which argue that regulations are designed by and operated for the benefit of producers; and (3)...the transfer theory, which says that regulation merely serves to take money from one group of citizens and give it to another group of citizens, the latter obviously being the more politically effective group.

The gist of recent research is that the public interest theory is contradicted by most of the common features of regulation. The theory that has been taught to generations of students, especially lawyers, does the most violence to reality. Most regulated industries were not monopolistic until after they were regulated. And regulatory commissions make decisions on grounds that have little if anything to do with stimulating competitive markets. A look at the history of the railroad, trucking, and airline industries is enough to shake anyone's confidence in the public interest view. Add to these state and local regulation of taxicabs, medicine, barbering and numerous service industries and the public interest theory is devastated.

Probably the main reason for the recent popularity among economists of the producer-protection view is that all of the industries...cited obtained regulation that was clearly designed to create cartels. But this theory is still too simple. Many special consumer groups have also benefited, such as rail passengers who travel at a fraction of costs, small remote towns that receive better airline service than they would under competition.... The more general transfer theory seems to be the better of the two "realistic" theories. The political process, in the form of regulation, intervenes in the economy for the purpose of transferring wealth.

A recent example of this process is the allocation of gasoline supplies during the Carter administration away from low-margin self-service retailers to higher-margin operators who had politically effective trade organizations in many states, political immunity from antitrust prosecution, and a strong and successful interest in using shortages to increase trade margins. Where allocation rules did not fully protect higher-margin operators, direct action was sometimes used. Thus, Standard Oil (Ohio) was ordered to increase prices by nine cents per gallon during the shortage period to prevent that company from using lower prices to increase market share.

CONCLUSIONS

1. Despite the difficulties with their use, global input–output matrices probably remain the most effective way to measure the aggregate contribution of the Distribution industries. Despite their substantial infirmities, it probably will continue to be necessary to use ratios of one sort or another to estimate the distribution contributions of the other economic sectors.

2. The need to develop theory about how markets and the actors in those markets do, in fact, operate using basically inductive and empirical methods continues to be great. The greater accord now being given to the views of Austrian, as contrasted with neoclassical, economics suggests that working with these economists and their concepts may prove beneficial to both marketing scholars and economists. Perhaps someday even U.S. economists will expose their students to the role of innovation and the nature of entrepreneurship as first expressed by Schumpeter more than 70 years ago and carried forward by modern Austrian economists.

3. Recognizing that there are many points at which corrective action to improve social performance seems to be needed, how does society take actions in the social interest that will have a good chance of achieving the desired, and not an opposing, result? Experimentation would appear to offer one avenue. But this is made difficult by the observed problems of aborting programs and regulations that fail to have the desired effect or are even harmful. An example is the strong

opposition of labor unions and activist groups to updating interest rate ceilings in some states when the existing ceilings had driven banks and other relatively low-rate lenders from the market. Keeping the legal rates well below the market level rather than protecting consumers, as alleged by their advocates, forced consumers to resort to the personal finance companies with their much higher rates, to loan sharks, or to doing without credit. A more recent example is the almost ideological opposition of alleged consumer interest groups to the restoration of competitive markets and competitive pricing in energy products, especially the almost fanatical clinging to a control system that was clearly harming consumers and preventing both efficient resource utilization and lower prices.

Thus, we are left with the unresolved question: What can be done to impact the system to improve social performance in view of all of the goal determination, operational, measurement, and political problems? In *Distribution in a High-Level Economy*, we were cautious—too cautious for at least one reviewer who had hoped for legislative recommendations. The greater understanding of the regulatory process that has emerged in recent years suggests that our caution was well justified. Happily, effectiveness and other performance issues are being addressed from increasingly broad conceptual perspectives, as this volume attests.

NOTES

1. For a discussion of the relationship of Alderson's discrepant markets to modern Austrian concepts of entrepreneurship, see Reekie and Savitt (1982).

REFERENCES

Alderson, Wroe. 1965. *Dynamic Marketing Behavior*. Homewood, IL: Richard D. Irwin.

———. 1957. *Marketing Behavior and Executive Action*. Homewood, IL: Richard D. Irwin.

Barger, Harold. 1955. *Distribution's Place in the American Economy Since 1869*. Princeton, NJ: Princeton University Press.

———. 1966. "Distribution in A High Level Economy: A Review Article." *Journal of Marketing Research* 3 (May) 202.

Bauer, Raymond A. 1960. "Consumer Behavior as Risk Taking." In *Proceedings of the 43rd National Conference of the American Marketing Association*. June, pp. 389–98.

Breyer, Ralph. 1934. *The Marketing Institution*. New York: McGraw-Hill.

Bucklin, Louis. P. 1975. "A Synthetic Index of Marketing Productivity." In *Proceedings of the 58th International Conference of the American Marketing Association*, April, pp. 556–60.

———. 1970. "National Income Accounting and Distributive Trade Cost." *Journal of Marketing* 34 (April):14–22.

Converse, Paul D., and Harvey W. Huegy. 1940. *Elements of Marketing*, 2nd rev. ed. New York: Prentice-Hall.

———. 1946. *Elements of Marketing*, 3rd ed. New York: Prentice-Hall.

Converse, Paul D., Harvey W. Huegy, and Robert V. Mitchell. 1952. *Elements of Marketing* 23 (April):355–62.

Cox, Reavis, Charles S. Goodman, and Thomas C. Fichandler. 1965. *Distribution in a High-Level Economy*. Englewood Cliffs, NJ: Prentice-Hall.

Galbraith, J. K., and R. H. Holton. 1955. *Marketing Efficiency in Puerto Rico*. Cambridge, MA: Harvard University Press.

Layton, Roger A. 1984. "Trade Flows in Australia, 1974–75, An Assessment of Structural Change." *Journal of Macromarketing* 4 (Spring):62–73.

———. 1981a. "Trade Flows in Macromarketing Systems: Part I. A Macromodel of Trade Flows." *Journal of Macromarketing* 1 (Spring):35–48.

———. 1981b. "Trade Flows in Macromarketing Systems: Part II. Transforming Input-Output Tables into Trade Flow Tables." *Journal of Macromarketing* 1 (Fall):48–55.

———. 1980. *Trade Flow Models in a Developing Regional Economy—A Case Study in Java*. Sydney: School of Marketing, University of New South Wales.

Mitchell, Edward J. 1977. "Energy and Regulation." *Dividend* 8 (Winter):15–17.

Mitchell, Robert B., and Chester Rapkin. 1954. *Urban Traffic: A Function of Land Use*. New York: Columbia University Press.

Reekie, W. Duncan, and Ronald Savitt. 1982. "Marketing Behavior and Entrepreneurship: A Synthesis of Alderson and Austrian Economics." *European Journal of Marketing* 16:55–66.

Revzan, David A. 1966. "Distribution in a High-Level Economy: A Review Article." *Journal of Business* 39:413–17.

Schumpeter, Joseph A. 1942. *Capitalism, Socialism and Democracy*. New York: Harper & Bros.

———. 1911. *Theorie der Wirtschaftlicher Entwicklung*, trans. by Redversch Opie (1934) as *The Theory of Economic Development*. Cambridge, MA: Harvard University Press.

Stewart, P. W., J. F. Dewhurst, with the assistance of L. Field. 1939. *Does Distribution Cost Too Much?* New York: Twentieth Century Fund.

Venkatesh, Alladi, and Philip C. Burger. 1984. "Toward an Integrated Theory of Consumer Regulation." *Journal of Macromarketing* 4 (Spring):29–40.

CHAPTER 10

Modeling Trade Flows
in a Developing Region

ROGER A. LAYTON

The study of trade or transaction flows in a macromarketing system has its origin in work by Cox and his colleagues (1965), describing the U.S. economy in 1947. Beginning with the 1947 Inter-Industries Study, Cox, Goodman, and Fichandler were able to estimate the dollar size of transaction flows between major sectors in the U.S. economy for that year. These flows were considerably larger in size than those shown in the corresponding input–output table; as these authors note, "For every dollar's worth of final sales to final buyers, the distributive mechanism had to arrange and carry out almost two dollars of intermediate purchases and sales" (p. 40).

More recently, a group of scholars at Michigan State University began to model urban food-marketing systems in Latin America. As Slater et al. (1979) note, this work in the late 1960s "was an effort to better understand the role of marketing and distribution in the development process as well as explore the impact of modernization of food marketing channels upon development." (p. 3). Emerging from these pioneering studies were simulation models "designed initially to assess tradeoffs between food marketing modernization and the displacement of labour employed, but underutilized in the traditional food marketing system" (p. 3).

Beginning in 1972, this effort in simulating flows in marketing systems was extended to describe the economic and social processes of development in Kenya and elsewhere, leading to the detailed SIMSIM model set out by Slater et al. (1979).

In parallel with this work in simulation modeling, Slater and his colleagues introduced and refined techniques in channel mapping that not only provided the data for many of the parameter estimates required by the simulation models, but also generated detailed qualitative and quantitative insights into the way channels worked in practice in the communities being studied.

The channel mapping methodology developed by Slater et al. and reported in the publications of the Latin American Marketing Project was used as a starting point for a series of social surveys covering households, retailers, wholesalers, and manufacturers, undertaken by Layton, Layton, and Western (1975), in Central Java in 1974, as part of an Australian government aid program to Indonesia. This work provided the empirical base for the trade flows model described later in this chapter.

In 1980, Layton (1980, 1981a), working with combined censuses of manufacturing, retailing, and wholesaling and with detailed input–output tables, all relating to Australia in 1968–69, was able to estimate a trade flows table with a sector structure very similar to that used by Cox, Goodman, and Fichandler (1965) for the U.S. economy in 1947. He went on to suggest a simple linear equation set that could be used to transform an input–output table into a trade flows table, assuming that the underlying structure of the marketing or distribution system as reflected in the coefficients of the transformation equations remains unchanged. This opened up the possibility of exploring the effect of change in the structure of industries, in technology (as reflected in the input–output coefficients), and in final demand patterns through a trade flows table.

In the present essay, the extended channel-mapping program undertaken in Indonesia in 1974 is used to develop estimates of input–output and trade flow tables for a region of Central Java. These tables are then used to explore the implications of possible development options for the traditional and modern components of the production and distribution sectors. In this context, the structure of the underlying model provides a framework for integrated regional economic and marketing systems planning, and the empirical work illustrates the methodology needed to turn the theoretical framework into an effective, data-based planning tool.

THE CILACAP REGION OF CENTRAL JAVA

Central Java is a low-income province in the Indonesian island of Java. For some years prior to 1974, the Australian government had been providing aid to the province in the form of river, harbor, and industrial estate development programs. Much of this work centered on the port town of Cilacap on the southern side of Java, and it was here that the social surveys were carried out that provided an empirical base for the trade flows modeling. In particular, it was proposed that an industrial estate be established in Cilacap and that as a first step a detailed feasibility study be conducted, in which the impact of industrialization would be considered, not only on employment, infrastructure, and the regional economy but also on social values and the structure and functioning of the traditional distribution sector.

For many years, Cilacap changed very little. Prior to the Great Depression, it was the third largest port in Java, exporting, among other commodities, considerable amounts of sugar. However, the depression resulted in the closure of most of the region's mills and the volume of goods moving through the port fell very sharply. This slump was then reinforced by the Japanese invasion, and although the provincial government constructed a large cotton-spinning factory there in the early 1950s, very little else occurred to initiate any growth prior to the study period in the mid-1970s. At that time, Pertamina commenced building an oil refinery and the Australian government provided assistance in clearing the port of wartime debris and dredging the harbor to allow larger vessels to enter. Little of this had had much impact on the lives of most of the people who lived either in the town or in the surrounding region, and it was becoming an urgent practical question to decide how to optimize the local benefits flowing from economic development.

Cilacap itself, a town of about 80,000 people, with a further 1,100,000 living in the surrounding region, is located in a somewhat isolated part of central Java, midway between Jogjakarta and Bandung. The region is bounded on the east by the Serayu River, on the north by the main railway to Jakarta, and beyond that by the mountains running through the center of Java, and on the west by a large area of swampy land. The town of Cilacap is built on a tongue of land and is linked with the inland by a railway spur line and two major (albeit occasionally impassable) roads and several minor roads. In the wet season, access can sometimes be more than a little precarious.

These physical features, which made economic development difficult, did, however, simplify the task of constructing input–output and trade flow tables, for the relevant boundaries were obvious and it was possible to obtain some measurement of the movement of goods by road, rail, and ship over the limited exit routes.

CONSTRUCTION OF AN INPUT–OUTPUT TABLE

An essential first step in the development of an integrated model of the trade flows among producers, traders, and households is to estimate an input–output table at producers' prices with an appropriate framework of sectors. As a second step, a trade flows table using the same set of sectors must be estimated; from these two basic analyses, a generalized input–output/trade flows model can be constructed that can then be used for the evaluation of alternative growth strategies.

In the case of Cilacap, the construction of the input–output table was greatly assisted by the availability of a detailed table for the Indonesian economy and by the unpublished work of Montgomery (1974) on the economy of Jogjakarta. While both studies suffer from the data defects that plague any such work in underdeveloped economies, they are the best available and have been used primarily for estimates of input–output coefficients. The Montgomery study in particular was helpful in that the author carried out field surveys in the vicinity of Jogjakarta in 1968–69 that led to direct estimates of the appropriate coefficients in several traditional sectors.

The sectors chosen for the Cilacap table followed the precedent set by Montgomery (1974). Since a major point of interest in the present study centered on the distinction between traditional and modern sectors, both producing and trade sectors were further disaggregated into modern and traditional components. In practice, the distinction between enterprises as to whether they were traditional or modern proceeded largely on the basis of the underlying management styles. Traditional enterprises, as well as being small in size, were usually family oriented, fatalistically inclined, operating from day to day on a cash-, not a profit-oriented basis. This group includes most handicraft or small local manufacturers, and most pasar traders, street vendors, and wayang traders. By way of contrast, the modern sectors in manufacturing could be clearly defined by naming the firms in each sector. The cotton-spinning mill became a separate sector, as did the two cassava-pelletizing plants and the iron ore sand-processing unit. On the trading side, all street-front shops in the shopping center, together with cooperatives, were classed as modern. In many respects, these traders were modern only by contrast with the pasar traders; however, these shops did not constitute a distinguishable group, which was predominantly Chinese in ethnic origin.

Agriculture was treated as a traditional activity and divided into paddy farming and other primary activities (including local fisheries). Traditional manufacturing was disaggregated into food and beverages (including snacks), mineral products (clay bricks, etc.), textile (local batik supplies), and other (including dog cart manufacturers, paper products, hoes and other implements, etc.). Finally, a service sector was included that covered such activities as banking, insurance, entertainment, and transport.

The choice of an appropriate time frame proved difficult. In the event, calendar 1973 was chosen as the period to which the tables would refer. The available data, however, ranged from 1967 to 1975. The Jogjakarta studies were based on 1969 and 1972 data; the official statistics for the Cilacap Kabupaten existed up to 1973; Bappenas Planning Study (BPS) survey data on family expenditure patterns related to 1971; and the Cilacap survey data were collected in late 1974. In 1973, furthermore, much of the construction work was still in the future and so it seemed best to adopt 1973 as the year of reference. All money flows were then converted to a 1973 basis, using a Jakarta-based index of price changes, knowing that Cilacap prices were moving in a similar, slightly lagged pattern.

With these decisions made, the detailed estimation of the two tables could proceed. The broad steps required by the input–output table were the following:

1. Total household income and expenditure estimates were derived, using Cilacap survey data on household expenditures, Jogjakarta estimates, and official statistics on income and expenditure. The final figure of Rp23,188 million gave a per capita figure rather less than Jogjakarta, which seemed reasonable.
2. Exports were built up from firm interviews and shipping, rail, and trade statistics. Imports were estimated from the same sources, with the addition of data derived from the two major pasars (markets) in the town.
3. Intermediate demands were estimated using technological coefficients from the Jogjakarta study applied to estimates of sector output. These latter estimates came from official Kabupaten Cilacap data, survey analysis, and interviews.
4. Wages were assessed from income distribution figures yielded by the Cilacap surveys and from interviews with major employers.
5. Trade sector estimates were derived from margin figures emerging from the surveys of traders and manufacturers. Sources of supply and customer characteristics were also available from the surveys, enabling a distinction to be made between traditional and modern sources and customers.

The steps listed above each required for completion a combination of judgment and hard data. The data available were generally inadequate and had been collected for a wide variety of reasons. Even the channel-mapping surveys were less helpful than might have been the case, largely because they were completed well before the framework set out here became available, and inevitably areas of questioning were overlooked that would now be asked. The final input–output table is shown in Table 10.1.

A glance at this table shows clearly the importance of the traditional sectors in the economy of Cilacap: Eighty-one percent of total output emerges from these sectors, and together they account for just over 99 percent of employment. Within the traditional sectors, farming stands out with 39 percent of total output and 78 percent of employment. Apart from the other manufacturing sector, all other traditional manufacturing sectors are strongly oriented toward the household marketplace. Export activity in these sectors is to an extent accidental. As it happened, 1973 was a year in which there was a slight rice surplus that was sold through official channels. Fishing is a major component of "other primary" and, depending on the season, generates a major part of that sector's export activity.

Value added by sector varies considerably. In the farm sectors, wages were a major component, and in the other traditional sectors, profits were dominant.

The isolation of the modern manufacturing sector is also apparent from the table. All these sectors produce solely for the export market, and in the case of the cotton mill, draw most of their raw materials from imports. The cassava-pelletizing plants (included in Sector 7, food) draw their raw materials from the rural parts of Cilacap, process these, and export to overseas markets. The iron ore sands operation exports directly to Japan under long-term contracts. The profits from these operations flow to entities outside the Cilacap region.

ESTIMATION OF THE TRADE FLOWS TABLE FOR CILACAP

In contrast with the input–output table, where emphasis is placed on the link between the production and household sectors, a trade flows table gives prominence to the role of the distribution sectors. Sales to these sectors by manufacturing and sales from distribution to manufacturing and households are measured and recorded.[1]

The construction of such a table for Cilacap drew on the data used in the input–output table. The broad steps required were the following:

1. Estimates of direct sales from manufacturers to other production sectors and to households were made, using data from the Cilacap surveys and from the Jogjakarta studies.
2. The difference between total output for each producing sector and total direct sales was then allocated to traditional and modern distributors on the basis of the Cilacap surveys of traders and manufacturers.
3. A similar allocation was made on the input side, again using survey data. These flows were then reconciled with margin information and with row or column totals.
4. A detailed sector-by-sector analysis of flows into the traditional and modern distribution sectors led to the flows between distribution sectors and to final demand. The flows noted in (3) and (4) were adjusted to take margins recorded in the input–output table into account.
5. Imports and exports were handled only by modern distributors, and the margin taken was derived from official Kabupaten statistics.

Although the steps just outlined are relatively straightforward, the practical difficulties stem from the inadequacies of the basic data that may not be apparent when each data element is looked at in isolation. Deciding on the best compromise is an integral part of the process of constructing these tables.

An estimate of the trade flows table for Cilacap is shown in Table 10.2.[2] From this table some points of interest can be noted. Compared with the U.S. and the Australian economies, where every dollar of sales to final demand generated $2.90 in total sales, the equivalent ratio in Indonesia is 2.50, that is, Rp1 million of final demand generated Rp2.50 million of local sales. Transactions among intermediate sectors accounted for Rp43527 million, 47 percent of the total volume of transactions. Households spent Rp23188 million, 58 percent on purchases through traditional outlets (pasars, street vendors, small local shops), 8 percent on purchases from the relatively modern retail sector, and the balance of 34 percent on purchases direct from suppliers. Distribution sector sales accounted for 40 percent of total sales volume, the equivalent Australian figure being 43 percent.

While these conclusions are of general interest, the longer-term structural insights into marketing system flows provided by a trade flows table rest on com-

TABLE 10.1. Cilacap Aggregated Input–Output Table for 1973 (Producers' Prices, millions rupiah)

	Farm		Traditional Manufacturers				Modern Manufacture						Total Inter Output	Income < 10,000 Rp	Income > 10,000 Rp	Total House-hold Demand	Exports	Total Use
	Paddy	Other Primary	Food Beverage	Mineral Prods.	Textile	Other	Food	Mining	Textile	Service etc.	Trad. Dist'n	Mod. Dist'n						
	1	2	3	4	5	6	7	8	9	10	11	12						
Paddy	146	20	916	—	—	—	—	—	—	—	—	—	1,082	2,921	3,566	6,487	365	7,934
Other Primary	692	936	1,780	—	71	213	2,020	—	—	118	—	—	5,830	2,371	4,054	6,425	2,190	14,445
Food Beverage	—	177	303	—	—	13	300	20	180	102	—	—	1,095	441	2,512	2,953	—	4,048
Mineral Products	—	3	1	29	—	389	10	—	—	83	—	—	515	55	200	255	—	770
Textile	—	9	2	1	79	96	20	10	90	10	—	—	317	397	1,200	1,597	—	1,914
Other	961	1,642	140	43	44	1,020	200	—	—	670	115	65	4,908	226	1,600	1,826	—	6,734
Food	—	—	—	—	—	—	—	—	—	—	—	—	—	—	—	—	5,242	5,242
Mining	—	—	—	—	—	—	—	—	—	—	—	—	—	—	—	—	897	897
Textile	—	—	—	—	—	—	—	—	—	—	—	—	—	—	—	—	4,583	4,583
Services etc.	302	486	163	43	39	195	100	122	366	1,883	430	315	4,444	1,073	995	2,068	—	6,512

160

	1	2	3	4	5	6	7	8	9	10	11	12	INTER					TOTAL
Trad. Dist'n.	70	220	231	7	20	150	—	—	—	216	14	2	930	339	867	1,206	—	2,136
Mod. Dist'n.	6	43	60	12	16	169	53	3	30	217	120	—	729	96	275	371	524	1,624
INTER, OUTPUT	2,177	3,536	3,596	135	269	2,253	2,703	155	666	3,299	679	382	19,850	7,919	15,269	23,188	13,801	56,839
Wages <10,000Rp	3,742	2,925	200	55	17	96	—	—	—	547	337	—	7,919					
Wages >10,000Rp	2,015	3,251	252	—	—	100	38	34	1,000	1,119	451	560	8,820					
WAGES	5,757	6,176	452	55	17	196	38	34	1,000	1,666	788	560	16,739					
Profits	1,518	1,042	—	580	74	752	—	—	—	1,107	669	682	6,424					
Ext. Pymts. Subsidies	-1,518	-1,042	—	—	—	—	2,501	668	717	440	—	—	1,766					
VALUE ADDED	5,757	6,176	452	635	91	948	2,539	702	1,717	3,213	1,457	1,242	24,929					
PRODUCTN.	7,934	9,712	4,048	770	360	3,201	5,242	857	2,383	6,512	2,136	1,624	44,779					
Imports	—	4,733	—	—	1,554	3,533	—	40	2,200	—	—	—	12,060					
TOTAL SUPPLY	7,934	14,445	4,048	770	1,914	6,734	5,242	897	4,583	6,512	2,136	1,624	56,839					
Employmt. 1973	360,900	12,800	1,300	400	4,660	200	240	3,000	—	40,643	—	36,000	460,143					

Source: Layton, R.A.; M. Layton, and J.S. Western. 1975. Cilacap Development Study, Vol. 3: Report on the Socioeconomics Study. Prepared for Bappenas, Republic of Indonesia, on behalf of the government of Australia under the Colombo Plan, Sydney.

TABLE 10.2. Cilacap Trade Flows Table for 1973 (million rupiah)

	Farm			Traditional Manufacture				Modern Manufacturer					Inter Total	Income < 10,000 Rp	Income > 10,000 Rp	Household Demand	Exports	Total Final Demand	Total
	1 Paddy	2 Other Primary	3 Food, Beverage	4 Mineral Products	5 Textile	6 Other	7 Food	8 Mining	9 Textile	10 Service etc.	11 Trad. Dist'n.	12 Mod. Dist'n.							
1. Paddy	102	14	641	—	—	—	—	—	—	—	1,977	659	3,393	2,045	2,496	4,541	—	4,541	7,934
2. Other Primary	423	572	1,088	—	43	130	1,234	—	—	72	1,563	3,553	8,678	382	652	1,034	—	1,034	9,712
3. Food Beverage	—	—	—	—	—	—	—	—	—	—	2,793	1,255	4,048	—	—	—	—	—	4,048
4. Mineral Products	—	—	—	—	—	—	—	—	—	—	293	477	770	—	—	—	—	—	770
5. Textile	—	2	—	—	20	24	5	3	22	3	140	130	349	3	8	11	—	11	360

	(1)	(2)	(3)	(4)	(5)	(6)	(7)	(8)	(9)	(10)	(11)	(12)	Total Inter							Col. Total
6. Other	114	195	17	5	5	122	24	—	—	80	788	1,634	2,984	27	190	217	—	—	217	3,201
7. Food	—	—	—	—	—	—	—	—	—	—	—	—	—	—	—	—	5,242	—	5,242	5,242
8. Mining	—	—	—	—	—	—	—	—	—	—	—	—	—	—	—	—	897	—	897	897
9. Textile	—	—	—	—	—	—	—	—	—	—	—	—	—	—	—	—	4,583	—	4,583	4,583
10. Service	302	486	163	43	39	195	100	122	366	1,883	430	315	4,444	1,073	995	2,068	—	—	2,068	6,512
11. Trad. Dist'n.	783	1,173	814	14	62	384	—	—	—	362	864	138	4,594	3,851	9,589	13,440	—	—	13,440	18,034
12. Mod. Dist'n.	453	1,094	873	73	100	1,398	1,340	30	278	899	7,729	—	14,267	538	1,339	1,877	3,079	—	4,956	19,223
Total Inter	2,177	3,536	3,596	135	269	2,253	2,703	155	666	3,299	16,577	8,161	43,527	7,919	15,269	23,188	13,801	—	36,989	80,246
Exports	—	—	—	—	—	—	—	40	2,200	—	—	9,820	12,060	—	—	—	—	—	—	12,060
Col. Total	2,177	3,536	3,596	135	269	2,253	2,703	195	2,866	3,299	16,577	17,981	55,587	7,919	15,269	23,188	13,801	—	36,989	92,576

Source: Layton, R.A., M. Layton, and J.S. Western, 1975. Cilacap Development Study, Vol. 3: Report of the Socioeconomics Study. Prepared for Bappenas, Republic of Indonesia, on behalf of the Government of Australia under the Colombo Plan, Sydney.

parative analyses that are lacking at the present time. It is hoped that the empirical application of the trade flows methodology illustrated in this chapter will lead to further studies in a range of marketing system alternatives and thus to relevant comparative analyses.

From a regional planner's viewpoint, the issues of interest turn on what is likely to happen to the production and distribution sectors as the economy changes. Will extra capacity be needed in certain production sectors? Can the traditional markets cope with the additional transaction flows generated by economic growth? Will bottlenecks emerge in the provision of space for the markets, in the availability of working capital, in the physical flows within and between markets? To the extent that these resource needs are related to total sales volumes through the relevant distribution sectors, a prediction of sales volume change in response to economic growth may help to identify critical components in the marketing system.

PREDICTING FLOWS IN MARKETING SYSTEMS

The input–output data set out in Table 10.1 can be divided into the following blocks:

Intermediate Sector Flows (AX)	Household Demand (D)	Exports (E)	Total Use (X)
Value Added (V)			
Imports (I)			
Total Supply (X^T)			

The intermediate sector flows comprise the 12-by-12 matrix of sales between sectors. Household demand consists of a 12-by-2 matrix of sector sales to the two household income groups, exports is a 1-by-12 vector of export sales by sector, and total use is a 1-by-12 vector of row totals. Value added in the subsequent analysis is a 2-by-12 matrix, with the first row relating to the earnings of low-income groups (less than Rp10,000 per month), and the second combining profits with the wages of the group earning Rp10,000 per month or more. Imports is a 1-by-12 row vector of imports by sector.

Associated with this input–output structure is a conformable partitioning of the trade flows table into blocks that correspond to the sector flows in the input–output table, that is,

Intermediate Sector Trade Flows (Z_P)	Household Demand Flows (Z_D)	Export (X_E)	Total (Q)
Imports (Z_M)			

In the setting of these two tables, the practical problems of growth planning require the simultaneous adjustment of both sets of flows in response to a development initiative. The input–output table directs attention to implications for production sectors and the trade flows table to the problems that may arise in channel flows. As an example, assume that one of the modern sector manufacturing enterprises such as the cotton mill expands its market considerably, increasing production perhaps by the addition of a further shift or by capacity extension. The first effect of this change will show up in the export column of both tables; from here there will be direct consequences felt by the local industries supplying the cotton mill (for example, local textiles or services) and by the household sector in the form of an increased flow of wage income. At this point, changes will be noted in the intermediate sector flows in both tables, and in the value-added and import components of the input–output table. At the next level, the increased wages will lead to increases in household consumption expenditure that will depend on the distribution of the wage gain between the two income groups. These household expenditure jumps will in turn lead to increased demand in all sectors supplying household needs, and these in their turn will generate wage effects, and so on. Each of these changes will be reflected in both tables, and assuming a stable situation, the cycle of changes will converge to a new equilibrium level, with increased production levels, increased flows through traditional and modern channels, and increased wages. The increase in production can be viewed against capacity limits (physical, financial, or human) in the manufacturing sector; the increased channel flows carry with them increased demands for space in the markets, increased traffic in already congested areas, increased needs for working capital that is already a major limiting factor, etc.

A similar argument would flow from an assumption that an industrial estate is established in the region, allocating to it a specified mix of industries. At the level of approximation involved in the model developed here, this initiative can be introduced as one or more new rows in the intermediate-producing sectors of the tables. The size of the initial flows will reflect assumptions about the technological coefficients associated with the industries in question, an issue that could in practice be tackled within the framework of detailed national input–output studies that have been carried out. These assumptions will appear first in the input–output table and then in the trade flows table. Wage effects will follow, the changes in household demand, further production and channel changes in flow levels, etc.

How, then, can these changes in production levels and channel flows be assessed? The model that follows illustrates the approach to the first of the two examples just discussed.

Let x_{ij} be the output of industry i used by industry j, measured in constant prices. Let z_{ij} be the corresponding flow of sales directly between industries i and j. Note that the industries considered include both production and distribution sectors.

Following the usual input–output structure, assume (1) that a particular product or commodity is supplied by only one industry, (2) that there are no joint products, and (3) that the inputs used by any industry are proportional to the output level of that industry. Of these assumptions, the third is the most troublesome in the context of development planning and needs to be kept in mind.

In the light of these assumptions, the relation between outputs and inputs for industry j can be written as

$$x_{ij} = a_{ij} X_j, \tag{1}$$

where a_{ij} is a technologically determined coefficient characterizing inputs to industry j, A is the matrix a_{ij}, and X_j is the output of industry j. Similarly, let V be a matrix of value-added ratios v_{kj}, where

$$v_{kj} = \frac{W_{kj}}{X_j} \tag{2}$$

and W_{kj} is the wage income of income group k in sector j. Also, let C be a matrix of consumption coefficients c_{ik}, where

$$c_{ik} = \frac{C_{ik}}{W_k}, \tag{3}$$

C_{ik} is the expenditure by income group k on the output of sector i, and $W_k = \sum_j W_{jk}$ is the income of the kth group.

Finally, assume that imports are proportional to the level of output, that is,

$$\mu_i = \frac{M_i}{X_i}, \tag{4}$$

where M_i is the import level for the ith sector, and

$$M = \begin{bmatrix} \mu_1 & & 0 \\ & \ddots & \\ 0 & & \mu_r \end{bmatrix} \tag{5}$$

Then, from the basic accounting framework,

$$X = AX - MX + CW + E. \tag{6}$$

Since $W = XV$,

$$X = AX - MX + CVX + E \tag{7}$$

and

$$X = (I - A + M - CV)^{-1}E, \tag{8}$$

where E is now taken as exogenously determined (as, for example, in the sales increase experienced by the cotton mill). This determines the equilibrium pattern of input–output flows that are associated with a specified level of exports, E.

Associated with the new input–output table will be a new trade flows table, where the elements z_{ij} are linear functions of each of the elements $x_{k\ell}$ in the input–output table, i.e.,

$$z_{ij} = \sum_k \sum_\ell \alpha_{k\ell} x_{k\ell}. \tag{9}$$

The $\alpha_{k\ell}$ are determined directly from the input–output and the trade flows tables, making an assumption of linearity similar to that required in the derivation of the a_{ij} from an input–output table. The $[\alpha_{ij}]$ values relating to direct flows from sector i to sector j are obtained as the ratio of entries in the trade flows table to corresponding entries in the input–output table; indirect flows are then split between the distribution sectors in proportions fixed for each industry. Flows between the distribution sector are taken as proportional to the total volume handled by each sector. As noted earlier, imports are assumed to be handled by modern distributors only.

For full details of these equations, see Layton (1980, 1981b).

An assessment of the effects of a change in E then proceeds as follows:

$$E \rightarrow X \rightarrow Z. \tag{10}$$

Further elaboration of the input–output and the corresponding trade flows models is possible to allow for capacity limits, employment, or other constraints and to consider more explicitly the time frame in which changes occur.

WHAT HAPPENS WHEN FINISHED COTTON EXPORTS JUMP BY 25 PERCENT?

As an illustration of the analysis suggested in the previous section, assume that the output of sector 9, the cotton-spinning mill, increases by 25 percent, that is, by Rp1,146 million. Since this export activity does not involve local distribution channels directly, the appropriate export vector E is

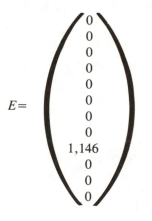

$$E = \begin{pmatrix} 0 \\ 0 \\ 0 \\ 0 \\ 0 \\ 0 \\ 0 \\ 0 \\ 1,146 \\ 0 \\ 0 \\ 0 \end{pmatrix}$$

Working from the matrix of input–output coefficients, the inverse,

$$(I - A + M - CV)^{-1},$$

can be computed. Using this matrix, the full multiplier effects of a change in export earnings on output levels can be assessed. For example, an increase of Rp1,000 million in the export sales of sector 9 (modern textiles) would in the long run generate an additional Rp371 million in the output of paddy rice, even though the immediate effect of sector 9 on sector 1 is nil. A comparison of the results for the three modern manufacturing sectors shows that sector 7 (largely cassava-pelletizing plants) would generate wider multiplier effects through an increase in export earnings than would an equal increase in the sales of beach sands (sector 8) or cotton thread (sector 9). This is certainly plausible as the cassava-pelletizing plants are much more closely integrated into the economic fabric of Cilacap than are either of the other two industries.

The new equilibrium output level,

$$X = (I - A + M - CV)^{-1}E,$$

can then be used to generate an incremental input–output table, reflecting the changes in all aggregates that occur as a consequence of the jump in sector 9 earnings. The effects of the change ultimately spread widely through the local economy. The output of paddy rice jumps by Rp425 million or just over 5 percent, the output of food and beverages by Rp251 million or 6 percent, and services by Rp425 million or 6.5 percent. Wages in the lower-income group increase by 4.9% and in the higher-income category by 6.3 percent.

The final step is to map the changes in marketing flow aggregates that result from a sector 9 export earnings jump using the equations linking the input–output and trade flows tables. The resulting incremental trade flows table is set out in Table 10.3, and shows sales through traditional distributors increasing by Rp1,042 million or 5.8 percent and through the modern distributors by Rp923 million or 4.8 percent. Sales to traditional distribution increase by amounts that differ by sector, and range from 4.0 (other primary) to 7.1 (textiles) percent. The household sector increases purchases from traditional outlets by 5.9 percent and from modern outlets by 5.8 percent. Generally, the increases were greater for shops that serviced the needs of the higher-income group.

The analysis highlights the strongly interconnected character of production and distribution in Cilacap. While the growth effects anticipated from an increase in cotton thread earnings could probably be accommodated within the existing production and marketing systems, further increments in other modern sectors could begin to strain capacities in both systems. There were (in 1974) signs of a spillover of the pasars into surrounding streets, a phenomenon that is common in many developing nations and a clear indicator of a system growing out of control owing to neglect. Apart from the spatial aspects of the changes envisaged here, a major practical problem will arise in increased needs for working capital, a need that is likely to be proportional to the volume of trade passing through the sector. The attitudes of banks and official agencies toward providing some of the capital needs of small retailers and manufacturers hinder rather than help the adaptive changes needed in the structure and function of marketing systems.

CONCLUSION

The combined input–output/trade flows model used in Cilacap provides a useful framework within which developmental changes can be evaluated. In many regional planning efforts in the past, an emphasis has been placed on production and infrastructure needs, with the trade sectors being largely ignored. The

TABLE 10.3. Changes to Trade Flows

	Sector												Inter Total	Household Demand			Exports	Total Final Demand		Row Total
	1	2	3	4	5	6	7	8	9	10	11	12		<10,000 Rp	>10,000 Rp	Demand		Demand	Adj.	
Sector 1	6	1	40	–	–	–	–	–	–	–	97	32	176	101	158	259	–	259	–10	425
2	23	23	67	–	3	7	–	–	–	5	63	143	334	19	41	60	–	60	–11	383
3	–	–	–	–	–	–	–	–	–	–	179	80	259	–	–	–	–	–	–8	251
4	–	–	–	–	–	–	–	–	–	–	16	27	43	–	–	–	–	–	–1	42
5	–	–	–	–	1	1	–	–	6	–	10	9	27	–	1	1	–	1	–4	24
6	6	8	1	–	–	6	–	–	–	5	41	86	153	1	12	13	–	13	–3	163
7	–	–	–	–	–	–	–	–	–	–	–	–	–	–	–	–	–	–	–	–
8	–	–	–	–	–	–	–	–	–	–	–	–	–	–	–	–	–	–	–	–
9	–	–	–	–	–	–	–	–	–	–	–	–	–	–	–	–	1,146	1,146	–	1,146
10	16	19	10	2	3	10	–	–	91	122	24	13	310	53	63	116	–	116	–1	425
11	42	44	51	1	4	20	–	–	–	24	50	13	249	188	608	796	–	796	–3	1,042
12	24	45	54	4	7	71	–	–	70	59	480	–	814	29	80	109	–	109	–	923
Total Inter	117	140	223	7	18	115	–	–	167	215	960	403	2,365	391	963	1,354	1,146	2,500	–41	4,824
Imports	–	–	–	–	–	–	–	–	550	–	–	469	1,019				–			1,019
Col. Total	117	140	223	7	18	115	–	–	717	215	960	872	3,384	391	963	1,354	1,146	2,500	–41	5,943

Source: Compiled by author from Table 10.1, p. 160-61, and Table 10.2, p. 162-63.

model suggested here is an attempt to redress this balance, providing an appropriate emphasis on the real needs of the marketing system. Where these needs are ignored, development may well be much less successful than had been hoped.

There are, in practice, considerable problems in the implementation of a model such as the one proposed here. Some of the difficulties in the Cilacap application arose because the field work did not proceed within the framework of data needed by the model. Sector definitions were not always the most useful; gaps were left in the survey instruments used with retailers and manufacturers; and in retrospect, official statistics that might have been available were overlooked. Perhaps one of the major advantages of working with a framework that links marketing and production sectors with households is simply that it will prompt the getting of the data really needed for intelligent planning decisions.

Looking beyond the practical application possible in the area of regional development planning, a replication of the basic analyses with some consistency in sector definition could help to pinpoint aspects of the evolution of marketing systems from peasant economies to fully industrialized states. A comparative analysis of the input–trade flows structure for different communities may help to identify constraints in the functioning of marketing systems, as well as focusing attention on those factors that are strongly influenced by environment.

These possibilities, however, still lie in the future. The immediate purpose of this chapter has been to suggest a way in which macroproduction and macromarketing systems can be studied simultaneously, taking into account the critical interdependencies that exist between these two systems and final demand.

NOTES

1. For details of trade flows methodology, see Layton (1980, 1981a,b).

2. A major area of uncertainty in this table lies in the split of sales volume within and between the two distribution sectors. There is evidence, according to Geertz (1963), that pasar traders sell goods from one to the other, sometimes through a chain of five to ten traders. In the Cilacap study, few of the pasar traders claimed any wholesale activity; this is reflected in the flows shown in the table. It seems likely, however, that this understates the real position.

REFERENCES

Cox, R., C. Goodman, and T. C. Fichandler. 1965. *Distribution in a High-Level Economy*. Englewood Cliffs, NJ: Prentice-Hall.

Geertz, C. 1971. *Agricultural Involution: The Process of Ecological Change in Indonesia*. Berkeley: University of California Press.

———. 1963. *Peddlers and Princes: Social Change and Economic Modernization in Two Indonesian Towns*. Chicago: University of Chicago Press.

Layton, R. A. 1981a. "Trade Flows in Macro Marketing Systems: Part I: A Macro Model of Trade Flows." *Journal of Macromarketing* 1:39-48.

——. 1981b. "Trade Flows in Macro Marketing Systems: Part II: Transforming Input Output Tables into Trade Flow Tables." *Journal of Macromarketing* 1:48-55.

——. 1980. "A Macro Model of Trade Flows in a Marketing System," Paper No. 727, April. West Lafayette, IN: Institute for Research in the Behavioral Economic and Management Sciences, Krannert Graduate School of Management, Purdue University.

Layton, R. A., M. F. Layton, and J. S. Western. 1975. *Cilacap Development Study, Vol. 3: Report on the Socio Economics Study.* Prepared for Bappenas, Republic of Indonesia, on behalf of the Government of Australia under the Colombo Plan, Sydney.

Montgomery, R. D. 1974. "The Link Between Trade and Labor Absorption in Rural Java: An Input Output Study of Jogjakarta," Ph.D. dissertation, Cornell University (see *Dissertation Abstracts*, Vol. 35, Dec. 1974).

Slater, C. C., D. G. Jenkins, L. A. Pook, and L. D. Dahringer. 1979. *Easing Transition in Southern Africa: New Techniques for Policy Planning.* Boulder, CO: Westview Press.

CHAPTER 11

Determining the Distribution of Retail Store Types within a Metropolitan Area: Macroretail Structure

CHARLES A. INGENE

INTRODUCTION

It has been a quarter-century since Reavis Cox offered two key insights into the spatial organization of the modern metropolis (1959). First, retail structure has an immediate influence upon how conveniently consumers can purchase goods and services. Second, socioeconomic characteristics of consumers affect the long-term structure of retailing. Despite the apparent importance of retail structure to consumer welfare and of socioeconomic structure to retail success, little empirical knowledge about retail structure and its socioeconomic determinants has been attained. This chapter is intended as the first step on the long road to obtaining a working knowledge of these phenomena.

Cox used the term "retail structure" to refer to the clustering of the entire range of retail store types into planned and unplanned shopping districts as well as to the dispersal of both individual stores and shopping districts throughout a metropolis. I will henceforth use the term *microretail structure* to refer to the intraurban, spatial aspects of retailing. Although there have been many studies of individual lines of retail trade (see Ghosh and Craig 1983) and of shopping centers (for example, Nevin and Houston 1980), little attention has been paid to the full breadth of microretail structure. There are many reasons for this lack of attention. Among them are (1) the obvious complexity of the topic, (2) the simple fact that each city has a somewhat unique microretail structure due to the vagaries of topography and historical evolution (Allen and Sanglier 1979), and (3) the absence of a theoretical or empirical explanation of why the statistical distribution of retail lines of trade differs across cities. I will henceforth refer

.to this statistical distribution as *macroretail structure*. An understanding of macroretail structure—what lines of trade appear in a metropolis—is a necessary prelude to an understanding of microretail structure.

This chapter is devoted to providing an understanding of the nature and determinants of macroretail structure across standard metropolitan statistical areas (SMSAs). Five specific topics are addressed. First, a theory of retail structure based upon observations from geography, marketing, and regional and urban economics is provided. Second, an extensive set of demographic and environmental variables is derived from the theory and the literature. Principal components analysis (PCA) is used to create a small set of orthogonal descriptors of the *socioeconomic structure* of SMSAs (Kernan and Bruce 1972). Cluster analysis is then employed in order to demonstrate that there are distinct regional regularities in the socioeconomic structure of SMSAs.

Third, the percentage distribution of retail lines of trade within each SMSA is factor analyzed (with principal components) in order to ascertain which retail types tend to occur in combination. Cluster analysis is then employed to demonstrate that regional regularities also exist in macroretail structure. Fourth, both regression and cluster analyses are used to show that macroretail structure is at least partially caused by socioeconomic structure and that regional regularities in the former are related to regional similarities in the latter.

Fifth, the final section provides a discussion of the results and sets forth a promising avenue for future research into retail institutions, product purchases, and the organization of distribution channels.

There are four critical reasons for investigating macroretail structure, socioeconomic structure, and their interaction. First, as Alderson and Cox (1948, p. 140) noted many years ago, "Marketing men should assume the task of working out concepts that have true significance in analyzing the nature of the distributive space through which goods and services are marketed and the nature of the forces that have brought the existing distributive pattern into existence." Second, an understanding of macroretail structure and its interaction with socioeconomic structure will provide a solid foundation for a thorough exploration of microretail structure. Third, consumer convenience and, indeed, social welfare are almost certainly affected by both macro- and microretail structure. Fourth, an appreciation of both macro- and microretail structure should ultimately be of value to senior retail management for the purposes of locational decisions and strategic planning.

MACRORETAIL STRUCTURE: THEORY AND EVIDENCE

Grocery stores account for 5 percent of all retail outlets in Lincoln, Nebraska, but three times that percentage of stores in Lake Charles, Louisiana. Eating establishments account for 13 percent of all retail outlets in Bay City, Michigan, but nearly twice that percentage in Honolulu, Hawaii. These two lines of trade are the exception: Almost all retail lines have a *greater* ratio from the SMSA in which they are most prevalent to the one in which they are least prevalent. This observation generates the question, Why do all SMSAs not have approximately the same percentage of retail outlets in every line of trade?

Determination of the statistical distribution of stores across lines of trade within an SMSA requires an understanding of three basic economic phenomena: first, the factors influencing the profitability of a single store; second, the factors affecting the total number of stores in a line of trade in the area; and third, the extent to which stores in two separate lines complement (or interfere with) each other. These three phenomena are addressed in turn, and then the limited empirical evidence on the statistical distribution of store types is briefly reviewed.

Store Profitability

Consumers consider purchasing at a store if and only if the utility from their purchases is sufficient to cover their "commodity and convenience costs." The former is the price of the merchandise; the latter is the value of their "time, physical and nervous energy, and money required to overcome the frictions of space and time" (Kelley 1958, p. 32). Thus, a consumer's demand for the merchandise of a store will be lower the further the customer is from the store (Huff 1964). While there are many demand curves that are consistent with this premise, a particularly convenient one that is widely used in location theoretic studies is (Beckmann 1968)

$$q=a-b(p+tr),\tag{1}$$

where

q=quantity demanded,
a=maximal demand quantity (at zero price and distance),
b=sensitivity to price and distance,
p=price at the store,
t=convenience cost per shopping trip, expressed in dollars per round-trip mile,
r=miles to the store.

The maximal distance the consumer is willing to travel to shop at the store is found from Equation 1 by setting $q=0$:

$$r^*= \frac{a/b-p}{t} ,\tag{2}$$

where r^* is the *range* of the store. The range rises with the maximal demand price (a/b), which is itself influenced by such factors as income, household size, and unemployment. [Ingene and Yu (1981) provide a thorough discussion of these factors.] The range declines with increases in convenience costs and with prices charged, given other elements of the retailing mix.

Store profits G are equal to markup times unit sales within the trade area, less overhead costs. Algebraically,

$$G=2\phi(p-c)\pi\int_0^{r*}r(a-bp-btr)\ dr-F, \tag{3}$$

where

F=overhead costs,
c=variable costs,

so

$(p-c)$=markup

and

ϕ=demand density=customers per square mile within the trade area.

It is assumed that the store is located at the center of its market area. Hence,

$$G=b\pi\phi(r*)^2(p-c)\ (\frac{a}{b}-p-\frac{2tr*}{3})-F. \tag{4}$$

It is easy to show that the profit-maximizing price rises with the maximal demand price and with variable costs, but falls the greater are transportation costs and the range of the store:

$$p*=\frac{a}{2b}+\frac{c}{2}-\frac{tr*}{3}. \tag{5}$$

Substituting Equation 5 into 4 gives profits as

$$G=\frac{\pi\phi(r*)^2}{4b}\left(\frac{a}{b}-c-\frac{2tr*}{3}\right)^2-F. \tag{6}$$

A critical point may now be made. The store is profitable if and only if its gross margin is sufficient to cover its overhead expense. In turn, this occurs only if the range $r*$ is greater than the *threshold market radius* for the store. The threshold is the radius r that sets G equal to 0. A high F and/or a low demand density will preclude a store from being successful unless the socioeconomic structure of the market area is particularly attuned to the store's merchandise offerings, as evidenced in a high a, a low b, and a low t. ·

Number of Stores

Managers consider opening a store at a location if and only if they expect the store to generate a positive profit. How many stores can squeeze into an SMSA before the average store in that line of trade begins to lose money? The question has been extensively analyzed by many authors, with results differing slightly according to the precise specification of the model (Beckmann 1971; Mills and Lav 1964; Ingene and Lusch 1981).

Central place theorists (for example, Christaller 1966; Lösch 1954) have argued that retailers in a city sell to the residents of the city, the surrounding rural hinterland, and nearby but smaller communities. This latter feature is the marketing phenomenon of "outshopping," first described by Reilly (1931) and extensively researched by Ferber (1958) and others. It follows that aggregate demand and the variety of retail stores in an SMSA depend not just on city size but also upon the specific details of smaller, surrounding cities (Beckmann and McPherson 1970).

Sociologists and geographers have rejected the standard economic assumption of identical preference functions across areas. Duncan et al. (1960) have argued that residents of large cities have different needs than the inhabitants of smaller communities. Rushton (1972) has also pursued this line of reasoning. This argument provides a rationale for the dispersal of retail store types to differ by city size.

Urban economists have focused on differences in overhead expenses, arguing that costs of doing business in large cities may be less than in smaller cities because of the presence of (1) social overhead capital, (2) more specialized labor, and (3) the existence of business services that allow some functions to be "spun off" to firms capable of providing them efficiently. These reduced costs are termed "urbanization economies" (Moomaw 1983). Evidence for the existence of such economies in the retail trades is provided by Ingene (1984b).

Finally, because retail structure—both micro and macro—is a function of past history as well as current realities, it may be anticipated that the retail structure of high-growth areas more accurately reflects current demand than does the structure of low-growth areas. Hall, Knapp, and Winsten (1961) and Chinitz (1961) have characterized this as indicative of the "entrepreneurial vibrancy" of high-growth areas. It may also be anticipated that areas that attract a considerable number of tourists will have a macroretail structure reflecting that fact.

Interaction Between Lines of Trade

In sharp contrast to the preceding pair of topics, relatively little analytical attention has been devoted to the topic of interaction between lines of trade. During the 1930s, Reilly (1931) and Christaller (1966) noted that customers engage in multipurpose shopping,[1] particularly when outshopping to a larger community. Eaton and Lipsey (1979) have demonstrated that this encourages the spatial agglomeration of stores, thereby harming the retail trades in small communities located near larger cities. Ingene (1985) argued that differing temporal attitudes among customers will encourage stores selling similar merchandise, but having different levels of service, to locate adjacent to one another. Mulligan (1984) presented an intriguing mathematical argument that when customers multipurpose-shop, changes in demand for one store will affect the profits of all stores, even if their merchandise is neither complementary nor substitutable.

Despite the value of these investigations, the fact remains that we have rather little empirical or analytical knowledge of why particular lines of trade tend to appear in conjunction or to avoid each other. All that seems certain is that through cost externalities (such as urbanization economies) and through demand-induced effects of multipurpose shopping, retailers in different lines of trade are in competition, even when they do not sell identical products.

Empirical Evidence

Apparently the first researcher to study the distribution of retail services across cities was Duncan (1952). Utilizing a statistical technique called "the coefficient of urbanization," he was able to show that some lines of retail trade were concentrated in larger cities, while others were more prevalent in smaller communities. Using 1948 data on sales, he found that large cities had a preponderance of (1) nongrocery food stores, (2) department stores, (3) apparel stores, and (4) jewelry and other specialty stores. In contrast, small cities had a disproportionate share of the sales of (1) general stores, (2) lumber and hardware stores, and (3) gasoline stations. Other retail types were approximately equally distributed across city size groups. In a followup study, Duncan and his associates (1960) concluded that "the differentiation and specialization of service [retail] trades with increasing city size can be explained to only a small degree by principles stemming from the central-place schema" (Duncan et al. 1960, p. 80). In the terminology of this chapter, city size does little to explain macroretail structure.

In a study of retail sales that was inspired by the socioeconomic typology of Hadden and Borgatta (1965), Bruce (1969) was able to derive ten clusters for the 79 SMSAs in his sample. He showed a significant relationship between cluster membership and (1) per capita sales as well as (2) per capita sales per store for the nine major lines of retail trade.

A considerable number of authors have researched the determinants of per capita sales in several lines of retail trade at the SMSA or city level. A thorough review is provided in Ingene (1984a). The essence of that research is that most factors have a differential impact across lines of trade. For example, high income positively influences per capita sales of department stores but negatively affects variety stores. Thus, specific institutional types appeal to different market segments. Ingene (1984a) also examined the impact of marketing mix factors on per capita sales. He found that they tend to enhance sales at all stores types, an intuitively appealing result.

In contrast to the sales results reported above, very little attention has been paid to the determinants of number of retail stores. Ingene and Lusch (1981) provide a review of this brief literature. I am unable to find any literature that simultaneously examines number of stores in several lines of trade [although Ingene (1983b) did look at restaurants and grocery stores], nor does there appear to be a literature on the percentage distribution of retail store types.

Summary

In summary, it may be anticipated that the socioeconomic factors that influence consumer demand, store profits, and the range and threshold values of a store type will affect macroretail structure. Similarly, those demand-related characteristics that influence multipurpose shopping behavior and those supply-side externalities that influence store costs should influence macrostructure.

The size of the metropolitan area and its degree of centrality should impact upon macroretail structure. Finally, the relative marketing mix efforts of retailers in different lines of trade ought to affect macrostructure. Each of these factors, except for the marketing mix, on which there is insufficient secondary information, is incorporated into the empirical research that follows.

SOCIOECONOMIC STRUCTURE

This section has two basic purposes: to describe a socioeconomic structure of U.S. metropolitan areas and to determine those SMSAs that are most similar in their structure. Data selection is described in the first subsection. Results of a factor analysis of the data, undertaken to create a parsimonious description of socioeconomic structure, are reported in the second subsection. The third subsection describes the results of a cluster analysis of the factors. The clustering reveals that those SMSAs that have the most similar socioeconomic structures tend to be regionally clustered. Brief observations on the results are offered in the final subsection.

Data Selection

Implicit in data selected for analysis are the results that will be obtained. Therefore, an effort was made to include data that have appeared in other studies or that might reasonably be expected to contribute to an understanding of macroretail structure. The primary constraint in data selection was the choice of 1977 as the year of analysis. This is the most recently available *Census of Retail Trade*.

In order to conserve space, the 35 variables selected for analysis are reported in Table 11.1, along with their mean, maximum and minimum values, and data sources. Thorough justification for most of the variables is provided in Ingene (1984a, pp. 44–47). Hence, only highlights are reported here.

Income, household size, and both population age and age of head of household provide insight into stages in the family life cycle (Wells and Gubar 1966). Ingene (1984a) has shown that the factors derived from these and other variables have a differential impact on household expenditures across eight lines of retail trade. Essentially, they influence the consumer's demand curves for the products and services of retail establishments.

The male percentage of the population and the population's racial composition are intended to capture sociocultural influences upon demand. Both were used by Ingene (1984a) in his retail expenditures study and by Green, Frank, and Robinson (1967) in their cluster analysis of U.S. cities. Price's seminal usage of factor analysis to classify cities (1942) included a gender variable, while Haddon and Borgatta's extensive factor analysis of cities used racial composition (1965).

Automotive ownership per household affects the convenience (transportation) costs of comparison shopping. Data on automotive registrations were obtained from unpublished figures of the U.S. Department of Transportation and of several state departments of motor vehicles.[2] Similar data have been used by Ingene (1984a) and Ingene and Lusch (1980, 1981).

Among the SMSA descriptors, population growth is intended to capture the vibrancy of each geographical area (Hall, Knapp, and Winsten 1961). It has been used by Ingene and Lusch (1981), Price (1942), Haddon and Borgatta (1965), and probably others. Population density and its statistical look-alike, automotive density, relate to demand density in Equations 3, 4, and 6 above. Haddon and Borgatta (1965) used the first, Ingene and Lusch (1981) the second.

The unemployment rate should reflect current job prospects for city residents and their need to rely upon savings to maintain a standard of living. It has been used previously by Haddon and Borgatta (1965), Green, Frank, and Robinson (1967), and Ingene and Yu (1981). Unemployment should affect the demand curve.

The final two variables are meant to capture the "centrality" of a central place (SMSA). The number of retail stores in the SMSA (termed URBAN) has been used by Ingene (1984b) as a measure of urbanization economies. It is a statistical look-alike with the more commonly employed "total population." The percentage of the work force engaged in retailing ($L\%$) measures the SMSA's retail centrality vis-à-vis smaller, nearby SMSAs. It is noteworthy that one of the largest $L\%$ values occurs for Sioux Falls, South Dakota (19.5 percent), while some of the lowest $L\%$ values (11.9 to 12.6 percent) occur in New Jersey: New Brunswick, Newark, Trenton, and Vineland. There appear to be no literature citations for $L\%$. Both URBAN and $L\%$ affect total demand levels in the SMSA; URBAN also influences costs via urbanization economies.

TABLE 11.1. Listing of Socioeconomic Variables

Variable	Brief Description	Minimum	Mean	Maximum	Source*
Income	Percent of households in income class				MEG
$3,000 to $4,999		2.9	6.16	10.1	
$5,000 to $7,999		4.0	9.31	16.2	
$8,000 to $9,999		3.0	6.66	11.8	
$10,000 to $14,999		9.1	18.50	25.0	
$15,000 to $24,999		18.5	28.16	38.6	
$25,000 to $49,999		6.3	18.01	39.2	
$50,000 plus		1.1	4.13	16.0	
Population Age	Percentage of population in age class				SBP
0 to 5		6.5	8.65	14.4	
6 to 11		7.2	9.81	11.6	
12 to 17		8.4	11.29	13.5	
18 to 24		9.4	13.91	30.4	
25 to 34		11.5	15.50	19.0	
35 to 49		12.4	16.27	19.7	
50 to 64		9.0	14.29	20.0	
Males	Median age in years	22.5	28.13	38.0	SBP
Females		24.2	30.42	43.7	

TABLE 11.1. (*continued*)

Variable	Brief Description	Minimum	Mean	Maximum	Source*
	Percentage of households with head in age class				SBP
25 to 34		14.8	22.79	30.2	
35 to 44		12.3	17.15	22.6	
45 to 54		13.0	17.24	22.8	
55 to 65		10.4	15.20	20.8	
65 plus		9.6	18.56	37.6	
Household Size	Percentage of households of different sizes				SBP
1		12.9	20.69	30.9	
2		25.3	30.47	42.4	
3		13.7	17.42	21.1	
4		10.9	16.25	22.1	
5		5.4	8.48	12.6	
Other Household Variables					
Male	Male percentage of population	46.5	48.61	53.1	SBP
White	White percentage of population	39.3	87.81	99.4	SBP
AUTOH	Automobiles per household	0.74	1.58	2.85	See text

182

SMSA Descriptors				
%GRO	Population growth rate, 1970-77	−5.5	8.88	43.9	SBP
ϕ	Population per square mile	24.7	418.45	6864.1	SBP, SMAD
Tϕ	Automobiles per square mile	16.6	218.69	1937.6	See text
U%	Unemployment rate	2.6	6.88	16.1	E & E
L%	Percent of all employees in the SMSA engaged in the retail trades	8.7	14.77	21.4	E & E, CRT
URBAN	Logarithm of number of retail stores in SMSA	6.3	7.85	10.9	CRT

*Sources: Compiled by the author from the following sources:

MEG: "Marketing Economics Guide." 1978. Marketing Economics Institute, New York, NY;

SBP: *Survey of Buying Power.* 1978. Data Service 1978, Sales and Marketing Management Magazine, New York, NY;

E&E: *Employment and Earnings* 1977, 1978. Washington, D.C. Department of Labor;

CRT: *Census of Retail Trade.* 1977. Geographic Area Series, Washington, D.C.: U.S. Department of Commerce;

SMAD: *State and Metropolitan Area Data Book.* 1978. Washington, D.C.: U.S. Dept. of Commerce.

Two points need to be made before progressing. First, each of the variables discussed above is an "immediate" measure. In contrast, macroretail structure—the distribution of retail stores across institutional types—is measured "immediately" but is actually the outcome of a historical process. Macrostructure inevitably adjusts slowly. Thus, for the socioeconomic structure variables used in this study to determine macroretail structure, it is necessary that the socioeconomic variables have changed rather slowly. Absence of data from previous years precludes a rigorous test of this hypothesis. Accordingly, the ensuing statistical tests comparing macroretail structure with socioeconomic structure must be regarded as nondefinitive.

Second, several variables that have been used in previous studies (for example, Haddon and Borgatta 1965; Green, Frank, and Robinson 1967) were not available to the author, since they can only be obtained from the decennial *Census of Population and Housing*. Particularly noteworthy are education, home ownership, and occupation. Their omission must be regarded as a weakness of this research. The absence of data on overhead costs and the limited information on variable costs, while irrelevant for socioeconomic structure, are also weaknesses in considering macroretail structure.

Factor Analysis

A principal components factor analysis with varimax rotation was performed on the 35 variables listed in Table 11.1. Twelve orthogonal factors were extracted. Thus, the rather considerable collinearity in the original data set has been eliminated. It should be noted that PCA is not theoretically based upon a causal model; hence, the extracted factors do not necessarily represent an underlying causal structure. In conjunction with this, PCA explains the variance in the variables, rather than the covariance between them. Varimax rotation generates a factor pattern that is less sensitive to excluded variables than are the results obtained with other rotational methods (Kim and Mueller 1978, p. 36).

Several criteria were used in deciding to extract 12 factors. First, it was felt that most of the variation of each variable should be accounted for. The success of this strategy can be seen in the communalities as well as in the fact that every variable has a significant loading on at least one factor. Second, it was felt that every factor should be readily interpretable. Third, attention was paid to the "rule of thumb" that there should be numerically at least two, and preferably three, variables for each factor. For this data set that meant between 12 and 17 factors. Fourth, an ordinary factor analysis was checked to be sure that variables that grouped together with PCA also grouped together with this other technique. That was the case. Finally, it should be recognized that the commonly applied scree test would dictate only nine factors. Use of this rule would have violated the first and second criteria.

SMSAs were deleted if there was a missing value for any variable. The unemployment rate and automotive ownership were the primary reasons for deletion. Except for New England, which was completely eliminated, there appears to be no systematic regional bias in the excluded SMSAs.

The reduced data set covered 184 SMSAs. Examination of initial cluster analysis results (reported later) showed a severe problem with one extreme outlier. Jersey City, New Jersey, was more than 11 standard deviations above the mean on the density–urbanity factor (described below). Following the suggestion of Punj and Stewart (1983), Jersey City was deleted and the results recomputed. Substantially better cluster results were obtained. Factor results with 183 SMSAs were nearly identical to those with 184 SMSAs. Hence, 183 SMSAs were retained for further analysis. Sixty-four percent of the U.S. population lives in these SMSAs.

The rotated factor loadings are reported in Table 11.2. As can be seen, communalities exceeded 0.76 for every variable. The 12 factors account for 91.6 percent of the total variation in this data set. To make the results easier to read, only factor loadings of at least 0.4 in absolute value are reported. Rotated eigenvalues are recorded at the bottom of the table.

The older population and household age brackets load positively on the first factor, while the younger categories load negatively on this factor. The percentage male also loads negatively, presumably reflecting life spans. Thus, the first factor is termed *seniors*. The lower-income brackets load positively on the second factor, while the higher-income categories load negatively. Hence, it is termed *poverty*. The third factor obviously captures *youth*. Apart from the age figures, there is some evidence of larger household sizes.

Population and automotive densities are extremely highly correlated with the fourth factor. Urbanity also loads positively. This factor is termed *density–urbanity*. Larger households constitute the fifth factor. It seems appropriate to call it *full nest*. People and households in the 35 to 54 age bracket make up the sixth factor: *middle age*.

The seventh factor is recent population *growth*. Two-person households seem to be common in high-growth SMSAs. The next factor is clearly *middle income*; the average household income for the 183 SMSAs is $17,335. *Unemployment* is the ninth factor; it is highest where there are more men.

The tenth factor is termed *racial composition*; it is the percentage white. The percentage of the work force engaged in retailing loads onto the eleventh factor. Following the logic presented earlier, it is termed *centrality*. The final factor is *mobility*, as indicated by automotive registrations per household.

Each of the 183 SMSAs can be characterized by means of its factor score on the 12 factors. For example, New York City has a high density–urbanity, but its citizens are not very mobile, at least as measured by private automobile ownership. While this type of description can be offered for every SMSA, it is considerably easier (and clearer) to perform a cluster analysis in order to learn which SMSAs are most similar.

TABLE 11.2. Rotated Factor Loadings for Socioeconomic Variables

Variable	Communality	Seniors	Poverty	Youth	Density–Urbanity	Full Nest	Middle Age	Growth	Middle Income	Unemployed	Racial Composition	Centrality	Mobility
Income													
%$3,000 to $4,999	0.9183		0.698						−0.436				
%$5,000 to $7,999	0.9638		0.772						−0.484				
%$8,000 to $9,999	0.9477		0.850						−0.439				
%$10,000 to $14,999	0.9128		0.922										
%$15,000 to $24,999	0.9620								0.920				
%$25,000 to $49,999	0.9507		−0.932										
%$50,000 plus	0.8508		−0.818										
Population Age													
%0 to 5	0.8210	−0.477		0.606									
%6 to 11	0.9446			0.884									
%12 to 17	0.9114			0.899									
%18 to 24	0.9648	−0.721		−0.435									
%25 to 34	0.9181	−0.747											
%35 to 49	0.9404						0.795						
%50 to 64	0.9658	0.909											
Male Age	0.9384	0.827											
Female Age	0.9418	0.859											
Household Age													
%25 to 34	0.9652	−0.896		0.433									
%35 to 44	0.9222						0.577						
%45 to 54	0.9254	0.411					0.566						

%55 to 64	0.9069	0.894											
65 plus	0.9617	0.773											
Household Size													
%1	0.9376		−0.495			−0.849							
%2	0.8774							0.622					
%3	0.8893					0.522	0.546						
%4	0.9123					0.751							
%5	0.9226			0.566		0.575							
Other Household Variables													
%Male	0.8336	−0.690								0.522			
%White	0.9535										0.919		
AUTOH	0.9726												0.933
SMSA Descriptors													
%GRO	0.8468							0.853					
φ	0.9453				0.932								
Tφ	0.9520				0.923								
U%	0.8608									0.827			
L%	0.8603											0.782	
URBAN	0.7603				0.695								
Rotated Eigenvalue		7.381	4.712	3.513	2.719	2.702	2.483	1.905	1.750	1.331	1.249	1.179	1.134
Percent Variance Explained	91.6%	21.1%	13.5%	10.0%	7.8%	7.7%	7.1%	5.4%	5.0%	3.8%	3.6%	3.4%	3.2%

Source: Compiled by the author.

187

Cluster Analysis

In a recent review article, Punj and Stewart (1983) discussed alternative methods of cluster-analyzing objects (SMSAs) and made specific recommendations designed to ensure the appropriate classification of those objects. They recommend a two-stage clustering procedure, "preliminary identification of clusters via Ward's minimum variance method, . . . followed by cluster refinement by an iterative partitioning procedure" (p. 134). Their advice is followed here.

Ward's method is a statistical technique that seeks to ensure that objects assigned to the same cluster are reasonably similar The results obtained with Ward's method, like all other clustering procedures, are somewhat dependent upon the definition of "similarity." The squared Euclidean distance is used in this chapter.

Ward's method, with a constant-level, partition-maximizing, expected distinctiveness rule, identified 15 separate clusters. A Z test on the separateness of the clusters showed them to be distinct at the 0.0525 level. These cluster results were then used to generate initial group centroids for a K means iterative clustering procedure, as recommended by Punj and Stewart (1983). The results stabilized after three iterations. Table 11.3 reports the final cluster centroids. These centroids may be interpreted as characterizing each cluster in terms of the 12 dimensions. For ease of reading, only centroid scores greater than 1.0 in absolute value are reported.

The statistics reported at the bottom of the table are the within-group homogeneity (Wi), the between-group distance (Bi), and an assessment statistic (Gi). Specific details on the three measures are contained in Klastorin (1983). All results are significant at the 0.001 level.

The first cluster may be characterized as SMSAs with full-nest households in rather dense urban areas. The second cluster is an extremely dense SMSA. The third cluster is high-growth SMSAs with many older citizens. The fourth cluster is not full nest; equivalently, it contains SMSAs with many single-person households. The fifth cluster is focused on SMSAs with a large number of children.

The sixth cluster is high in unemployment, but low in centrality. That is, the SMSAs in this group do not serve as places for outshopping by people living in the surrounding area. The seventh cluster is extremely high in private automobile ownership. The eighth cluster consists of older people and households, but, unlike the third cluster, these are not growth areas. The ninth cluster consists of poor SMSAs. The tenth cluster is high in unemployment, but average in centrality.

The eleventh and thirteenth clusters are average in all respects. The former leans somewhat toward a middle-aged populace, the latter toward middle-income households. The twelfth cluster is particularly interesting: It is not young, not old, and not middle aged! Careful examination of the factor loadings (Table 11.2)

TABLE 11.3. Socioeconomic Structure: Cluster Centroids

Cluster Number	Seniors	Poverty	Youth	Density–Urbanity	Full Nest	Middle Age	Growth	Middle Income	Unemployed	Racial Composition	Centrality	Mobility	Number of SMSAs in Cluster
1	-1.96			2.14	2.09					1.07			5
2		-1.05		8.27		-2.30		-1.03			-1.17	-3.52	1
3	2.51	-1.69		1.00		-1.56	4.11				1.22		3
4				1.00	-3.04								4
5	-1.15	1.45	2.36	1.22				-1.56		1.31	1.00		4
6									1.10		-1.39		16
7						-1.16				-1.07	-1.12	5.13	3
8		1.27											18
9		1.19						-1.19					14
10									1.33				12
11													19
12	-1.11		-1.56			-1.13							14
13													38
14										-1.92			21
15		-2.02											11

Note: SMSA, standard metropolitan statistical area.
Statistics: $W_1 = -6.53$, $B_1 = 10.76$, $G_1 = -19.43$, $G_2 = -47.81$, $G_3 = -14.04$, Wilks lambda = 0.0000, Hotelling's trace = 18.64.
Source: Compiled by the author.

189

points to a large population between 18 and 24 years of age, in short, college communities. Recalling the definition of racial composition from Table 11.2 reveals the fourteenth cluster to consist of SMSAs having a large nonwhite population. Finally, the last cluster contains SMSAs in which households have an above-average income.

Table 11.4 lists the membership of every cluster based on socioeconomic structure. This listing provides face validity for the cluster characterizations based on their centroids. To conserve space, the table also reports the membership of every cluster based on macroretail structure. These latter results are derived and discussed in the next section.

Observations

Perhaps the most intriguing result of the research reported thus far is the strong *regionality* of the cluster memberships. Four-fifths of the first cluster are *suburbs of New York City*, while the second cluster is *New York City*. The third cluster contains the high-growth *retirement communities of Florida*. The fourth cluster contains the *large, West Coast SMSAs*. Three of the four members of the fifth cluster are *Mexican–American SMSAs of Texas*, where the number of children is high (as it is in Salt Lake City, the fourth member of this cluster).

Nearly three-fourths of the members of the sixth cluster are *moderate-sized SMSAs in the industrial heartland*. Eighty percent of the members of the eighth cluster are in or adjacent to *Pennsylvania*. Half the members of the ninth cluster are *impoverished SMSAs in the Middle Atlantic region*. The tenth cluster is focused on the *West*. It is rather surprising to see this area as characterized by high unemployment. Presumably this is due to in-migration exceeding economic growth, although more research is needed before this conclusion can be regarded as definitive.

The eleventh cluster consists of SMSAs in the *Southeast and Southwest*. Most SMSAs in the twelfth cluster are immediately identifiable as containing *large state universities*. The large thirteenth cluster spans the nation, except for the East and South. The fourteenth cluster is readily recognizable as *nonwhite, Southern SMSAs*. (Honolulu is a member because Orientals are classified as nonwhite in this data base.) The final cluster comprises cities in *California*, plus three cities in the North Central region with a large union presence, plus the District of Columbia with its well-paid government employees and Houston with its space center.

In summary, the cluster analysis that has classified these 183 SMSA's into 15 discrete groups has revealed strong regional characteristics. There are intraregional similarities and interregional differences in socioeconomic structure. Of course, there is more to this structure than a strictly regionalist perspective might indicate, as many SMSAs link with clusters based outside their own census region. Nonetheless, the regional nature of the results is striking. Whether there is an equally strong regionality to macroretail structure remains to be seen.

TABLE 11.4. Standard Metropolitan Statistical Area (SMSA) Cluster Assignment

SMSA Name	State	Socio-economic Cluster	Macro-Retail Cluster	SMSA Name	State	Socio-economic Cluster	Macro-Retail Cluster
Anaheim	CA	1	7	Allentown	PA	8	12
Long Branch	NJ	1	15	Altoona	PA	8	12
Nassau-Suffolk	NY	1	15	Beaumont	TX	8	12
New Brunswick	NJ	1	15	Charleston	WV	8	12
Newark	NJ	1	15	Erie	PA	8	5
				Harrisburg	PA	8	1
New York	NY	2	15	Johnstown	PA	8	12
				Miami	FL	8	15
Fort Lauderdale	FL	3	15	Northeastern	PA	8	1
Tampa-St. Petersburg	FL	3	11	Philadelphia	PA	8	15
West Palm Beach	FL	3	15	Pittsburgh	PA	8	15
				Reading	PA	8	12
Los Angeles	CA	4	7	South Bend	IN	8	4
Portland	OR	4	11	Wheeling	WV	8	12
San Francisco	CA	4	7	Williamsport	PA	8	1
Seattle	WA	4	8	Wilmington	DE	8	6
				York	PA	8	12
Corpus Christi	TX	5	11	Youngstown	OH	8	3
El Paso	TX	5	11				
Salt Lake City	UT	5	1	Albany	NY	9	3
San Antonio	TX	5	11	Asheville	NC	9	13
				Atlantic City	NJ	9	15
Battle Creek	MI	6	8	Baltimore	MD	9	3
Bay City	MI	6	15	Binghamton	NY	9	3
Canton	OH	6	1	Buffalo	NY	9	3
Eugene	OR	6	8	Chattanooga	TN	9	13
Flint	MI	6	1	Elmira	NY	9	4
Jackson	MI	6	8	Fort Smith	AR	9	5
Kalamazoo	MI	6	9	St. Joseph	MO	9	6
Kenosha	WI	6	3	Syracuse	NY	9	3
Lansing	MI	6	9	Utica-Rome	NY	9	1
Modesto	CA	6	5	Waco	TX	9	5
Muskegon	MI	6	8	Wichita Falls	TX	9	5
Poughkeepsie	NY	6	10				
Racine	WI	6	3	Albuquerque	NM	10	11
Salem	OR	6	8	Bakersfield	CA	10	11
Stockton	CA	6	1	Denver	CO	10	7
Vineland	NJ	6	5	Las Vegas	NV	10	11
				Orlando	FL	10	13
Jackson	MS	7	13	Phoenix	AZ	10	11
Paterson	NJ	7	15	Reno	NV	10	11
Trenton	NJ	7	15	Riverside	CA	10	10

TABLE 11.4. (*continued*)

SMSA Name	State	Socio-economic Cluster	Macro-Retail Cluster	SMSA Name	State	Socio-economic Cluster	Macro-Retail Cluster
Salinas	CA	10	7	Appleton	WI	13	4
San Diego	CA	10	7	Boise City	ID	13	10
Tacoma	WA	10	8	Cedar Rapids	IA	13	1
Tucson	AZ	10	11	Chicago	IL	13	1
				Cincinnati	OH	13	3
Atlanta	GA	11	13	Cleveland	OH	13	3
Charlotte	NC	11	2	Columbus	OH	13	3
Dallas	TX	11	5	Davenport	IA	13	1
Galveston	TX	11	11	Dayton	OH	13	3
Greensboro	NC	11	13	Decatur	IL	13	4
Greenville	SC	11	13	Des Moines	IA	13	9
Huntington	WV	11	13	Detroit	MI	13	1
Huntsville	AL	11	5	Dubuque	IA	13	4
Knoxville	TN	11	13	Evansville	IN	13	6
Lexington	KY	11	6	Fort Wayne	IN	13	1
Little Rock	AR	11	5	Gary-Hammond	IN	13	1
Lynchburg	VA	11	12	Green Bay	WI	13	4
Nashville	TN	11	13	Indianapolis	IN	13	6
Newport News	VA	11	2	Kansas City	MO	13	6
Parkersburg	WV	11	4	La Crosse	WI	13	4
Raleigh	NC	11	9	Lancaster	PA	13	12
Richmond	VA	11	2	Louisville	KY	13	6
Roanoke	VA	11	2	Milwaukee	WI	13	3
Tulsa	OK	11	5	Minneapolis	MN	13	9
				Oklahoma City	OK	13	5
Ann Arbor	MI	12	9	Omaha	NE	13	3
Austin	TX	12	11	Peoria	IL	13	9
Bloomington	IN	12	10	Rochester	NY	13	1
Champaign	IL	12	9	Rockford	IL	13	6
Fargo-Moorhead	ND	12	9	St. Louis	MO	13	1
Fayetteville	AR	12	10	Sioux City	IA	13	8
Lincoln	NE	12	6	Sioux Falls	SD	13	9
Lubbock	TX	12	5	Spokane	WA	13	8
Madison	WI	12	4	Springfield	IL	13	1
Muncie	IN	12	6	Topeka	KS	13	6
Santa Barbara	CA	12	7	Waterloo	IA	13	9
Springfield	MO	12	5				
Terra Haute	IN	12	12	Augusta	GA	14	13
Wichita	KS	12	7	Baton Rouge	LA	14	11
				Birmingham	AL	14	13
Akron	OH	13	3	Charleston	SC	14	13
Amarillo	TX	13	5	Columbia	SC	14	13

TABLE 11.4. (*continued*)

SMSA Name	State	Socio-economic Cluster	Macro-Retail Cluster	SMSA Name	State	Socio-economic Cluster	Macro-Retail Cluster
Columbus	GA	14	13	Shreveport	LA	14	5
Honolulu	HI	14	14	Tuscaloosa	AL	14	13
Jacksonville	FL	14	13				
Lake Charles	LA	14	10	Fresno	CA	15	11
Macon	GA	14	13	Grand Rapids	MI	15	8
Memphis	TN	14	13	Houston	TX	15	11
Mobile	AL	14	13	Oxnard	CA	15	7
Monroe	LA	14	13	Sacramento	CA	15	7
Montgomery	AL	14	13	Saginaw	MI	15	15
New Orleans	LA	14	11	San Jose	CA	15	7
Norfolk	VA	14	2	Santa Rosa	CA	15	10
Pensacola	FL	14	11	Toledo	OH	15	3
Pine Bluff	AR	14	4	Vallejo	CA	15	7
Savannah	GA	14	13	Washington	DC	15	7

Source: Compiled by author.

MACRORETAIL STRUCTURE

This section has two basic purposes: to describe the macroretail structure of U.S. SMSAs and to determine those SMSAs that are most similar in their structure. The first subsection briefly describes the data. The second subsection reports the results of a principal components factor analysis of 28 lines of retail trade. The third subsection details the results of a cluster analysis based on the factor scores. Observations are offered in the final subsection.

Data

The *Census of Retail Trade* reports information on 57 lines of retail trade. Nineteen of these are at the four-digit Standard Industrial Classification (SIC) code level. The other 38 are at the three-digit level. On a geographical area basis, the Bureau of the Census suppresses data whenever information on a line of trade would reveal the details of particular stores or businesses. Thus, in order to obtain the maximum number of SMSAs, several of the smaller lines of trade were deleted from the data base used here. Details on the data base are included in Table 11.5.

TABLE 11.5. Listing of Retail Store Types

Line Code Number	Standard Industrial Classification Code	Description	Minimum (%)	Mean (%)	Maximum (%)
002R	526,7	Retail Nurseries, Mobile Home Dealers	0.27	1.07	2.57
003	521,3	Building Material & Supply Stores	0.79	2.47	4.71
006	525	Hardware Stores	0.19	1.28	2.57
009R	533,9	Variety, Miscellaneous General Merchandise	0.37	1.75	3.67
010	531	Department Stores	0.21	0.84	1.45
013R	54-541	Food Stores except Grocery Stores	1.13	3.28	8.08
014	541	Grocery Stores	5.04	9.34	14.98
028	551	Motor Vehicle Dealers—New and Used	0.92	2.06	4.66
032	552	Motor Vehicle Dealers—Used Only	0.32	1.23	2.88
033	553	Auto & Home Supply Stores	1.05	2.93	5.81
036	555,6,7,9	Miscellaneous Automotive Dealers	0.42	2.00	4.27
041	554	Gasoline Service Stations	5.85	11.39	15.24
042R	564,5,6,9	Family Clothing, Shoe, Other Apparel	1.98	3.67	5.46

Code	SIC	Retail Type	Min	Mean	Max
043	561	Men's and Boys' Clothing Stores	0.65	1.59	2.78
044	562,3,8	Women's Clothing and Specialty Stores, Furriers	1.41	3.36	6.33
063	5712	Furniture Stores	1.19	2.40	4.41
064	5713,4,9	Home Furnishing Stores	0.71	1.81	3.29
068	572	Household Appliance Stores	0.42	0.96	1.91
069	573	Radio, Television and Music Stores	1.16	2.26	4.04
075	5812	Eating Places	12.75	18.39	23.64
083	5813	Drinking Places (Alcoholic Beverages)	0.81	5.91	17.54
084	591	Drug and Proprietary Stores	1.96	3.41	4.86
088	592	Liquor Stores	0.39	2.52	7.20
089	593	Used Merchandise Stores	0.41	1.24	2.29
090R	5942,3,5,6,7,8,9	Book, Stationary, Hobby, Camera, Gift, Luggage and Sewing Stores	2.34	4.09	7.86
091	5941	Sporting Goods Stores and Bicycle Shops	0.54	1.46	2.82
094	5944	Jewelry Stores	0.71	1.54	5.53
118	5992	Florists	0.39	1.58	2.53
		SMSA minimum, mean, maximum for the preceding 28 retail types	93.1	95.81	97.7

Note: SMSA, standard metropolitan statistical area.
Source: Compiled by the author.

Several points should be made. First, 36 of the three-digit lines of trade and 16 of the four-digit lines are included. Excluded are nonstore retailers (vending machines, mail order), fuel and ice dealers, cigar stores, news dealers, and miscellaneous retail stores. Nearly 96 percent of all retail stores in the average SMSA are included. Second, to obtain such a high coverage rate, it was often necessary to use retail lines that are reported by the Census Bureau in aggregated form, for example, home furnishing stores that comprise floor covering, drapery and curtain, and miscellaneous home furnishing stores. It was also occasionally necessary to accept lines of trade reported in a residual form. An instance is retail nurseries and mobile home dealers, obtainable only by subtracting hardware and building material stores from SIC code 52. All instances of this latter form are noted by an "R" at the end of the line code number listed in Table 11.5. Third, as a result of these various combinations, there are 28 specific "lines of trade" incorporated into the data base used here. These 28 lines were available for 272 SMSAs. To ensure compatibility with the socioeconomic structure factors and clusters, only 183 were used. However, principal components results with 272 SMSAs are similar to those with the reduced data set. Fourth, consistent with the concept of macroretail structure developed earlier, all data were in the form of the percentage of all retail stores in the SMSA that was in the specific line of trade.

Factor Analysis

A principal components factor analysis with orthogonal, varimax rotation was performed on the variables listed in Table 11.5. The logic for this technique is identical to that reported under Socioeconomic Structure above.

Rotated factor loadings are reported in Table 11.6. Lines of trade are denoted by their line code numbers from Table 11.5. Fifteen factors were extracted, accounting for 85.7 percent of the total variation in the data. Communalities for each line of trade range upward from 0.76. To ease the task of reading Table 11.6, only factor loadings of at least 0.4 in absolute value are reported.

The first factor consists of variety stores, miscellaneous general merchandise stores, grocery stores, and furniture stores plus, to a lesser extent, used car dealers, auto and home supply stores, retail nurseries, and mobile home dealers. Negative loadings were obtained for drinking establishments and nongrocery food stores (bakeries, meat markets, etc.). After some consideration, the first factor was termed *basic* retailing.

Building material and supply stores, retail nurseries, mobile home dealers, and miscellaneous automotive dealers load heavily on the second factor. The last category consists of boat, motorcycle, and recreational vehicle dealers. Except for nurseries, all of them sell durable goods that are used proactively. Hence, the second factor is termed *active durables*. This label contrasts with *passive durables* that has been applied to the seventh factor. It consists of household appliance stores and new and used car dealers.

The third factor consists of the entire range of *apparel* stores. *Used goods* stores are the primary component of the fourth factor. Large factor loadings for sporting goods, radio, television, and music stores are obtained for the fifth factor. It is termed *recreation*-oriented retailers. The sixth factor is labeled *jewelry*. In addition to jewelry stores, various specialized retailers of apparel and other goods load onto it.

The eighth factor is composed primarily of home furnishing stores that do much of their business with people in the process of *redecorating* their homes or apartments. *Department* stores load most heavily on the ninth factor. It is of some interest to note that used car dealers appear in conjunction with department stores. No reason is offered. The remaining factors, *drugs, eating out, gasoline, liquor, hardware*, and *flowers*, have rather straightforward labels.

From the viewpoint of macroretail structure, the first through seventh and the ninth factors describe those retail lines of trade that tend to occur in combination with each other. The other factors reflect retailers that tend to "stand alone." Whether these combinations and singularities are driven by consumer demand, metropolitan area size, and multipurpose shopping remains to be seen in the next section. Prior to turning to that topic, we first investigate the degree to which macroretail structure appears to be similar in various SMSAs.

Cluster Analysis

Ward's method, with a constant-level, partition-maximizing, expected distinctiveness criterion, identified 15 separate clusters. The appearance of 15 macroretail structure clusters *and* 15 socioeconomic structure clusters must be regarded as a coincidence. A Z test on the separateness of the macroretail clusters did not show them to be significantly distinct.

The results of Ward's method were then used to generate group centroids for a K means iterative clustering procedure. The results stabilized after five iterations. Table 11.7 reports the final cluster centroids. Once again, only centroid values of at least 1.0 in absolute value are recorded. The various within-group, between-group, and assessment statistics reported at the bottom of the table are all highly significant. Hence, the K means results, unlike the Ward results, do show distinct macroretail-based clusters. Both techniques generated clusters that are internally consistent.

An examination of the cluster centroids reveals that the macroretail structure clusters are not nearly as distinctive as the ones based on socioeconomic structure. The most distinct cluster is the fourteenth. It has an extremely high percentage of jewelry stores and a high percentage of liquor stores and florists, but a distinct absence of many of the other lines of trade. However, the fourteenth cluster has only one member: Honolulu, noted as a tourist center for both the West Coast and the Orient. Other clusters with a certain distinctiveness are now discussed briefly.

TABLE 11.6. Rotated Factor Loading for Retail Variables

Line Code Number	Communality	Basic	Active Durables	Apparel	Used Goods	Recreation	Jewelry	Passive Durables	Redecorate	Department	Drugs	Eating Out	Gasoline	Liquor	Hardware	Flowers
002R	0.8103	0.417	0.536													
003	0.8604		0.847													
006	0.8942															
009R	0.7979	0.733														
010	0.8620									0.831						
013R	0.7945	−0.577														
014	0.8687	0.652														
028	0.8034							0.595								
032	0.8746	0.447								0.578						
033	0.8148	0.565			0.477											
036	0.7864		0.656													
041	0.9190												0.874			
042R	0.8602			0.416			0.570								0.863	
043	0.8644			0.893												

198

Item	F1 (3.534)	F2 (1.926)	F3 (1.836)	F4 (1.729)	F5 (1.683)	F6 (1.644)	F7 (1.552)	F8 (1.406)	F9 (1.374)	F10 (1.336)	F11 (1.325)	F12 (1.228)	F13 (1.189)	F14 (1.183)	F15 (1.045)
044	0.8263	0.778					0.881								
063	0.7630				0.639										
064	0.8851														
068	0.8889										0.930				
069	0.7980	−0.754													
075	0.9488		0.682							0.872					
083	0.8969														
084	0.9082												0.944		
088	0.9556							0.866							
089	0.8534			0.846											
090R	0.8575					0.522				−0.472					
091	0.8728														
094	0.8089				0.880										
118	0.9183				0.787										0.829
Rotated Eigenvalue	3.534	1.926	1.836	1.729	1.683	1.644	1.552	1.406	1.374	1.336	1.325	1.228	1.189	1.183	1.045
Percentage Variance Explained (total 85.7%)	12.6%	6.9%	6.6%	6.2%	6.0%	5.9%	5.5%	5.0%	4.9%	4.8%	4.7%	4.4%	4.2%	4.2%	3.7%

Source: Compiled by the author.

199

TABLE 11.7. Macroretail Structure: Cluster Centroids

Cluster Number	Basic	Active Durables	Apparel	Used Goods	Recreation	Jewelry	Passive Durables	Redecoration	Department	Drugs	Eating Out	Gasoline	Liquor	Hardware	Flowers	Number of SMSAs
1	1.02									1.17						17
2		-1.27							1.30		-2.05		1.28			5
3	-1.16															16
4					1.34				1.41							10
5		1.05		1.30											-1.05	15
6					1.01								-1.58			11
7													-1.03			13
8								1.03					1.04			10
9			1.08											1.48		11
10		2.26		-1.65												7
11																18
12							1.94									11
13	1.51															23
14	-2.59	-1.87		-1.74		7.85				-1.51	-1.34	-1.07	1.49	-1.42		1
15	1.03		1.03					1.12							1.62	15

Note: SMSA, standard metropolitan statistical area.

Statistics: $W1 = -17.40$, $B1 = 9.87$, $G1 = -17.78$, $G2 = -45.90$, $G3 = -23.46$, Wilk's lambda $= 0.0001$, Hotelling trace $= 15.86$.

Source: Compiled by the author.

The second cluster is distinguished as having a relative shortage of restaurants, cafeterias, and fast food establishments. SMSAs in the fourth cluster have an above-average percentage of department and recreationally oriented stores. Only the fifth cluster shows a high percentage of used goods stores. SMSAs in the sixth cluster are noteworthy for their relative absence of liquor stores.

The ninth cluster is focused on hardware stores, while the tenth shows a preponderance of "active durables" and an absence of used goods stores. SMSAs in the twelfth cluster have a high level of "passive durable" goods stores. Finally, the thirteenth cluster is focused upon the basic retail lines of trade.

Even though many of the clusters do not seem to be particularly distinct, at least in terms of our ability to apply meaningful labels to them, the fact remains that they are significantly different from one another in a statistical sense. This suggests that there may be regional characteristics to the clusters. This is the topic to which we now turn.

Observations

An examination of cluster membership, recorded in the last column of Table 11.4, indicates definite regional concentrations for many of the clusters. Some of these concentrations are quite compact, while others span a substantial geographical area. For only one cluster is there an absence of any obvious regionality.

The *first* cluster stretches in an arc from upstate New York, through Pennsylvania, Ohio, Michigan, Indiana, Illinois, Missouri, and Iowa. Fifteen of the 17 members of this cluster lie in the arc. The *second* cluster is much more tightly bunched, consisting of SMSAs in Virginia and North Carolina. It might be termed the "Upper South." The *third* cluster contains four SMSAs in upstate New York, seven in Ohio, three in Wisconsin (Milwaukee and two neighbors), plus two others.

The *fourth* cluster is centered on Wisconsin (four SMSAs), with nearby members in Iowa, Illinois, and Indiana, the other three SMSAs being scattered. The *fifth* cluster is concentrated in the "Southwest," Texas, Oklahoma, Arkansas, and Louisiana accounting for 10 of the 14 members. The *sixth* cluster may be termed the "Midwest," since all but one SMSA lie in the states of Indiana, Illinois, Kentucky, Missouri, Nebraska, and Kansas.

The *seventh* cluster may be termed "California," 10 of its 14 SMSAs being located there. Of the ten SMSAs in the *eighth* cluster, five are located in the Pacific Northwest (Washington and Oregon) and four in Michigan. The *ninth* cluster is focused upon the "Upper Midwest," all but one member lying in the Dakotas, Minnesota, Iowa, Illinois, or Michigan.

The seven SMSAs composing the *tenth* cluster are scattered across the nation. It is the only one of the clusters to have no obvious regional nature. The *eleventh* cluster might be termed a "Sunbelt" version of the first cluster. All but one of its members lie in the broad belt from California through Nevada,

Arizona, New Mexico, Texas, and Louisiana on to Florida. The *twelfth* cluster is much more concentrated, eight of its SMSAs being in Pennsylvania or West Virginia.

The *thirteenth* cluster may be termed the "Deep South," all but one of its members being located in Florida, Georgia, the Carolinas, Louisiana, Mississippi, Alabama, or Tennessee.

The *fourteenth* cluster is Honolulu, as mentioned earlier. The *fifteenth* cluster is particularly interesting. It contains all the SMSAs included in this data base that are part of the New York standard consolidated statistical (SCSA),[3] the Philadelphia SCSA (except for Wilmington, part of the sixth cluster), the Miami SCSA, West Palm Beach (adjacent to the Miami SCSA), Atlantic City (adjacent to the Philadelphia SCSA), Pittsburgh, and the adjacent SMSAs of Saginaw and Bay City, Michigan.

In summary, there is a strong regionality to the clusters defined on the basis of macroretail structure, although it is certainly not the same regionality defined on the basis of socioeconomic structure. Two questions remain: First, is there a significant overlap of the two pairs of clusters? Second, do the socioeconomic structure factors help to explain the macroretail structure factors? These questions are addressed in the next section.

STRUCTURAL INTERACTION

A joint consideration of socioeconomic structure and macroretail structure generates two immediate questions. First, are the regional clusters of SMSAs created with the socioeconomic structure similar to the clusters formed by macroretail structure? Second, does socioeconomic structure help to explain the cross-sectional variation in macroretail structure? This section addresses these questions.

Cluster Comparison

For ease of exposition, the assignment of SMSAs to distinct clusters will be termed a "partition." The first partition is based on socioeconomic structure, the second partition on macroretail structure. If the two partitions were identical, then every pair of SMSAs that appeared together in the first partition would also appear together in the second partition. At the other extreme, even if the partitions were unrelated, some pairs of SMSAs would appear together in both partitions on a random basis. It is possible to assess statistically the similarity of the two partitions. Following a technique developed by Klastorin and Ledingham (1981, pp. 34–36), it can be shown that a Z test for similarity is equal to 17.97, a number significantly greater than zero at the 0.001 level.

Thus, we may safely conclude that the two partitions are significantly more similar than would be expected on a random basis. The assignment of SMSAs to clusters on the basis of socioeconomic structure is indeed similar to the assignment based on macroretail structure. This suggests that the former may be related to the latter, a proposition that can be investigated with regression analysis.

Regression Analysis

Results of the ordinary least-squares regression of the 12 socioeconomic factors upon each of the 15 macroretail factors are contained in Table 11.8. Because the independent variables are factor scores derived from an orthogonal rotation, there is no collinearity between them. Since the independent variables were created by the same process, each regression equation is itself independent of any influences from the others.

The hypothetical average SMSA has a value of zero on all of the dependent and independent variables. Thus, a beta coefficient such as Poverty's 0.176 in the basic regression should be read as follows: An SMSA that is 1 standard deviation above average in poverty can be expected to be 0.176 standard deviation above average in its percentage distribution of stores engaged in basic retailing. The constant term is, by definition, equal to zero in each regression.

As can be seen from Table 11.8, the presence of a disproportionate percentage of *seniors* has a negative influence on the percentage of stores selling used goods, recreational items, jewelry, and gasoline. However, seniors have a positive effect on "passive durable" goods, drugstores, and eating establishments.[4] In contrast, the presence of a high percentage of the *middle-aged* tends to depress the number of stores engaged in the sale of "active durables" and recreational items, eating establishments, and hardware stores. The middle aged have a positive impact upon basic retailing and florists. Finally, the presence of a *youthful* population diminishes the percentage of stores engaged in basic retailing, "passive durables," and merchandise used in redecorating and florists, while positively affecting drugstores and eating establishments. Thus, just as products demand change as people move through their life cycles (Wells and Gubar 1966), so does patronage of differing retail store types. Because retailing is competitive, these demand differences have an influence on macroretail structure.

Household size, as measured by the *full-nest* variable, has a positive impact on basic retailing, department stores, and eating establishments but a negative effect on used goods and recreational equipment stores.

Poverty enhances the number of basic and used goods retailers and department stores. This last result is somewhat surprising in light of Ingene's finding (1984a) that poorer households spend less at department stores. It may be that this result is due to the "department" factor being a composite of department stores and used car dealers. Poverty has a negative influence upon recreational goods retailers, those selling items used in redecorating, and hardware stores. In contrast, *middle-income* households enhance the number of recreational and

TABLE 11.8. Regressions of Macroretail Structure Factors upon Socioeconomic Structure Factors

Socioeconomic Structure Factors	Basic	Active Durables	Apparel	Used Goods	Recreation	Jewelry	Passive Durables	Redecorate
Seniors	-0.043 (-0.91)	0.019 (0.29)	-0.063 (-0.90)	-0.278 (-4.25)[a]	-0.337 (-5.38)[a]	-0.170 (-2.39)[b]	0.228 (3.44)[a]	0.34 (0.52)
Middle Age	0.078 (1.67)[c]	-0.274 (-4.27)[a]	-0.074 (-1.07)	0.101 (1.54)	-0.118 (-1.89)[c]	0.026 (0.36)	-0.039 (-0.59)	-0.009 (-0.14)
Youth	-0.092 (-1.97)[c]	-0.002 (-0.03)	-0.111 (-1.60)	0.060 (0.92)	0.023 (0.37)	-0.073 (-1.02)	-0.149 (-2.24)[b]	-0.252 (-3.82)[a]
Full Nest	0.240 (5.14)[a]	-0.050 (-0.78)	0.032 (0.46)	-0.270 (-4.12)[a]	-0.141 (-2.26)[b]	-0.026 (-0.37)	0.084 (1.27)	-0.081 (-1.23)
Poverty	0.176 (3.77)[a]	0.054 (0.85)	-0.102 (-1.46)	0.160 (2.45)[b]	-0.274 (-4.38)[a]	-0.040 (-0.55)	0.010 (0.15)	-0.146 (-2.22)[b]
Middle Income	-0.298 (-6.38)[a]	0.023 (0.35)	-0.034 (-0.49)	-0.156 (-2.39)[b]	0.130 (2.08)[b]	-0.137 (-1.91)[c]	0.111 (1.67)[c]	0.031 (0.48)

Racial Composition	−0.490 (−10.48)ᵃ	0.311 (4.86)ᵃ	−0.210 (−3.02)ᵃ	−0.002 (−0.03)	0.086 (1.37)	−0.114 (−1.59)	0.226 (3.41)ᵃ	0.040 (0.60)
Unemployed	−0.167 (−3.57)ᵃ	−0.107 (−1.67)ᶜ	−0.134 (−1.92)ᶜ	−0.031 (−0.48)	−0.007 (−0.12)	0.044 (0.62)	0.077 (1.15)	0.025 (0.39)
Mobility	−0.059 (−1.25)	−0.000 (−0.00)	0.122 (1.75)ᶜ	0.068 (1.04)	−0.049 (−0.78)	0.148 (2.07)ᵇ	0.063 (0.95)	0.104 (1.58)
Growth	0.241 (5.15)ᵃ	0.181 (2.83)ᵃ	−0.022 (−0.32)	0.194 (.297)ᵃ	0.100 (1.60)	0.099 (1.39)	−0.190 (−2.86)ᵃ	0.257 (3.90)ᵃ
Density–Urbanity	−0.306 (−6.53)ᵃ	−0.273 (−4.26)ᵃ	0.234 (3.37)ᵃ	−0.115 (−1.76)ᶜ	−0.175 (−2.79)ᵃ	0.113 (1.58)	−0.243 (−3.66)ᵃ	0.287 (4.37)ᵃ
Centrality	−0.099 (−2.11)ᵇ	−0.076 (−1.18)	0.103 (1.49)	0.030 (0.45)	0.211 (3.37)ᵃ	0.135 (1.88)ᶜ	−0.010 (−0.15)	−0.098 (−1.48)
$\bar{R}^2$	0.601	0.253	0.119	0.220	0.288	0.072	0.199	0.212
(F)	(28.88)ᵃ	(6.15)ᵃ	(3.05)ᵃ	(5.28)ᵃ	(7.13)ᵃ	(2.18)ᵇ	(4.76)ᵃ	(5.09)ᵃ

TABLE 11.8. (continued)

Socioeconomic Structure Factors	Department	Drugs	Eating Out	Gasoline	Liquor	Hardware	Flowers	# of Significant Results	
								Positive	Negative
Seniors	-0.013 (-0.20)	0.157 (2.27)[b]	0.268 (4.06)[a]	-0.170 (-2.49)[b]	0.060 (0.84)	-0.002 (-0.03)	-0.044 (-0.63)	3	4
Middle Age	-0.069 (-1.04)	0.071 (1.03)	-0.199 (-3.02)[a]	-0.009 (-0.14)	-0.080 (-1.12)	-0.190 (-2.77)[a]	0.118 (1.69)[c]	2 (2)	4 (1)
Youth	-0.041 (-0.62)	0.176 (2.55)[b]	0.248 (3.76)[a]	0.025 (0.36)	0.043 (0.60)	-0.092 (-1.34)	-0.157 (-2.24)[b]	2	4 (1)
Full Nest	0.137 (2.08)[b]	0.044 (0.63)	0.174 (.264)[a]	-0.037 (-0.55)	0.054 (0.75)	0.018 (0.27)	0.107 (1.53)	3	2
Poverty	0.273 (4.15)[a]	0.001 (0.01)	-0.008 (-0.13)	-0.072 (-1.05)	0.017 (0.24)	-0.115 (-1.68)[c]	-0.082 (-1.18)	3	3 (1)
Middle Income	0.108 (1.64)	-0.054 (-0.78)	-0.080 (-1.22)	0.205 (2.99)[a]	0.203 (2.85)[a]	0.062 (0.90)	0.029 (0.37)	4 (1)	3 (1)

Racial Composition	0.080 (1.22)	−0.117 (−1.70)[c]	−0.102 (−1.54)	−0.072 (−1.05)	−0.056 (−0.78)	0.092 (1.34)	−0.114 (−1.63)	2	3 (1)
Unemployed	−0.325 (−4.95)[a]	−0.118 (−1.71)[c]	0.072 (1.09)	−0.201 (−2.94)[a]	0.083 (1.16)	−0.166 (2.42)[b]	−0.276 (−3.95)[a]	0	8 (3)
Mobility	0.013 (0.19)	0.044 (0.64)	0.169 (2.56)[b]	0.162 (2.37)[b]	−0.042 (−0.59)	−0.103 (−1.50)	0.126 (1.80)[c]	5 (2)	0
Growth	−0.128 (−1.95)[c]	+0.169 (−2.45)[b]	0.014 (0.21)	−0.121 (−1.77)[c]	0.193 (2.71)[a]	−0.231 (−3.37)[a]	−0.066 (−0.95)	5	5 (2)
Density–Urbanity	−0.163 (−2.48)[b]	0.075 (1.08)	−0.046 (−0.70)	−0.198 (−2.90)[a]	−0.134 (−1.87)[c]	−0.079 (−1.15)	−0.055 (−0.80)	2	8 (2)
Centrality	−0.006 (−0.10)	−0.250 (−3.62)[a]	0.070 (1.07)	−0.007 (−0.10)	0.090 (1.26)	−0.184 (−2.69)[a]	0.011 (0.16)	2 (1)	3
$\bar{R}^2$	0.215	0.135	0.209	0.148	0.070	0.146	0.113		
(F)	(5.15)[a]	(3.36)[a]	(5.00)[a]	(3.64)[a]	(2.14)[b]	(3.59)[a]	(2.94)[a]		

[a] prob < 0.01.
[b] prob < 0.05.
[c] prob < 0.10.

Note: Two-tail tests except for the *F* tests on the regressions.
Source: Compiled by the author.

"passive durable" goods retailers, as well as gasoline stations and liquor stores. However, middle-income households lessen the percentage of stores engaged in basic retailing, in selling used goods, and in selling jewelry.

A large white percentage of the population, as measured by *racial composition*, increases the percentage of stores selling "active" and "passive" durables, while decreasing the percentage of basic retailers, apparel stores, and drugstores. *Unemployment* has a particularly straightforward effect. It lowers the percentage of stores in eight lines of trade: basic, active durables, apparel, department stores, drugstores, gasoline stations, hardware stores, and florists.

Mobility has a pronounced positive effect on the percentage of stores in five lines of trade: apparel, jewelry, eating establishments, gasoline stations, and florists. The gasoline result is, of course, driven by the presence of so many automobiles.

Recent *growth* of population spurs the development of basic retailing, "active durables," used goods, redecorating items, and liquor stores, but harms the relative development of "passive durable" goods stores, department stores, drugstores, gasoline stations, and hardware stores.

Dense, urban areas evidence more apparel stores and retailers engaged in selling redecorating merchandise. However, negative influences are seen for basic and "active durable" goods retailers, used goods stores, recreational goods stores, "passive durable" goods, department and liquor stores, as well as gasoline stations. It is believed that the availability of mass transit is the driving feature in this last case, although there does not appear to be an adequate data base that would allow testing of that proposition.

Finally, *central places* (SMSAs with a large percentage of their work force engaged in retailing) show a relative shortage of basic retailers, drugstores, and hardware stores, but an abundance of recreation goods and jewelry stores.

The total number of significant positive and negative signs for each independent variable is given in the final two columns of Table 11.8. In all, there are 33 positive and 47 negative signs; this is 18.3 and 26.1 percent, respectively, of all the signs. The total number of significant signs, 80 (44.4 percent), is considerably greater than the 10 percent that would be expected by chance. It should be noted that while most researchers would assign significance only at the 0.05 level, it seems better to point out those signs that are "nearly significant" (0.051 to 0.10 level) and let readers draw their own conclusions (Leamer 1978). There are 18 such cases (10 percent). They are counted (in parentheses) in the final pair of columns in Table 11.8.

Adjusted $\bar{R}^2$ figures are reported in the last row of Table 11.8. All 15 regressions are significant, although liquor and jewelry stores are rather weaker than the others. $\bar{R}^2$'s values range from 0.07 to 0.601 with a simple average of precisely 0.2. It is safe to conclude that socioeconomic structure, as measured by these 12 factors, does account for a significant proportion of the cross-sectional variation in macroretail structure. However, by the same token, we must acknowledge that considerable variation remains unaccounted for. Excluded phenomena that may be important explanatory variables include (1) socioeconomic factors such as home ownership, education, occupation, and ethnicity, (2) various macromarketing mix factors such as store size, the capital-to-labor ratio, and advertising, and (3) environmental factors such as mass transit, legal restrictions on operating hours (blue laws), and the degree of state control exercised in the alcoholic beverage area.

DISCUSSION AND CONCLUSION

This chapter has (1) developed the concept of macroretail structure, (2) examined the influence of a set of socioeconomic factors on that structure, and (3) demonstrated that both macroretail structure and socioeconomic structure evince distinct regional patterns. Three questions raised by these findings are discussed in this section. First, are the regional patterns as straightforward as is suggested by such common parlances as "Northwest," "Southwest," "Sunbelt," and so forth? Second, what is the relationship between microretail structure and its macrolevel counterpart? Third, what avenues for future research seem most promising?

Regional Patterns

While there are distinct regional patterns in socioeconomic and macroretail structure, there are also certain rather sharp differences that point up how complex the concept of regionality is. Consider, for example, the seven SMSAs located in Florida that are part of this data base. On the basis of the macroretail structure-based clusters, Orlando and Jacksonville are most like the "Deep South," while Tampa–St. Petersburg and Pensacola are linked to the "Sunbelt." The other trio of SMSAs, Miami, West Palm Beach, and Fort Lauderdale, are clearly associated with the large, Northeastern metropolises centered on New York, Philadelphia, and Pittsburgh.

In a similar vein, six of the Texas SMSAs are part of the Sunbelt, while five are grouped with other SMSAs in the West South Central census division. California, Michigan, and New York, among other states, have several SMSAs that transcend any narrow geographical concept of regionality.

These observations point up two facets about our thinking on regions. First, the Census Bureau classifications of sections of the country (East South Central, West South Central, etc.) no longer form perfectly valid clusters of similar SMSAs, although these classifications continue to maintain some validity. The newer, more popular taxonomy of regions (Sunbelt, Industrial Heartland, etc.) is superimposed on its predecessor. Some SMSAs are better considered by the old classificatory scheme, others by the new taxonomy. Second, there are instances of SMSAs that are geographically quite separate, yet that are clearly quite similar in structure. Miami–New York–Philadelphia–Pittsburgh is one such "region"; the Pacific Northwest and some moderate-sized SMSAs in Michigan form another. These geographically dispersed clusters occur because the very concept of region is multidimensional; it transcends the solitary dimension of location to embrace the underlying theme of internal similarity. It is necessary to consider the full dimensionality of "regions" if we are to understand the various possible structures of U.S. metropolises.

It is suggested that U.S. "regions" are undergoing a continual transformation, changing both in terms of what they are and in terms of their membership. One avenue for future research is to establish a more complete data base than has been employed here, in order to determine a complete and accurate taxonomy of regionality. A second avenue for research is to establish both how and why regional membership is changing, including how new regions are created. For example, retirements and vacations from Northeastern SMSAs to the Miami area may be responsible for moving the latter metropolis into conformity with the former ones.

Micro-Macro Relationship

It must be acknowledged that the macroretail research reported here cannot explain microretail structure. However, it can provide a foundation for future micro-level studies by offering an explanation of the rather substantial cross-sectional variation in the percentage of stores in each line of retail trade.

Consider for a moment an SMSA with a substantial percentage of its outlets concentrated on convenience goods retailing (for example, grocery stores). Such areas may have a microretail structure that is inherently dispersed spatially. In contrast, an SMSA with a large proportion of its outlets in shopping goods retailing (for example, department stores) may be much less dispersed because such retailers tend to agglomerate. If this proves to be the case, then it follows that consumer convenience in shopping is affected by macroretail structure. This in turn will affect consumer satisfaction with the entire retail system (Ingene 1983a).

The concept of centrality provides a second method of differentiating the microretail structure of SMSAs. We have shown that areas that are the focus of outshopping from the surrounding hinterland have a different macroretail structure than do those SMSAs that themselves outshop. It follows that SMSAs low in centrality may be characterized as having a preponderance of their stores in spatially dispersed convenience goods retailing. In contrast, SMSAs that are high in centrality may evince a high level of spatial agglomeration both because they tend to have a high proportion of shopping goods retailers and because agglomeration is the only efficient method of serving outshoppers.

Future Research

There are innumerable opportunities for additional research. Some of these opportunities represent straightforward extensions of the research reported herein. Other more exciting opportunities lie in substantial extensions of this research. The former possibilities are catalogued first.

1. Acquisition of data on additional variables such as education, occupation, and home ownership will yield further, more refined insights into socioeconomic structure. This refined structure will in turn alter the number of geographic clusters we obtain, as well as causing some SMSAs that appear to be members of the same cluster to be revealed as actually not being linked.

2. The simultaneous factoring of the socioeconomic and macroretail variables will generate different factor analytic results and different clusters of SMSAs. While such an approach will preclude ascertaining why specific macroretail structures occur, it may yield additional insights into the nature of U.S. metropolises.

3. Macroretail structure may also be defined on the basis of the percentage distribution of sales across lines of trade. Such an approach may be used to gain further insights into which retail store types are supported by which socioeconomic groups.

4. The approach taken herein may be replicated with 1982 data. Provided that the 1977 results are included as explanatory variables, it may be possible to support Allen's assertion (1981, p. 61) that "the spatial organization of a region does not result uniquely and necessarily from the 'economic and social' [forces]...but also represents a 'memory' of particular, specific deviations from average behavior."

Some of the more exciting possible areas for research, listed in the order in which they must be researched, are as follow:

5. Merchandise line code statistics from the *Census of Retail Trade* can be used to learn *what* products are purchased, rather than *where* they are purchased. The latter, of course, has characterized 100 percent of all published research on retailing that has relied upon governmental data.

6. Merchandise line code statistics can be used in conjunction with retail line of trade data. This approach will answer the question, What products are purchased and in what lines of retail trade are they purchased? The answer should give insights into consumer demands for goods and the services associated with those goods.

7. Once the preceding point is well understood, it should be possible to examine spatial–regional differences in channels of distribution. Different products require different types of distribution. Similarly, different retail types demand different levels of distributive support. In the consumer goods industries, regional differences in macroretail structure and macroproduct purchases almost certainly cause regional differences in distribution. Grether (1983) has recently written of the importance of the distribution–retail interaction in a spatial–regional setting.

Summary

Macroretail structure is the percentage distribution of retail store types within a metropolitan area. This chapter has shown that there is considerable variation in macroretail structure across U.S. SMSAs. Further, this variation is not geographically random. There are distinct regional patterns of macroretail structure. These patterns are related to the regional pattern of socioeconomic structure. Finally, macroretail structure is partially explained by socioeconomic structure.

While progress has been made in our understanding of the structure of retailing, the road to a complete knowledge of this topic is long. Much work remains to be done. Some of the work that awaits us has been cataloged in this section. To quote Reavis Cox (1959, p. 362), once we have traversed this road, "the resultant effects upon [our knowledge] of the structure of retailing are likely to be drastic."

NOTES

1. Multipurpose shopping is the practice of shopping at stores in different lines of trade on the same shopping expedition.

2. Appreciation is expressed to the state and federal officials for their gracious cooperation. Several have requested that the standard disclaimer be made: Results reported herein do not necessarily represent their views or the positions of their agencies.

3. An SCSA is a group of adjacent SMSAs. Like SMSAs, SCSAs are defined by the Census Bureau.

4. It may be that tourism is greater in areas with many senior citizens; this provides an alternative explanation for the regression results. I am indebted to my colleague John Wheatly for this observation.

REFERENCES

Alderson, W., and R. Cox. 1948. "Towards a Theory of Marketing." *Journal of Marketing* 13 (October): 137–52.

Allen, P. 1981. "The Evolutionary Paradigm of Dissipative Structures." In *The Evolutionary Vision: Toward a Unifying Paradigm of Physical, Biological and Sociocultural Evolution,* edited by E. Jantsch, pp. 25–72. Boulder, CO: Westview Press.

Allen, P., and M. Sanglier. 1979. "A Dynamic Model of Growth in a Central Place System." *Geographical Analysis* 11 (July): 256–72.

Beckmann, M. 1971. "Equilibrium Versus Optimum: Spacing of Firms and Patterns of Market Areas." *Northeast Regional Science Review* 1:1–20.

———. 1968. *Location Theory.* New York: Random House.

Beckmann, M. and J. McPherson. 1970. "City Size Distribution in a Central Place Hierarchy: An Alternative Approach." *Journal of Regional Science* 10:25–33.

Bruce, G. 1969. "The Ecological Structure of Retail Institutions." *Journal of Marketing Research* 6 (February):48–53.

Bucklin, L. 1963. "Retail Strategy and the Classification of Consumer Goods." *Journal of Marketing* 27 (January):50–55.

Chinitz, B. 1961. "Contrasts in Agglomeration: New York and Pittsburgh." *American Economic Review* 51 (May):279–89.

Christaller, W. 1966. *Central Places in Southern Germany,* trans. by C. W. Baskins. Englewood Cliffs, NJ: Prentice-Hall.

Cox, R. 1959. "Consumer Convenience and the Retail Structure of Cities." *Journal of Marketing* 23 (April):355–62.

Duncan, O. 1952. "Urbanization and Retail Specialization." *Social Forces* 30 (March):267–71.

Duncan, O., W. Scott, S. Liebersen, B. Duncan, and H. Winsborough. 1960. *Metropolis and Region.* Baltimore: Johns Hopkins University Press.

Eaton, B., and R. Lipsey. 1979. "Comparison Shopping and the Clustering of Homogeneous Firms." *Journal of Regional Science* 19:421–35.

Ferber, R. 1958. "Variations in Retail Sales Between Cities." *Journal of Marketing* 22 (January): 295–303.

Ghosh, A., and S. Craig. (1983). "Formulating Retail Strategy in a Changing Environment." *Journal of Marketing* 47 (Summer):56–68.

Green, P., R. Frank, and P. Robinson. 1967. "Cluster Analysis in Test Market Selection." *Management Science* 13 (April):B387–B400.

Grether, E. 1983. "Regional-Spatial Analysis in Marketing." *Journal of Marketing* 47 (Fall):36–43.

Hadden, J., and E. Borgatta. 1965. *American Cities: Their Social Characteristics.* Chicago: Rand McNally.

Hall, M., J. Knapp, and C. Winsten. 1961. *Distribution in Great Britain and North America.* London: Oxford University Press.

Huff, D. 1964. "Defining and Estimating a Trading Area." *Journal of Marketing* 28 (July):34–38.

Ingene, C. 1985. "Temporal Influences upon Spatial Shopping Behavior of Consumers." *Papers of the Regional Science Association,* Vol. 54, pp. 71–87. Urbana: IL: University of Illinois Press.

———. 1984a. "Structural Determinants of Market Potential." *Journal of Retailing* 60 (Spring):37–64.

———. 1984b. "The Effect of Scale, Localization and Urbanization Economies on Productivity in Retailing." In *1984 AMA Educator's Conference Proceedings,* edited by R. Belk and R. Peterson, Chicago: American Marketing Association.

———. 1983a. "Consumer Expenditures and Consumer Satisfaction with the Spatial Marketing System." *Journal of Macromarketing* 3 (Fall):41–54.

———. 1983b. "Intertype Competition: Restaurants Versus Grocery Stores." *Journal of Retailing* 59 (Fall):49–75.

Ingene, C., and R. Lusch. 1981. "A Model of Retail Structure." In *Research in Marketing,* Vol. 5, edited by J. Sheth, pp.101–64. Stamford, CT: JAI Press.

———. 1980. "Market Selection Decisions for Department Stores." *Journal of Retailing* 56 (Fall):21–40.

Ingene, C., and E. Yu. 1981. "Determinants of Retail Sales in SMSAs." *Regional Science and Urban Economics* 11 (November):529–47.

Kelley, E. 1958. "The Importance of Convenience in Consumer Purchasing." *Journal of Marketing* 22 (July):32–38.

Kernan, J., and G. Bruce. 1972. "The Socioeconomic Structure of an Urban Area." *Journal of Marketing Research* 9 (February):15–18.

Kim, J., and C. Mueller. 1978. *Factor Analysis: Statistical Methods and Practical Issues.* Beverly Hills: Sage.

Klastorin, T. 1983. "Assessing Cluster Analysis Results." *Journal of Marketing Research* 20 (February):92–98.

Klastorin, T., and R. Ledingham. 1981. *Program CLAN: Documentation.* Mimeo, April, University of Washington.

Leamer, E. 1978. *Specification Searches.* New York: John Wiley & Sons.

Lösch, A. 1954. *The Economics of Location,* trans. by W. Woglem with W. Stopler. New Haven, CT: Yale University Press.

Mills, E., and M. Lav. 1964. "A Model of Market Areas with Free Entry." *Journal of Political Economy* 72 (June):278–88.

Moomaw, R. 1983. "Spatial Productivity Variations in Manufacturing: A Critical Survey of Cross-Sectional Analysis." *International Regional Science Review* 8 (June):1–22.

Mulligan, G. 1984. "Agglomeration and Central Place Theory: A Review of the Literature." *International Regional Science Review* 9 (September):1–42.

Nevin, J., and M. Houston. 1980. "Image as a Component of Attractiveness to Intraurban Shopping Areas." *Journal of Retailing* 56 (Spring):77–93.

Price, D. 1942. "Factor Analysis in the Study of Metropolitan Centers." *Social Forces* 20 (May):449–55.

Punj, G., and R. Stewart. 1983. "Cluster Analysis in Marketing Research: Review and Suggestion for Application." *Journal of Marketing Research* 20 (May):134–48.

Reilly, W. 1931. *The Law of Retail Gravitation.* New York: Knickerbocker Press.

Rushton, G. 1972. "Map Transformations of Point Patterns: Central Place Patterns in Areas of Variable Population Density." *Papers of the Regional Science Association* 28:111–32.

U.S. Department of Commerce, Bureau of the Census. 1980. *Census of Population and Housing.* Washington, D.C.: U.S. Government Printing Office.

———. 1977. *Census of Retail Trade.* Washington, D.C.: U.S. Government Printing Office.

Wells, W., and G. Gubar. 1966. "The Life Cycle Concept in Marketing Research." *Journal of Marketing Research* 3 (November):355–63.

CHAPTER 12

Cities as Agencies of Distribution: The Vital Role of Exports

RICHARD F. WENDEL

One approach to weighing the prospects of the city as an agency of distribution is to examine its history. Marketing history is "one of the most important of the dark continents that lie before us awaiting exploration" (Cox 1960, p. 239). History presents a way of looking at cities as agencies of marketing as "institutions in the true sociological usage of the term...patterns of human behavior and communication clustered about some physical facility" (Alderson and Cox 1948, p. 143).

"What is a city? How did it come into existence? What processes does it further: what functions does it perform: what purposes does it fulfull?...The origins of the city are obscure, a large part of its past buried or effaced beyond recovery, and its further prospects are difficult to weigh" (Mumford 1961, p. 1). The relationship of cities and marketing is old, time out of mind.

PURPOSE, METHOD, AND SCOPE

Among the many functions a city performs is that of being an agency of distribution. Yet, "cities tend to be overlooked when anyone draws up a list of the agencies that do the work of marketing.... Systematic analysis of the ways [cities] facilitate exchange among economic specialists [is] scarce and fragmentary" (Cox, Goodman, and Fichandler 1965, p. 85).

Purpose

The purpose of this analysis is to trace the role of exports in facilitating urban specialization on the hypothesis that the pace and timing of city development

are determined by export marketing. This chapter examines how export marketing contributed to the formation and sustained existence of cities, past and present. Each city examined has been chosen to show how exports facilitated its development as an agency of distribution, a concept proposed by Reavis Cox, who
also pointed to marketing history as a method of analysis appropriate for this task.

Historical Research Method

"Historical research and writing are basically descriptive: they begin with
narration of events in a time sequence.... 'What is the correct method for historical research?'.... All research should be based on scientific method" (Savitt
1980, pp. 52, 54). "The scientific method has been well-defined as the method
of tested and therefore testable hypotheses; and testable in this context means
falsifiable by comparison with empirical evidence. The method has never proved
any statement about the object world to be true. It has proved some very important statements to be false" (Cox 1964).

Historical research must often substitute verification for falsification.
"Verification procedures are the equivalent of hypothesis testing. Verification
is accomplished by comparison of qualitative factors, which may or may not be
associated with numerical values.... Most historical research involves the
qualitative comparison of events over time or between different places" (Savitt
1980, p. 56).

Only two of today's cities resemble the city–states of the past: Singapore,
a true city–state, and Hong Kong, which only acts like one. Export–import information for Singapore and Hong Kong exists, but data on those for ancient
Rome are largely effaced beyond recovery. Methods of verification used in
historical research overcome such data limitations and allow the hypothesis to
be tested and comparisons to be made between cities of the past, even the distant past, and those of the present.

Scope

The cities examined range from the most rudimentary type through advanced
centers of the Middle Ages and the nineteenth century United States, to those
of today. Adam Smith, (1776, p. 392) observed that "the commerce and
manufactures of cities, instead of being the effect, have been the cause and oc-
casion of the improvement and cultivation of countries."

In comparing the commerce and manufactures of cities of the past and present, by looking to their ever-lengthening trade routes, their collection of wider
and wider assortments of goods, and their development of ways to facilitate exchange, it should be possible to piece together some of the "scattered bits of information...that can tell...how and when and through whose efforts this fantastically complicated set of activities...we call marketing came into existence"
(Cox 1960, p. 237).

CITY-FORMING INDUSTRIES

"It is customary to draw a distinction between two types of economic activity in cities. . . . Industries that 'export' goods and services have been called 'city-forming industries'. The other basic group of industries that performs services for the city's own people has been called 'city-serving' industries. . . . Important in particular for city-forming industries is the city's ability to draw upon widely scattered sources for a great variety of materials and services" (Cox, Goodman, and Fichandler 1965, pp. 91–92).

Imports versus Exports

Most cities must turn outside themselves to obtain many things. "Large clusters of population are possible with little or no 'foreign' trade. Even today, towns with a good many thousands of people that do little trade with the outside may be found" (Cox 1965, p. 95). Their's is a highly localized trade.

A city may "import," from near or far, things that it could produce. Such "imports" may either be for city consumption or for processing into "exports." City imports and exports are concealed in national income accounts. "So little is this acknowledged that, although the realities are there for all to see, that we do not even have a word meaning 'both the domestic and foreign purchases alike' of a city" (Jacobs 1984, p. 43). To overcome this problem, this analysis often uses the term "long-distance trade" to make clear the kind of marketing being discussed.

URBANIZATION AND EXPORTS

The traditional view of the origins of markets and marketing is based on Smith's notion of a human (1776, pp. 13,15): "Propensity. . .to truck, barter, and exchange one thing for another" among neighbors. Alderson (1964, p. 100) came closer to what archaeological evidence suggests. "The true beginning of trade was when the specialist began to compete with the generalist and gradually to replace him." Trade goods from afar abound in early human campsites.

> The bronze products of Mesopotamian workshops made their way into the deep forests where [Europeans] still lived in the primitive simplicity of the Stone Age.
> These business pioneers. . .produced excellent axes: in one deposit in Brittany, four thousand standardized hatchets, neatly bundled together with wire have been recovered. (Clough and Cole 1946, p. 24)

Such sites are far older than any extant evidence of nearby cities, towns, or villages. From archaeological and anthropological evidence, going far afield to hunt for food and other goods appears to be a better explanation of marketing's origins than does a built-in propensity to exchange. "The true starting point [of markets] is long-distance trade, a result of the geographical location of goods, and of the 'division of labor' given by location. Long-distance trade often engenders markets, an institution which involves acts of barter, and, if money is used, of buying and selling" (Polanyi 1944, p. 58).

Urbanization and Export Marketing Among the Ancients

Sometime in the New Stone Age, permanent settlement replaced wandering as the way most people lived. Later a series of technological advances allowed what has been called the "Urban Revolution." Copper was worked, the wheel invented, animals domesticated. The first ships set sail. Efforts at writing began. Villages, then towns and cities appeared. Monetization, market days, and fairs began to appear in the ancient world. The stage was being set for cities to equalize the pull of demands with the push of supply through the specialized activities of collecting, sorting, and dispersing goods according to relative demands for them.

Cities as Agencies of Accumulation

"The city of the dead antedates the city of the living" (Mumford 1961, p. 7). Burial places, first for celebrated warriors, hunters, or other leaders and then for group members, appear to have been people's first fixed meeting places. To these, primitive peoples returned at intervals. Whether to commune with or to placate the spirits of the dead is indeterminable. Places of periodic assembly became places of periodic ceremony. Offerings, first to the spirits of the dead and then to those who guarded them, followed. Building walled sanctuaries to protect offerings was the next step. Exchange of offerings among sanctuary guardians and between them and visitors probably came next. Initially, "imports" of offerings and "exports" of spiritual solace not only brought cities into existence, but provided substance for continued existence of these "cities" of the dead. Traces of necropolises are fragmentary in the Old World, but many can be found in Meso-America, where this phase of urban development had barely ended at the time of the Spanish Conquest. The Olmec city of Teotihuacán was such a city. So, too, probably, was Mayan Palenque; so, certainly, was Zapotec Monte Albán, which was never inhabited by the living (Meyer 1973).

How "cities of the dead" were transformed into anything like cities of today is unknown. It took place before writing was invented. In time, sanctuaries became walled enclaves separating their spiritual guardians from the profane world outside. The accumulated treasures of offerings within sanctuaries were targets for pillage.

"The oldest city thus far discovered...Jericho...was found only in 1957. [It was] founded about 8000 B.C.... in the south of Palestine" (Willis 1973, p. 16). Walls 20 feet high and a 6-foot-deep by 25-foot-wide dry moat cut into the living rock protected it. A tall tower with three-foot-wide inner steps commanded the town as a citadel. These fortifications were beyond the military technology of the day. "It is only for their gods that men exert themselves so extravagantly. But what first was designed to ensure the god's favor, may have paid off in practice as more effective military protection" (Mumford 1961, p. 37).

Jericho had no identifiable marketplace. Goods from Anatolia and the Sinai found in its citadel are as likely to have come there through robbery as from trade. While Jericho is the oldest city whose remains have been found, it cannot have been alone. Yet, the word "merchant," designating an "official of a temple privileged to trade abroad," does not appear until about 6,000 years after Jericho (Mumford 1961, p. 35).

Wars to take citadels protecting a god's treasure and to maintain divine favor are the stuff of early legend. Priam's accumulated treasure was as much the reason Homer's Greeks attacked Troy as was recovering Helen.

Cities as Agencies of Distribution

In historic times, "where there is a town, there will be division of labor, and where there is any marked division of labor, there will be a town. No town is without its market, and there can be no regional or national markets without towns" (Braudel 1981, pp. 480–81). Before the town came the village.

The Village

A city is not a village writ large. A village is a small cluster of families. It has little division of labor. What one family does, all others do as well. It is a place where tradition shapes practice. Little change is generated from within. External events—war, famine, and the political adventures or misadventures of outsiders—are what cause villages to wax or wane. Who makes what and who has claim over goods produced are settled outside of markets through tradition.

> The Indian village of the past was not a market economy. Each person performed his job largely determined by his caste, and shared in the village's produce on the basis of a complete system of shares. There was no market valuation of either the services of artisans or the produce of farmers. In such an economy there was no place for selling. The attitudes developed over the centuries of this type of...thinking cannot be changed quickly.... Lack of understanding of a market economy is still a major factor." (Westfall and Boyd 1960, p. 15)

Silent Trade

Just as tradition offers an alternative to Smith's notion of a human propensity "to truck, barter and exchange one thing for another" as an explanation for marketing's origin, so, too, does silent trade:

In silent trade, one party would put down its products at an appointed spot and then retire into the bush. The second party would then come up, observe what had been deposited and then put down what it regarded as goods of equivalent value. The second party then would retire to give the first party time to examine the proposed exchange. If satisfied, the visitors would pick up the goods offered in exchange and depart. If not satisfied, they would remain in the vicinity until the second party had sufficiently augmented the goods it was offering. (Alderson 1964, p. 99)

Alderson chose the silent trade to show how prices might have been negotiated prices, but evident in his example are the processes of collecting, sorting, and dispersing that the coming of cities would enhance. The silent trade is the contemporary marketing of much of Africa, of South America's jungles, of the Australian outback, and of underdeveloped places the world over (Wendell 1979).

War as a Method of Distribution

"War and domination, rather than peace and cooperation, were ingrained in the ancient city" (Mumford 1961, p. 44). Human sacrifice to ensure crop and/or human fertility forced primitive peoples to look beyond their own groups for victims. Protecting temple treasure was an imperative civic duty. Amassing more to appease the gods was almost as important. Warrior–priest–kings made palaces of the citadels and made gods of themselves, or, at the very least, representatives of gods on earth. To protect or to obtain treasure, it might be necessary to fight, for "trade" was one sided. The very presence of city populations—standing armies in reserve—could intimidate weaker neighbors in scattered village settlements or in smaller cities into making tribute.

"It was as difficult to begin a civilization without robbery as it was difficult to maintain it without slaves in ancient times" (Durant 1939, p. 10). The labor force needed to build holy places to honor gods was usually beyond what the small populations of early cities could supply. Expeditions to collect the slaves needed to build holy places, to obtain sacrifices for the gods, to garner goods for noble, priestly elites probably had as much to do with the invention of warfare as had human aggressiveness or protection of territorial rights to grazing and croplands. Organizing raids to seize goods by force was a first step in the changeover from self-sufficiency to interdependence through markets (Alderson and Mesopotamia boasted on public monuments of enriching temple treasure city needs is well documented. Writing had begun. City kings of Greece, Egypt, and Mesopotamia boasted on public monuments of enriching temple treasures troves through pillage of cities. Within cities, weapons-owning minorities came to share economic and social power with local god–priest–kings.

Trade

The Greeks started out as robbers and pirates, but some ended up as great traders. "The ancients knew a lot about hunting, fighting and lovemaking, but took a long time to learn that trade could raise living standards more certainly and effectively than plunder" (Fisk 1967, p. 29). Athenians were among the earliest to learn this lesson. They "contributed their unique evolution . . . to the poverty of Attica. 'Attica, whose soil was poor and thin, enjoyed a long freedom from civil strife, and therefore retained its original inhabitants', the historian Thucydides wrote . . . . It did not attract invaders" (Willis 1973, pp. 73–74). "Only adventurous trade, and patient culture of the olive and the grape, made civilization possible in Attica" (Durant 1939, p. 107).

While exports of olive oil and wine, both state monopolies, made life possible, selective imports of ideas, science, and techniques from older civilizations made Athens into the "glory that was Greece." From the Lydia of King Croesus, Greek traders brought home the idea of a state-sponsored coinage. In Egypt, at their trading post of Cyrene, Athenians learned the hollow casting that made their deposits of lead and copper valuable (Durant 1939, p. 68). From Egypt they learned new methods of textile manufacture and architecture. Pottery-making skills learned in Egypt turned their poor soil into an asset in international markets.

Phoenician merchants were the middlemen who diffused the knowledge and technologies of Egypt and Mesopotamia among the Greeks. They brought with them to Greece a tradition of long-distance trade. Greeks learned of Babylonia's system of weights and measures, geometry and astronomy, and ways of measuring time—sundials and waterclocks—from Tyrian and Carthaginian traders. Phoenician shipwrights taught the Greeks to build the merchant vessels-turned-warships that defeated the Persians at Salamis. Phoenicia's most precious gift to Greece was the first true, sound-symbol alphabet (Ogg 1948, p. 79) that it had developed for keeping "business accounts and tallies" (Welles 1921, p. 229). The Greeks added vowels. From the Greek alphabet came all those of the West.

Winning at Salamis secured freedom of the seas for Greek traders. "The Athenian fleet that remained after Salamis now opened every port in the Mediterranean to Greek trade, and the commercial expansion that ensued provided the wealth that financed the leisure and culture of Periclean Athens . . . its Golden Age" (Durant 1939, p. 242). Not long after, trading contact with the Gauls was established at what is now Marseilles and a trading post called Emporium was opened in southern Spain.

Warriors versus Traders

The rivalry between Rome and Carthage exemplifies the struggle among the ancients between war and trade as methods of maintaining or increasing standards of living. Rome developed an enormous commercial life but enriched itself through conquest. Carthage, a great marketing center, was home to one of history's most famous generals, Hannibal.

The economic base of Roman life at the beginning...was of necessity quite simple. Rome controlled only about 400 square miles of territory, and already its population was too large for the land available. Famines were frequent, and [satisfying] hunger for wheat became a fixed goal of all Roman policy" (Willis 1973, p. 151). Carthage held the granaries in Sicily, Sardinia, and Africa that could feed Rome.

Founded as a trading post by merchants from nearby Utica and distant Tyre about the same time that Rome began, Carthage quickly outstripped its parents in size and sway. Unlike some Greeks and nearly all Romans who felt trade an unfit occupation for a "citizen" (Aristotle) or a "free man" (Cicero), Carthaginians dominated northern Africa, Sardinia, western Sicily, and the south of Spain through mercantile skills. Commitment to trade extended to its armies which were made up of mercenaries. Neither Rome nor Carthage was democratic: Rome was dominated by warrior aristocracy; Carthage was a mercantile oligarchy.

Carthaginian traders ranged throughout the western Mediterranean and beyond the Straits of Gibralter to the Azores, Britain, and the Baltic, and perhaps to the Malabar Coast of India. Carthage with its population of 700,000 to 1,000,000 (Durant and Mommsen 1928) was the first city to demonstrate clearly the role of cities as a social device for minimizing the distance that goods move in small lots (Vaile, Grether, and Cox 1952, p. 142). Long before Rome, it posed a constant threat to Greek traders in the western Mediterranean.

Carthage was destroyed in 146 B.C. Corinth fell to Rome that same year. Corinth had replaced Athens as Greek entrepreneur. The taking of Corinth was signalized by every horror usual in Roman warfare.... It was rendered famous beyond similar catastrophes by the amount of valuable plunder and by the brutal recklessness with which trophies of Grecian art were destroyed.... With the fall of Corinth fell the last shadow of the liberties of Greece" (Merivale 1876, p. 202). 146 B.C. marked the end of a round in the "struggle between trader and warrior" that had "continued over almost a millenium between the period when the trader furnished swords to the barbarians and the terrible hour when the trader succumbed to his armed customers.... History villified the trader-rulers and exalted...the warriors" (Beard 1938, p. 29). The warriors had won.

Urbanization and Export Marketing in the Middle Ages

"The Middle Ages...were a *continuation* and a *formulation*. They were a continuation of old Rome in race, language, institutions, law, literature, the arts. They were also a continuation of cultures independent of Rome. The Franks and the Saxons, the Greeks and the Arabs, contributed their own civilizations...to make the new civilization that we inherit" (Bishop 1970, p. 1). The civilization that emerged offered new answers to old problems.

An Empire Built on Trade: Constantinople

Constantinople was the great city of the Middle Ages. It continued Greco-Roman civilization, but was also a source of innovation. Founded by Constantine in 324, it lasted until 1453 when it fell to invading Turks. It operated as a marketing center, from ancient times well into the late Middle Ages. Rome, for all its sizable commerce, was a parasitic military state to the end. The ''New Rome,'' Constantinople, frequently warred, but built its wealth through international marketing.

Unplagued by warriorly disdain for trade, Byzantines took up Greek trading traditions. Aristocrats were among its major traders. ''One empress ran a perfume factory in her bedroom'' (Willis 1973, p. 266). For 1,100 years, it was Christendom's richest and most important city. Byzantines styled themselves Romans, but spoke Greek. They developed the Greek Orthodox Church and saved the classics of Roman law and literature for the future through their Greek translations. After its fall, Constantinople remained the model for other cities of the Middle Ages.

Constantinople's great advantage in international marketing was its location. It lay athwart two of the Old World's major trade routes. The first was from east to west, between Europe and China and India. The second ran from wheat-growing, former Greek colonies in southern Russia to the cities of the Mediterranean.

Constantinople's most prized trade good was Chinese silk. After the Emperor Justinian commissioned missionaries returning from China to smuggle silkworms and mulberry tree seeds out in the mid-sixth century, domestic silk replaced the Chinese imports. With supplies at hand, the Eastern Empire became a manufacturing center. The second most important trade was in spices: pepper, nutmeg, cinnamon, and cloves from southeast Asia.

In addition to wheat, southern Russia sent furs, slaves, and salt through the city on their way west. The Hunic invasions of southern Russia slowed but did not stop the city's East-West trade. ''The greatest volume of the shipping trade was in the hands of foreigners, most of whom came all the way to Constantinople itself to sell their goods. Special provision was made...for lodging these foreigners, who were expected to stay apart...in segregated national compounds, so that the police and customs officials could keep an eye on their activities'' (Willis 1973, p. 263). When Russia could no longer provide them, ''Venetian vessels came to supply Byzantium with wheat, wine, wood, salt, and slaves, and took back the Eastern luxuries that the West craved. In 1085, Venice was granted its own quarter in Byzantium, and exemption from customs duties in the Eastern Empire'' (Bishop 1970, p. 46).

Intermunicipal Trade: Venice, the Hanse, and the Fairs of Champagne

''Right up to [1500] what may appear to us as national trade was not national, but municipal. The Hanse were not German merchants, they were a corporation of trading oligarchs hailing from a number of North Sea and Baltic towns. . . . The trade of Antwerp or Hamburg, Venice or Lyons, was in no way Dutch or German, Italian or French. London was no exception: It was as little 'English' as Luebeck was 'German''' (Polanyi 1944, p. 63). Venice was a leader in Europe's economic revival.

Venice

"Venice was. . .an independent republic for over 1,000 years—longer than the period separating us from the Norman conquest—during much of which she had been. . .the principal crossroads between East and West, the richest and most prosperous centre of the civilized world'' (Norwich 1982, pp. xxi–xxii). Venice was not the first, but was the most successful of Italy's city-states run as marketing enterprises. Pisa, Florence, Genoa, and Milan were all involved in large-scale international marketing between the Near East and Europe before Venice gained control of safe routes to Byzantium and Flanders. "Venice itself had grown out of the realities of forced migration, war, conflict, piracy, and trade. Though it commanded men's allegiances. . .by its splendor and order, it made no pretenses to being an ideal city: it was merely the best that a succession of energetic merchants and industrialists, who courted money and power, and the luxuries that money and power will buy, were able to conceive'' (Mumford 1961, p. 325).

The Most Serene Republic of Venice began in 726 when its first duke, *doge* in Venetian Italian, was elected. It lasted until dissolved by Napoleon in 1797 (Norwich 1982, p. 13). Prior to electing its first doge, Venice was nominally a vassal state of Constantinople. Electing its first doge loosened but did not end Venice's Byzantine political ties. Preserving the fiction of Byzantine suzerainty allowed Venice to avoid becoming embroiled in mainland politics and wars. It freed the city up to penetrate Byzantium's huge market. Venice did with more success than its maritime rivals, Genoa and Pisa.

Venice prospered modestly from East–West trade, but "beyond all question the fantastic adventure of the Crusades. . .really launched the trading fortunes of Christendom and of Venice'' (Braudel 1984, p. 109). Towns and merchants had done much to revitalize European trade, but the Crusades accelerated the pace of change. "Crusaders, coming from. . .draughty castles and boring manorial routines, thought they would find in the East only untutored heathen savages. They were astonished to be met by a people far more civilized, infinitely more luxurious, and much more money-oriented than they'' (Heilbroner 1970, p. 46). Like Constantinople before it, Venice profited by its location. It was the major port for the Crusades. Crusaders en route to the Holy Land came to Venice fully equipped with horses, armor, and passage money. Transports built to take them to the Levant returned with trade goods. Christian states established in the Near East by the Crusaders became gateways to the riches of the Orient. Spices, pepper, and silks, so sought after in the West, could be obtained through the Crusader states without going through Constantinople. Venice succeeded in directing a Crusader sack of Constantinople in 1204 (Heilbroner 1970, p. 46). Greatly enriched by Byzantine plunder, Venice became still richer by taking over much Byzantine trade (Norwich 1982, pp. 12–39; Braudel 1984, pp. 109–10).

By the end of the thirteenth century, Venice was the number one power in Europe. Venetian control over Europe's two emerging trade and industrial regions in the Baltic and Italy brought it that power. In 1423 a dying doge advised his fellow republicans that "looking after one's ducats, dwellings, and doublets was the road to true power, for it was better to become 'masters of the Gold of Christendom'...by trade and not by arms" (Braudel 1984, p. 121). "Venice's budget was equal to that of Spain (though quite what 'Spain' means in this context is disputed) almost equal to that of England, and far exceeded those of the other Italian cities deemed to be her peers: Genoa, Florence, and Milan" (Braudel 1984, p. 120). At this time, Venice appeared as another Constantinople or as Rome reborn. One French visitor described it as "the most triumphant city I have ever seen" (Willis 1973, p. 31).

The Hanse

Northern Europe replaced southern Russia as the major source of the grain, hides, wool, tallow, salt meat and fish, hemp, timber, furs, tin, and other metals that Italy's northern cities turned into trade goods to send to the ports of the Near East (Adams 1901, pp. 284–85). The Hanse was the North. Many of its member cities—Danzig, Hamburg, Bremen—ringed the Baltic. It reached into Russia and, through Bruges, along the Atlantic in its search for trade. Bruges became the chief place of exchange between North and South after Genoa sent a Mediterranean trade convoy there in 1277 (Braudel 1984, p. 114).

"The Age of Faith" was a major reason for the rise of the Hanse. The Hanse's tallow candles illuminated its churches; its salt herring allowed Christendom's faithful to keep its dietary laws. "Lent...was the most profitable time— fish was essential, and fresh fish was scarce inland. Fridays throughout the year were almost as good.... As late as the mid-sixteenth century, it was still (theoretically) possible for an Englishman to hang for eating meat on a Friday. The Hanseatic League dominated...Baltic commerce in salt fish" (Tannahill 1973, p. 211).

Organization was the Hanse's great advantage over the cities of Italy. "At its height, it dominated politically and economically the basin of the North...all the way from Novogorod in Russia to London and Bruges...in Flanders, [where] the two greatest streams of European commerce, coming respectively from the Mediterranean and the Baltic, coalesced, making Bruges the leading world emporium until supplanted in the sixteenth century by Antwerp" (Schevill 1930, p. 30).

The Fairs of Champagne

While the Hanse on the north and Venice on the south were the poles of burgeoning international marketing, the heart of the market for the goods each offered was inbetween. To facilitate exchanges between them, in the days before regular sea and land routes were established between the Mediterranean and the North Sea, the fairs of Champagne came into existence. There were six of them. Each lasted two months (Pirenne 1969, p. 89). While they were not the only European fairs, they were the most important. "The great fairs were tremendous occasions, a mixture of social holiday, religious festival, and time of intense economic activity. At some fairs, like those in Champagne...a wide variety of merchandise was brought for sale; silks from the Levant, books and parchments, horses, drugs, spices.... The fair was a kind of traveling market, established in fixed localities for fixed dates, in which merchants from all over Europe conducted genuine international exchange" (Heilbroner 1970, pp. 32–33).

> The originality of the Champagne fairs lay less...in the super-abundance of goods on sale than in the money market and the precocious workings of credit.... Money-changers, usually Italians, really called the tune.... All compensatory payments balancing sales and purchases, all deferred payment between one fair and another, all loans to lords and princes, the settlement of bills of exchange...passed through their hands.... All the international and most modern aspects of the Champagne fairs were controlled...by Italian merchants." (Braudel 1984, p. 112)

The Champagne fairs began to falter in the great recession that followed the Black Death in the fourteenth century, when, as one writer of the time wrote, "a third of the world died" (Gottfried 1983, p. 77). The final blow fell when the sea link between the Mediterranean and North Sea established in 1277 came into greater use and after Venice gained control of the Brenner Pass.

The "Commercial Revolution

The term "Commercial Revolution" describes the shift of the center of gravity of the West from the Mediterranean to the Atlantic seaboard (Polanyi 1944, p. 65). "As the center of...activities shifted, and the weight of Asia and America was thrown into the European scale, its balance was altered for all time.... The outworn framework of mediaeval society broke down under the pressure.... This movement, partly begun, partly accelerated by a huge tidal wave of sudden wealth from overseas...laid the foundations of a new economy" (Abbott 1918, p. 107-8). The result was a symbiosis of capitalism with seaboard location, which "became the vehicle to power for Portugal, Spain, Holland, France, England and the United States" (Polanyi 1944, p. 28). Particularly affected were Venice, the Hanse, and Lisbon.

Lisbon: Lisbon possesses one of Portugal's two good harbors. Rudimentary exports of wine, salt, and dried fruit from its hinterland in exchange for cloth and luxuries were in place by the twelfth century. "Lisbon's rise in the thirteenth century was that of a port of call which gradually assimilated the lessons of an active, maritime, peripheral and capitalist economy" (Braudel 1981, p. 403). By 1385 Lisbon's merchants were powerful enough to gain a place in the government. By Henry's time—he was born in 1394—Lisbon was Portugal's capital. The majority of its 40,000 residents were occupied with international marketing and related trades (Willis 1973, p. 412).

Merchant participation in government precipitated an expedition against Ceuta in North Africa—a Moslem bottleneck in Lisbon's trade with the Far East and sub-Saharan Africa. The expedition took the form of a Crusade against the Infidel. After Ceuta's capture, Henry was dazzled by the "gold, silver, copper, brass, silks, and spices all brought by caravan" (Boorstin 1983, p. 160). "After the taking of Ceuta, he always kept ships. . . . [One reason he did so] was that if there chanced to be. . .havens into which it would be possible to sail without peril, *many. . .products of this realm might be taken there, which traffic would bring great profit to our countrymen*" (Bagley and Prestage 1896, pp. 27–29; italics added).

Portugal undertook its voyages of discovery in an attempt to cut into Venice's spice trade. "In those days, spices, particularly pepper, were in great demand for preserving carcasses slaughtered in the autumn because of winter feed problems. The spice islands of the Moluccas are situated in the East Indies. . . . Pepper was brought to Europe via Malaya, India, Egypt and then overland to the Mediterranean. . . . Pepper purchased for one ducat in the Moluccas sold for 105 ducats in Venice" (Innes 1969, pp. 23–24).

Henry's example inspired Lisbon merchants, partly financed by their kings, to continue a step-by-step exploration to reach the Far East. They arrived at Calcutta in 1498. In 1500 the first of the great Portuguese East Indian fleets was organized. On its way to the Far East, it accidentally discovered Brazil.

"So quickly was the effect of the Portuguese. . .felt that by 1503, the price of pepper in Lisbon was only one fifth of what it was in Venice" (Boorstin 1983, p. 178). When Venetian galleys arrived at Alexandria in 1504, "they found not a single sack of pepper waiting for them" (Braudel 1984, p. 143). Venice no longer held "the gorgeous East in fee." Its days of dominating Western trade were over.

Lisbon could shatter the Venetian hegemony, but could not supplant it. Well located for voyages of exploration, Lisbon, on the edge of the known world, was poorly located as a center of distribution, for "nine out of ten consumers of pepper and spices lived in the north" (Braudel 1984, pp. 142, 145). Merchants from Germany, Italy, and the Netherlands flocked to Lisbon to share in the fruits of the Portuguese triumph. It was short lived. Columbus, on his second voyage, found an American variety of pepper in Haiti. It was different from the East Indian species, but could substitute for it (Tannahill 1974, p. 237).

The cost of the long voyage to the Indies and lack of nearby markets prompted even Portuguese ships to bypass Lisbon for Antwerp. Antwerp became the Low Countries' chief port when the enterprising Valois duke, Philip the Good, made it the substitute port for Bruges (Pirenne 1969, p. 183). Bruges' harbor was silting up and not deep enough for the large *koggen* of the Hanse (Braudel 1982, p. 246). "Within twenty-five years, the nations of Europe were complaining just as much over the Portuguese monopoly as they had over the Venetian (Tannahill 1974, p. 240). Columbus' New World substitute began to compete "and a collapse in export prices for spices and sugar caused by an over-supply" ended Lisbon's "brief, heady period of glory" (Willis 1973, p. 420).

Bruges and Antwerp

Bruges became the Burgundian capital in 1419. The dukes made it the jewel of the Netherlands. They had a flair with cities. They turned Beaune, their duchy's Capetian capital, into the international wine center it remains to this day. At Dijon they turned the remnants of a fourth-century Roman garrison town into a "metropolis and major European trade clearinghouse with routes toward Paris, the Mediterranean, Germany, Switzerland, and Italy, well-served by roads and water-ways" (Michelin 1977, p. 95) that competes with Lyons. Upon inheriting most of the Netherlands, the dukes eliminated in their territories the internal tolls that plagued merchants of the Middle Ages.

Bruges struck one "young English wool merchant John Paston as a fairyland: 'I never heard of none like it, save King Arthur's court'" (Willis 1973, p. 317). Wines from its vineyards and woolens from its cities kept the duchy independent until the death of Charles the Rash in 1477. Long before the dukes, Bruges was in the circuit of Flemish fairs that puts its merchants and weavers into contact with English wool exporters. Through these exporters, Bruges gained access to both markets in England and to those in the English king's possessions in Normandy and Acquitaine. Access to these markets attracted the Hanse. Hanseatic raw materials in turn attracted traders from northern Italy. Italian traders connected Bruges through Levantine ports to trade routes to India and beyond.

With the Reformation, Antwerp became a center of Lutheranism. To extirpate what he saw as heresy, Phillip had Antwerp placed under siege in 1585. It fell and was sacked in 1587. Amsterdam—as Calvinist as Antwerp was Lutheran—became the new center of resistance to Spain. When Antwerp fell, "it obtained generous terms. . . . Merchants were permitted either to stay or to leave the city, taking their property with them" (Schevill 1930, p. 187). Most of Antwerp's refugees arrived in Amsterdam with their capital and commercial contacts intact.

Amsterdam

Amsterdam epitomized the innovative, enterprising cities of the Low Countries. The last of the medieval cities (Braudel 1984, p. 288), it was the "pacemaker of the western world" (Schevill 1930, p. 211) for nearly 200 years. It was a curious mix of the medieval and modern worlds.

"There is one city that bears witness to the commercial spirit at its best...Amsterdam. The fact that it was not widely imitated shows that it was not capitalism alone, but a complex of institutions, personalities and opportunities that came together at a unique moment, that made the city capitalism's outstanding urban achievement" (Mumford 1961, p. 439).

Amsterdam, a small, obscure fishing port with a smaller population than almost any other town in Holland in 1500, was the leading commercial and financial center of the West with a population of nearly 200,000 by 1660 (Braudel 1981, p. 528). It imposed its will directly upon Holland and indirectly throughout the Low Countries.

Two developments had prepared Amsterdam for greatness: In the middle of the fifteenth century, the herring fisheries that had enriched the Hanse shifted from the Baltic to the North Sea. Fishing boats and the warships sent to guard them in working the Dutch "Gold Mine" gave Amsterdam a splendid merchant marine. Around 1570 or so, "the *vlieboot* or *fluyt*...a sturdy ship of great capacity...[and] handled by a small crew—twenty per cent smaller than other ships of equal tonnage" was developed (Braudel 1984, p. 191). Its savings in wages and food—the biggest expenses on a long voyage—ensured Amsterdam's triumph over the Hanse.

While the shift of the herring fisheries and development of the flyboat prepared Amsterdam for greatness, Flemish and Dutch defiance of the Duchy of Burgundy in the person of Philip II of Spain made it into a world city. Philip became Duke of Bungundy and King of Spain when his father, the Holy Roman Emperor, Charles V, abdicated in 1556 (Schevill 1930, p. 119). Charles was a native of Burgundian Flanders. He had allowed local nobles to run Low Country politics, had encouraged tax-producing trade activities, and had turned a blind eye to increasing Protestantism. Philip's views of his responsibilities as Duke, tax collector, and as His Most Catholic Majesty differed sharply from his father's. Simultaneously, he tried to reduce the political power of Low Country aristocrats, to increase tax revenues from marketing and manufacturing, and to save souls from the heresies of Luther and Calvin. The resulting revolt lasted 80 years. Throughout the revolt, Amsterdam prospered by trading with both sides (Willis 1913, p. 460).

Amsterdam stood ready to take advantage of the refugees' arrival. "Fifty per cent of the first deposits of the Bank of Amsterdam, created in 1609, came from the southern Netherlands" (Braudel 1984, p. 187). Its merchant marine, together with the refugees' capital, mercantile skills, and market contacts, made Amsterdam Antwerp's replacement as the commercial and financial center of the West. From Amsterdam sailed the fleets that expelled Lisbon's merchantmen from the Indies and set up a Dutch trading empire, "on the Phoenician model," that extended from Batavia in the East Indies to New Amsterdam in North America (Braudel 1984, p. 215). In 1616, they took over from the Portuguese in Japan—more than 300 years before it was "opened" to the West by Commodore Perry.

Amsterdam's ability to borrow ideas from others, to improve upon them, and to depart from old ways contributed to its greatness. Its greatest departure from the past was in scale of operations. Previously, long-distance trade had been on a small scale and in luxuries. In the day of the Champagne fairs, "the total amount of goods [coming] into France in a year...would not fill a modern freight train; the total amount of merchandise carried by the great Venetian fleet would not fill one modern steel freighter" (Heilbroner 1961, p. 13). Amsterdam's pride was in being "the Cornbin of Europe" (Braudel 1984, p. 207). The flyboat was an ideal craft for shipping raw materials and foodstuffs. It made the Dutch, as Daniel Defoe called them, "*The Carryers of the World*" (Beard 1962, p. 285). Much of the naval stores it carried ended up in the ship-building yards of Rotterdam. Of 20,000 or so ships in Europe in the mid-seventeenth century, 16,000 were Dutch (Beard 1938, p. 287).

The toll-free trading zone, borrowed from the Valois dukes, made Holland the urban region it is today. "Amsterdam and Rotterdam, together with most of the country's small cities and many of its towns have jointly formed a single overwhelmingly important region which the Dutch call Ring City because the amalgamation of cities and joint city region encircles as a 'hole' formed by agricultural land and the inland sea" that endures to this day (Jacobs 1983, p. 174).

From Venice Amsterdam borrowed the idea of making the Bank of Amsterdam a bank of deposit. The bank combined with Dutch Calvinism made it possible for "great merchants...to draw on the savings of their less well-to-do relatives when...equipping East Indiamen" (Willis 1973, p. 461). Calvinism promoted thrift, "made saving...a virtue...[and]...investment...an instrument of piety as well as of profit" (Heilbroner 1970, p. 51). Amsterdam became a "center where the savings of hundreds of thousands of poorer people were invested. Land...was scarce and expensive, and thus not a normal source of investment" (Willis 1973, p. 461).

The idea of a Dutch East India Company was borrowed from that of the similarly named English joint stock venture chartered four years earlier. It accepted investment from anyone in permanent company shares rather than shares in each single-company venture (Clapham 1945, p. 692). This enlivened trade at the Amsterdam Stock Exchange begun as an imitation of the original in Bruges. Italian merchants resident at Bruges introduced the Dutch to the double-entry bookkeeping developed in the north of Italy in the fourteenth and fifteenth centuries. The list seems endless. If an idea seemed to have merit, the Dutch would try it.

Commercial leadership had passed quietly from Amsterdam to London by the third quarter of the 18th century, as Boswell (1764, p. 288) noted: "Most of their principal towns are sadly decayed.... Instead of finding every mortal employed you meet with multitudes of poor creatures...starving in idleness." The causes of the Dutch decline were many.

Exports and Urbanization in English America

"The discovery of America, and that of a passage to the East Indies...are the two greatest and most important events recorded in the history of mankind...uniting the most distant parts of the world...enabling them to relieve one another's wants, to increase one another's enjoyments, and to encourage one another's industry" (Smith 1776, p. 590).

The Virginia and Plymouth companies, both chartered in 1606, and that of Massachussetts Bay were private ventures. The Virginia Company produced no cities that acted as agencies of distribution. The Massachussets Bay Company after absorbing the Plymouth produced several.

The Virginia Company

England's first attempt at colonization, "an all-male expedition...[at] Roanoke Island...in 1585 failed when supplies from England failed to arrive on time. A second attempt at Roanoke, including women and children, was made in 1587. The Spanish Armada of 1588 interrupted contact until 1591. When the tiny settlement was finally reached again, it was deserted" (Murrin 1974, p. 184). Roanoke's failure showed that colonization needed outside nurturing. England's kings lacked the means to do so. London's merchants had the means, but wanted to profit from investment. A profitable export crop was needed to enlist merchant support. By 1606 tobacco exports looked promising.

Under the cultivation methods used in its day as Virginia's major export, tobacco required extremely large land holdings. Growing tobacco removes nitrogen and potash from soil. It these are not replaced, the soil becomes useless for further cultivation of tobacco or any other crop; so tobacco land had to be new land. Virginia's tobacco aristocracy had, of necessity, to be land speculators.

The land of the Virginia Tidewater worked against formation of cities. The Tidewater is cut by many rivers deep enough to carry ocean shipping. In a time of primitive land transportation, deep-water plantation docks made delivery of goods "from London, Bristol, &c, with less Trouble and Cost, than to one living five Miles in the Country in England" (Boorstin 1958, p. 107). Virginia needed no cities of its own. London was as much "Town" to its planters as it was to English squires. It was from London and not the rising new American distributive centers of Philadelphia or Boston that Washington and other rich planters ordered household furnishings, clothes, books, and carriages (Flexner 1965). Each plantation was a "company town" focused on exporting tobacco to England.

The need for large land holdings led to an intermarried upper class. "In the list of ninety-one men appointed to the Governor's council from 1680 until the American Revolution, there appear only fifty-seven different family names, nine...providing nearly a third" (Boorstin 1958, p. 109). The House of Burgesses was the workbench of the aristocracy as well. "Gentlemen freeholders" voted in any county in which they met the property qualification. "Many great Virginians, including...Washington, Patrick Henry, John Marshall, and Benjamin Harrison used their extensive and dispersed landholdings to advance their political fortunes" (Boorstin 1958), p. 116).

The South produced no Boston, Providence, New Haven, or Newport. Cities in the South appeared only after postrevolutionary factors had replaced those of London and grew only after cotton had been added to tobacco as a cash crop for export. "The belated rise of Southern cities...had unique effects: it actually tended to make Southern leadership less cosmopolitan, more rural and more withdrawn" (Boorstin 1965, p. 172).

The Massachusetts Bay Company

"In 1628, Puritan leaders secured a patent from the Council of New England to trade and settle in Massachusetts. Immediately, a shipload of settlers set sail. In 1629, the colony was designated the Massachusetts Bay Company by royal charter" (Catton and Catton 1978, pp. 88, 90). Colonial America ran consistent trade deficits with Britain between 1745 and 1774. At their peak in 1771, British exports to the colonies amounted to more than £4 billion. The peak year for exports to Britain, just under £2 billion, was 1775 (U.S. Bureau of the Census 1960). How did the colonists make up the difference? By going outside the mercantilist system legislated in the seventeenth-century Acts of Trade and Navigation. "A steady stream of ships beat their way down to the French and Spanish Indies laden with dried fish, lumber, naval stores, and horses, and brought back molasses which was then processed into rum.... Local consumption of this item was enormous, but lagged behind production. By 1750, Boston alone was exporting more than 2,000,000 gallons a year" (Glusker and Ketchum 1971, pp. 55–56).

Export Marketing and Urbanization in the United States

The revolution eliminated almost all trade. Winning eliminated favorable treatment at British ports. "The demand for staple exports...the basis of colonial well-being, was no longer expanding. Tobacco, which accounted for one-third of the value of colonial exports [stabilized]. . . . Rice exports actually declined. . . . Exports of wheat and flour. . .showed no tendency toward expansion." "The obstacles to rapid economic growth. . .were a small and scattered market and a foreign market which gave little indication of expansion. . . . The comparative advantage of the United States was confined, with a few exceptions of which shipbuilding and shipping were the most significant, to primary goods" (North 1961, pp. 19, 22). Loss of shipping during the war was an even greater blow, but New England traders proved resilient.

In 1784, a Boston ship carried the new American flag to St. Petersburg (Boorstin 1965, pp. 2,9). On August 23 of that year, a ship of Salem registry, *The Empress of China*, six months out of New York arrived off Macao. By 1807 Salem had succeeded Amsterdam in the pepper trade (Root and de Rochemont 1976, p. 102). It was "the world headquarters for trade in the tiny peppercorn. . . . In 1791 the United States re-exported less than 500 pounds of pepper; in 1805, it re-exported 7,500,000 pounds. . .nearly the whole crop of Northwest Borneo (Boorstin 1965, p. 8). Pepper was just one of Salem's trade goods. "From Salem, vessels traded with the west coast of Africa, brought copal for varnish from Zanzibar. . .and rubber and overshoes from Brazil. . .picked up sandalwood in Hawaii or otterskins in British Columbia as currency for Chinese tea" (Boorstin 1965, p. 8).

A typical Salem shipmaster was "a buyer and seller of goods of all kinds from castor oil and cowitch (an herbal specific for intestinal disorders) through rum, coffee, and cotton to garden seeds of curious kinds and the best stockings and shawls to be purchased in the Paris market; he was a dealer in foreign exchange in a number of currencies, including. . .those domestic valuations which were expressed in such terms as '27 1/2 lawfl money is £13.2.6 or $43.75 cts'" (MacLeish 1956, p. 38).

Salem brigs, Boston barks, Nantucket whalers, and New York clippers made the United States the "greatest mercantile sea power in the world" in the first half of the nineteenth century (Jensen 1973, p. 79). The growth of the United States as an international marketer was interrupted only once during this period, between 1815 and 1818 when English manufacturers denied U.S. markets by the War of 1812 dumped their unsold goods. "As a result. . .the decade 1810–1820 was the only one in our history in which urbanization did not increase" (North 1961, p. 62).

The first American clipper ship, built for the China trade, was launched in 1845 (Villiers 1955, p. 17). It had three times the tonnage of the largest Venetian trading galley and unmatched speed (Jensen 1973, p. 88). In 1849 the clipper "*Lightning* set a record for the greatest distance ever logged in a single day, a mark which steam vessels were unable to equal for many years" (Root and de Rochemont, p. 153). Clippers were ideal ships for luxury goods—like tea—that had a high value to bulk and for perishables. The first U.S. steamship had been launched in 1818. Slowly, beginning in the late 1850s, British steamships took over more and more of the world's carrying trade; what they lacked in speed they made up in greater cargo capacity. They outcompeted the clippers on shipping costs.

Nineteenth-Century Cities

"Northern and Southern coastal cities grew rapidly before 1840 but functioned mostly to facilitate movement of agricultural surpluses to distant and foreign markets and to bring to rural and village hinterlands the valued manufactured goods of Europe and artisan wares of the American city" (Filler 1974, p. 136).

"Legally cities are the children of states, but in the West many offpsring antedated their parents...[and] rural interests clearly predominated" (Wade 1959, pp. 73–74). The predominant rural interest was in finding markets for rural goods, which gave Western cities rare power. The East dominated U.S. international marketing, but international marketing dominated the West. "Merchandise from Europe and luxuries from the Orient landed at town wharves where they met the produce of nearby farmers waiting shipment...to New Orleans" (Wade 1959, p. 35). There was no market for Western produce among Westerners—whatever one farmer could produce, others could produce as well. Produce of the new lands began moving down the Ohio and Mississippi to New Orleans for export before the revolution.

As the West opened for settlement, urbanization more than kept pace. "The development process of Europe was recapitulated, much more rapidly, in the northern part of the United States.... First...Boston, which started by exporting timber...and fish, and Philadelphia which exported grain, were the first American cities to start wriggling, like Venice...out of this simple...dead end form of trade. Even as colonial cities, they began copying their simpler imports...and exporting these to one another and to other...settlements.... As new cities like Cincinnati, Pittsburgh, and Chicago formed, they entered the network" (Jacobs 1984, p. 145). For Cincinnati the slow-moving but powerful Ohio and for Pittsburgh the surrounding mountains acted like protective tariffs for their infant industries.

Chicago

In many ways, Chicago was the city of nineteenth-century America. Located at the shortest portage between the Great Lakes and the river system that empties into the Gulf of Mexico, it began as a stopover for voyageurs carrying furs from French Canada to, then, French New Orleans for export. New Orleans was a center for exports to Europe when acquired by the United States in 1803, but by 1815 it became a reshipment center for the U.S. East, the West Indies, and South America (North 1961, p. 141).

In the late 1830s, canals began to change the direction of Chicago's trade from north–south to west–east. Initially, Midwestern exports and "exports" moved southward; canal-borne "imports" came to it from the East. Chicago was a natural junction point for these outgoing and incoming goods. With the coming of the railroads and the opening of the Western lands to beef grazing and wheat raising, Chicago boomed. "Built in two generations by producers and marketers of lumber and meat products, by traders . . . by speculators, promoters and social workers" (Bursk, Clark, and Hidy 1962, p. 28), Chicago increased from around 3,000 people in 1833 to 3,000,000 or so by 1933: "The Century of Progress" celebrated in its Depression-era World's Fair.

Carl Sandburg (1916) made Chicago famous as the "Hog Butcher for the World . . . Stacker of Wheat, [and] Player with Railroads." In each of these, international marketing played a significant part.

Pork was the most important U.S. meat from domestic animals for three centuries (Root and de Rochemont 1976, p. 59), but it was as world beef butcherer that Chicago started in meat packing. It took over as world beef butcher from Paris following the Civil War (Boorstin 1983, p. 320). What secured Chicago's lead was development of the refrigerator car. It was developed simultaneously, but independently, as part of rival chilled meat-shipping systems by Philip Armour and Gustavus Swift. Refrigerator cars delivered dressed beef carcasses in good shape to eastern markets beginning in 1875 (Root and de Rochemont, p. 209). Two years later, beef was being exported in the refrigerator ships that had been developed to ship frozen New Zealand lamb to London (Tannahill 1974, p. 357). The U.S. population in 1880 was too small to eat all the beef the West could raise (Boorstin 1983, p. 320).

"The engineering genius involved in [the killing, cleaning, grading, and cutting up of steers] was even more obvious when Chicago packers began processing hogs, for though . . . cattle had started them on their way, it was inevitable that they would move on to all other meats" (Root and de Rochemont 1976, p. 210). Swift and Company had added operations in Tokyo, Osaka, Shanghai, Hong Kong, Manila, and Singapore to its English and French distribution outlets for Chicago-butchered beef and pork before 1900 (Boorstin 1983, p. 321).

Technology, especially Cyrus McCormick's reaper, helped to make Chicago the center of the international wheat trade. "America was encouraged to expand her wheat lands—wheat not maize—because Europe wanted wheat" (Lowenberg et al. 1968, p. 59). Just as opening western range lands to cattle had produced more than could be consumed domestically, so opening the prairies to wheat cultivation created another crop for export. To carry these crops to eastern ports for shipment abroad railroads was essential. The railroads built to carry away exports drew farmers from the Plains and cattle drivers from the western ranges into the mainstream of U.S. life. The trains stopped in Chicago to have the grain they carried ground and their cattle butchered before being shipped on to eastern cities and ports. On the way back, they brought mail order catalogs from Montgomery Ward and Sears, Roebuck. Mail order catalogs lessened farmer isolation. Money earned through export marketing helped to pay for catalog orders. Chicago became the center of the U.S. mail order business.

Chicago never overtook New York's lead as its boosters said it would (Boorstin 1965, p. 279), nor has it Los Angeles' current growth of booming Pacific Basin exports (Carlson 1985, p. 37), but it has a glorious past, if uncertain future, in international marketing.

SUMMARY AND CONCLUSIONS

This analysis set out to test the hypothesis that the pace and timing of city development are determined by export marketing. Comparison of qualitative factors to draw conclusions was chosen as the method of analysis because of the lack of comparable data among the marketing histories of the cities selected to test the hypothesis. A summary of city forming innovations is displayed in Table 12.1. Statements of the implications for national policy and for marketing theory conclude this analysis.

What the Record Shows

The record shows that exports are, indeed, city forming and that urbanization's pace is particularly connected with export marketing. Table 12.1 summarizes some of the "scattered bits of information...that can tell...how and when...this fantastically complicated set of activities...we call marketing came into existence" (Cox 1960, p. 237). Table 12.1 shows that the development of marketing was neither steady nor always forward.

Time after time, innovations that had been in place earlier had to be reinvented. The reasons for this are many, among them war and, perhaps, just forgetting. Standardization of firearms production with interchangeable parts is usually ascribed by Americans to Eli Whitney in nineteenth-century New Haven, yet was common practice in Nürnberg in the 1540s (Beard 1938, p. 219). Cities that became great through exports waned when their day as exporting centers passed. Why is this true? What marketing functions do cities acting as agencies of distribution perform?

First, cities add utility to goods by bringing them from afar and assembling assortments either for local consumption or for transmission to other centers of distribution. Second, intercity links at long distance enable distant trading partners to relieve one another's wants, raise living standards, and encourage full employment of human and natural resources. Third, long-distance trade encouraged voyages of discovery that added to the world's supply of goods, enriching the lives not just of those nations that did the exploration, but all nations. Fifth, world amalgamation of markets holds the same potential benefits that amalgamation of national markets did in the past: unification of laws and standards and stimulation of commerce and industry. Finally, the gains of trade—as the

TABLE 12.1 City-Forming Innovations in Selected Cities

City— Era, Peak Population	Principal Trade Goods	Trading Area	Significant City-Forming Innovations in Use, Type of Government
Ancient Cities			
Carthage 740–146 B.C. 700,000 to 1,000,000	Grain Spanish silver, Cornish tin, silk, pepper	Western Mediterranean + Britain and India	Alphabet, long-distance trade, freighters, rudimentary accounting, celestial navigation, coinage, standard weights and measures, water clock, business as an honorable calling, plutocratic timocracy
Athens 480–399 B.C. 100,000 to 125,000	Olive oil, wine, lead, copper pottery	Eastern Mediterranean, Sicily, southern Russia, North Africa	State-sponsored coinage, aristocracy
Medieval Cities			
Constantinople 430 to 1452 A.D. 1,000,000	Spices, silk (from China and local manufac- ture), icons	Eastern Mediterranean, southern Russia	Import substitution, factory system, patriciate

237

TABLE 12.1 (continued)

City—Era, Peak Population	Principal Trade Goods	Trading Area	Significant City-Forming Innovations in Use, Type of Government
Venice ca. 550 to 1797 120,000+ in 1204	Salt, saltmeat, spices, silk, (imports and local manufacture), glassware, German silver	Eastern Mediterranean, Asia Minor, southern Germany, Champagne (through Marseilles)	Commodities and futures exchanges, bank of deposit, patriciate
The Hanse 1000 to 1550 Lübeck and Nürnberg, 20,000; 90 other cities around 5,000 each	Herring, furs, tallow, hemp, tin, iron, naval stores, grain, salt, saltmeat	Baltic Basin + London and Novogorod	Cogship, merchant oligarchy
Modern Cities Lisbon 100,000	Spices—pepper, Guinea gold	Japan, Africa Brazil	Caravel, quadrant, routier cartography, bourgeois-like aristocracy

238

Amsterdam 1510 to 1699 200,000	Herring, naval stores, ships, spices— pepper, woolens, linens	Japan, East Asia, India, North & South America	Flyboat, marine insurance, stock exchange, limited liability joint stock company, toll-free regions, double-entry bookkeeping, carrying trade, merchant oligarchy
Boston 1630 to 1850 ca. 300,000	Cod, naval stores, lumber, rum horses, ice	United Kingdom, West Indies, Mediterranean, Africa, India	Clipper ship timocracy
Chicago 1833 to 1933 ca. 3,000,000	Beef, pork, grain, flour, farm implements	U.S. East Coast and beyond	Refrigerator railway car, modern slaughterhouse, mail order merchandising, plutocracy

Source: Compiled by the author.

histories of Carthage, Constantinople, and Venice indicate—are longer lived than those of conquest.

Contemporary Singapore demonstrates that the benefits of long-distance trade for an autonomous state are not a thing of the past. Singapore, expelled by Malaysia in 1965 has gone from poverty to opulence (Ellis 1977; Hodgson 1981). It now enjoys a living standard second only to that of Japan in Asia and is rapidly closing the gap (Crossette 1984). Like Venice and Amsterdam, political control is narrow. There is only a pretense of democracy by the standards of the United States and other Western nations, but Singaporeans seem quite free of discontent because income opportunity is quite open (Hodgson 1981; Crossette 1984).

City Forming Through Exports and National Policy

None of the cities successful in using exports as a city-forming industry had a plan. Each seems to have adapted itself to marketing opportunities as they presented themselves. "As the market can be seen as the mother of inventions" (Fisk 1967, p. 698), so, perhaps, it can also be said to mother discovery of marketing opportunity.

The People's Republic of China appears to agree that exports can produce economic development. It has created four special economic zones to lure foreign investment, technology, and management skills. The zones are independent of all Chinese control save that of foreign policy and currency regulation. The treaty recently concluded between the People's Republic and the United Kingdom over Hong Kong goes even further. When the People's Republic takes over in 1997, residents of Hong Kong will become residents of a very special economic zone. They will retain their current form of government—with Chinese rather than British supervision, separate passports, and the Hong Kong dollar (Copper 1984). Hong Kong has never been politically independent. Like Singapore, it seems a nearly apolitical community.

Few governments might be so willing as China to create specially privileged zones for fostering urban growth and development. Few see their problems as severe as China's. Cities are engines of riches that nations exploit to overcome differences among their regions, but the implication of the histories examined here is that such practices literally kill the geese that lay the golden eggs. Rather than encouraging flight of resources from cities, as the policies of the United States and many other nations do, this analysis indicates that concentration of resources in cities, particularly those involved in export marketing, contributes to more effective employment of resources and yields higher returns from each resource employed than does resource dispersal.

City Forming Through Exports and Marketing Theory

Exchange between rather than within groups seems to be the likely origin of marketing. The notion that marketing had its origins within communities is placed in serious doubt by historical analysis. There is a certain ease to explaining the development of markets and marketing as resulting from a division of labor within communities and, then, by extension to interregional and international marketing, but this explanation does not seem in accord with the facts. It is not that the division of labor as the source of exchange is invalid, but rather that it should be applied to inter- rather than intragroup exchange. Illustrations now used to make the point of how the division of labor contributes to exchange would need only minor modification to reflect the world as it is. Replacing fancy with fact about marketing's international origins ought to benefit not only marketing theory but marketing practice.

REFERENCES

Abbott, Wilbur Cortez. 1918. *The Expansion of Europe: A History of the Foundations of the Modern World*, Vol. 1, pp. 107–8. New York: Holt.

Adams, George Burton. 1901. *Civilization During the Middle Ages*. New York: Charles Scribner's Sons.

Alderson, Wroe. 1964. *Dynamic Marketing Behavior*. Homewood, IL: Richard D. Irwin.

Alderson, Wroe, and Reavis Cox. 1948. "Towards a Theory of Marketing." *Journal of Marketing* 13 (October): 143.

Alderson, Wroe, and Michael H. Halbert. 1968. *Men, Motives, and Markets*, p. 58. Englewood Cliffs, NJ: Prentice-Hall.

Bagley, C. R., and Edwin Prestage. 1896. *Azurara's Chronicle of the Discovery and Conquest of Guinea*, pp. 27–29. London: Hakluyt Society.

Beard, Miriam. 1962. *A History of Business*. 2d ed. Ann Arbor: University of Michigan Press.

Bishop, Morris. 1970. *The Middle Ages*. New York: American Heritage Press.

Boorstin, Daniel J. 1983. *The Discoverers*. New York: Random House.

——. 1965. *The Americans, Vol. 2: The National Experience*. New York: Random House.

——. 1958. *The Americans, Vol. 1: The Colonial Experience*. New York: Random House.

Boswell, James. 1764. *Boswell in Holland*, p. 288. London: W. Heinemann, (1957 edition).

Braudel, Fernand. 1984. "The Perspective of the World." In *Civilization and Capitalism, 15th–18th Century, Vol. 3*, trans. by Sian Reynolds, pp. 109, 121. New York: Harper & Row.

——. 1982. "The Wheels of Commerce." In *Civilization and Capitalism, 15th–18th Century, Vol. 2*, trans. by Sian Reynolds, pp. 120–210. New York: Harper & Row.

——. 1981. "The Structures of Everyday Life." In *Civilization and Capitalism, 15th–18th Century, Vol. 1*, trans. by Sian Reynolds, pp. 480–81. New York: Harper & Row.

Bursk, Edward C., Donald T. Clark, and Ralph W. Hidy, eds. 1962. *The World of Business*. New York: Simon & Schuster.

Calmette, Joseph. 1949. *The Golden Age of Burgundy*, trans. by Doreen Weightman. London: Weidenfeld and Nicolson.

Carlson, Eugene. 1985. "Los Angeles' Growth Differs from Other Major Cities." *Wall Street Journal* January 15, p. 37.

Catton, Bruce, and William B. Catton. 1978. *The Bold and Magnificent Dream: America's Founding, 1492–1815*. Garden City, NY: Doubleday.

Church, R. W. 1893. *The Beginning of the Middle Ages*, p. 15. New York: Charles Scribner's Sons.

Clapham, Sir John. 1945. "The Antecedents and the First Three Years of the Bank." In *The World of Business, Vol. 2*, edited by Edward C. Bursk, Donald T. Clark, and Ralph W. Hidy, p. 697. New York: Simon & Schuster.

Clough, Shepard B., and Charles W. Cole. 1946. *Economic History of Europe*, p. 24. Boston: D.C. Heath.

Cooper, John F. 1984. "Hong Kong Doesn't Provide a Pattern for Taiwan." *Wall Street Journal* November 5, p. 33.

Cox, Reavis. 1964. "Introduction." In *Theory in Marketing: Second Series*, edited by Reavis Cox, Wroe Alderson, and Stanley Shapiro, p. 1. Homewood, IL Richard D. Irwin.

——. 1960. "The Dark Continents of Marketing." In *Marketing Concepts in Changing Times*, edited by Richard M. Hill, p. 239. Chicago: American Marketing Association.

Cox, Reavis, Charles S. Goodman, and Thomas C. Fichandler. 1965. *Distribution in a High-Level Economy*. Englewood Cliffs, NJ: Prentice-Hall.

Crossette, Barbara. 1984. "The Opulence of Singapore." *New York Times Magazine*, December 16, pp. 122–24, 142–43, 146–48.

Davidson, Marshall B. 1975. *The World in 1776*. New York: American Heritage.

Durant, Will. 1939. *The Life of Greece*. New York: Simon & Schuster.

Ellis, William S. 1977. "Malaysia: Youthful Nation with Growing Pains." *National Geographic* 151 (May):635–79.

Filler, Louis. 1974. "Urban Society." In *The Study of American History, Vol. 2*, edited by Ernest Kohlmetz, p. 136. Guilford, CT: Dushkin.

Fisk, George. 1967. *Marketing Systems*. New York: Harper & Row.

Gottfried, Robert S. 1983. *The Black Death*, pp. 77–80. New York: Free Press.

Hodgson, Bryan. 1981. "Singapore: Mini-Size Superstate." National Geographic 159 (April):540–61.

Heilbroner, Robert L. 1970. *The Making of Economic Society*, 3rd ed. Englewood Cliffs, NJ: Prentice-Hall.

——. 1961. *The Worldly Philosophers*, p. 12. New York: Simon & Schuster.

Flexner, James Thomas. 1965. *George Washington: The Force of Experience, 1732–1775*. Boston: Little, Brown.

Glusker, Irwin and Richard M. Ketchum. 1971. *American Testament*, pp. 55–56. New York: American Heritage Press.

Jacobs, Jane. 1984. *Cities and the Wealth of Nations*. New York: Random House Inc.

Lowenberg, Miriam E., E. Neige Todhunter, Eva D. Wilson, Moira C. Feeney, and Jane R. Savage. 1968. *Food and Man*. New York: John Wiley & Sons.

MacLeish, Archibald. 1956. "Portrait of a Yankee Skipper." *American Heritage* 8 (December):38–43, 97.

Merivale, Charles. 1876. *General History of Rome*, p. 202. New York: Harper & Brothers.

Meyer, Karl E. 1973. *Teotihuacan*, pp. 50–75. New York: Newsweek.

Michelin Tyre Co. 1977. *Belgique Duchée* Luxembourg 1st ed. Paris: B. Michelin.

Mommsen, Theodor. 1928. "Rome." In *History of Nations*, Vol. 3, edited by Henry Cabot Lodge, p. 93. New York: P. F. Collier.

Mumford, Lewis. 1961. *The City in History*. New York: Harcourt, Brace & World.

Murrin, John M. 1974. "The Colonial Era." In *The Study of American History, Vol. 1*, edited by Ernest Kohlmetz, p. 20. Guilford, CT: Dushkin.

North, Douglass C. 1961. *The Economic Growth of the United States*. Englewood Cliffs, NJ: Prentice Hall.

Norwich, Lord John Julius. 1982. *A History of Venice*. New York: Alfred A. Knopf.

Ogg, Oscar. 1948. *The 26 Letters*. New York: Thomas Crowell.

Pirenne, Henri. 1969. *Histoire Economique et Social du Moyen Age*, trans. by R. F. Wendel. Paris: Presses Universitaires de France.

——. 1925. *Medieval Cities*, p. 161. Princeton, NJ: Princeton University Press.

Pneu Michelin. 1977. *Bourgogne/Morvan*, trans. by R. F. Wendel. Tours: Imprimerie MAME.

Polanyi, Karl. 1944. *The Great Transformation*, p. 58. Boston: Beacon Press (1957 edition).

Potter, David M. 1954. *People of Plenty*, p. 78. Chicago: University of Chicago Press.

Ricardo, David. 1817. *Principles of Political Economy and Taxation*, p. 256. London: I. M. Dent & Sons (Everyman's Library Edition, 1962).

Root, Waverly Lewis and Richard Rochemont. 1976. *Eating in America: A History*. New York: Morrow.

Sandburg, Carl. 1916. *Chicago Poems*, p. 3. New York: Henry Holt.

Savitt, Ronald. 1980. "Historical Research in Marketing." *Journal of Marketing* 44 (Fall):52–58.

Schevill, Ferdinand. 1930. *A History of Europe*. New York: Harcourt, Brace and Company.

Seward, Desmond. 1978. *The Hundred Years War: The English in France, 1337–1453*. New York: Atheneum.

Smith, Adam. 1776. *An Inquiry into the Nature and Causes of the Wealth of Nations*, p. 15. New York: Random House (Modern Library Edition, 1937).

Tannahill, Reay. 1973. *Food in History*. New York: Stein and Day.

Tyler, William R. 1971. *Diion and the Valois Dukes of Burgundy*, pp. 9, 10. "The Seafaring Tradition." *American Heritage*. 24 (August):18–27. Norman: OK. University of Oklahoma Press.

U.S. Bureau of the Census. 1960. *Historical Statistics for the United States. Colonial Times to 1957*, p. 757. Washington, D.C.: U.S. Government Printing Office.

Vaile, Roland S., Ewald T. Grether, and Reavis Cox. 1952. *Marketing in the American Economy*. New York: Ronald Press.

Wade, Richard C. 1964. *Chicago: The Growth of a Metropolis*. Chicago: University of Chicago Press.

———. 1959. *The Urban Frontier: The Rise of Western Cities, 1790–1830*. Cambridge, MA: Harvard University Press.

Welles, H. G. 1921. *The Outline of History, Vol. 1*, p. 229. New York: Macmillan.

Wendell, Richard F. 1979. "New Worlds for Marketers: Speculations on Marketing's Origins and Future." In *International Marketing: Managerial Perspectives*, edited by Subhash Jain, and Lewis R. Tucker, p. 77. Boston: CBI.

Westfall, Ralph, and Harper W. Boyd. 1960. "Marketing in India." *Journal of Marketing* 25 (October) 15:11–17.

Willis, F. Roy. 1973. *Western Civilization: An Urban Perspective*. Lexington MA: D.C. Heath.

Willsion, George F. 1945. *Saints and Strangers*. New York: Reynal & Hitchcock.

PART IV

Methods for Advancing Marketing Knowledge

Time, Space, and Competition: Formulations for the Development of Marketing Strategy

RONALD SAVITT

INTRODUCTION

It is nearly four decades since the publication of "Towards a Theory of Marketing" by Wroe Alderson and Reavis Cox (1948). From that article, Alderson and Cox, working together, separately, and with others, went on to shape the field of marketing as it is known today. Reavis Cox's contributions are spread across the various parts of marketing, and his writings and ideas have been instrumental in providing a clear understanding of marketing as one of the set of social institutions. Within his work are new and exciting ideas about the elements and constructs of marketing as well as concepts directly usable by marketing managers.

The present chapter deals with concepts that have run through much of Cox's contributions. Time and space have been a common theme in his detailed study on house-building materials (Cox and Goodman 1956), as part of the major synthetic effort with Roland S. Vaile and E. T. Grether (Vaile, Grether, and Cox 1952), and in the monumental study of distribution in a high-level economy (Cox, Goodman, and Fichandler 1965).

MARKETING AND COMPETITION

Introduction

Marketing scholars have paid little attention to the development of a theory of competition based on marketing concepts. Rather, we have continued to rely upon the constructs from economic theory. While economic models of competition have been helpful in structuring the framework of the competitive process, they have not proven elegant enough to help us understand market behaviors. The purpose of this discussion is to better understand the competitive process and hence lay the foundation for more powerful theories in marketing, especially those dealing with the development of marketing strategy. This need has not gone unnoticed in the literature, though most efforts in this area have not fully recognized that the new ideas are available to expand the unique elements present in marketing (Anderson 1982).

This analysis will focus upon dynamic elements rather than the static components found in the general and partial equilibrium analysis of traditional marketing theory. The dynamic dimension is change in time and space. Although these elements have been part of the marketing literature, they have not been viewed as central to the understanding of marketing behavior. Greater concern has been shown for space in contrast to time, although in the fullest dimension, spatial analysis still remains a mystery in marketing (Grether 1983). Time, on the other hand, has been greatly neglected by economic theory and by marketing, so much that its neglect is a puzzle to the observer (Rizzo 1979).

Central to the development of any marketing-based theory of marketing strategy is the full recognition and complete acceptance of the most important contribution of marketing theory, namely, the heterogeneity of markets and the resultant behavioral goals of market participants for heterogeneity. Unlike economic theory, marketing theory explains market and market behavior in terms of differentiation.

Marketing can be viewed in three ways: Namely, it represents an institution in society, it represents a business function, and it represents a philosophy of management. Regardless of the level of analysis, the central concern is to understand the behavior of market participants. Unlike economic theory, marketing does not view markets that reach equilibrium points; indeed, marketing theory shows that markets rarely clear through matching heterogeneous supply and demand. Instead of reaching positions of similarity, as found in traditional equilibrium theory, and instead of reaching positions of limited difference, as found in partial equilibrium theory, marketing is about extreme differentiation and about the creation of market disruptions in which entrepreneurs (either buyers or sellers) can thrive.

There are gaps within the operation of the matching process, and it is the role of the entrepreneur to search for opportunities by first creating discrepancies and then fulfilling satisfaction by offering goods and services that extinguish them. The essence of this type of marketing behavior assumes that competition is the search for meaningful differential advantage on the part of both buyers and sellers. Hence, for decision makers, the attainment of efficiency and satisfaction implies some "matching" of the discrepancies between heterogeneous supplies and heterogeneous demand. This matching always has discrepancies, it is never total; the clearance of markets is the exception of market functioning rather than the substance of marketing (Reekie and Savitt 1982).

Marketing Competition

Competition is normally defined as the rivalry between and among firms and customers for the custom of consumers and suppliers, respectively. In the decision-making process, customers are generally viewed as making decisions about the allocation of income toward various expenditures, and at that level, firms are in competition with one another for the resources allocated by consumers.

The central premise of this argument is that time and space represent first-order activities in the decision-making process. The argument is that time and its cohort, space, are primary decisions made by firms and consumers. Consumers make time allocation decisions before financial allocation decisions. Time, above all, is the single scarcest resource; activity groups requiring time to perform and a place to perform them (space) are made before the allocation of financial resources. For example, time determines whether a family will take a vacation; finances will determine its nature.

The rivalry between marketing firms is aimed at the occupancy of time of customers. They are in competition with other firms and other activities for the scarce resource time. In order to occupy time, they must organize their resources to occupy space, because the occupancy of space explicitly means the occupancy of time. Time is the most precious of all resources, and the most rational behavior of firms in competition with one another is to try to maximize the time that its offerings have with customers. A firm pursuing this action betters its own chance for survivability and at the same time weakens the survivability opportunities of its competitors. In this context, competition or rivalry takes on new dimensions since it reorganizes priorities around time domination and points toward marketing behaviors to maximize customer time, which denies competitors access to this resource. The strategies that naturally follow are threefold: namely, to maximize the occupancy of the time domain of any customer in the purchase of X's product, to maximize the occupancy of the consumption time of any customer of X's product, and to maximize the blockages that consume time to prevent customers in general from purchasing or consuming the offerings of A to J's products.

Developing competitive offerings that have as a central appeal "time saving" for the customer may be a dangerous strategy for the seller unless the seller is prepared to fill in or occupy the time that has been saved. As with financial resources in which there is real savings, the value of the savings to the customer is valuable only to the extent that total well-being can be increased. Similarly, to the firm, the net result of the savings is valuable only if by the freeing of the saving the customer is able to consume more from that seller. It is no different with time savings. For example, a new house-cleaning technology that saves an hour a day for a householder has limited potential, and perhaps even great danger, to the seller if, as a result, the householder is now able to allocate the time to the consumption of competitive products. Hence, a concern of the new technology ultimately must be the ability of having subsequent offerings that absorb the time that has been freed.

While in all cases it may not be possible to develop and offer time-absorbing offerings to capture the newly freed time, the firm must develop strategies that prevent competitiors from gaining the "new" time or affecting the possible ways in which customers can use this time. Revzan (1961, pp. 19–21), in a slightly different context, that of marketing channels, developed this proposition; he referred to it as blockages. The concept as originally proposed was the reciprocal of linkages that are the formal and informal connections between various middlemen and their customers. Blockages, on the other hand, represent the attempt by firms either "individually or collectively, or both, to set up obstructions to the formative linkages" (p. 20). Whatever the form of these blockages, they are formulated to minimize the time available for customers to be engaged with offerings of competitors.

The interesting point is that firms have a greater ability to establish and shape their environments, a point that has received some recognition (Zeithaml and Zeithaml 1984). Focus on time and space means that marketing firms must shape their own environments if they are to be the successful participants in market transactions. Time and space as revealed in subsequent arguments have the capacity to be molded; they offer and enjoy the concept of plasticity. The concept strongly suggests that the environment is not simply a given but a marketing variable that can be affected with the same degree as the more traditional ones. It goes beyond the notion of stretching, which is found in elasticity (expansion and contraction), and reaches toward the concept of environmental molding. Plasticity refers to the molding or "form-giving" process often called "demand shaping." It incorporates time, since in order to create shape, time must pass. It also recognizes that once shape takes place, it is subject to change or reshaping. The goals of marketing firms can be simplified: to shape consumer preferences for their individual offerings.

The reciprocal is to reshape the preferences of consumers whose choice is for offerings other than their own. In the analogy of the competitive process, it is the recognition that demand must not become fixed for alternative offerings while at the same time maintaining as much solidity among those individuals who have preference for the firms's product. This view of the competitive process focuses on the ability of market participants to affect markets. "Much less attention has been devoted to the fact that demand can be remolded into quite different forms. The investigation of plasticity of demand has generally been left to the market analyst rather than to the economist" (Penrose 1959, p. 81).

In summary, some basic axioms about the conditions in which competition occurs can be stated: (1) Marketing systems may be operationally independent in space, but the firms may be operating in multiple geographic markets. (2) Firms may be operating in several markets that are not part of a single marketing system. (3) A firm may offer a wide product line that includes complementary and substitute items. (4) A firm may be selling several brands of the same product; these may be substitutes for one another (Carman 1977, p. 115). (5) Firms have different perceptions of time and space and hence will differ in terms of their planning horizons. (6) Finally, firms have different perceptions about other marketing system participants, expecially buyers. The corollary, of course, in terms of consumers is that they possess similar conditions defined from their perspective.

THE TIME–SPACE PERSPECTIVE

Introduction

The time–space perspective comes from the work of Hägerstrand at the Swedish School at Lund. His work focuses on the organization of activities into temporal and spatial terms that can be used to define the performance of human activities. He argues that human activities form environments that have a hierarchical ordering to the extent that "those who have access to power in a superior domain frequently use this to restrict the set of possible actions permitted in the inside subordinate domains. Sometimes they can also oblige the subordinate domains to remove constraints or to arrange for certain activities against their will" (Hägerstrand 1970, pp. 16–17). In essence, the environments in which human action takes place have temporal and spatial characteristics and these characteristics and hence the environment can be shaped.

Time represents the transition from one event to another; it describes the actual transformation of one situation into another (Shackle 1958, p. 15). Within the concept of time are the descriptors that define the environment in which actors behave and that define the limits of behavior. While time presents movement and expressly has structural and behavioral elements, there is no absolute. Time in terms of its structure, the starting and ending points, and its behavior, the movement between these points, is subjective, namely, defined through individual perceptual processes. Firms have the ability to define their own time and affect the perceptions of the time definitions of their customers; so do customers, though their ability to affect the time perceptions of suppliers is probably not as great. Suppliers have the ability to influence their customers in the ways in which they proceed through time. Changes are difficult to overcome by the individual or by competitors. In the most general situation, Pred (1977, p. 209) has stated: "The constraints which must be overcome in order to enable the formation of any single activity bundle of interaction are synonomous with the necessary (but not the sufficient) conditions which must be met for the occurrence of that activity bundle or interaction.''

The Domain

A domain is the "time–space" entity within which activities and events are under the control and/or influence of specific individuals or organizations. "Domains are intended to protect artificial or natural resources, to restrict population density, and to form an efficient arrangement of bundles" (Pred 1973, p. 42). The ability of an individual or an organization to navigate through the domain is a function of the constraints that affect action. There are three major classes of constraints. *Capability constraints* circumscribe the amounts of time needed to take care of physiological necessities and hence limit the distance (space) that an individual can cover within a given time span within given transport technologies. *Coupling constraints* are those related to such activities in which individuals must join other individuals (organizations, as well) in order to form production, consumption, social, and other activity bundles. Finally, *authority constraints* arise as a result of the fact that it is very difficult to pack more than one or several activities into a limited space "space occupation is exclusive and that all spaces have a limited packing capacity. Authority constraints subsume those general rules, laws, economic barriers, and power relations which determine who does or does not have access to specific domains at specific times to do specific things" (Pred 1977, p. 208).

The structure of a domain is a perceptual phenomenon in which the members of the domain, as well as those attempting to affect the domain, play important roles in creating a definition. A domain in its narrowest sense can be viewed as a time period such as a day of 24 hours. Given a set of known processes, only certain activities can be accomplished in that time period; however, a change of the environment can be accomplished by extending or contracting the nature of the activities undertaken in the 24-hour period. The course of the day can be affected by rearranging and molding the activities that a person must undertake to go through the period. The day can appear to have more time if onerous activities are shortened or changed, or, on the other hand, the day can be made to seem longer if such activities are increased in number or intensity. As such changes take place in the movement in time through the day, space occupancy varies. As some of the time requirements shift and shrink, for example, then there is time freed and concomitantly there are changes in space occupancy patterns.

Changes in time utilization and space occupancy can be affected by the individual who occupies the domain and by other groups and/or individuals in other domains that have some hierarchical and lateral position to other domains. At a micro level, an employer can affect the domains of workers by shifts in the environment. Consider what happens if a firm decides to move the plant four miles further from the locus of the houses of the work force. Their total domain structure has been affected. On a more macro level, similar effects take place as the result of marketing programs such as the development and expansion of the hypermarkets (Dawson 1984). While extension examples can be put forward, the importance of the points is that domains or environments in which marketing decisions are formed can and are affected by the results of such decisions.

The "Path"

The central unit of analysis in time–space domains is the "path." The path is the trajectory of the domain through time and space. Each path can be visualized as a continuous line with a starting point or birthplace and ending point or deathplace. These can be defined in absolute terms such as days, months, or years or by perceptual terms such as the perceived time that each path takes (Thrift 1977). The ability to describe the path provides the basis for understanding domains.

An example of this is to take the individual and his or her behavior given the events of a day. Given a base point, say, the home, that an individual cannot leave before a certain time and to which he or she must return to before a certain time, it is possible to trace the path of activities that the individual undertakes and to identify the activities through which the individual moves as well as identify those through which passage may be limited or impossible. The example establishes the amount of time that the individual has, namely, the difference between the departure time from home and the arrival time at home at the end of the day. Being able to properly describe the path is foremost in understanding the effects of domains. That is why individual behavior, either customer or firm, is the best element for illustrating the concepts.

The time that it takes an individual to move through the domains will be related to the maximum speed at which he or she can move from the base point and back again. These conditions determine the outer limits of the time–space prism available for performing specific activities. A simple example of this is found in Figure 13.1.

The time–space prism depicts the situational determinants of an individual's path through the environment given certain assumptions. The shape of the prism is described by the individual's speed of travel to the destination, the distance to the destination, and the time required to complete any activity at any of the stations in the prism such as a, b, c, or d. "Thus an individual's prism is an amalgam of point of departure, a speed constraint, the projects and activities to be performed and the coupling constraints imposed by the time-space destina-

FIGURE 13.1. The Time–Space Domain

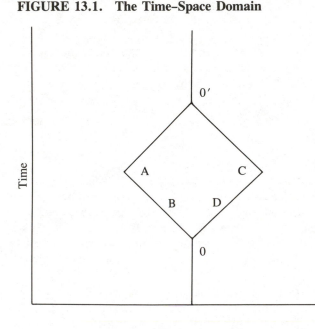

Source: Nigel Thrift, "Time and Theory in Human Geography, Parts I and II," *Progress in Human Geography* 1 (1977):433, Figure 6.

tions (such as hours of opening). Prisms are not only of use at the individual level, but also enable one to analyze time allocation and spatial allocation" (Thrift 1977, p. 433).

The environment of the prism is described by *O*, the origin of the activities, and by *O′*, which is the origin that the individual must reach after the completion of the activities. The various stations in the prism are so described to suggest that in spite of the fact that all are within the prism, not all of them can be undertaken in the given time period. For example, completion of *A* means that none of the others can be accomplished since the individual cannot go back in time to perform those activities. The choice of *B* first would suggest that *D* and *C* could be completed but not *A*, since two events, namely, *C* and *A*, cannot be completed at the same time.

The present example relies upon the assumption of an objectively measured and described prism. This is only for the purpose of the example. What must be added is the subjectivity that is clearly a part of the description of the prism. While there may be only 24 hours in a day, the sequence of events can be affected; also, the perceptions about the sequences and the importance of their performance can be dramatically affected. The shape of the prism can be changed to be narrower, that is, viewed as taking more time and less space, or it can be made wider. Also, the stations of activities can be changed to be placed in a way in which more or all or most can be performed in some more efficient or effective manner or perceptions can be created about them to suggest that such can transpire. What is important to recognize is that the environment can be changed; these changes can only be, however, up to the limits of the physical environment—two events cannot take place at the same time in the same place.

The path has a trajectory, which can be traced from the past and discussed as part of present actions. It also implies something about future behaviors to the extent that those pursuing the path believe that it will remain on the same trajectory into the future or it will change to the extent that those affecting it can change its direction or change the domain elements. Since future events are difficult to predict, the path of the domain may vary dramatically as the result of outside factors such as a gasoline shortage or poor crops. Similarly, the path can be affected by institutions or individuals who will directly benefit by changing the perceptions of others to believe that the speed or the direction of the domain in its trajectory path will change. While sudden and dramatic changes in the path may not be easily made in the short run, more substantial changes can be accomplished in longer periods. Such changes can be made by affecting the ways in which the domain moves, such as new technologies, or through changes that affect the expectations of market participants.

The ability of firms to affect the time processes will affect the choice processes of consumers. Here are found the opportunities for developing competitive strategies. Although this is a generally static perspective, the dynamic implications are to be seen. The introduction of "quick checkout" lanes in supermarkets is one recognition of this principle; other examples also merit inclusion, such as the Canadian supermarket operator who located "convenience" stores on the outer parts of shopping centers and supermarket locations to allow customers to avoid the confusion of the major operations as well as to be able to avoid the domination of public policy that affected store hours on Sundays. In both of these examples are clear signs of the competitive developments that are possible by affecting the time–space domains of individuals and hence affecting the outcome of competition.

Space

Space represents the location at which events take place, and they, like the element of time, have real physical characteristics and perceptual characteristics of those passing through them and those observing the sequence of events. Space is based on the recognition of images that individuals use to define it. Each individual will necessarily have a different definition for space and that definition will change through time. The perceptions of space are affected by time processes and the information flows received by the viewers. These images are called mental maps (Gould and White 1974, p. 49).

In the absolute sense, physical laws dictate the capacity of a specific location to be occupied by an event, a principle that is well understood. However, space occupancy is a perceptual phenomenon, and it is reasonable to suggest that a firm can convince the viewer that such space is occupied when in reality it is only partially occupied or even perhaps unoccupied. This may be achieved through the use of information and the creation of images. Space occupancy can be affected by the rapidity and speed at which events move through space. These arguments lead to the proposition that a specific space can be molded to fit the needs of the actor that wants to affect the flow of events. These abilities are directly created by affecting the perceptual conditions about the image of the space.

Whether it be the individual or the firm, the perception of space is a highly subjective phenomenon. There are, however, both perceived and real boundaries at any time. The former represent the extent to which the decision maker establishes points that he or she uses in discriminating between relevant and irrelevant points. This is simply cognition and can be called cognitive space. It may encompass vast or relatively limited areas. These definitions will vary from product to product and behavior to behavior. We all know of individuals who are thought to be provincial because their spatial boundaries are limited. The same is true for firms. The fact that all firms do not enter the same markets (points at which buyers are located in time and space) cannot be argued on the basis of economic factors alone. Some firms, some countries, do not perceive opportunities over large areas. It is unrealistic to argue that cost functions alone set spatial boundaries. In international business, some firms enter foreign markets because they have a greater perception of space. In this context, we can more easily identify the perceptual factors. What we need to do is measure the individual factors that lead to such definitions.

On the other hand, a clear distinction must be made between the perceived or behavioral environment and the objective environment. The behavioral environment represents that segment of the objective environment that is perceived by the individual or firm; it is that part of space from which information signals are received and interpreted by the perceptual mechanism of the decision maker. Only a small amount of the information transmitted from the objective environment is received: "It is this that determines the nature of the individual's behavioral environment, and it is this and only this, that is relevant to purposive behavior" (Lloyd and Dicken 1972, p. 138). Events, phenomena, or places outside the behavioral environment have no relevance to, and no effects on, conscious decision making.

Firms and Time–Space Perceptions

Each individual and firm will have a unique region, that is, a defined perception of space. These regions are confined at any point or in any sequence of time points by the domain. A domain, as we have seen, is an area that has time and space dimensions that incorporate the performance of specific activities or functions. There is a temporal hierarchy among domains. Certain activities must be performed before others. Each individual or firm has a multidimensional set of domains. These domains are also characterized by power or superiority as well as hierarchical order. The new result of this is that some individuals and firms will be able to affect the functions of others.

Every firm is surrounded by an environmental framework or pattern of resource and activity alternatives that must be dealt with if want satisfaction is to take place. These alternatives are unevenly distributed in the Aldersonian sense, and they are known to the extent that information-seeking behavior takes place. They are relative to the individual, and individual behavior can generally be characterized to the extent that it is either geocentric or ethnocentric, that is, the degree to which the individual is outward looking or inward looking (Perlmutter 1967, pp. 33–44). The extent of the behavior depends on the individual's perceptions, the availability of information, which in itself is dependent upon the outward or inward search behavior, and the available resources.

The movements of a firm through space can be traced historically, but they cannot be exactly forecasted. Some statements about the hierarchy of domains over firms can be made, though these are estimates at best. An example of this is the life of the individual: "Thus, in earning a living and filling his informational, social and recreational needs and wants each individual wanders over an individual path which commences at a birth point and terminates at a death point" (Pred 1973, p. 37). In the search for want satisfaction, individuals will follow more or less repeated rhythms within a known sequence of paths; however, because of changes in their environments and their perceptual skills, individuals will make sudden changes in their paths. Such changes will not be common to all on an a priori basis.

TIME, SPACE, INFORMATION, AND ENTREPRENEURIAL BEHAVIOR

A Review of Premises

If time represents the most limited of resources, then space is the second most limited resource; it is extendable only to the extent that "new space" can be carved from unused space. Time and space form environmental structures that have objective definitions and subjective definitions by users. Perceptions about time and space are affected by flows of information, and both the quantity and quality of information affect the perceptions about time and space. In this context, it is important to realize that time and space perspectives and the resultant perceptions about occupancy can be affected by either buyers or sellers.

A key characteristic of markets and their participants is their diversity. Asking two individuals to describe a known item will show the extent to which market diversity and discrepancies appear. Unlike the assumptions of equilibrium theory that underlie much of normative marketing analysis, a more correct description of markets is, as we know from Alderson, radical heterogeneity. That is a condition that is present and serves as the basis of entrepreneurial behavior, which will be shown to be the basis for marketing behavior in the strategic sense.

Market participants, buyers and sellers, use information as a means of communicating with each other and more importantly as means of creating market opportunities. The entrepreneur does not seek homogeneity, but creates and exploits heterogeneity. Unlike the "firm" of equilibrium economics and much of marketing, the role of the management is to seek and exploit market discrepancies. These are accomplished by affecting perceptions of time and space occupancy for customers and competitors.

The Nature of Information

Traditional economics uses price as the market-clearing mechanism. Alderson incorporating the work of Stigler restates the premises to focus on information as the factor that allows the market-matching process to take place (Stigler 1961). The problem with that approach is that three important concepts are improperly defined as irseparable, when indeed each has its own important existence (Loasby, 1976, pp. 7-9). "Risk represents a condition where all possible states of the future are assumed unknown and a probability distribution can be defined for those states. With these data the economist can forecast the equilibrium using the expected value criterion" (Reekie and Savitt 1982, p. 60). Uncertainty is the situation in which all of the possible outcomes cannot be stated with such certainty, but in which a variety of probability distributions with associate weights can be constructed.

In reality, such a list does not exist, which is Loasby's state of "partial ignorance" (1976, p. 6). The knowledge of the future is better described in terms of ignorance insofar as there is no way of determining the future. While in the very short run, the manager can attempt to estimate what future outcomes might be, as required by the adherence to the marketing concept, the future is more difficult to deal with. Instead of attempting to rely solely upon what customers perceive and what they say they want, prudence dictates that the entrepreneur affect the flow of information to mold the environment by affecting the perceptions of time and space occupancy. As Alderson suggests, an offering is only "adequately identified" for a customer if in his or her ignorance the "supplier has guessed right" (Alderson 1958, p. 61). "Guessing" is simply a means of overcoming ignorance, which is not based on a computative process—it is intuitive. "It is the process of entrepreneurship in which the successful guesser or entrepreneur makes a profit, the unsuccessful a loss'' (Reekie and Savitt 1982, p. 60).

Marketing as Entrepreneurial Behavior

Both buyers and sellers in the discrepant market behave in a way as to differentiate themselves from other members of their respective groups. Though buyers and sellers may employ similar techniques, information, and processes, the emphasis is on movement toward diversity rather than homogeneity. Exchange transactions become the central way in which the differences come to pass; buyers and sellers seek to create and maintain positions in the time–space domain that are unique and invulnerable from attack by others.

Exchange transactions (or marketing) should be approached from the perspective of seeking out and exploiting opportunities created by the discrepancy of markets and the limited information of the very short run and the state of ignorance of the long run. The exploitation process from the point of view of the firm is to affect the consumer by changing perceptions about time and space in the future. This really amounts to affecting or changing the environment rather than allowing the environment to be a static element to be considered rather than to be managed.

As a more dynamic process, marketing as entrepreneurship becomes a system in which the entrepreneur attempts to continue to upset the system of relationships by creating new market discrepancies and then exploiting them with consumers who are open to exploitation. This process requires a commitment to clear and precise observation of market conditions and a focus on individuals and their differences rather than their similarities. This requires a new managerial perspective that moves marketing analysis away from the accepted principles of seeking homogeneous market segments.

This does not imply that all marketing activities should or can be carried out focused solely on the individual level. Basic principles of economics and scale economies dictate the need for specialization; and no matter how much we might want to revoke those principles, they cannot be. What happens is that the more homogeneous groups (or segments, in more common marketing parlance) are built up from the analysis of the market discrepancies rather than imposed by the assumptions of homogeneity that are part of market segmentation. It is at the level of the individual or at the level of the group that has common interests that the discrepancies can be discovered.

One need look no further than the 19th century history of retail cooperatives in the United Kingdom to see how consumers, too, can perceive entrepreneurial opportunities and exploit them. The fact that the retail cooperatives came to employ resources of land and labor and have accumulated trading capital to purchase other forms of stocks and equipment may mean that some entrepreneurial acts in the modern consumer cooperative are inspired by resource owners such as managers or capitalists but the proximate entrepreneurship was undoubtedly that of consumers. (Reekie 1979, p. 114)

In the setting of Austrian economics, the entrepreneur provides a corrective function in the marketing. "Entrepreneur means man acting in regard to the changes occurring in the market" (Mises 1963, p. 254). The position taken here is even stronger: namely, that the entrepreneur (the marketer) aids in the disruption of the market process as well as in the corrective process. The marketer does this by being able to affect the perceptions of time and space held by customers, potential consumers, and actual and potential competitors.

In this context, serving needs, perceived needs of customers, is not acceptable, given that understanding about the future is limited, as we have seen previously. What the marketer must engage in is the affective action of the time and space position of other market participants, which makes them search for solutions. In this way, the activities of the firm are to create a dissonance prior to the consumption situation and then respond with a solution.

A LOOK AHEAD TO ENTREPRENEURSHIP AND MARKETING STRATEGY

Entrepreneurship has been described as the creation and exploitation of marketing opportunities by market participants. Creation of such opportunities is based on the premise that the environment is malleable and plastic and can be molded by market participants. Exploitation depends upon observation of market discrepancies and/or the potential for creating such discrepancies and the pursuit of them in such a fashion as to upset and affect the plans of other market participants. This type of activity is made possible because of the limited knowledge of future events. Entrepreneurship is an active, rather than a passive, process and requires a willingness to make guesses about outcomes.

In order to formulate strategies, market participants start with the assessment of the environment, which is defined in terms of time–space domains, since these elements and their internal constructs represent the structures that affect market behavior. These elements are characterized by vast degrees of heterogeneity and have both objective and perceptual definitions. Changes in either represent the basis for laying marketing strategies.

These strategies develop along the lines of the constraints on the time–space domains introduced earlier. The first marketing strategy is the capability strategy, which is affecting the amounts of time—actual, potential, or perceived—needed to complete the transaction and the following consumption process (for customers) or the production process (for those engaged in the creation of utilities).

Such strategy is organized around premises that disrupt the time relationships among market participants. Second, coupling strategy is based on the development of relationships in anticipation that the future will be less productive without such arrangements. It works because of the limited knowledge about the state of future environments. The third strategy is the authority strategy; It focuses on the ways in which market participants organize space, primarily, who shall occupy it and how it shall be occupied.

In each of these strategy types, the underlying principle is that the environment can be affected rather than accepted as an element that affects the strategy development process. The ability to affect the environment is based on the great desire for heterogeneity by market participants.

REFERENCES

Alderson, W. 1958. *Marketing Behavior and Executive Action*. Homewood, IL: Richard D. Irwin.

Alderson, W., and R. Cox. 1948. "Towards a Theory of Marketing." *Journal of Marketing* 13 (October):137–52.

Anderson, Paul F. 1982. Marketing, Strategic Planning and the Theory of the Firm." *Journal of Marketing* 46 (Spring):15–26.

Carman, J. M. 1977. "Theories to Describe Some Competitive Conditions in Which the Firm Operates." In *Behavioral Models for Marketing Action*, edited by F. M. Nicosia, and Y. Wind, pp. 148–62. Dryden Press.

Cox, Reavis, and C. S. Goodman. 1956. "Marketing of Household Building Materials." *Journal of Marketing* 21:36–61.

Cox Reavis, C. S. Goodman, and T. C. Fichandler. 1965. *Distribution in a High-Level Economy*. Englewood Cliffs, NJ: Prentice-Hall.

Dawson, John A. 1984. "Structural-Spatial Relationships in the Spread of Hypermarket Retailing." In *Comparative Marketing Systems*, edited by Erdener Kaynak and Ronald Savitt, pp. 156–82. New York: Praeger.

Gould, P., and R. White. 1974. *Mental Maps*. Baltimore: Penguin Books.

Grether, E. T. 1983. "Regional-Spatial Analysis in Marketing." *Journal of Marketing* 47 (Fall):36–43.

Hägerstrand, T. 1970. "What About People in Regional Science?" *Papers of the Regional Science Association* 24:7–21.

Lloyd, P. E., and P. Dicken. 1972. *Location in Space: A Theoretical Approach to Economic Geography*. New York: Harper & Row.

Loasby, B. J. 1976. *Choice, Complexity and Ignorance*. Cambridge: Cambridge University Press.

Mises, L. 1963. *Human Action*. Chicago: Regency Press.

Penrose, E. T. 1959. *The Theory of the Growth of the Firm*. Oxford: Basil Blackwell.

Perlmutter, Howard V. 1967. "Social Architectural Problems of the Multinational Firm." *Quarterly Journal of AIESEC International* 3 (Fall).

Pred, A. 1977. "The Choreography of Existence on Hägerstrand Time-Geography and

Its Usefulness.'' *Economic Geography* 53 (April):207–21.

———. 1973. ''Urbanization, Domestic Planning Problems and Swedish Geographic Research.'' *Progress in Geography* 5:1–76.

Reekie, W. D. 1979. *Industry, Prices and Markets*. Oxford: Philip Alan.

Reekie W. D., and Ronald Savitt. 1982. ''Marketing Behaviors and Entrepreneurship: A Synthesis of Alderson and Austrian Economics.'' *European Journal of Marketing* 16:(July).

Revzan, David A. 1961. *Wholesaling in Marketing Organization*. New York: John Wiley & Sons.

Rizzo, Mario J. 1979. ''Disequilibrium and All That: An Introduction Essay.'' In *Time, Uncertainty and Disequilibrium*, edited by Mario J. Risso, pp. 1–18. Lexington: MA Lexington Books.

Shackle, G. L. S. 1958. *Time in Economics*. Amsterdam: North-Holland.

Stigler, George J. 1961. ''The Economics of Information.'' *Journal of Political Economy* 69:213–25.

Thrift, N. 1977. ''Time and Theory in Human Geography, Part I.'' *Progress in Human Geography* 1:65–101.

Vaile, R. S., E. T. Grether, and R. Cox. 1952. *Marketing in the American Economy*. New York: Ronald Press.

Zeithaml, Carl P., and Valarie A. Zeithaml. 1984. ''Environmental Management: Revising the Marketing Perspective.'' *Journal of Marketing* 48:46–53.

CHAPTER 14

Parameter Theory and Science in Marketing

STIG INGEBRIGTSEN
MICHAEL PETTERSSON

INTRODUCTION

Reavis Cox and Wroe Alderson made a significant contribution to the debate about marketing theory and marketing as a science in "Towards a Theory of Marketing" (1948).[1] In the editor's note, Alderson and Cox invited comments on their views, stressing disciplines that can inspire marketing theory. This chapter is an attempt to address this challenge, although a time lag of 37 years separates our response. From a different generation and with different backgrounds, we wish to establish marketing as a science with a theory of its own.

This chapter consists of three main sections. The first section interprets the "1948" essay on two levels: as a general economic interpretation and as an account of the scientific perspective from which Alderson and Cox base their theoretical framework. As is often the case with an interpretation of a theory of science, it would have been desirable for Alderson and Cox to have stated their premises more explicitly.

The second section presents a specific attempt at theory contruction. We have chosen to discuss "parameter theory" from 1955 [2] to confront a U.S. view of marketing with a Scandinavian view from approximately the same period. In our opinion, the "1955" theory is based on an ideal of science, world picture, and image of the human approximating the Alderson and Cox ideal. To a certain extent, it may be seen as a response to Alderson and Cox's desire to establish a marketing theory. We are dealing with one of the central treatises of what Mickwitz has called the "Copenhagen School."[3] Since it includes variables other than price as determinants of demand, it is a multiparameter theory, a logical extension of the one (price) parameter theory that appears in macro- as well as microeconomics.

Lastly, the third section will return to the central issues of the Alderson and Cox essay. The discussion concludes with comments on the scientific basis of the Copenhagen School theory. Since the scientific basis of the Copenhagen School is the same as the Alderson and Cox ideal, our comments apply to both works. A crucial question is raised concerning what scientific criteria are and should be, and particularly which criteria to choose, given the complex problems marketing theorists wish to discuss. An attempt is made to portray a different ideal of science and world picture and a different image of humans than the model in these earlier discussions of marketing theory.

In "Towards a Theory of Marketing," Alderson and Cox stress the need for developing a "marketing theory." Alderson and Cox accepted the applied aims of marketing, but they regarded theory based on scientific methods as better able to comply with the demands of business because marketing behavior exhibits law-like regularities. We emphasize that they wished to develop marketing into a science proper. If so, their wish may have been superfluous because the question is not whether marketing is to be a science, but whether it is capable of meeting business demands for solutions to problems of business. Businesspeople are unconcerned whether this problem solving is carried out on the basis of scientific theories or not, if solutions are effective.

TOWARDS A THEORY OF MARKETING

General Economic Interpretation

The Alderson and Cox essay can be seen as a contemporary (1948) view of and as an indication of future development of marketing. Their essay emphasizes an increased interest in marketing theory and points out the following circumstances as their rationale for this interest: (1) the lack of principles and theories: "marketing literature offers its readers very few true and important 'principles' and 'theories'"[4] (p. 138) and (2) a widespread feeling of not having been able to pose or identify problems or draw up procedures or practices for solving marketing problems: "too little even in setting fundamental and significant problems for themselves, to say nothing of working out procedures for solving problems once they have been formulated" (p. 138).

The "method of attack" has not been satisfactory. A possible starting point in Northrop's "logic research"[5] is pointed out by Alderson and Cox, stressing that if such a "creative analysis of the problems of marketing" is not followed, marketing will become a "haphazard accumulating of facts" or at best "an empirical art" (p. 138).

Alderson and Cox choose theoretical subjects demonstrating that the existing "theory" ("so-called principles stated in manuals of management") cannot account for or explain the data observed. For example "Problems of Price Discrimination" is mentioned and it is emphasized that "conventions" are accepted as if they were "objective facts." Furthermore, it is pointed out that price determination is a question of negotiation rather than impersonal balancing of supply and demand. In relation to "Spatial Aspects of Marketing" as well as to "Temporal Aspects of Marketing," they emphasize that "it is clear that new concepts and new analyses based on new and more realistic assumptions are required."

In relation to "Economic Entities," it is pointed out that economic entities are not always "observable or measurable" and that they are "arbitrarily assumed to exist" (p. 141), that is, conventions. Furthermore, they contend that "competitive" is often replaceable by "cooperative" behavior. Economists have focused only on "competitive behavior" and not on "cooperative behavior," relevant to a discipline like marketing. Even if attention has been paid to organizations that call themselves cooperative, this has not resulted in a "theory of cooperation" in the broad sense.

The assumption of maximization as continuous functions is also questioned. In real world decisions discontinuous–discrete functions characterize the managerial alternatives that can be discussed. In their words, "little or no weight is given to the fact that decisions are really discontinuous" (p.141). Even if "marketing men" have known this to be a fact, they have done little to develop theories on this background.

In "Attitudes and Motivations of Buyers and Sellers," inadequate and unrealistic concepts of human behavior are identified. Alderson and Cox claim that marketing itself has just as good opportunities as psychology to observe "human beings in action as buyers and sellers" (p. 147). Their starting point for propounding a potential theory of marketing must therefore be behavior, particularly observable consumer behavior. They state that it is important to pay attention to the way in which behavior is organized, who makes what decisions, and how they are made, and to observe how the consumer's behavior (perhaps also of a group) interacts with the seller's behavior in a system organized in a particular way. Thereby, buyer behavior as well as seller behavior and the organization of both determine how we organize our mix of parameters of action, that is, for advancing a parameter of action theory proper. Finally, much criticism of marketing is dismissed as superfluous, "wasteful," by pointing out that the market is not static if and when it is first established, but something that is necessarily in "continuous adjustment, improvement," etc.

Realizing that a continuation of the status quo implies that "marketing must remain fragmentary, superficial and inaccurate," Alderson and Cox look for inspiration for the construction of "profound theoretical formulations" (p. 142). They state that the possibilities are good for advancing a theory soon, if the following disciplines are examined thoroughly:

"Economic Theory" including especially "institutional economics."

"Group behaviorism" in the sociological sense. This would mean that "the agencies of marketing would become patterns of human behavior and communication clustered about some physical facility."

"Game Theory." Transactions are divided into "routine" and "fully negotiated" by Commons. Von Neumann and Morgenstern have elaborated "fully negotiated transaction" in a mathematical framework under the label of game theory (p. 143).

In addition to the concepts mentioned, inspiration can be obtained in disciplines like anthropology, sociology, ecology, etc.

For Alderson and Cox, the concept of "group behaviorism" is a starting point for an integrated "marketing theory." This concept is broader than the narrow psychological concept of Pavlov and Watson, as it focuses on the sociological concept of "the organized behavior system." Thus, the crux of a "marketing theory" is said to be an understanding of behavior, system, and organization in relation to marketing.

The concept of "group behaviorism" has proven valuable in other social sciences. "Group behaviorism" (p. 146) is appreciated by Alderson and Cox because of its lack of analogies to the equilibrium systems of physics and because it centers on "individual behavior that tends to perpetuate organized behavior systems."

Alderson and Cox referred to a proposed test of the relevance of the "group behaviorism" concept in an "exploratory survey" to satisfy two basic needs: (1) to permit the setting up of theoretical subjects in marketing according to Northrop's norms and (2) to permit the setting up of generalizations that allow testing. This refers to an analysis of equilibrium in the shape of efficiency optima for every task performed by the market in accordance with the "functional approach to a study of marketing" (p. 149).

Finally, they ask if a marketing theory is forced to wait until a "reformulation of economic theory has progressed further" (p. 151). Here they criticize economics for its lack of dynamic approach; that is, economists often regard technological aspects as being outside their sphere of interest and thus outside the domain of economic theory. Alderson and Cox want both economic and marketing theories that deal explicitly with "this interaction between the system and the processes which take place within it" (p. 151).

We hope that our summary of the Alderson and Cox article reflects their strong interest in changing things. The 1948 article critical of the situation then prevailing expressed optimism with regard to attaining the proposed objectives provided that the stated directions were followed.

After 37 years it is alarming to find that these arguments can still be advanced. Of course, a great deal has changed since 1948, but many of the central and severe criticisms have not been resolved. Among them are identification of problems, scientific criteria, new concepts and methods as a function of new problems, discussion of discontinuous–discrete functions, image of humans, and an independent framework for the observations of behavior of marketing.

Specific Theory of Science Interpretation

Now we examine the Alderson and Cox theory essay in terms of a theory of science. We want to state elements of the theory of science as they appear explicitly and implicitly in the essay. We seek to establish more precisely what Alderson and Cox understand by science. This will facilitate an understanding and evaluation of the economic content of their essay. The aspects on which we focus are natural elements in a total paradigmatic analysis.[6] Because we cannot examine all the elements in the paradigm, we have chosen to focus on elements central to establishing on scientific premises an independent marketing theory. It is essential to specify the framework for this scientific theory. In a broad sense, we must infer their world picture and image of humans in order to make an explicit evaluation. Hence, our attention is first directed to their world view, next to their image of humans and, then their views on science.

World View

Alderson and Cox's rejection of the criticism of marketing as being "wasteful" presents a world picture that is both explicitly and implicitly liberalistic–capitalistic. They assess marketing as a necessary means to continued existence of markets. It should be pointed out, however, that Alderson and Cox mention several times that weight should often be put upon "cooperative rather than upon competitive behavior" (p. 141). They do not explain how far cooperative behavior should be extended or whether cooperation is a description of the market solely from the "marketing channel" point of view, "accomplishing a common, overall task" (p. 144). Cooperation might be interpreted to be a pure power or competitive situation. "Cooperative behavior" can be a macrodescription of a market on a sociological and political level, or from a micro point of view it is experienced as a power or competitive struggle. Therefore, we do not find a distinctly normative message supporting cooperation in the Alderson–Cox view.

The same ambiguous phenomenon appears concerning the fundamental objectives of business. Here again, it is difficult to decide whether Alderson and Cox's is a purely descriptive argument or whether it is also somewhat normative. In question is their reference to Boulding's speculations about regarding "the principle of organizational preservation" as fundamental instead of maximization of returns. Support for the normative interpretation rests on "the individual's struggle for socio-economic status" (p. 146). It leads to a consideration of the image of humans held by both Alderson and Cox, since they do not state their attitude explicitly.

Image of Humans

On the one hand, it appears that the human behaviors of buyers and sellers are of interest and presumably these alone. On the other, they refer to Kurt Lewin and his topological concepts as offering "some promise of setting up procedures that may lead to more effective understanding of human motivation" (p. 146). Thus, it is questionable that the pure theory of behavior rather than procedures for studying behavior is the center of their interest in group behavior.

The descriptive-versus-normative question is a central issue in the image of humans and an element of their paradigm of science. The universal methodological problem of a pure description is decisive because it is impossible to avoid taking a position on the image of humans implied in the chosen method and system of analysis. The normative aspects arise because the content of the analysis will be a consequence of the implied image of humans. Hence, a descriptive analysis is inescapably normative. It is surprising that Alderson and Cox do not speak more explicitly of the image of humans in the normative sense, in light of their explicit statement of the interaction between the system and the processes of the system.

Views of Science

The view of science as the descriptive element appears relatively clearly from "Towards a Theory of Marketing." Time and time again, Alderson and Cox emphasize the lack of theories and theoretical problems and methods for problem solving. They explicitly state that marketing is in "the first stage of scientific study, namely that of the gathering of vast compilations of fact" (p. 149). Although this characterization is not very positive, it is more positive than for economic theory as a whole, which is characterized as being a step further back, "in a prescientific or metaphysical stage. It has occupied itself with the effort toward logical deductions from assumptions" (p. 149). Thus, their scientific outlook is more positive in relation to marketing than in relation to economics as a whole.

Ideal of Science

The ideal of science is the normative element. How is the discipline to develop in order to achieve scientific status? Alderson and Cox try to remedy the lack of scientific method for problem solving by involving Northrop and his logic of research. They take the following scientific process from Northrop:

1. Analyze the problem imaginatively, since its nature will dictate the method that must be used to solve it
2. From (1) springs an understanding of the sorts of fact that must be assembled to answer it and of the methods by which it can be assembled
3. Actual assembly of the facts required

4. Description and classification of these facts
5. Derivation from them of fruitful and relevant hypotheses
6. Verification of the hypotheses thus deductively derived by inductive appeal to further facts

This scientific process (p. 138) corresponds to the methodological ideal of classical mechanics, that is, the analytical method, which has been very favorably received in classical physics and several other classical sciences. By way of introduction, the first "analysis" is "imaginative," because a definite method of analysis has not yet been decided on; that is, the problem should determine the method. Since Alderson and Cox mention only a single method, this point can not be decisive. However, there is a departure from classical analytical methods in their suggestion that the problem should determine the choice of method, because in classical science it is the analytical method that defines scientific status.

The choice of a starting point in a classical scientific ideal harmonizes well with the choice of a psychology and a sociology similar to that of Pavlov or Watson, who also operate with a classical scientific ideal as a starting point. The classical scientific ideal seeks to generalize and lay down regularities.

There is also evidence of how J. Q. Stewart and his social physics have exerted influence. At the same time, it is also clear that Alderson and Cox are conscious of limitations of the classical ideal of physics since they stress the importance of separating the equilibrium concept of group behaviorism from that of physics. "Thus, while it may make use of equilibrium concepts, it does not depend primarily on analogies drawn from the equilibrium systems discussed in physics" (p. 147).

The above-mentioned scientifically inspired process also appears: "Neither economics nor marketing can lay claim to being scientific until they attain the stage of continuous interaction between theory and research. The assumptions on which theory rests must more and more spring from careful empirical generalization. The facts which research gathers must more and more be relevant to hypotheses adopted on theoretical grounds" (p. 149). Thus, empiricism is the decisive factor in their theoretical framework. The theory is verified through empirical tests, and it is in the light of empiricism that the hypotheses, the empirical generalizations, are advanced.

The question of when a new theory "makes its appearance" is answered by Northrop saying "when existing theories fail to satisfy students because they do not account for or take into consideration all of the relevant observed facts" (p. 138). Many scientists have discussed the problem of scientific evolution. Among them Kuhn advances his paradigmatic theory of development in the light of the development in classical physics.[7] According to Kuhn, scientific research takes place in long normal science periods interrupted only by revolutionary periods, when the existing–prevailing paradigm is no longer able to explain severe problems sufficiently. This theory of development is valid only for disciplines already in the scientific stage, and thus it cannot be directly applied to marketing, which must be described as being preparadigmatic, since there is no one generally accepted paradigmatic ideal or norm.

More serious problems emerge in connection with the classical mechanical ideal expressed by Alderson and Cox's empirical view of science. Without having defined "problems," "objective," "world picture," and "image of humans," they choose Northrop's logic of science as a starting point. It seems as if Alderson and Cox do not follow the procedure prescribed by their own method. Certain parts of the reality of marketing do not fit directly into the classical physics ideal. Alderson and Cox express reservations in relation to the concept of equilibrium. The wish for "patterns" of explanation founded on the structure of causal explanation implies difficulties when discontinuity is introduced.

THE "COPENHAGEN SCHOOL OF MARKETING"

General Economic Interpretation

From the preceding interpretation of the Alderson and Cox essay, it appears that a scientific theory of marketing was missing in 1948.

In 1955 Rasmussen published "Pristeori eller parameterteori" ("Price Theory or Parameter Theory"),[8] which became one of the bases of the "Copenhagen School." The starting point for Rasmussen was Chamberlain's concept of monopolistic competition. Rasmussen stated that only with the theories of the heterogeneous market has it become possible to fuse marketing with managerial economics. He also asserted that it is a necessity to build marketing around the theory of monopolistic competition. A decisive aspect of monopolistic competition in relation to marketing is the realism of this type of market and the corresponding description.

Another important point in Rasmussen's work is his concept of parameters of action, which he defined as an economic factor the value of which the individual is free to determine and which is independent.

Three main problems appear to Rasmussen:

1. An analysis of the parameters of action of the firm and of the concept of competition
2. Construction of the concept of the consumer unit and the model of the stage of development for the marketing or sale of a product (life cycle)
3. Construction of the conditions of equilibrium for the various parameters of action in the firm

It is very important for Rasmussen to coordinate the parameters of action of the firm so that price becomes only one among many parameters. One of Rasmussen's aims was to put the parameters of advertising, service, quality, etc., on an equal footing with the parameter of price by stating a number of partial relations between the individual parameters and the corresponding demand. The choice of this partial strategy is due primarily to the fact that the different attempts of total parameter views of both macro- and microeconomics had operated with price–quantity diagrams up until then. The application of price–quantity diagrams in this connection has been possible because parameters other than price have been transformed into the costs generated by the application of the parameter in question. This clearly indicates that in general the price has been in focus as *the* decisive parameter of action. It was this view that Rasmussen contradicted.

In addition to his wish for a multi-parameter theory, Rasmussen specifies a demand–oriented multiparameter theory. By this he means that "consumers' criteria" should be decisive and the basis of the transformation into "producers' criteria" (corresponding to parameters of action) and not the other way around. Rasmussen recognizes measurement problems in connection with the "consumers' criteria" starting point, but thinks that examining the costs of the parameters of action will solve the problem corresponding to a change to producers' criteria. To Rasmussen this difficulty is a problem of measurement and not a fundamental epistemological problem.

A theoretical field of the greatest importance is the product life cycle. It is suggested that there is a mutual influence: Demand determinants influence the product life cycle, and in the other way around the latter's influence on demand determinants influence sale. Of course, this includes a distinction between short-term and long-term goods. Over and above the concept of action the concept of elasticity[9] appears as the most central in Rasmussen. The problem of the conditions of equilibrium in the partial parameter functions of the firm is solved by means of the concept of elasticity (demand elasticities only). The concept of elasticity is also important when defining competion. He accepts the notion common among economic theorists that there is competition between the firms in question if one or more of the cross elasticities is numerically different from zero.

In the attempt of Rasmussen to define and elucidate the concept of competition, he states that the sales of the individual firm depends on the value of a number of parameters of action, the price being only one among many and of the ability of the individual firm to influence the sales of the others through *all* these parameters of action.

Beyond this, Rasmussen distinguishes between narrow competition, which relates to the cross-elasticities in connection with supply of *substituting* products, and broad competition, which relates to competition for the buyers' tight budgets.

The cross-elasticities cannot be used as a dividing line between these elasticities, however, since both concepts of elasticity are present in the cross-elasticities. Rasmussen thinks that common sense might help distinguish between narrow and broad (extended) competition.

Rasmussen focuses on parameters of action in narrow competition by means of the kinked demand curve. In keeping with his wish for a multi-parameter theory, Rasmussen presents competitors' reactions to the shape of the kinked demand curve for all the continuously variable parameters of action. He thereby shows absolute consistency as to the potential heterogeneity of the market. He attempts to point out the equality of all the parameters of action, without advancing partial theories for any individual parameters (or collectively for a total parameter of action theory). He stresses the importance of regarding all parameters as equal, working out the elasticities of quality, advertising, and other continuously variable parameters.

A Comparative Theory of Science Interpretation

Rasmussen's theory responds to Alderson and Cox's "Theory of Marketing" by attempting to establish the product life cycle. His prerequisites are based on Duesenberry's "demonstration effect" resting on the assumption of "keeping up with the Jones'." Rasmussen's image of the human is an expression of a strong determinism external to the individual. Rasmussen's choice of Kleppner's advertising procedure is a further argument for the product life cycle based on external determinism.

This theoretical construction is parallel to the image of humans stated in the behaviorist school of psychology. Hence, Rasmussen and Alderson and Cox share approximately the same ideal of scientific method for developing theory: the hypothetical deductive method. In comparison with the ideal of science advanced by Alderson and Cox, Rasmussen's ideal maintained that a theory must be a systematic interpretation of the causal relations and interactions under examination. Both attach importance to an independent theory resting on a realistic view of the market. Both move in a normative direction in the form of generalization. However, we deal with two different views on levels of organization to be analyzed. The Copenhagen School is the more macroeconomic of the two.

It is difficult to postulate either a demand orientation or a production orientation for Alderson and Cox's organizing concept of "group behaviorism." This concept may suggest a starting point in behavior with a view either to meeting heterogeneous demand or to achieving a rational organization of work in the firm. Hence, the question of priority cannot be answered by focusing on either demand or supply assumptions about price formation, decision-making processes, descriptions of behavior, etc. Their focus on the heterogeneous market may signal that the assumption that all buyers are alike is rejected and that thus perhaps gradually a demand or marketing orientation could receive emphasis.

It is appropriate to compare the starting point of Alderson and Cox with that of Rasmussen. While Rasmussen's book from 1955 attempts to point out concrete lines–directions for the construction of a fully elaborated partial parameter theory, the essay of Alderson and Cox is an outline of the foundation on which such a theory can be developed. The two writings are not antagonistic but can be seen as development of a single line of thought. Rasmussen has an explicitly stated a demand-oriented starting point. Thus, "parameters of action" in principle are adapted to meet existing demand. The theoretical starting point in "consumers' criteria" is clear in Rasmussen's work compared with that of Alderson and Cox.

On the other hand, Alderson and Cox's strong emphasis is on the sociological aspects, on objects other than maximization of returns for business, and focuses on cooperation instead of competition. In theory development, they sought to study fields that were unexamined until recent years.

Fundamental points of resemblance are the starting point in Chamberlain ("monopolistic competition") and with it the focus on the heterogeneity of the market and the existence of preferences. Furthermore, the theory of behavior plays an important part in both starting points, although on different organizational levels. It is also clear that the primary wish both of Rasmussen and of Alderson and Cox is to elaborate a comprehensive model, a general parameter theory so that business can organize its marketing mix in order to attain its objectives. This might mean satisfying "consumers' criteria" by meeting the demands of the buyers or satisfying the objectives of business, for example, maximization of returns or survival or a combination of both. With some justice, it might thus be concluded that the decisive scientific ideal is identical. Both Alderson and Cox's and Rasmussen's crucial premise in elaborating theories and models is to formulate generalizations for use in business. Other wishes [10] are suppressed in favor of a scientific ideal that has proved its strength in the material world by discovering "law-like" regularities and generalizations. However, this ideal is problematic in the light of both Alderson and Cox's and Rasmussen's avowed intentions of explaining marketing behavior from a starting point in human behavior and needs. Unless human behavior and needs are themselves characterized as purely materialistic, the classical physics ideal fails to fit the phenomena under study.

EPISTEMOLOGICAL PROBLEMS OF CHOICE IN FORMULATING A SCIENTIFIC MARKETING THEORY

Alderson and Cox's call for a "Theory of Marketing" and Rasmussen's response attempt to begin by examining (1) the basis of marketing theory in economics and (2) an ideal of science. Although the theoretical areas considered differ, both theories are based on the ideal of science developed in physics, a purely materialistic conceptualization.

In this section an attempt will be made to discuss central elements in the classical physics ideal of science in a fundamental epistemological sense and in relation to the desired development in marketing, to move from a "producer's" to a "consumer's" perspective in marketing. The discussion examines interdependence between the substance, problems, aim, methodology, world picture, image of humans, view on science, and ideal of science.

Rasmussen generalized the kinked demand curve to apply also to each marketing action parameter. His theory of competitor behavior has been reoriented toward a more holistic view by Nielsen (1972).[11] His conceptualization allowed a competitor's behavior to relate to all competitors, all products, all markets, all parameters, their values and time of reaction.

Rasmussen's total system optimization solution is hindered by such practical matters as measurability and limited knowledge to the extent the theory building based on total system optimization difficulties will arise on account of the limited knowledge about interrelations between the individual action parameters.[12] Among the crippling limitations of competitive theory identified by Rasmussen[13] is the dependence on marginal reasoning as a convenient and neat paraphrase of the prerequisite of maximization of profit. If one tries to obtain other objectives than profit maximization, competitive theory breaks down. Rasmussen (in 1970) points out that it is therefore more promising to argue in favor of a total systems optimization strategy.

In his choice of definition of an action parameter, Rasmussen declares that he starts from Frisch's determination of concepts from which independence between the parameters is required. This independence should be related to the determination of parameters and not to the parameter effect. This, Rasmussen states, will include both substitution and complementarity between the action parameters.

Furthermore, the connections between action parameters and sale are regarded as causal relations. In other words, marketing actions produce a "hypodermic effect" on sales. This is termed deterministic causality. In classical mechanics, relations involve an isolatable system, complete reversibility, "unidirectionality," and no learning, characteristics rarely found in economic relations. However, deterministic causality must be chosen as the structure of explanation if generalization and postulation of "law-like" regularities are to describe marketing relationships.

The wish to optimize based on deterministic causes is extremely questionable. As total independence between marketing action parameters is not presupposed, their functional connection in producing the overall outcome cannot be the result of a simple addition of the individual parameter effects on demand or consumer preferences. This implies that, irrespective of optimization being sought whether by means of a parameter-combining overall outcome or by means of a number of partial marketing functions, optimization of the marketing mix cannot be carried out by determinist cause-and-effect analysis as in classical physics.

There are two central points in the above argument: (1) that simple addition applies only to independent parameters and (2) that causality is generally based on the implication of continuity. In cases of discontinuity, as Alderson and Cox have pointed out that marketing decisions are, it cannot be determined whether unidentified causes appear in the gaps. If this conception is confronted with the realities of economics, the further question of construing economic relations as causal relations arises, because continuous variation has hardly ever been registered in economics. It has not even been approximated as in physics, despite longitudinal measurement at points in time as in consumer panel diary measurements.

In our opinion, both Alderson and Cox and Rasmussen begin analyses with an examination of demand. In market analysis, experience confirms the effectiveness of entering the problem by first identifying "consumers' criteria" instead of "producers' criteria." As a step in the direction of an orientation toward demand, Rasmussen points out the need for transforming "consumers' criteria" into "producers' criteria." However right and reasonable it might be to start from "consumers' criteria," this creates serious problems of cognition in connection with marginal analysis. It is not only a matter of interaction between the producers' marketing action parameters, but also of the producers' interaction with the potential consumers expressing heterogeneous market demands. The number of possible consumer interpretations will make the number of constellations that can be covered by a market demand curve unpredictable. Only under a mechanistic image of humans, can a demand theory be analyzed in two-dimensional coordinates like price–quantity curves.

Beginning an analysis with "consumers' criteria" would imply that the consumers' experience controlled the choice of model structures, including the number of dimensions as well as content of the individual dimensions to be measured. Such prerequisites appear to be unrealistic. For this reason, parameter theories should be regarded as purely deductive systems. These Alderson and Cox argue against and cite as a basis for evaluating economics to be prescientific.

Because of the methodological problems in formulating and testing parameter theories, another approach to a theory of marketing is warranted. "General System Theory," presented for the first time in 1948 by von Bertalanffy[14] tried to cope with the above-mentioned methodologic problems. This alternative view on method is also pointed out by Alderson and Cox. A central element of "General System Theory" is antireductionism requiring the problems to be solved at the level of system aggregation at which they have been identified. This antireductionistic view rejects Rasmussen's partial treatment of parameters of action. Rasmussen's view implies that a problem can be divided and reduced to a single parameter under which subproblems will be more simple. In parameter theory, the original problem is solved by "adding" the subsolutions. In "General System Theory," systems consist of components with their couplings or relations, which are the focus of analytical effort. Said in another way, the methodological aim is solving general problems characterized by interaction and nonlinear relations of functions. It appears from "The Alpbach Symposium,"[15] however, that there are severe difficulties connected with the establishment of an operational "General System Theory."

One of the fundamental problems of "General System Theory," as we see it, is the critical question of causality as the organizing cognitive structure. Causality is connected with dependent and continuous functional relations between variables. In "General System Theory," deterministic causality yields to interaction and evolutionary change. It is doubtful that "General System Theory" consciously or unconsciously maintains a causal structure of cognition. It is thus relevant to examine the ideal of causality. Although causality is presented as the organizing cognitive structure in marketing theory formulated under the classical physics of science, a changed concept of substance beginning in the late 1920s initiated discussion about maintaining causality as the organizing cognitive structure for quantum physics. A further question is whether the concept of substance in quantum physics will be more in harmony with the problems in marketing than the concept of substance in classical physics.

To abandon causality as the organizing cognitive structure, as it recurs in almost all of our learning, creates conceptual difficulties. The belief in causality has been an enduring concept in scientific research. For this reason, it is quite natural that scientists like Einstein and Bohm[16] sought to maintain causality as the organizing cognitive structure of physics. Later Bohr and Heisenberg abandoned causality in their interpretation of modern nuclear physics, quantum physics. In the interpretation by the Copenhagen School, Bohr and Heisenberg introduce the ideal of complementarity as a consistent generalization of the ideal of causality.

Bohr defines complementarity in relation to phenomena that are at first sight characterized as mutually exclusive,[17] since they are complementary in the sense that they collectively exhaust any information about the atomic object. Causality becomes a special case of complementarity when the original conditions are present. In other words, when the fundamental discontinuity is small relative to the subject under analysis, it is permissible to disregard it. This means the reintroduction of continuous relations, because the universal quantum of action discovered by Planck implies a minimum quantity.

The underlying problem in connection with this discussion of cognition in physics is discontinuity. Every observation inevitably involves an interaction between "measuring tool" and "object" that it will not be possible to expound precisely on grounds of principle (the quantum of action). As a consequence of this fundamental impossibility, Bohr argues that "object" and measuring tool must be regarded as a whole and introduces the concept of phenomenon to describe this whole.

The development of quantum physics in the shape of quantum mechanics commences with the introduction of an extremely abstract way of thinking, a formalism, disconnected from the traditional conceptualization based on intuitive understanding. Quantum mechanics seeks a consistent statistical treatment of atomic problems that become known to use solely as intensifying mechanisms that force the atomic quantities to manifest themselves in the classical four-dimensional time–space system. In this formal thought mode, Bohr states: "The conjugate variables are replaced by operators subject to a non-commutative Algorithm involving Planck's constant as well as the symbol $\sqrt{-1}$."[18]

This physicist's way of treating discontinuity and interaction does not directly solve the corresponding problems in marketing because application of the mathematical formalism poses severe problems. These problems stem from the fact that formalism is related only to "matter," the inanimate. In contrast, unless a material image of the human is chosen, marketing has to deal also with the immaterial aspects of humans. As discontinuity and interaction must be the rule rather than the exception in group behavior, the epistemological discussions in physics about these problems should give rise to their consideration in marketing to avoid choosing a material image of humans.

The choice of image of humans thus appears to be central in building economic theory. It is not a question of the "real world" and our brains being causal or noncausal, but a question of our knowledge about the "real world" and our brains being described as causal or noncausal. It is a question of choice not only as regards methodological problems but also as regards ontological problems. In other words, a number of choices must be made both in solving problems and in their interrelationship. This has also been pointed out by Bohr, who stresses that we always act as both actors and audience on the stage of life.

As a consequence of rejecting causality as the organizing cognitive structure, it is tempting to accept the concept of complementarity as an alternative. However, the formalism developed to solve the methodological problems of contradictory descriptions in quantum physics cannot be transformed to marketing theory because the formalism is related only to the inanimate. To solve the methodological problems in relation to the animate, marketing theory must establish unambiguous communication built on explicit elements of paradigms and prerequisites. To establish a scientific demand-oriented marketing theory predicated on a realistic description of monopolistic competition in heterogeneous markets, even with a narrow consideration of the competitive choices available to the firm, serious methodological problems remain.

It would probably be more realistic, therefore, to adopt an overall view of the relations between the firm and its environment where the dimensions of the relations must range from competition via negotiation to cooperation or full integration. A given move may evoke any response as regards both the nature and the dimension of the interaction between buyers and sellers. With the difficulties in choosing a starting point in "consumers' criteria" in mind, an extremely complicated system of relations requires explicit choices to explain a given system. Any marketing system will always be a subsystem segment, no matter how total a theory is advanced. Hence, explicit choices as regards system delimitation also emphasize the relations to larger systems that influence a chosen system and that are modifiers of evolved theories within that system.

There is also the question of observer–observed in all action research. In any form of study–observation of relations, the fundamental interaction between observer and observation will appear. Thus, it is impossible to talk about an "object'' without seeing it as part of the chosen way of observing. This also resulted in the introduction of the concept of phenomenon in physics explaining the whole consisting of ''object'' and measuring tool. In marketing theory, this includes the observer's prerequisites; the evaluation of marketing as either a superfluous or a necessary element if the market is to function. Another aspect of ''object'' versus ''phenomenon'' in marketing involves what an observation really deals with. What does a communication about a given observation really communicate: Does it communicate about the ''object'' or about the interaction between ''object'' and observer as experienced by the observer? This question asks what is really happening during an action research process: What changes occur in observer, in observed, and in measurements taken before, during, and after the action process?

In an economic theory not based solely on a material image of humans, that is, a holistic view, the concept of complementarity is also relevant. Typically, simultaneous observations of both the material and the immaterial aspects are mutually exclusive, but both views are necessary for a complete description. Thus, it appears that the choice of starting point (for example, the material or the immaterial) will be decisive in the choice of a paradigm for developing marketing theory.

A final problem in constructing demand-oriented marketing theory concerns pursuit of an optimization strategy. In order for an optimization process, such as the marginal analysis, to reach a solution, it is often necessary to build an over-simplified model of reality. Even with simplified models it is not possible to avoid the methodological problem of discontinuity and system breaks. Pursuing an optimization strategy in business is operationally difficult. A more feasible strategy would seek the objective of flexibility, including flexibility in the structure of the organization.

We have previously stressed that the choice regarding the identification of problems is inevitable, and it appears that choices also have to be made as regards problem solving. This could lead to the abandonment of optimization strategies as the organizing structure, substituting instead *original* dialectics,[19] which eventually would imply that the subjective choice appears inevitable.

To some extent, the problem can be expressed as the choice between strong, deductive statements and weak hypothetical–deductive statements. The choice may also be described from the point of view of ''reality.'' Is ''reality'' viewed as continuous and causal or discontinuous and acausal? Since the description must start from some view of ''reality,'' a descriptive language must exist in accordance with that chosen view. Otherwise, a special language may be developed and adapted as, for example, the mathematical matrix calculus to the quantum mechanics of physics. The question always remains, however, of whether a theory or model says anything about ''reality'' or about our view of ''reality.'' Thus, it appears that it will not always be appropriate to describe a phenomenon by means of a scientific language, not to mention a specific scientific language.

In some situations, depending on phenomenon, substance, aim, image of humans, etc., it may thus be necessary in relation to marketing to use a language of experience open for interpretation instead of noncontradictory and unambiguous mathematical logical languages. This consequence must be seen as a logical result of the choices made in the conceptualizing paradigm.

NOTES

1. Wroe Alderson and Reavis Cox. 1948. "Towards a Theory of Marketing." *Journal of Marketing* 13 (October):137–52.
2. Arne Rasmussen, "Pristeori eller parameterteori" ("Price Theory or Parameter Theory"). (Kobenhavn, 1955).
3. See Gosta Mickwitz, "Copenhagen School and Scandinavian Theory of Competition and Marketing," in *Readings in Danish Theory of Marketing*, edited by Max Kjaer-Hansen (Copenhagen, 1966); also E. T. Grether, "Chamberlain's Theory of Monopolistic Competition and the Literature of Marketing," in *Monopolistic Competition Theory: Studies in Impact*, edited by R. E. Kuenne (London, 1967).
4. If nothing else is mentioned in this section, the quotations are from Alderson and Cox, "Towards a Theory of Marketing."
5. F. S. C. Northrop, *The Logic of the Sciences and the Humanities* (New York, 1947).
6. According to Jan Barmark ("Varldsbild och Vetenskabsideal," Goteborg, 1976; "World Picture and Ideal of Science"), a paradigm comprises five elements: world picture and image of humans, view on science, ideal of science, ethics and aesthetics; see also Hakan Tornebohm, *Paradigms in Fields of Research* (Goteborg, 1977).
7. Thomas S. Kuhn, *The Structure of Scientific Revolutions* (Chicago: University of Chicago Press, 1962).
8. Rasmussen, "Pristeori eller parameterteori."
9. The concept of elasticity with regard to price is defined as $(dq/q)/(dp/p)$. The concept of cross-elasticity with regard to firm B's price and firm A's quantity is $(dqA/qA)/(dpB/pB)$.
10. For example, Alderson and Cox's wish to develop a marketing theory based on more realistic assumptions and Rasmussen's superior aim for a real demand or need orientation.
11. Jan Aarso Nielsen, "Om deskriptiv konkurrentadfaerdsteori fra en normativ afsaetningsokonomisk synsvinkel," *Markedskommunikasjon* nr. 3, 1972 ("On a Positive Competitor Behavior Theory Seen from a Normative Marketing Point of View").
12. See further Rasmussen's discussion of the problem of optimization in relation to marketing in *Readings in Danish Theory of Marketing*, pp. 116–27: "How Critical Are Optimal Points of Marketing?"
13. Arne Rasmussen, "Udviklingslinier i den okonomiske konkurrenceteori," *Erhvervsokonomisk Tidsskrift* nr. 2–3, 1970 ("Trends of Development in the Economic Competition Theory").
14. Van Bertalanaffy, Ludwig. 1968. General Systems Theory. New York: G. Braziller.
15. A. Koestler and J. R. Smythies, *Beyond Reductionism* (London, 1972).
16. David Bohm, "On the Intuitive Understanding of Nonlocality as Implied by Quantum Theory," *Foundations of Physics* 5 (1975):93–109.
17. Niels Bohr, "The Rutherford Memorial Lecture," in *Essays 1958–1962 on Atomic Physics and Human Knowledge* (London, 1963).
18. Bohr, *Essays 1958–1962*, p. 55.
19. See Socratic analysis as distinct from dialectical materialism.

CHAPTER 15

Externality Focus of Macromarketing Theory

ROBERT W. NASON

INTRODUCTION

In 1976 Charles Slater gave formal recognition to the discipline of macro-marketing by creating the first Annual Macromarketing Theory Seminar (Nason and White 1981). In the years since that first gathering, scholars have struggled to shape the new discipline and its research agenda with only modest success (Hunt 1976, 1981; Hunt and Burnett 1982; Shawver and Nickels 1981; Dholakia and Nason 1984).

The purpose of this essay is to recognize the antecedents of macromarketing as a springboard for focus—particularly the work and concerns of Reavis Cox during the 1950s and 1960s. From these roots, macromarketing can be seen not as a revolution, but as an evolution with implications for attention to externalities of the marketing transaction. From this focus, the central question of how to deal with negative externalities will be raised and a broad direction suggested.

MACROMARKETING—AN EVOLUTION

Macromarketing is the formalization of what Reavis Cox saw as important in the discipline of marketing. He both welcomed and feared the preoccupation with "managerial" marketing. His hope was that focus on the objectives of the firm would yield managements more capable of providing consumer satisfaction more efficiently. Yet he foresaw the possible myopia of overemphasis of firm objectives in dictating the direction of the discipline.

Science, like nature but unlike engineering or technology, is not concerned with individuals. It seeks to create not a large file of case reports but a small number of formulas, each as simple as possible, that summarize what one can say about an entire population after observing a large number of individuals. In the process of generalization we inevitably suppress much of what is known about individuals. We learn some important things about the forest but very little about the trees. In contrast, it is usually a specific tree upon which consultants and managerial scientists focus their attention. (Cox 1964, p. 7)

Reavis Cox was very concerned with the social value of marketing technology and systems. He clearly recognized the subservient role of business to the interests of society and the further subordination of marketing under the goals of the firm. He clearly saw the suboptimization problems as well as the incentive benefit of the means–ends dilemma—firms versus society. He put the argument as follows:

Much of our concern over the social objectives of marketing grows out of the fact that we are not satisfied as students and observers to confine ourselves to the problem of helping marketing serve as well as it can the narrowest interest of the most narrowly defined entity we can find to talk about—the individual worker or the particular firm. We must at some point subsume our ideas as to the functions of marketing into our ideas of what our whole society is supposed to achieve for us. (Cox 1962, p. 23)

It takes us back to the old, familiar but often neglected idea that economic activity is engaged in not for its own sake but because something we call consumption happens at the end of the process. It argues that the true standard against which performance is to be measured is not the profitability of the enterprises that sell what the economy produces, but the quality, variety and quantity of satisfaction created for those who use it. (Cox 1962, p. 18)

The discipline did veer strongly toward micromarketing analysis predominately to serve the firm. Marketing theory and societal analysis were all but overrun by the deluge of micromarketing studies. At the same time, however, new issues emerged in the awareness of the role of marketing in economic development and in externalities. The turmoil of the 1960s and 1970s caused firms and citizens alike to ask questions about the social impacts of marketing.

The questions were different in specifics but similar in concept. Instead of questions on the efficiency and productivity of marketing in the U.S. economy, questions were asked about the beneficial role of marketing in countries of the less-developed world. Instead of questions on general social impacts, a series of questions on specific social impacts were substituted—questions on such as the following:

Resource depletion
Pollution

Conservation and reuse
Deception
Disclosure
Exaggeration
Obsolescence
Discrimination

The new discipline of macromarketing emerged in name, but as a continuation of work on the social effects of marketing championed by Reavis Cox. In this sense, the discipline of marketing is clearer about the objectives of inquiry, if not radically altered in content. The micro branch clearly takes its direction from the needs of operating organizations, be they private or public, profit or nonprofit. Macromarketing, too, is purposeful and goal directed, but it takes its direction from a different set of clients, namely, those concerned with public policy and public welfare. It is the client orientation, be it a government of a less-developed country or a regulatory agency of a developed country, that gives macromarketing new vitality and purpose as an applied discipline. To the degree that macromarketing aligns itself more closely with its clients' needs, it will gain both in support and in usefulness.

It is not necessary to have a client perspective. One can study marketing for its own sake. But, marketing is not a science of natural physical phenomena in either macro or micro senses. All that marketers deal with is human made—products, services, organizations, behavior systems. There is no pure or abstract right or wrong, if we could only find it. There is only individual organizations and nations (superorganizations) with their vast diversity of objectives. Therefore, investigation takes on the most focus and meaning when it is dealing with the problem faced by clients empowered, at least to some degree, to choose among alternative courses of action. Macromarketing then is or should be just as decision oriented as micromarketing.

This is not to say that scholars should not pursue generalizations about marketing as of interest in themselves. However, generalizations will eventually serve macro and/or micro clients. We should strive for that applicability if macromarketing is to develop theories.

For example, the pioneering work of Reavis Cox on the flows, costs, efficiency, and productivity of marketing (distribution) has clear public policy implications (Cox 1948, 1959; Cox and Goodman 1956; Sevin et al. 1951; Cox, Goodman, and Fichandler 1965). The question, "Does distribution cost too much?", arises because of concern on some parts that marketing costs are high, or higher than they should be. The implication is that public policy should be drafted to in some way constrain the system or provide incentives for improved performance. If the marketing costs are not shown to be too high relative to benefits, then perhaps ill-designed constraints can be headed off.

Little of the theory or knowledge gained in marketing is irrelevant to the micro or macro clients. Yet few macromarketers have focused sufficiently on relevant issues of public policy to allow their work to become central in the analytical process. The resurgence of macromarketing has been to some degree a response to growing awareness of public policy needs, but the linkage needs to be strengthened. In conclusion, then, macromarketing has emerged because real world concerns are not adequately dealt with by other modes of analysis. Its reason for existence is to work toward integration of analysis from society's complex objectives around the engine of its economic performance—the market transaction. The clear and unequivocal clients are those who must make the complex and difficult decisions about appropriate constraints of market actors. Therefore, macromarketing should be very much focused on public policy regarding market behavior.

EXTERNALITY FOCUS FOR MACROTHEORY

With the growth of population density, affluence, and technology of a society comes the unavoidable increase in number and severity of externalities. Economists since Mill, Marshall, and Pigou have recognized externalities in increasing cost and decreasing cost industries (Davis and Hulett 1977, p. 4). The seminal work of Kapp (1950) identified natural economic effects of economic activity. More recently, economists have included a broader set of externalities relating to "third party" or "spillover" effects of transactions—effects on those not a party to the transaction (Lin 1976, p. 1).

> The essence of an externality is that there is an effect on some person of a transaction to which he is not a party. Since the attainment of Pareto-efficiency through the operation of a competitive market is brought about by each party to a transaction adjusting to the price parameters, the fact that there are people affected by the transaction but not parties to it means that the appropriate adjustments will not be made, and the points attained in such a process will not in general be Pareto-efficient. (Alexander 1970, p. 24)

Krupp (1973, pp. 21–22) defines externalities another common way, as a function of aggregation:

> The problem of externalities concerns the interdependence that emerges when individual units are aggregated with consequences not predictable under theorems derived from the individual units. Externalities are introduced at the point in theory where deductive explanation becomes unsatisfactory.

Neither of these definitions addresses another sort of market failure, what we might call externalities to the parties to the transaction, those effects to the parties that were not anticipated by them at the time of the transaction. These are sometimes referred to as "incomplete transactions" (Harris and Carman 1983). They include certain effects of monopoly and monopolistic competition. Economists tend to assume these externalities away by arguing that the primary parties are the best judge of their needs and desires and can achieve their objectives reasonably well; that is, they internalize these possible externalities. However, the discipline of marketing is built on countless studies that demonstrate the falseness of this assumption. Externalities do exist to the parties of the transaction, and any treatment of externalities must include that reality.

Further, the phenomenon of externalities is not just a theoretical problem at the fringe of mainstream economics (Staaf and Tannian 1973, p. vii) but a reality of market operation whether pure or imperfect. External effects occur as a result of *every* transaction. Thus, as externalities grow in frequency and severity, the diverse impacts of them must be understood, analyzed, and coordinated so that public policy can be developed to deal with those aspects deemed important and actionable.

Marketing provides the understanding of the transaction process from ecclectic roots in many disciplines. Macromarketing provides the umbrella focus around which micromarket behavior and social objectives of interest groups within society can be merged to generate more useful research and coordinate understanding for the formulation of public policy. The mission of macromarketing is fundamentally tied to the importance of externalities. Without externalities there would be little rationale for the discipline.

How, then, should externalities be defined? For the purpose of macromarketing analysis, an externality is any effect, positive or negative, resulting from a market transaction that is not anticipated by the parties to the transaction in their calculus of their own goal achievement. Conversely, an internality is any prior consideration by the parties to the transaction in the calculation of their goal achievement from the transaction. The term "social cost–benefit" has been commonly used to describe the consequences of market action. However, the use of the term "externality" in this chapter is intended to clarify the nature of those effects as external to the market transaction—the fundamental unit of marketing action. Figure 15.1 depicts these definitions and some of their ramifications.

The first quadrant (I) identifies those aspects of the market transaction that have intended or foreseen impacts on the parties to the transaction as seen by those parties. Thus, a seller looks to short-and long-run market and financial objectives in the consummation of a transaction. Iikewise, the buyer assesses known benefits and costs of the transaction for net advantage or satisfaction. Each of the parties has a hoped-for positive outcome. The effects on the transacting parties, both negative and positive, which are considered in the calculation of expected outcome from the transaction are said to be internalities. What effects are internalized is a function of a large range of factors but is generally guided by the principle of self-interest. Important in what is internalized may be such di-

FIGURE 15.1. Categories of Externalities

	FORESEEN EFFECTS	UNFORESEEN EFFECTS
DIRECT EFFECTS TO PARTIES TO THE TRANSACTION	**I** Seller Objectives (profit. . .) Buyer Objectives (satisfaction/value)	**II** Financial Losses (Recalls, suits. . .) Dissatisfaction (Harm, regret. . .)
INDIRECT EFFECTS TO ALL OTHER PARTIES	**III** Health Deterioration Asset Deterioration Corrosion/Despoliation Consumer Capital Resource Depletion • • •	**IV** Discrimination Health & Safety Product Work Accident • • •

Source: Adapted from Klein 1977, p. 7, Figure 1-1.

verse factors as intelligence, knowledge, information access, values, morals, social pressure, law, and government sanctions. It is the role of the market to allow the multitude of internalized factors, as they differ from party to party and as they change over time (in kind and in weight), to result in transactions.

However, it is clear that the parties to the transaction have both limitations in foresight and limitations in terms of interests in society served. In other words, the parties to a transaction tend to serve their own interests with imperfect knowledge of effects on themselves or others. The result is externalities. There are three somewhat overlapping categories of externalities that must be considered.

The second quadrant (II), unforeseen effects on the parties to the transaction, represents externalities generally ignored, as noted earlier, by economists in their treatment of the subject. The vast literature of consumer behavior and industrial buying behavior belies the notion that the parties to a transaction can and do internalize all the effects over time of the transaction. It takes no great power of intellect to recognize the preposterousness of the proposition. Much of the research on procurement, information processing, and decision making are in fact attempts to reduce the externalities of unforeseen effects on the decision makers involved. Neither perfect information nor perfect analysis exists, and thus externalities to some extent by definition will impact the parties involved in the transaction. There also may be externalities that cannot be anticipated given the reality of the capability of the parties. Such areas have been given some attention in marketing, especially since the 1960s, and can be categorized as follows:

1. Competitive restrictions
    Price fixing
    Collusion
    Concentration
2. Imperfect information
    Deception–fraud
    Bait and switch
    Withholding of information
    Product performance
3. Imperfect analysis
    Information processing and overload
    Inadequate technical ability
    Insufficient time horizon
    Optimism (accidents will not happen to me)

One needs only to point to thalidomide, asbestos, and safety-related auto defects to understand the potential severity of externalities on the transacting parties— often both sides of the transaction lose.

The third quadrant (III), foreseen effects on indivduals and organizations not party to the transaction, is also an area of much criticism of the market operation. There are conquences of every transaction to suppliers, employees, and segments of the public at large. What is more, some are known by the transacting parties prior to the transaction. For example, most pollution and resource depletion resulting from the manufacture and consumption of goods are known to exist by the parties to the transaction. Businesses know what industrial wastes they dispose of as consumers know how they dispose of packaging and products. Generally, smokers know that there are side-stream effects to others. Drivers know that auto emissions pollute. Users of throwaway products know that the material is lost. Likewise, businesses know the impact, positive or negative, of their decisions on employees, suppliers, competitors, and communities. Perhaps because these effects are known and foreseeable, they tend to get the most public attention when they are ignored by the parties to the transaction.

The fourth quadrant (IV) involves unforeseen effects on nonstransacting parties. These externalities are harder to deal with than those of quadrant III, as the effect is only understood some time after the transaction has been completed. Unforeseen effects on individuals and institutions not party to the transaction result from several causes:

1. Aggregation of many transactions when no one has a significant effect but all together do (for example, auto emissions)

2. Technological advancement where the full ramifications of a new process, substance, or product cannot be forecast (for example, new chemicals or food additives)
3. Changes in the social environment where values and morals shift to reverse acceptable and unacceptable behavior, desires, and phenomena (both ways, for example, racism and sexism)
4. Changes in economic and technical environments where resources are created and destroyed in value (for example, oil reserve finds, automation technology, computer chips, etc.)

One of the raging controversies over unforeseen effects deals with the question of how much testing is required in order to understand the externalities from any new product or technology. The 1979 Three Mile Island nuclear leak and the 1984 Union Carbide Chemical Plant runaway reaction in Bhopal, India, are graphic examples of such unforeseen externalities even if some specialists feel they predicted the events and therefore they were known.

This taxonomy of externalities serves to show the diversity of externalities but, more important, it identifies the key causal factors that need to be considered in any kind of remediation plan. These major factors are summarized in Figure 15.2.

FIGURE 15.2. Externalities: Key Causal Factors

	FORESEEN EFFECTS	UNFORESEEN EFFECTS
DIRECT EFFECTS TO PARTIES TO THE TRANSACTION	I	II Imperfect Information Imperfect Analysis Imperfect Knowledge
INDIRECT EFFECTS TO ALL OTHER PARTIES	III Self-Interest	IV Quadrant II plus Aggregation Across Transactions Value and Moral Shifts in Society Technological Change

EXTERNALITY REMEDIATION

The identification and analysis of market externalities are at the core of macromarketing, but remain an academic exercise unless social policy decision makers are involved as clients and questions of remediation are subjected to the same depth of analysis. Each externality implies its own set of possible solutions, which in turn have levels of potential effectiveness and externalities. Thus, development of a remediation strategy is no less dependent on analysis of the main intended effects and externalities than was assessment of the need for remediation. Macromarketing thus not only requires information on market externalities but the ability to place those externalities in the context of the market and social systems involved so that effective and coordinated plans can be developed for remediation—if desirable. The role of macromarketing is strikingly parallel to that of micromarketing information systems–strategic planning concepts. Figure 15.3 depicts the scope of macromarketing. Of course, the complexities and rigidities in the macromarketing sphere dwarf in size those of the typical micromarketing model, but that is no justification for ignoring the normative process. One of the contributions of macromarketing may well be in identifying that process more clearly.

The fundamental issue of internalization is succinctly put by Reavis Cox (1962, p. 21). ''The social problem often becomes one of seeing how individual people with their self-centered interests tied into narrowly circumscribed units can be induced to seek social objectives broader than their own immediate wants.''

The strategies for remediating externalities fall basically into one or more of the following categories:

Voluntarism
Pressure of interest groups
Government coercion
Government reward
Government nationalization

Voluntarism is based on the acceptance by marketers of social values in society. Interestingly, Adam Smith envisioned the necessity of strong moral, religious, and social shared values in order for the market to work (Dixon 1981, p. 20). Certainly the voluntary internalization of acceptable behavior is a vital control of externalities, yet it has proven to be uneven and insufficient generally. Many companies have addressed externalities voluntarily and must be commended in their concern for safety, minorities, communities, and the environment. However, the market model makes it difficult to internalize social costs when not all competitors are willing to do so. The struggle with industrial pollution standards provides a graphic example. Therefore, voluntarism tends to

FIGURE 15.3. Applied Macromarketing

Execution ← ———————————— Public Policy Plan ←

↓

Market Behavior	Investigation	Analysis
Internalities	Identification	Who affected
Externalities	Measurement	Importance
Physical Environment		Alternative remediation
Culture & Values	Feedback	Agency
Satisfaction	Monitoring	Remediation performance evaluation
		Revision
Institutions		Continuation
Equity		Removal

work only when costs are low or when they are pursued for other hoped-for objectives.

Interest group pressure is another plank in internalizing social cost of marketing decision makers. Such pressure can come from industry trade associations, on the one hand, or various unrelated interest groups, on the other. Tactics range from public embarrassment from demonstrations and exposure to secondary boycott programs, sabotage, and the like. Again, this force is uneven and usually addresses only specific externalities that overall may or may not have broad priority.

The third means, most commonly used, is that of governmental coercion. In this category falls much of the vast legislative and regulatory structure of government where prohibitions and punishments are spelled out and enforcement is attempted. The strategy is to force internalization of externalities by not allowing the externality to occur often by making the cost of noncompliance greater than the cost of compliance. From the marketer's standpoint, the best solution is to figure out how not to internalize the externality and, simultaneously, how to avoid the penalty cost levied for not doing so. That is, the incentive for the marketer is to use ingenuity to find loopholes, create loopholes, calculate the internalization versus violation cost trade-off, etc. (Nason and Armstrong, 1972). If penalties are low and enforcement weak and spotty or politically influenced, then the incentive is to beat the system by not internalizing the externality. Costs of both enforcement and the externality increase to society as a result. Again, compliance with pollution laws established and enforced by the Environmental Protection Agency provides a legion of well-known examples where violation was more the rule than was compliance—especially if original timetables are viewed as the objective. The nature of coercion makes it a lose–lose situation for the marketer. The marketer either increases costs by compliance or increases costs because of penalties. Therefore, the real incentive is to try to avoid both. This places the ingenuity of the marketer in direct opposition to the internalization process. It is no wonder that the coercion structure is as costly as it is with questionable equity and effectiveness. The added bureaucracy to both business and government in order to handle the paperwork needs of such a system is a growing threat to our economic health (Commission on Federal Paper Work 1977). Of course, not all of the burden can be laid at the feet of the coercive model. The history of abuse response legislation and regulatory policy is only in part a function of the model of coercive restraint.

The incentive or reward model is also a feature of the U.S. regulatory structure. Government tax incentives, subsidies, procurement, and services all are well known, if not as prevalent as coercive techniques. Incentive systems have some fundamental advantages over coercion for inducing internalization of externalities. First, incentives usually accrue to the marketer after the externality is internalized. The marketer must perform first to obtain the advantage. Second, the nature of incentives places the marketer in a position of determining the least costly method to achieve the internalization required for the incentive or the reward. Thus, incentives breed efficiency because the ingenuity of the marketer is focused on reducing cost and thus maximizing the benefits of the incentives. Third, if the incentive is less than the cost of internalization, the marketer has the choice of postponing compliance until technology or ingenuity makes the venture profitable or the reward is increased. Finally, in this case where compliance is postponed, the public goals are not achieved immediately, but the costs to business and society in terms of bureaucracy are not increased either. The system itself is not likely to add costs as is the coercive model.

Internalization of externalities through incentive systems has conceptual attractiveness as a promising direction for control of externalities. However, the means of doing so has real operational difficulties. Perhaps direction can be taken from Cox (1962, p. 18), Tawney (1920), and Heilbroner (1970), among others, who remind us that the economic entity is a means to society's ends, the servant to the master of human well-being. It follows that if the well-being of society is not only determined in economic terms, the means to human ends should not be allowed to focus only on economic criteria. Further, the economic servant has a right to prosper only if it is contributing to the human welfare objectives on net. Finally, it can be argued that the greater the welfare benefit of the economic entity to society, the greater should be its own rewards.

First-party effects are those internalized by the transaction automatically, and thus are not subject to further analysis here. Each party uses its own calculus and objectives in that setting of the transaction. However, other externalities may represent costs to society and should be internalized to the degree feasible. Pigou (1932) argued that taxes represent a charge to the firm for its externalities. He suggested a system of taxes and subsidies to internalize the costs of social capital used by business as an expense. The implication is that if business can replace its use of social capital, then its tax rate will drop, allowing the owners and managers more reward for their efforts. Either the cost of internalizing these social costs or the tax burden would have to be incorporated in the price of the product or service. Thus, the cost of the product reflects a truer valuation of the cost to society. The higher cost is likely to be reflected in higher prices, which would skew demand away from products with major social cost impact. Thus, the market actually is strengthened in its allocative function. The more externalities are internalized or paid for through taxes, the truer is the allocative process of the market.

The operational linking of externalities and the tax rate is a problem of immense difficulty. It requires the setting of performance standards for each externality and specifying the reduction of the tax burden with various levels of achievement by the marketer. If the marketer were able to internalize some of the externality, its tax rate would decrease commensurately. The cost of externality to society would decrease as well.

Since Pigou's suggestion, there has been theoretical effort in economics to develop such as incentive system (for example, Baumol 1972; Buchanan and Tullock 1975; Balcer 1980; Landsberger and Meilijson 1982). However, little practical advancement has been made. More centralized planning and coordination would be needed than has evolved in the multifaceted system of the United States. Yet, the simple elegance of the concept is intriguing and merits further serious study. A few scholars have made first stabs at fleshing out more detail, but the efforts as yet are crude in comparison with what is needed (Abt 1977, p. 28; Nason 1978; Higgins 1977). If such a system can be developed, then the self-interests of the servant institutions and their focus on profit will drive them to increasing social performance in ingenious and low-cost ways without resorting to altruism or coercion. Inventiveness of business will be applied to reducing costs of internalization of externalities as with other operational cost reductions and operational improvements. That is the promise of an incentive system. Whether it can be realized remains to be seen.

CONCLUSION

The purpose of this chapter has been to explore the importance of macromarketing as an applied client-oriented discipline through the analysis and remediation of marketing externalities. It has been argued that the core of macromarketing must be the study of externalities and the development of a system of internalization of market externalities. It is the position of the author that through the development of an incentive tax-related internalization system, the market can more efficiently serve the needs of society, in terms of both reduced externalities and improved allocative efficiency.

REFERENCES

Abt, Clark C. 1977. *The Social Audit of Management.* New York: Amalom.

Alexander, Sidney S. 1970. "Comment." In *The Analysis of Public Output,* edited by Julius Margolis, pp. 24–30. New York: Columbia University Press.

Balcer, Yves. 1980. "Taxation of Externalities: Direct Versus Indirect." *Journal of Public Economics* 13 (February):121–29.

Baumol, W. J. 1972. "On Taxation and the Control of Externalities." *American Economic Review* 62 (June):307–22.

Buchanan, James M., and Gordon Tullock. 1975. "Polluters' Profits and Political Response: Direct Controls Versus Taxes." *American Economic Review* 65 (March):139–47.

Commission on Federal Paper Work. 1977. *A Report of the Commission on Federal Paper Work: Final Summary Report.* Washington, D. C.: U. S. Government Printing Office, October 3.

Cox, Reavis. 1964. "Introduction." In *Theory in Marketing,* edited by Wroe Alderson and Stanley J. Shapiro, pp. 1–14. Homewood, IL: Richard D. Irwin.

———. 1962. "Changing Social Objectives in Marketing." In *Emerging Concepts in Marketing,* Proceedings of the Winter Conference of the American Marketing Association, edited by William S. Decker, Pittsburgh: pp. 16–25.

———. 1959. "Consumer Convenience and the Retail Structure of Cities." *Journal of Marketing* 23 (April):355–62.

———. 1948. "The Meaning and Measurement of Productivity in Distribution." *Journal of Marketing* 12 (April):433–41.

Cox, Reavis, and Charles S. Goodman. 1956. "Marketing of Housebuilding Materials." *Journal of Marketing* 21 (July):36–61.

Cox, Reavis, Charles S. Goodman, and Thomas C. Fichandler. 1965. *Distribution in a High-Level Economy.* Englewood Cliffs, NJ. Prentice-Hall.

Davis, J. Ronnie, and Joe R. Hulett. 1977. *An Analysis of Market Failure: Externalities, Public Goods, and Mixed Goods.* Gainesville, FL: University Presses of Florida.

Dholakia, Nikhilesh, and Robert W. Nason. 1984. "Research Issues in Macromarketing: A Blueprint for Progress." *European Journal of Marketing* 18:41–55.

Dixon, Donald F. 1981. "The Micro-Macro Dilemma (An Eighteenth Century View)." Presented to the 1981 Macromarketing Conference, Emory University, August 13–16.)

Harris, Robert G., and James M. Carman. 1983. "Public Regulation of Marketing Activity: Part I: Institutional Typologies of Market Failure. *Journal of Macromarketing* 3 (Spring):49–58.

Heilbroner, Robert L. 1970. *The Marketing of Economic Society,* 3rd ed. Englewood Cliffs, NJ: Prentice-Hall.

Higgins, James M. 1977. "A Proposed Social Performance Evaluation System." *Atlanta Economic Review* 27 (May–June):4–9.

Hunt, Shelby D., and John J. Burnell. 1982. "The Macromarketing/Micromarketing Dichotomy: A Taxonomical Model." *Journal of Marketing* 46 (Summer):11–26.

———. 1981. "Macromarketing as a Multidimensional Concept." *Journal of Macromarketing* 1 (Spring):7–8.

———. 1976. "The Nature and Scope of Marketing." *Journal of Marketing* 40 (July):17–28.

Kapp, K. William. 1950. *Social Costs of Private Enterprise*, Cambridge, MA: Harvard University Press.

Klein, Thomas A. 1977. *Social Costs and Benefits of Business*. Englewood Cliffs, NJ: Prentice-Hall.

Krupp, Sherman. 1973. "Analytic Economics and the Logic of External Effects." In *Externalities: Theoretical Dimensions of Political Economy*, edited by Robert J. Staaf and Francis X. Tannian, pp. 19–24. New York: Dunellen.

Landsberger, Michael, and Isaac Meilijson. 1982. "Incentive Generating State Dependent Penalty System." *Journal of Public Economics* 19 (December):333–52.

Lin, Steven A. Y., ed. 1976. *Theory and Measurement of Economic Externalities*, pp. 1–5. New York: Academic Press.

Nason, Robert W. 1978. "Reward Adjustment for Corporate Social Performance." In *Macro-Marketing: Distributive Processes from a Societal Perspective, An Elaboration of Issues*, edited by Phillip D. White and Charles C. Slater, pp. 69–87. Boulder CO: Graduate School of Business Administration, University of Colorado.

Nason, Robert W., and J. Scott Armstrong. 1972. "Role Conflict in Marketing: Society's Dilemma with Excellence in Marketing." *Wharton Quarterly* 7 (Fall):13–16.

Nason, Robert W., and Phillip D. White. 1981. "The Visions of Charles C. Slater: Social Consequences of Marketing." *Journal of Macromarketing* 1 (Fall):4–18.

Pigou, A. C. 1932. *The Economics of Welfare*, 4th ed., London: Macmillan.

Sevin, Charles H., Reavis Cox, Edward R. Hawkins, and Richard M. Clewett. 1951. "An Outline of Distribution Costs." *Journal of Marketing* (July):51–55.

Shawver, Donald L., and William G. Nickels. 1981. "A Rationalization for Macromarketing Concepts and Definitions." *Journal of Macromarketing* 1 (Spring):8–10.

Staaf, Robert, and Francis X. Tannian. 1973. *Externalities: Theoretical Dimensions of Political Economy*. New York: Dunellen.

Tawney, Richard H. 1920. The Acquisitive Society. New York: Harcourt, Brace, and Howe.

Index

About the Contributors

Johan Arndt (deceased) was Professor of Business Administration at the Norwegian School of Management, Oslo. Recent books include *Management, Production and Marketing Services* and *Internal Marketing*, both published in Sweden by Liber. Articles by Professor Arndt on consumer behavior, advertising marketing theory, and management have appeared in the *Journal of Marketing, Journal of Marketing Research, Journal of Industrial Economics*, and the *Journal of Macromarketing*. Teaching appointments include Columbia University, University of California at Berkeley, University of Missouri at St. Louis, and the Norwegian School of Economics and Business in Bergen.

Robert Bartels is Professor Emeritus of Marketing and International Business at Ohio State University, Columbus, Ohio. His current areas of interest are comparative economics and marketing, marketing philosophy, and directions of marketing thought. His principal publications are *The History of Marketing Thought, Marketing Theory and Metatheory*, and *Global Development and Marketing*.

Jean J. Boddewyn is Professor of Marketing and International Business at the Baruch College of the City University of New York. His Ph.D. is from the University of Washington. His research interests have centered on comparative marketing and the regulation and self-regulation of advertising around the world. Some of his publications include *Comparative Management and Marketing* and *Comparison Advertising: A Worldwide Study*.

C. Samuel Craig is Associate Dean for Academic Affairs and Professor of Marketing at New York University's Graduate School of Business Administration. Among his international studies are a coauthored book, *International Marketing Research* (1983), and "Determinants of Multinational Corporation Performance" (1983) in the *Journal of International Business Studies*. His current research focuses on retail location and media models as well as international marketing.

305

Edward W. Cundiff is the Charles H. Kellstadt Professor of Marketing in the School of Business Administration at Emory University, Atlanta, Georgia. His major contributions to the discipline in the past include *Marketing in the International Environment* and *Fundamentals of Modern Marketing,* published by Prentice-Hall. His major research has been in comparative marketing and economic development.

Nikhilesh Dholakia is Professor of Marketing at the University of Rhode Island. His research interests include macromarketing, economic development, and marketing theory. He is a coauthor of *Essentials of New Product Management* (Prentice-Hall, 1986) and a coeditor of *Changing the Course of Marketing* (JAI Press, 1985). He obtained his Ph.D in marketing from Northwestern University.

Ruby Roy Dholakia is Professor of Marketing at the University of Rhode Island. She obtained her Ph.D. in marketing from Northwestern University. She has published in the areas of communication, consumer behavior, and macromarketing. In addition to these areas, her research interests include economic development and consumer socialization.

Susan P. Douglas is Professor of Marketing and International Business at New York University. She has authored over 60 articles and professional publications on cross-national studies of consumer behavior and multinational strategic planning published both in the United States and Europe. Her article on "Life Style and Media Planning" was awarded the Jours de France Gold Medal for Advertising Research in 1977. In addition to serving as a consultant to firms in the United States, Europe, and Far East, she is a founder–member and past president of the European Marketing Academy.

George Fisk, the editor of this book, serves as Georgia Power Professor of Marketing at Emory University, Atlanta, Georgia. He was the founding editor of the *Journal of Macromarketing.* He researched under the supervision of Reavis Cox at the University of Pennsylvania. Among books he has written are *Marketing Systems* and *Marketing and the Ecological Crisis.* He has also edited numerous books including *New Essays in Marketing Theory* and *Social Responsibility in Business: Scandinavian Viewpoints.* He previously served as Visiting Professor at the University of Lund (Sweden) and the Norwegian School of Business Administration in Oslo.

Charles S. Goodman is Professor of Marketing at the University of Pennsylvania. With Reavis Cox, he researched the marketing of house-building materials and coauthored *Distribution in a High-Level Economy.* His current work is "On Output Measures of Retail Performance." His article, "Do the Poor Pay More?" won the Alpha Kappa Psi Award for the best article in the *Journal of Marketing* for 1968.

Ewald T. Grether is remembered for his major contributions to the resale price control controversy including *Price Control Under Fair Trade Legislation.* He was for many years Dean and Flood Professor of Economics in the School of Business Administration at the University of California, Berkeley. With Roland S. Vaile and Reavis Cox, he coauthored *Marketing in the American Economy* (1952). His recent research has focused on regional–spatial analysis, but over the years his interests have included marketing and public policy.

Stanley C. Hollander is Professor of Marketing at Michigan State University. Among his coauthored books are ten editions of *Modern Retail Management* and publications coedited on marketing and retail regulation. His 1954 Ph.D. dissertation, *Discount Retailing: Deviations from the One Price System in American Retailing,* is included in a series on American Business History, the area of his current research interest.

Stig Ingebrigtsen lectures on marketing at the Copenhagen School of Economics and Business Administration. With Michael Pettersson he has coauthored papers on marketing theory, among which are included, "Epistemological Problems in Marketing," a precursor to the essay included in this volume. His research interests focus on marketing metatheory. He has edited a collection of readings, *Reflections on Danish Theory of Marketing* (1981).

Charles A. Ingene is Associate Professor and Director, Center for Retail, Transportation and Distribution Management, at the University of Washington, Seattle. His "Labor Productivity in Retailing: What Do We Know and How Do We Know It?" in the *Journal of Marketing* (Fall 1985) and "Structural Determinants of Market Potential" in the *Journal of Retailing* (Spring 1984) reflect his current research interests.

Roger A. Layton is Professor of Marketing and Head of the School of Marketing at the University of New South Wales. His recent research has been in the area of input–output analysis and trade flows in the field of macromarketing, with several papers from this work being published in the *Journal of Macromarketing*. His publications include *Readings in Marketing—A Systems Perspective* (1978) published by McGraw-Hill in Australia and editorship of a long-running series of volumes on marketing developments in Australia called *Australian Marketing Projects,* published annually by the National Committee for the Hoover Award for Marketing.

Robert W. Nason is Professor and Chairperson of the Marketing Department at Michigan State University. He has served as Associate Editor of the *Journal of Macromarketing* since its initial appearance in 1981. With the late Charles Slater, he coauthored *Market Processes in the Recife Area of Northeast Brazil,* a research area of continuing interest along with externalities and constraint systems, as illustrated in the essay he authored for this book.

Michael Pettersson lectures on marketing at the Copenhagen School of Economics and Business Administration. With Stig Ingebrigtsen, he coauthored in 1980 "An Intradisciplinary Research of Marketing," in 1981 "Epistemological Problems and Marketing," and in 1982 "The Response Function." They are together attempting to relate pluralistic ideals of science to issues of ethics and esthetics posed by marketing behavior.

Ronald Savitt is the John L. Beckley Professor of American Business at the University of Vermont. His research interest in retail management has resulted in the publication of papers such as "The Wheel of Retailing and Retail Product Management" in the *European Journal of Marketing* (1984).

Richard F. Wendel is Professor of Marketing in the School of Business Administration at the University of Connecticut at Storrs. Between 1974 and 1984, he was editor of *Annual Editions: Readings in Marketing.* Currently he is preparing *Selling: Personality, Persuasion, Strategy* for its third edition to appear in 1986.